4th edition

~What's ~What

A guide to acronyms for cardiovascular trials

ASTRA

Although extensive efforts have been made to ensure accuracy of the information in this book, the reader is advised to consult the original papers, which have been cited in all cases.

Fourth edition
Third revised printing
ISBN 91-85520-97-7

Published by Astra Hässle AB, S-431 83 Mölndal, Sweden

Copyright © 1998 Astra AB

Prepared by Excerpta Medica for Astra

Excerpta Medica is a member of the Reed Elsevier group.
Local offices:
Amsterdam, Barcelona, Hong Kong, Milan, Munich, Osaka, Oxford, Paris, Princeton, Sydney, Tokyo, Washington

Printed in The Netherlands by
Koninklijke Wöhrmann BV, Zutphen 1998

We must continuously update and verify our knowledge if we want to fulfil the purposes of the medical profession. Medical scientists will never stop searching for new reasons behind human illness, such as genetics, epidemiology, physiopathological mechanisms and risk factors, or looking for new solutions, be they pharmacological or non-pharmacological treatments. That explains why, every year, thousands of physicians are performing new trials. It has become impossible for most of us to recall the details of all the trials in cardiovascular medicine, either completed or ongoing, including acronyms, drugs involved, results in terms of significance, etc.

What's What is a reference guide to acronyms of mainly clinical studies in cardiovascular medicine. The most important data are reported for the major trials in this area, from ACAPS to WWICT, as well as selected references.

In this 4th edition, over a hundred new studies have been added, and the studies published in the 3rd edition have been updated. As in previous editions, some minor studies that are identified by acronyms, as well as some major studies that do not have acronyms or have not been referenced for several years, are covered in a briefer format in an Appendix (p 371–378). Indices (p 379–405) are included to facilitate cross-referencing by author name, drug and disease.

We would like to thank all the readers who have provided us with useful information by returning the reply card attached to the back cover. Please continue to advise us of any clinical cardiovascular trials with acronyms that are about to begin or that we may have overlooked.

We are very pleased to have completed this 4th edition of *What's What* as a service to the medical profession.

ACAPS
Asymptomatic Carotid Artery Plaque Study

Authors	**(a)** The ACAPS group **(b)** Furberg CD, Adams HP Jr, Applegate WB, Byington RP, Espeland MA, Hartwell T, Hunninghake DB, Lefkowitz DS, Probstfield J, Riley WA, Young B **(c)** Probstfield J, Margitic SE, Byington RP, Espeland MA, Furberg CD
Titles	**(a)** Rationale and design for the Asymptomatic Carotid Artery Plaque Study (ACAPS) **(b)** Coronary Heart Disease/Myocardial Infarction: Effect of lovastatin on early carotid atherosclerosis and cardiovascular events **(c)** Results of the primary outcome measure and clinical events from the Asymptomatic Carotid Artery Progression Study
References	**(a)** *Control Clin Trials* 1992;**13**:293–314 **(b)** *Circulation* 1994;**90**:1679–87 **(c)** *Am J Cardiol* 1995;**76**:47C–53C
Disease	Carotid atherosclerosis
Purpose	To assess the effects of lovastatin and warfarin on carotid atherosclerosis progression in asymptomatic high-risk individuals. Secondary objective: to assess the effect of the treatments on the incidence of major atherosclerotic events
Study design	Randomised, double-blind, placebo-controlled, factorial
Follow-up	3 years
Patients	919 subjects (48% women), aged 40–79 years (mean 62 years), with moderately elevated serum low-density lipoprotein (LDL) cholesterol (≥ 130 and ≤ 189 mg/dl) and a thickening of the arterial wall (≥ 1.5 and < 3.5 mm) without previous MI, severe angina, stroke, or TIA
Treatment regimen	Lovastatin, 10–40 mg/day, and/or warfarin, 1 mg/day, or placebo
Concomitant therapy	Aspirin, 81 mg/day
Results	Mean LDL fell by 28% at 6 months in the lovastatin group ($p < 0.0001$ vs placebo) and remained stable throughout the follow-up. Regression of early atherosclerosis was seen after 12 months in the lovastatin-only group, compared to the placebo group ($p < 0.001$). No progression occurred in the lovastatin-placebo groups. A negative interaction ($p = 0.04$) was observed in the group receiving both lovastatin and warfarin. The incidence of major cardiovascular events and all-cause mortality was significantly ($p < 0.05$) lower in the lovastatin group compared to the placebo group

ACAS
Asymptomatic Carotid Atherosclerosis Study

Authors	**(a)** The Asymptomatic Carotid Atherosclerosis Study group **(b)** Executive Committee for the Asymptomatic Carotid Atherosclerosis Study
Titles	**(a)** Study design for randomized prospective trial of carotid endarterectomy for asymptomatic atherosclerosis **(b)** Endarterectomy for asymptomatic carotid artery stenosis
References	**(a)** *Stroke* 1989;**20**:844–9 **(b)** *JAMA* 1995;**273**:1421–8
Disease	Asymptomatic carotid stenosis (haemodynamically significant)
Purpose	To determine whether the addition of carotid endarterectomy to aggressive medical management can reduce the incidence of cerebral infarction in patients with asymptomatic carotid artery stenosis
Study design	Randomised, open, parallel-group
Follow-up	5 years
Patients	1662 patients, aged 40–79 years, with unilateral or bilateral surgically accessible stenosis in the region of the bifurcation of the common or internal carotid artery of at least 60%
Treatment regimen	Carotid endarterectomy or no surgery
Concomitant therapy	Aspirin, 325 mg/day, plus risk factor reduction counselling
Results	After a median follow-up of 2.7 years, the aggregate risk over 5 years for ipsilateral stroke and any perioperative stroke or death was estimated to be 5.1% for surgical patients and 11.0% for patients treated medically. This means an aggregate risk reduction of 53%
Comment	As a consequence of the trial reaching statistical significance in favour of endarterectomy, the study was halted and the investigators were advised to reevaluate patients who did not receive surgery

ACCEPT
Accupril Canadian Clinical Evaluation and Patient Teaching

Authors	Larochelle P, Hayness B, Maron N, Dugas S
Title	A postmarketing surveillance evaluation of quinapril in 3742 Canadian hypertensive patients: the ACCEPT study
Reference	*Clin Ther* 1994;**16**:838–53
Disease	Hypertension
Purpose	To evaluate the efficacy and safety of the ACE inhibitor quinapril in hypertension
Study design	Open
Follow-up	6 months
Patients	3742 patients, median age 56 years, median duration of hypertension 5 years
Treatment regimen	Quinapril, 10 mg/day initially, titration to blood pressure response, mostly at 2-week intervals, for a maintenance dose of 10–20 mg daily, not to exceed 40 mg/day
Results	Of 2979 patients receiving quinapril at 3 months, 77% were stabilised. Of 2517 patients receiving quinapril at 6 months, 84% were stabilised. There were larger decreases in diastolic and systolic blood pressure in patients who continued quinapril than in those who stopped it. Response to quinapril was similar in newly diagnosed patients and those with a history of hypertension. 980 patients (26.2%) reported adverse events, most frequently cough, which was considered definitely connected with quinapril in 3.6% of cases. Serious adverse events occurred in 55 patients (1.5%) and were considered possibly connected with quinapril in three cases. Adverse events were reported significantly more frequently by patients who received the detailed consent form than by those who received the abbreviated one ($p = 0.004$)

ACCORD
Angioplastie Coronaire, CORvasal and Diltiazem study

Authors	Lablanche J-M, Grollier G, Lusson J-R, Bassand J-P, Drobinski G, Bertrand B, Battaglia S, Desveaux B
Title	Effect of the direct nitric oxide donors linsidomine and molsidomine on angiographic restenosis after coronary balloon angioplasty: The ACCORD study
Reference	*Circulation* 1997;**95**:83–9
Disease	Angina or myocardial ischaemia with a significant stenosis
Purpose	To study the effect of linsidomine and molsidomine on restenosis after percutaneous transluminal coronary angioplasty (PTCA)
Study design	Randomised, open, stratified for centre and single- or multivessel disease
Follow-up	6 months
Patients	723 patients
Treatment regimen	Treatment group: linsidomine, 1 mg/h iv, started 3–18 h before PTCA. The dose was reduced if blood pressure decreased > 10%. The infusion continued 24 h after PTCA, and 2 h before infusion stop molsidomine, 4 mg orally, was given. Molsidomine, 4 mg tid, was continued until follow-up angiography. Control group: diltiazem, 60 mg tid, started 3 h before PTCA and continuing until follow-up angiography
Concomitant therapy	Aspirin, 250 mg daily, and iv heparin during PTCA
Results	Pretreatment with linsidomine and molsidomine was associated with a modest but statistically significant improvement in the immediate angiographic result compared to diltiazem pretreatment (minimal luminal diameter 1.94 vs 1.81 mm). This improvement was maintained at the 6-month follow-up. Restenosis, defined as ≥ 50% stenosis, occurred less often in the linsidomine/molsidomine group (38.0% vs 46.5%, p = 0.026)

ACCT
Amlodipine Cardiovascular Community Trial

Authors	Kloner RA, Sowers JR, DiBona GF, Gaffney M, Wein M
Title	Sex- and age-related antihypertensive effects of amlodipine
Reference	*Am J Cardiol* 1996;**77**:713–22
Disease	Mild to moderate hypertension
Purpose	To assess whether there were age, sex, or race differences in response to amlodipine in patients with mild to moderate hypertension
Study design	Open
Follow-up	16 weeks
Patients	1084 patients (79% white and 21% black), aged 21–80 years
Treatment regimen	Amlodipine, 5–10 mg daily
Results	At the end of the 4-week titration/efficacy phase, mean ± SD blood pressure had decreased by -16.3 ± 12.3/-12.5 ± 5.9 ($p \leq 0.0001$). Amlodipine produced a goal blood pressure response (sitting diastolic ≤ 90 mm Hg or a 10 mm Hg decrease) in 86% of the patients. The response was greater in women (91.4%) than in men (83.0%, $p \leq 0.001$) and greater in patients ≥ 65 years (91.5%) than in those < 65 years (84.1%, $p \leq 0.01$), but there was no significant difference between whites and blacks (86.0% vs 85.9%, respectively). The sex differences were not fully explained by differences in age, weight, dose (mg/kg), race, baseline blood pressure, or compliance, and there were no differences between women connected with use of hormone replacement therapy. Amlodipine was well-tolerated, mild to moderate oedema being the most frequent adverse effect

ACIP
Asymptomatic Cardiac Ischemia Pilot study

Authors	**(a)** Pepine CJ, Geller NL, Knatterud GL *et al* **(b)** Knatterud GL, Bourassa MG, Pepine CJ *et al* **(c)** Rogers WJ, Bourassa MG, Andrews TC, Bertolet BD, Blumenthal RS, Chaitman BR, Forman SA, Geller NL, Goldberg AD, Habib GB, Masters RG, Moisa RB, Mueller H, Pearce DJ, Pepine CJ, Sopko G, Steingart RM, Stone PH, Knatterud GL, Conti CR **(d)** Bourassa MG, Knatterud GL, Pepine CJ, Sopko G, Rogers WJ, Geller NL, Dyrda I, Forman SA, Chaitman BR, Sharaf B, Davies RF, Conti CR **(e)** Pratt CM, McMahon RP, Goldstein S, Pepine CJ, Andrews TC, Dyrda I, Frishman WH, Geller NL, Hill JA, Morgan NA, Stone PH, Knatterud GL, Sopko G, Conti CR **(f)** Davies RF, Goldberg AD, Forman S, Pepine CJ, Knatterud GL, Geller N, Sopko G, Pratt C, Deanfield J, Conti CR
Titles	**(a)** The Asymptomatic Cardiac Ischemia Pilot (ACIP) Study: design of a randomized clinical trial, baseline data and implications for a long-term outcome trial **(b)** Effects of treatment strategies to suppress ischemia in patients with coronary artery disease: 12-week results of the Asymptomatic Cardiac Ischemia Pilot (ACIP) study **(c)** Asymptomatic Cardiac Ischemia Pilot (ACIP) study: outcome at 1 year for patients with asymptomatic cardiac ischemia randomized to medical therapy or revascularization **(d)** Asymptomatic Cardiac Ischemia Pilot (ACIP) study. Improvement of cardiac ischemia at 1 year after PTCA and CABG **(e)** Comparison of subgroup assigned to medical regimens used to suppress cardiac ischemia (the Asymptomatic Cardiac Ischemia Pilot (ACIP) study) **(f)** Asymptomatic Cardiac Ischemia Pilot (ACIP) study two-year follow-up. Outcome of patients randomized to initial strategies of medical therapy versus revascularization
References	**(a)** *J Am Coll Cardiol* 1994;**24**:1–10 **(b)** *J Am Coll Cardiol* 1994;**24**:11–20 **(c)** *J Am Coll Cardiol* 1995;**26**:594–605 **(d)** *Circulation* 1995;**92**(suppl II):II-1–7 **(e)** *Am J Cardiol* 1996;**77**:1302–9 **(f)** *Circulation* 1997;**95**:2037–43
Disease	Silent ischaemia
Purpose	To compare the 12 weeks' anti-ischaemic effect of angina-directed medical therapy, angina plus ambulatory ECG-directed medical therapy, and revascularisation
Study design	Randomised
Follow-up	12 weeks, 1 year

Patients	618 patients (204 'control', 202 ischaemia-guided therapy, 212 revascularisation). Patients must have at least 1 major coronary artery narrowing $\geq 50\%$, stress-related ischaemia, 1 episode or more of silent ischaemia on a 48-h ambulatory ECG
Treatment regimen	'Control': antianginal therapy to relieve angina plus blinded placebo. Medical, ischaemia-guided: antianginal therapy to relieve angina and ischaemia on 48-h ECG. Revascularisation: percutaneous transluminal coronary angioplasty (PTCA) or coronary artery bypass grafting (CABG). If necessary blinded antianginal therapy
Results	At 12 weeks, ambulatory ECG ischaemia was no longer present in 39% of patients assigned to the angina-guided strategy, 41% of patients assigned to the ischaemia-guided strategy and 55% of patients assigned to the revascularisation strategy. All strategies reduced the number of ischaemic episodes and total duration of ST-segment depression during follow-up ambulatory ECG monitoring. For most patients in the two medical strategies, angina was controlled with low to moderate doses of anti-ischaemic medication. Following revascularisation, 65% of patients did not require angina medication. Despite more severe coronary disease and more ischaemic episodes at baseline, ischaemia was significantly improved in the CABG patients compared to the PTCA patients, and significantly fewer patients had angina (90% vs 68%, p = 0.001); these differences were maintained to 1 year. At 1 year, mortality rate was 4.4% in the angina-guided group, 1.6% in the ischaemia-guided group, 0% in the revascularisation group (overall p = 0.004; angina-guided vs revascularisation, p = 0.003). The revascularisation group had significantly fewer hospital admissions and non-protocol revascularisations at 1 year, but the frequency of MI, unstable angina, stroke and congestive heart failure was not different between the groups. The incidence of death, MI, non-protocol revascularisation, or hospital admission at 1 year was 32% (angina-guided), 31% (ischaemia-guided) and 18% (revascularisation) (p = 0.003). Two years after randomisation the total mortality had increased to 6.6% in the angina-guided group, 4.4% in the ischaemia-guided group, and 1.1% in the group with revascularisation strategy

ACME
Angioplasty Compared to Medicine

Authors	Parisi AF, Folland ED, Hartigan P
Title	A comparison of angioplasty with medical therapy in the treatment of single-vessel coronary artery disease
Reference	*N Engl J Med* 1992;**326**:10–6
Disease	Stable angina pectoris, coronary artery stenosis
Purpose	To study whether percutaneous transluminal coronary angioplasty (PTCA) is better than medical treatment for coronary artery stenosis
Study design	Randomised
Follow-up	6 months
Patients	212 patients (107 drug therapy and 105 PTCA)
Treatment regimen	Oral isosorbide dinitrate with sublingual glyceryl trinitrate and/or β-blockers and/or calcium antagonists. PTCA group: calcium antagonists before and during 1 month after PTCA, heparin at PTCA and glyceryl trinitrate during and 12 h after the procedure
Concomitant therapy	Aspirin, 325 mg/day
Results	Paired exercise tests were performed by 199 patients. Both groups showed an increase in total exercise duration: 0.5 min for the drug therapy group and 2.1 min for the PTCA group ($p < 0.001$). In the drug therapy group, the maximal heart rate-blood pressure product decreased 2800 units compared to an increase of 1800 units for the PTCA group ($p < 0.0001$). Angina was reduced by 15 attacks/month in the PTCA group and 7 attacks/month in the drug therapy group ($p < 0.06$). The quality of life score improved by 8.6 units in the PTCA group and by 2.4 units in the drug therapy group ($p = 0.03$)

ADEG
Antiarrhythmic Drug Evaluation Group study

Authors	**(a)** Zuanetti G, Latini R, Neilson JMM, Schwartz PJ, Ewing DJ **(b)** Antiarrhythmic Drug Evaluation Group
Titles	**(a)** Heart rate variability in patients with ventricular arrhythmias: effect of antiarrhythmic drugs **(b)** A multicentre, randomised trial on the benefit/risk profile of amiodarone, flecainide and propafenone in patients with cardiac disease and complex ventricular arrhythmias
References	**(a)** *J Am Coll Cardiol* 1991;**17**:604–12 **(b)** *Eur Heart J* 1992;**13**:1251–8
Disease	Ventricular arrhythmia, cardiac disease
Purpose	To compare the long-term benefit/risk profiles of flecainide, propafenone and amiodarone in patients with complex ventricular arrhythmias and heart disease and to study the effect of the drugs on heart rate variability
Study design	Randomised, open, parallel-group, partly crossover
Follow-up	2 years
Patients	141 patients, mean age 59 years. 109 (77%) completed the study. 40 patients entered a washout protocol
Treatment regimen	Flecainide, 200 or 450 mg/day, or propafenone, 300 or 900 mg/day, or amiodarone, 200–400 mg/day, after an initial loading dose of $\geq$ 600 mg/day for 1 week
Results	After 2 years, of the 76 patients (54%) responding, 60 never changed drug (49% of those given amiodarone, 46% of those given flecainide and 30% of those given propafenone, as first drug). There were 50 adverse reactions resulting in drug withdrawal (17% of the amiodarone group, 21% of the flecainide group and 35% of the propafenone group). Cardiovascular adverse events were significantly less common with amiodarone ($p < 0.03$). The different effects of the drugs on heart rate variability may contribute to their overall effect on mortality

AFTER

Aspirin/Anticoagulants Following Thrombolysis with anistreplase (Eminase) in Recurrent infarction

Authors	Julian DG, Chamberlain DA, Pocock SJ
Title	A comparison of aspirin and anticoagulation following thrombolysis for myocardial infarction (the AFTER study): a multicentre unblinded randomised clinical trial
Reference	*BMJ* 1996;**313**:1429–31
Disease	AMI
Purpose	To compare the effect on cardiac death and reinfarction of aspirin with anticoagulant therapy
Study design	Randomised, open, controlled
Follow-up	30 days, 3 months
Patients	1036 patients (aim 1856). Time since onset of symptoms: ≤ 6 h
Treatment regimen	All patients anistreplase, 30 U, then randomised to either aspirin, 150 mg/day, or heparin, 1000 U/h iv for 24 h, beginning 6 h after anistreplase, plus oral anticoagulants to maintain an international normalised ratio in the range 2.0–2.5. Both regimens were continued for 3 months
Results	There were no significant differences in the incidence of cardiac events between the two groups. After 30 days, cardiac death or reinfarction occurred in 11% of the anticoagulation group and 11.2% of the aspirin group. At 3 months, the corresponding rates were 13.2% (anticoagulation) and 12.1% (aspirin). Severe bleeding or stroke by 3 months was more common in the anticoagulation group than in the aspirin group (3.9% vs 1.7%; p = 0.04)
Comments	The trial was stopped earlier than intended because of the slowing rate of recruitment

AIMS
APSAC Intervention Mortality Study

Authors	**(a)** and **(b)** The AIMS group
Titles	**a)** Effect of intravenous APSAC on mortality after acute myocardial infarction: preliminary report of a placebo-controlled clinical trial **(b)** Long-term effects of intravenous anistreplase in acute myocardial infarction: final report of the AIMS study
References	**(a)** *Lancet* 1988;**i**:545–9 **(b)** *Lancet* 1990;**335**:427–31
Disease	AMI
Purpose	To investigate the effects of anisoylated plasminogen streptokinase activator complex (APSAC) on survival rates for up to 1 year after AMI
Study design	Randomised, double-blind, placebo-controlled
Follow-up	1 year
Patients	Aim 2000 patients, but only 1004 patients (502 in each group) recruited (see comments), aged ≤ 70 years
Treatment regimen	APSAC, 300 U iv bolus over 5 min within 6 h of onset of symptoms
Concomitant therapy	Heparin iv. Ancillary therapy administered according therapy to normal practice. β-blockers given on discharge from hospital
Results	At 30 days, 6% of patients in the APSAC group had died compared to 12% in the placebo group. At 1 year, the mortality rates were 11% and 18%, respectively. Major complications of AMI were less common in the APSAC group than in the controls
Comments	It was considered unethical to continue to randomise patients to a placebo treatment arm because of the 47% reduction in the 30-day mortality in patients receiving APSAC. Patient entry to the trial was terminated in November 1987

AIRE
Acute Infarction Ramipril Efficacy study

Authors	**(a)** The Acute Infarction Ramipril Efficacy (AIRE) study investigators **(b)** Ball SG, Hall AS, Murray GD **(c)** Cleland JGF, Erhardt L, Murray G, Hall AS, Ball SG
Titles	**(a)** Effect of ramipril on mortality and morbidity of survivors of acute myocardial infarction with clinical evidence of heart failure **(b)** ACE inhibition, atherosclerosis and myocardial infarction – the AIRE study **(c)** Effect of ramipril on morbidity and mode of death among survivors of acute myocardial infarction with clinical evidence of heart failure. A report from the AIRE study investigators
References	**(a)** *Lancet* 1993;**342**:821–8 **(b)** *Eur Heart J* 1994;**15**(suppl B):20–5 **(c)** *Eur Heart J* 1997;**18**:41–51
Disease	AMI with heart failure
Purpose	To compare the effects of ramipril with placebo on total mortality in patients surviving AMI and with early clinical evidence of heart failure. Secondary objective: to compare the incidences of progression to severe or resistant heart failure, nonfatal reinfarction and stroke between the two groups
Study design	Randomised, double-blind, parallel-group, placebo-controlled
Follow-up	More than 6 months with an average of 15 months
Patients	2006 patients (1014 ramipril and 992 placebo), aged ≥ 18 years, with a definite AMI 3–10 days before randomisation and clinical evidence of heart failure at any time since AMI. Patients with severe or resistant heart failure were excluded
Treatment regimen	Ramipril, 2.5–5 mg bid, or placebo
Results	Mortality from all causes was significantly lower for patients on ramipril compared to patients on placebo. The risk reduction was 27% (p = 0.002). Ramipril reduced the risk of sudden death by 30% (p = 0.011) and of death from circulatory failure by 18% (p = 0.237). The magnitude of the effects on sudden death and death due to circulatory failure were not significantly different, but 38% of the reduction in overall mortality was from the subgroup with sudden death who had developed prior severe resistant heart failure. The mortality reduction was already apparent at 30 days and consistent across a range of subgroups. Ramipril did not alter the rate of stroke or reinfarction
Comments	The study continued into the AIREX study

AIREX
AIRE Extension study

Authors	Hall AS, Murray GD, Ball SG
Title	Follow-up study of patients randomly allocated ramipril or placebo for heart failure after myocardial infarction: AIRE Extension (AIREX) study
Reference	*Lancet* 1997;**349**:1493–7
Disease	AMI with heart failure
Purpose	To assess the long-term (3 years after the end of AIRE) survival benefits of ramipril compared to placebo in the UK patients from the AIRE study
Study design	Retrospective, controlled
Follow-up	3 years
Patients	603 patients (302 initially on ramipril and 301 initially on placebo)
Treatment regimen	See treatment for the AIRE study
Results	Death from all causes had occurred in 117/301 previously placebo-treated patients and 83/302 previously ramipril-treated patients. This is a statistically significant relative risk reduction of 36%

ALLHAT
Antihypertensive and Lipid-Lowering treatment to prevent Heart Attack Trial
Ongoing trial

Authors	Davis BR, Cutler JA, Gordon DJ, Furberg CD, Wright JT Jr, Cushman WC, Grimm RH, LaRosa J, Whelton PK, Perry HM, Alderman MH, Ford CE, Oparil S, Francis C, Proschan M, Pressel S, Black HR, Hawkins CM
Title	Rationale and design for the Antihypertensive and Lipid Lowering treatment to prevent Heart Attack Trial (ALLHAT)
Reference	*Am J Hypertens* 1996;**9**:342–60
Disease	Hypertension and hypercholesterolaemia
Purpose	Antihypertensive part: to assess the incidence of fatal coronary heart disease and nonfatal MI in patients treated with chlorthalidone, amlodipine, lisinopril, or doxazosin. Lipid-lowering part: to assess the all-cause mortality in half of the above patients treated with either pravastatin or 'usual care'
Study design	Antihypertensive: randomised, double-blind Lipid-lowering: randomised, open
Follow-up	Mean 6 years
Patients	Aim 40,000 high-risk hypertensive patients, aged ≥ 55 years, about 45% women, at least 55% black
Treatment regimen	Antihypertensive: step 1: chlorthalidone, 12.5 mg initially, then 12.5–25 mg, or amlodipine, 2.5 mg initially, then 2.5–10 mg, or lisinopril, 10 mg initially, then 10–40 mg, or doxazosin, 1 mg initially, then 2–8 mg. Lipid-lowering: pravastatin, 40 mg in the evening plus NCEP diet, or NCEP diet alone
Concomitant therapy	Step 2 and step 3 antihypertensive agents, if required
Results	To be expected in 2002

AMICUS
Austrian Multicenter Isradipine Cum Spirapril study

Author	Magometschnigg D
Title	Isradipine in the treatment of mild to moderate hypertension: the Austrian Multicenter Isradipine Cum Spirapril study (AMICUS)
Reference	*Am J Hypertens* 1993;**6**(suppl):49S–53S
Disease	Mild to moderate hypertension
Purpose	To assess the safety and efficacy of isradipine in the treatment of patients with mild to moderate hypertension in general practice
Study design	Open
Follow-up	26 weeks
Patients	595 patients (282 women and 313 men), aged 20–79 years
Treatment regimen	Isradipine, 1.25–2.5 mg bid, plus, if necessary, spirapril, 3 mg once daily, or pindolol, 5 mg once daily
Results	Normalisation of blood pressure was achieved in 80.5% of cases. This result was obtained with the lower isradipine dose in 249 cases (4.18%), the higher isradipine dose in 215 cases (36.1%) and with isradipine plus spirapril or pindolol in 112 cases (18.5%). There was no clinically relevant change in heart rate. A total of 100 adverse effects were reported in 73 patients (12.3%), of which 18 were severe

ANBP2
Australian National Blood Pressure study 2
Ongoing trial

Authors	Management Committee on behalf of the High Blood Pressure Research Council of Australia
Title	Australian comparative outcome trial of angiotensin-converting enzyme inhibitor- and diuretic-based treatment of hypertension in the elderly (ANBP2): objectives and protocol
Reference	*Clin Exp Pharmacol Physiol* 1997;**24**:188–92
Disease	Hypertension
Purpose	To determine whether in hypertensive patients aged 65-84 there is any difference in total cardiovascular events (fatal and non-fatal) between antihypertensive treatment with an ACE inhibitor-based regimen and treatment with a diuretic-based regimen over a 5-year treatment period
Study design	Randomised, open with blinding of endpoint assessment
Follow-up	5 years
Patients	Aim 6000 patients, aged 65–84 years
Treatment regimen	ACE inhibitor group: step 1: ACE inhibitor (enalapril); step 2: β-blocker or calcium antagonist or α-adrenoceptor antagonist; step 3: either of two drug classes not used in step 2 or a diuretic; step 4: drug from a class not used in step 2 or 3 Diuretic group: step 1: diuretic; step 2: β-blocker or calcium antagonist or adrenoceptor antagonist; steps 3 and 4: as in ACE inhibitor group
Results	To be expected in 2002

APIS
Antihypertensive Patch Italian Study

Authors	The Antihypertensive Patch Italian Study (APIS) Investigators
Title	One year efficacy and tolerability of clonidine administered by the transdermal route in patients with mild to moderate essential hypertension – a multicentre open label study
Reference	*Clin Auton Res* 1993;**3**:379–83
Disease	Mild to moderate hypertension
Purpose	To evaluate the efficacy and safety of clonidine therapeutic transdermal system (TTS) in the Italian population
Study design	Open
Follow-up	12 months
Patients	101 patients (51 men and 50 women), aged 30–71 years (mean 53 years ± 10)
Treatment regimen	The initial dose was a patch of 3.5 cm^2 delivering clonidine, 100 µg/day (TTS-1) for 2 weeks. Non-responders received a 7 cm^2 patch delivering clonidine, 200 µg/day (TTS-2). After another 2 weeks, non-responders received a 10.5 cm^2 patch delivering clonidine, 300 µg/day (TTS-3) for 2 weeks. Then non-responders to TTS-3 received chlorthalidone, 25 µg/day orally in addition. After 2 months, the patient was maintained on the effective dose until the end of the study
Results	The decrease in systolic and diastolic blood pressure was significant (p = 0.01) after 12 months of treatment. 56% of patients achieved blood pressure control with TTS-1 or TTS-2. 10% of the patients required TTS-3 and 6% needed additional chlorthalidone. At 90 days, the non-responder rate was 5%. 24 patients (32%) complained of a skin reaction and 21 of these (10 men, 11 women) were withdrawn from the study because of this. No serious side effects were observed. No rebound phenomena occurred in the week after discontinuation of treatment

APRICOT
Antithrombotics in the Prevention of Reocclusion In Coronary Thrombolysis

Authors	**(a)** Meijer A, Verheugt FWA, Werter CJPJ, Lie KI, van der Pol JMJ, van Eenige MJ **(b)** Veen G, Meyer A, Verheugt FWA, Werter CJPJ, de Swart H, Lie KI, van der Pol JMJ, Michels HR, van Eenige MJ **(c)** Meijer A, Verheugt FWA, van Eenige MJ, Werter CJPJ
Titles	**(a)** Aspirin versus Coumadin in the prevention of reocclusion and recurrent ischemia after successful thrombolysis: a prospective placebo-controlled angiographic study. Results of the APRICOT study **(b)** Culprit lesion morphology and stenosis severity in the prediction of reocclusion after coronary thrombolysis: angiographic results of the APRICOT study **(c)** Left ventricular function at 3 months after successful thrombolysis. Impact of reocclusion without reinfarction on ejection fraction, regional function, and remodeling
References	**(a)** *Circulation* 1993;**87**:1524–30 **(b)** *J Am Coll Cardiol* 1993;**22**:1755–62 **(c)** *Circulation* 1994;**90**:1706–14
Disease	AMI
Purpose	To assess the effect of aspirin or warfarin on reocclusion and recurrent ischaemia after thrombolysis
Study design	Randomised, placebo-controlled
Follow-up	3 months
Patients	300 patients, aged < 71 years, with chest pain > 30 min < 4 h and ST-segment elevation indicative of MI. Patients were eligible when the infarct-related artery was patent with residual grade 1–3 stenosis, as determined by angiography
Treatment regimen	Continuation of iv heparin plus warfarin adjusted to international normalised ratio of 2.8–4.0 (open-label); aspirin, 325 mg/day, or placebo (double-blind)
Concomitant therapy	Streptokinase, 1.5 × 10⁶ U iv over 30–60 min, or anistreplase (APSAC), 30 U/5 min iv. After thrombolytic treatment heparin, 20,000 U/24 h iv. Standard coronary care according to the ISIS-1 protocol
Results	Reocclusion rates at 3 months: aspirin 25%; warfarin 30%; placebo 32%. Compared to placebo, aspirin significantly reduced reinfarction and revascularisation rates. The efficacy of warfarin seemed less than that of aspirin. Angiographic features of the lesion after successful thrombolysis significantly predicted the risk of reocclusion. In a subset analysis, persistent patency at 3 months after anterior infarction significantly improved ejection fraction. Reocclusion prevented recovery of infarct zone contractility

APSI
Acebutolol et Prévention Secondaire de l'Infarctus

Authors	Boissel J-P, Leizorovicz A, Picolet H, Peyrieux J-C
Title	Secondary prevention after high-risk acute myocardial infarction with low-dose acebutolol
Reference	*Am J Cardiol* 1990;**66**:251–60
Disease	AMI
Purpose	To investigate the effects of long-term acebutolol, a β-blocker with mild intrinsic sympathomimetic activity, in the prevention of late death in high-risk patients surviving AMI
Study design	Randomised, double-blind, placebo-controlled
Follow-up	Aim 1 year; average 318 days
Patients	607 patients (443 men and 164 women; 298 acebutolol and 309 placebo), aged < 76 years (mean 62.9 years). Mean time since onset of symptoms: 10.5 days
Treatment regimen	Acebutolol, 200 mg bid, or placebo
Results	There were 17 deaths in the acebutolol group and 34 in the placebo group (ie, a 48% decrease; p = 0.019). Vascular mortality decreased by 58% (p = 0.006). All cardiovascular causes of death, including congestive heart failure, were less common in the acebutolol group. The objective was not achieved (see comments), but patients in the acebutolol group were at a higher risk than average in nine previous trials with β-blockers giving a significant result (12% instead of 7%). In addition, total mortality did not decrease in nine subgroups (increasing mortality risk of 2–23%)
Comments	At the time of the second interim analysis, the placebo group 1-year mortality was much lower than expected (12% instead of 20%) and the ethical board recommended premature discontinuation of the trial

APSIS
Angina Prognosis Study in Stockholm

Authors	**(a)** Rehnqvist N, Held C, Forslund L **(b)** Rehnqvist N, Hjemdahl P, Billing E, Björkander I, Eriksson SV, Forslund L, Held C, Näsman P, Wallén NH
Titles	**(a)** Influence of antianginal therapy on premature ventricular contraction and ST-segment depression in patients with chronic angina pectoris **(b)** Effects of metoprolol vs verapamil in patients with stable angina pectoris. The Angina Prognosis Study in Stockholm (APSIS)
References	**(a)** *New Trends Arrhythmias* 1990;**6**:663–70 **(b)** *Eur Heart J* 1996;**17**:76–81 (erratum **17**:483)
Disease	Stable angina pectoris
Purpose	To study the prognosis for patients with stable angina pectoris according to their medical history and clinical findings and to compare the effects of treatment with metoprolol or verapamil on atherosclerotic endpoints and psychosocial variables
Study design	Randomised, double-blind, parallel-group
Follow-up	6 years
Patients	809 patients (248 women) < 70 years
Treatment regimen	Metoprolol CR, 200 mg once daily, or verapamil SR, 240 mg bid. The dosages were reduced by half if side effects developed
Results	During the period of follow-up, 22 patients (5.4%) died in the metoprolol group and 25 (6.2%) in the verapamil group. The total number of non-fatal cardiovascular events was 204. There was no difference between metoprolol and verapamil with regard to cardiovascular and atherosclerotic events. Men had a much poorer prognosis than women, both for cardiovascular and atherosclerotic events. However, there was a preponderance of women in the subgroup undergoing angiography due to incapacitating angina not followed by a procedure. The primary psychological endpoints were the same for metoprolol and verapamil but differed significantly from the controls

APTH

Ambulatory blood Pressure and Treatment of Hypertension

Ongoing trial

Authors	(a) Staessen J, Amery A (b) Bieniaszewski L, Staessen JA, Polfliet J, Thijs L, Fagard R
Titles	(a) APTH – a trial on ambulatory blood pressure monitoring and treatment of hypertension: objectives and protocol (b) Treatment of hypertensive patients according to the conventional or ambulatory pressure: a progress report on the APTH trial
References	(a) *Acta Cardiol* 1993;**48**:25-42 (b) *Acta Cardiol* 1996;**51**:243-51
Disease	Hypertension
Purpose	To test the hypothesis that antihypertensive treatment based on ambulatory blood pressure (ABP) monitoring may be more beneficial than treatment guided by conventional sphygmomanometry (CBP)
Study design	Randomised, double-blind for 6 months, then open
Follow-up	1 year
Patients	Aim 400 patients, aged $\geq$ 18 years, with diastolic blood pressure $\geq$ 95 mm Hg on two consecutive measurements
Treatment regimen	Dose titration to maintain adequate diastolic blood pressure 1st step: lisinopril, 10 mg once daily 2nd step: addition of lisinopril, 10 mg (total 20 mg once daily) 3rd step: addition of hydrochlorothiazide, 12.5 mg once daily 4th step: addition of amlodipine, 5 mg once daily Target pressure: CBP group: a sitting diastolic pressure 80–89 mm Hg on conventional sphygmomanometry; ABP group: daytime (10 am to 8 pm) mean ambulatory diastolic pressure 80–89 mm Hg
Results	Interim report on 207 patients: at 1 month, lisinopril was discontinued more frequently in the ABP group than in the CBP group (p = 0.004). At 2 months, blood pressure control was not significantly different between the two groups

ARIC
Atherosclerosis Risk In Communities study
Ongoing trial

Authors	Sharret AR and the ARIC Investigators
Title	The Atherosclerosis Risk In Communities (ARIC) study. Introduction and objectives of the hemostatic component
Reference	*Ann Epidemiol* 1992;**2**:467–9
Disease	Atherosclerosis
Purpose	To investigate aetiological risk factors associated with atherosclerosis and its clinical outcomes
Study design	Observational, epidemiological
Follow-up	Up to 10 years
Patients	15,801 patients, aged 35–74 years
Comments	This study has been the basis for a vast number of publications. A small selection of the references are listed below.

Haemostasis
– Shahar E, *Arterioscler Thromb* 1993;**13**:1205–12

Lipids
– Brown SA, *Arterioscler Thromb* 1993;**13**:1558–66

Cardiac autonomic function
– Liao D, *Am J Hypertens* 1996;**9**:1147–56

TIA/stroke
– Chambless LE, *Am J Epidemiol* 1996;**144**:857–66

Coronary heart disease
– White AD, *J Clin Epidemiol* 1996;**49**:223–33

ARMS
APSAC Reocclusion Multicentre Study

Authors	Relik-van Wely L, Visser RF, van der Pol JMJ *et al*
Title	Angiographically assessed coronary arterial patency and reocclusion in patients with acute myocardial infarction treated with anistreplase: results of the Anistreplase Reocclusion Multicenter Study (ARMS)
Reference	*Am J Cardiol* 1991;**68**:296–300
Disease	AMI
Purpose	To investigate the effects of anisoylated plasminogen streptokinase activator complex (APSAC or anistreplase) on coronary artery patency following AMI
Study design	Open
Follow-up	24 h
Patients	156 patients. Time since onset of AMI: < 4 h
Treatment regimen	Anistreplase, 30 U iv over 5 min
Concomitant therapy	Heparin, 1000 U/h from 3 h after anistreplase
Results	After 90 min, 106 of 145 patients (73%) had patent infarct-related vessels. After 24 h, 98 of 102 patients (96%) had a patent infarct-related vessel. The incidence of reinfarction within 2 months was 11.5%

ASAAC
Acetylsalicylic Acid versus Anticoagulants study

Authors	Weber MAJ, Hasford J, Taillens C, Zitzmann A, Hahalis G, Seggewiss H *et al*
Title	Low-dose aspirin versus anticoagulants for the prevention of coronary graft occlusion
Reference	*Am J Cardiol* 1990;**66**:1464–8
Disease	Coronary artery disease, coronary graft occlusion
Purpose	To compare the occlusion rates of grafts or bypass vessels, perioperative blood loss and clinical results in patients treated with platelet inhibitors or anticoagulant therapy after coronary artery bypass
Study design	Randomised, open, parallel-group
Follow-up	3 months
Patients	235 patients (122 aspirin and 113 anticoagulant)
Treatment regimen	Aspirin, 100 mg/day, started 24 h before coronary bypass surgery, or heparin in a constant dose of 10,000 U/24 h, started 6 h after surgery, plus phenprocoumon 48 h after surgery. Heparin was discontinued after a prothrombin of 30% had been reached
Concomitant therapy	All platelet-inhibiting medication was discontinued 10 days before surgery
Results	22% of 218 vein graft distal anastomoses in the aspirin group and 29% of 272 in the anticoagulant group were occluded. At least one occluded distal anastomosis was present in 38% of 74 patients in the aspirin group and in 39% of 86 in the anticoagulant group. For grafts with endarterectomy, the occlusion rate was lower in the aspirin group (12% vs 22%; $p \leq 0.05$). Perioperative blood loss in the aspirin group was 1211 ± 814 ml in the first 48 h, compared to 874 ± 818 ml in the anticoagulant group ($p \leq 0.001$)

ASCB
Asymptotic Cervical Bruit study

Authors	**(a)** The Asymptomatic Cervical Bruit study group **(b)** Côté R, Battista RN, Abrahamowicz M, Langlois Y, Bourque F, Mackey A **(c)** Mackey AE, Abrahamowicz M, Langlois Y, Battista R, Simard D, Bourque F, Leclerc J, Côté R
Titles	**(a)** Natural history and effectiveness of aspirin in asymptomatic patients with cervical bruits **(b)** Lack of effect of aspirin in asymptomatic patients with carotid bruits and substantial carotid narrowing **(c)** Outcome of asymptomatic patients with carotid disease
References	**(a)** *Arch Neurol* 1991;**48**:683–6 **(b)** *Ann Intern Med* 1995;**123**:649–55 **(c)** *Neurology* 1997;**48**:896–903
Disease	Carotid atherosclerosis
Purpose	To examine the determinants of vascular events in asymptomatic patients with carotid atherosclerosis identified by cervical bruits and to test the effect of aspirin on stenoses $\geq 50\%$
Study design	Randomised, double-blind, placebo-controlled
Follow-up	2 years for the aspirin part, 6 years for the epidemiological part
Patients	715 neurologically asymptomatic patients with cervical bruits for the epidemiological part; of these, 372 had a carotid stenosis $\geq 50\%$ and were randomised to aspirin or placebo
Treatment regimen	Aspirin enteric-coated, 325 mg/day, or placebo
Results	The annual rate of all ischaemic events and death from any cause was 12.3% for the placebo group and 11.0% for the aspirin group (p = 0.61). In the epidemiological study part it was found that progression of carotid stenosis particularly to more than 80% was associated with a higher rate of both ipsilateral neurologic events and overall combined vascular events. The data suggest that severity of carotid stenosis is the main risk factor for neurologic and other events
Comments	An interim analysis was made in April 1994. As the results showed that aspirin did not decrease the risk for adverse outcomes, the trial was stopped

ASIST
Atenolol Silent Ischemia Study

Authors	**(a)** and **(b)** Pepine CJ, Cohn PF, Deedwania PC *et al*
Titles	**(a)** The prognostic and economic implications of a strategy to detect and treat asymptomatic ischemia: the atenolol silent ischemia trial (ASIST) protocol **(b)** Effects of treatment on outcome in mildly symptomatic patients with ischemia during daily life. The Atenolol Silent Ischemia Study (ASIST)
References	**(a)** *Clin Cardiol* 1991;**14**:457–62 **(b)** *Circulation* 1994;**90**:762–8
Disease	Silent ischaemia, coronary artery disease
Purpose	To assess the influence of frequency and duration of symptomatic and asymptomatic ischaemic episodes on the occurrence of fatal and nonfatal cardiac events and to analyse the response to atenolol treatment
Study design	Randomised, double-blind, placebo-controlled
Follow-up	Mean 10.4 years
Patients	306 patients (152 atenolol, 154 placebo) with coronary artery disease, mild or no angina, abnormal exercise tests and ischaemia on ambulatory monitoring
Treatment regimen	Atenolol, 100 mg once daily, titratable to 50 mg once daily should side effects develop, or placebo
Results	After 4 weeks of treatment the number and average duration of ischaemic episodes per 48 h of ambulatory monitoring decreased significantly in atenolol-assigned patients compared to placebo-assigned. Event-free survival improved in atenolol-treated patients ($p < 0.0066$), who had an increased time to onset of first adverse cardiac event (120 vs 79 days) and fewer total first events compared to placebo ($p = 0.001$). The most powerful univariate and multivariate correlate of event-free survival was absence of ischaemia on ambulatory monitoring at 4 weeks

ASK
Australian Streptokinase Trial

Authors	**(a)** and **(b)** Donnan GA, Davis SM, Chambers BR *et al* **(c)** Infeld B, Davis SM, Donnan GA, Lichtenstein M, Baird AE, Binns D, Mitchell PJ, Hopper JL
Titles	**(a)** Australian Streptokinase Trial (ASK) **(b)** Streptokinase for acute ischemic stroke with relationship to time of administration **(c)** Streptokinase increases luxury perfusion after stroke
References	**(a)** In: del Zoppo GJ, Mori E, Hacke W, eds. Thrombolytic Therapy in Acute Ischemic Stroke II. Berlin: Springer, 1993:80–5 **(b)** *JAMA* 1996;**267**:961–6 **(c)** *Stroke* 1996;**27**:1524–9
Disease	Acute ischaemic stroke
Purpose	To test whether iv streptokinase administered within 4 h of acute ischaemic stroke will significantly reduce subsequent morbidity and mortality
Study design	Randomised, double-blind, placebo-controlled
Follow-up	3 months
Patients	340 patients (aim 600), mean age 68.5 years, with acute ischaemic stroke < 4 h
Treatment regimen	Streptokinase, 1.5×10^6 U iv over 60 min, or placebo
Concomitant therapy	Oral aspirin, 100 mg/day, started within 4 h of streptokinase. Standard medical treatment. No heparin, warfarin or similar anticoagulants within 48 h of study therapy
Results	There was a trend towards higher incidence of death and disability in the streptokinase group, 48.3% vs 44.6% for placebo. This was particularly so for those treated after 3 h. In 24 of the patients, having acute middle cerebral cortical infarction, streptokinase was associated with a greater amount of non-nutritional reperfusion than was placebo
Comments	Recruitment of patients was stopped after 340 patients in total were enrolled because of significantly worse outcomes for patients treated 3–4 h after symptom onset

ASPECT
Anticoagulants in the Secondary Prevention of Events in Coronary Thrombosis

Authors	**(a)** Anticoagulants in the Secondary Prevention of Events in Coronary Thrombosis (ASPECT) research group **(b)** Azar AJ, Cannegieter SC, Deckers JW, Briët E, van Bergen PFMM, Jonker JJC, Rosendaal FR
Titles	**(a)** Effect of long-term oral anticoagulant treatment on mortality and cardiovascular morbidity after myocardial infarction **(b)** Optimal intensity of oral anticoagulant therapy after myocardial infarction
References	**(a)** *Lancet* 1994;**343**:499–503 **(b)** *J Am Coll Cardiol* 1996;**27**:1349–55
Disease	AMI
Purpose	To assess the effect of long-term treatment with oral anticoagulants in the secondary prevention of mortality and morbidity after AMI
Study design	Randomised, double-blind, placebo-controlled
Follow-up	0.5–6 years (mean 3 years)
Patients	3404 survivors of MI (1700 anticoagulants and 1704 placebo), enrolled within 6 weeks after hospital discharge
Treatment regimen	Coumarins (nicoumalone or phenprocoumon) to achieve an international normalised ratio of 2.4–4.8, or placebo
Results	There were 170 deaths among the anticoagulant-treated patients and 189 in the placebo group. Compared to placebo, long-term anticoagulant therapy led to a significant reduction in recurrent MI and cerebrovascular events. Major bleeding complications were seen in 73 patients who received anticoagulants and 19 patients who received placebo. The incidence of the combined outcome (bleeding or thromboembolic complications) was lower with international normalised ratios between 2 and 4 than with international normalised ratios of < 2 or > 4, and was lowest with an international normalised ratio of 3–4 (3.2 events/100 patient-years)

ASPIRE
Action on Secondary Prevention through Intervention to Reduce Events

Authors	ASPIRE steering group
Title	A British Cardiac Society survey of the potential for the secondary prevention of coronary disease: ASPIRE (Action on Secondary Prevention through Intervention to Reduce Events). Principal results
Reference	*Heart* 1996;**75**:334–42
Disease	Coronary disease
Purpose	To determine the potential for secondary prevention of coronary disease in the United Kingdom by influencing risk factors
Study design	Retrospective, cross-sectional
Follow-up	6 months (minimum)
Patients	2583 patients, aged 26-70 years, with approximately 300 men and 300 women in each of four diagnostic categories: elective coronary bypass grafting, elective percutaneous transluminal coronary angioplasty, AMI, acute myocardial ischaemia
Results	When interviewed at least 6 months after leaving hospital, many patients still presented risk factors: 10–27% were still smoking, 75% remained overweight, up to 25% remained hypertensive, more than 75% had elevated total cholesterol levels (> 5.2 mmol/l). Only one-third of infarct patients were taking β-blockers, and up to 20% of those who had suffered acute myocardial ischaemia were not taking aspirin. There is thus considerable potential to reduce the risk of further major ischaemic events in patients of this type by more effective lifestyle intervention, rigorous management of blood pressure and cholesterol levels, and the appropriate use of prophylactic drugs

ASSET
Anglo-Scandinavian Study of Early Thrombolysis

Authors	**(a)** and **(b)** Wilcox RG, von der Lippe G, Olsson CG, Jenssen G, Skene AM, Hampton JR
Titles	**(a)** Trial of tissue plasminogen activator for mortality reduction in acute myocardial infarction. Anglo-Scandinavian Study of Early Thrombolysis (ASSET) **(b)** Effects of alteplase in acute myocardial infarction: 6-month results from the ASSET study
References	**(a)** *Lancet* 1988;**ii**:525–30 **(b)** *Lancet* 1990;**335**:1175–8
Disease	AMI
Purpose	To investigate the effects of rt-PA on mortality after AMI
Study design	Randomised, double-blind, placebo-controlled
Follow-up	1–12 months
Patients	5013 patients (2514 rt-PA and 2499 placebo), aged 18–75 years
Treatment regimen	rt-PA, 10 mg bolus within 5 h of onset of symptoms, followed by an infusion of 50 mg/h for the first hour and 20 mg/h for the next 2 h
Concomitant therapy	Heparin, 5000 U bolus before and an infusion of 1000 U/h for 21 h after administration of rt-PA or placebo. Anticoagulants, aspirin and other antiplatelet drugs not permitted. β-blockers permitted on discharge from hospital
Results	After 1 month, 7.2% of the rt-PA group and 9.8% of the placebo group had died. This represented a 26% reduction in mortality in the rt-PA group. After 6 months, the mortality rates were 10.4% (rt-PA) and 13.1% (placebo), which represents a relative reduction of 21%. In patients with proven AMI, these rates were 12.6% and 17.1%, respectively. Treatment with rt-PA made no difference to subsequent cardiac events after 1 month. Bleeding from non-infusion site was the major difference between the two groups. Bradycardia occurred in 27 patients in the rt-PA group and 5 patients in the control group

ATACS
Antithrombotic Therapy in Acute Coronary Syndromes

Authors	**(a)** Cohen M, Adams PC, Parry G, Xiong J, Chamberlain D, Wieczorek I, Fox KAA, Chesebro JH, Strain J, Keller C, Kelly A, Lancaster G, Ali J, Kronmal R, Fuster V **(b)** Cohen M, Parry G, Adams PC, Xiong J, Chamberlain D, Wieczorek I, Fox KAA, Kronmal R, Fuster V
Titles	**(a)** Combination antithrombotic therapy in unstable rest angina and non-Q-wave infarction in nonprior aspirin users: primary end points analysis from the ATACS trial **(b)** Prospective evaluation of a prostacyclin-sparing aspirin formulation and heparin/warfarin in aspirin users with unstable angina or non-Q wave myocardial infarction at rest
References	**(a)** *Circulation* 1994;**89**:81–8 **(b)** *Eur Heart J* 1994;**15**:1196–203
Disease	Unstable angina pectoris, non-Q-wave MI
Purpose	**(a)** To assess whether the combination of aspirin plus anticoagulation vs aspirin alone, when added to conventional antianginal therapy, reduces cardiac morbidity and mortality in non-prior aspirin users **(b)** To compare two different formulations of aspirin in the prevention of recurrent angina
Study design	**(a)** Randomised, open, parallel-group **(b)** Randomised, double-blind, parallel-group
Follow-up	12 weeks
Patients	**(a)** 214 non-prior aspirin users, randomised as soon as possible after admission **(b)** 144 prior aspirin users (72 controlled-release and 72 conventional aspirin)
Treatment regimen	**(a)** Aspirin, 162.5 mg/day; or aspirin, 162.5 mg/day, plus heparin, 100 iv bolus, followed by infusion for 3–4 days, followed by aspirin, 162.5 mg/day, plus warfarin (international normalised ratio 2–3) **(b)** Controlled-release, prostacyclin-sparing aspirin, 75 mg daily, or conventional aspirin, 75 mg daily
Concomitant therapy	**(a)** Standard antianginal regimen **(b)** Anticoagulation: iv heparin 3–4 days plus change to warfarin
Results	**(a)** At 14 days, total ischaemic events were significantly reduced in the combination group compared with aspirin alone (10.5% and 27%, $p = 0.004$), and this difference was maintained to 12 weeks (13% and 25%, $p = 0.06$). Bleeding complications were slightly more common with combination therapy

(b) Prostacyclin-sparing aspirin offers no clinical benefits over conventional aspirin

Comments	A pilot study, also named ATACS, was published in *Am J Cardiol* 1990;**66**:1287–92

ATLAS
Assessment of Treatment with Lisinopril And Survival
Ongoing trial

Authors	Komajda M, Wimart MC, Thibout E
Title	L'étude ATLAS (Assessment of Treatment with Lisinopril And Survival); justification et objectifs
Reference	*Arch Mal Coeur Vaiss* 1994;**87**(II):45–50
Disease	Congestive heart failure
Purpose	To compare the effects of two lisinopril dosages on mortality and morbidity in patients with chronic heart failure
Study design	Randomised, double-blind, parallel-group
Follow-up	Aim 3–4.5 years
Patients	Aim 3000 patients > 18 years, with chronic heart failure of NYHA classes II, III and IV, and an ejection fraction $\leq 30\%$
Treatment regimen	Run-in phase: lisinopril, 2.5–15 mg once daily Double-blind phase: all patients will receive lisinopril, 5 mg once daily (open dose), plus lisinopril, 30 mg, or placebo once daily (double-blind dose)
Results	Not yet available

AVID
Antiarrhythmics Versus Implantable Defibrillators study
Ongoing trial

Authors	The AVID investigators
Title	Antiarrhythmics Versus Implantable Defibrillators (AVID) – rationale, design, and methods
Reference	*Am J Cardiol* 1995;**75**:470–5
Disease	Ventricular fibrillation or ventricular tachycardia
Purpose	To compare the efficacy of antiarrhythmic medication and implantable cardioverter-defibrillators in terms of mortality, quality of life and cost
Study design	Randomised, open
Follow-up	Mean 2.6 years
Patients	200 in pilot trial (completed). Aim 1000 additional patients, all high-risk patients without correctable cause of index event
Treatment regimen	Implantation of advanced-generation cardioverter-defibrillator, or medication with amiodarone (empiric dosage) or sotalol (dosage guided by Holter/electrophysiological responses)
Results	To be expected in 1999

BAATAF
Boston Area Anticoagulation Trial for Atrial Fibrillation

Authors	**(a)** The Boston Area Anticoagulation Trial for Atrial Fibrillation investigators **(b)** Singer DE, Hughes RA, Gress DR, Sheehan MA, Oertel LB, Maraventano SW, Blewett DR, Rosner B, Kistler JP **(c)** Kistler JP, Singer DE, Millenson MM, Bauer KA, Gress DR, Barzegar S, Hughes RA, Sheehan MA, Maraventano SW, Oertel LB, Rosner B, Rosenberg RD
Titles	**(a)** The effect of low-dose warfarin on the risk of stroke in patients with nonrheumatic atrial fibrillation **(b)** The effect of aspirin on the risk of stroke in patients with nonrheumatic atrial fibrillation: the BAATAF study **(c)** Effect of low-intensity warfarin anticoagulation on level of activity of the hemostatic system in patients with atrial fibrillation
References	**(a)** *N Engl J Med* 1990;**323**:1505–11 **(b)** *Am Heart J* 1992;**124**:1567–73 **(c)** *Stroke* 1993;**24**:1360–5
Disease	Non-rheumatic atrial fibrillation
Purpose	To assess the efficacy of low-dose warfarin in preventing strokes in patients with non-rheumatic atrial fibrillation
Study design	Randomised, open, controlled
Follow-up	Mean 2.2 years
Patients	420 patients (212 warfarin and 208 controls) of whom 72% were men, mean age 63 years
Treatment regimen	Low-dose warfarin (target prothrombin time: 1.2–1.5 times control), or no treatment
Concomitant therapy	Aspirin allowed in the control group, but not in the warfarin group
Results	Prothrombin times in the warfarin group were within the target range 83% of the time, except for the first 4 weeks of medication. Mean levels of prothrombin activation factor were 71% lower in the warfarin group than in the control group ($p < 0.001$). Control patients taking aspirin had prothrombin activation factor levels similar to those in control patients not taking aspirin. There were 2 strokes in 446 person-years with warfarin (annual rate 0.45%) and 8 strokes in 206 person-years with aspirin (annual rate 3.9%), and 5 strokes in 271 person-years in patients taking neither aspirin nor warfarin (annual rate 1.8%). The relative rates of stroke controlled for other determinants were 0.135 (warfarin/aspirin), 1.95 (aspirin/no aspirin or warfarin) and 0.263 (warfarin/no aspirin or warfarin). Total mortality rate

was 2.25% and 5.97% in the warfarin and control groups, respectively. Minor bleeding occurred in 38 patients in the warfarin group compared to 21 in the control group

| **Comments** | The study was discontinued in April 1990 because of the strong evidence favouring warfarin. This decision was taken by an external Data-Monitoring Committee and ratified by the executive committee of the trial |

BASIS
Basel Antiarrhythmic Study of Infarct Survival

Authors	**(a)** Burkart F, Pfisterer M, Kiowski W, Follath F, Burckhardt D, Jordi H **(b)** Pfisterer M, Kiowski W, Burckhardt D, Follath F, Burkart F **(c)** Kiowski W, Brunner H, Pfisterer M, Burckhardt D, Burkart F **(d)** Pfisterer M, Kiowski W, Brunner H, Burckhardt D, Burkart F
Titles	**(a)** Effect of antiarrhythmic therapy on mortality in survivors of myocardial infarction with asymptomatic complex ventricular arrhythmias: Basel Antiarrhythmic Study of Infarct Survival (BASIS) **(b)** Beneficial effect of amiodarone on cardiac mortality in patients with asymptomatic complex ventricular arrhythmias after acute myocardial infarction and preserved but not impaired left ventricular function **(c)** Langzeiteffekt der Amiodaron-Therapie nach Myokardinfarkt bei komplexen ventrikulären Rhythmusstörungen **(d)** Long-term benefit of 1-year amiodarone treatment for persistent complex ventricular arrhythmias after myocardial infarction
References	**(a)** *J Am Coll Cardiol* 1990;**16**:1711–8 **(b)** *Am J Cardiol* 1992;**69**:1399–402 **(c)** *Schweiz Med Wochenschr* 1993;**123**:533–6 **(d)** *Circulation* 1993;**87**:309–11
Disease	MI with asymptomatic complex ventricular arrhythmias
Purpose	To investigate the effect of prophylactic antiarrhythmic treatment on mortality and arrhythmic events. Secondly, to assess whether the effect of low-dose amiodarone was dependent on left ventricular (LV) function
Study design	Randomised, controlled
Follow-up	1 year on therapy; 55–125 months after discontinuation of therapy
Patients	312 patients (100 individual treatment, 98 amiodarone and 114 no treatment), aged < 71 years, with persisting, asymptomatic, complex, ventricular arrhythmias on a 24-h ECG taken before hospital discharge
Treatment regimen	Individual antiarrhythmic treatment, dose-titrated quinidine or mexiletine (in case of drug failure ajmaline, disopyramide, flecainide, propafenone or sotalol were tried, and if these failed, amiodarone was tried), amiodarone treatment, 200 mg/day, or no therapy
Concomitant therapy	Standard treatment for ischaemic heart disease when necessary

Results The probability of survival for patients given amiodarone was significantly greater than for control patients ($p < 0.05$). Arrhythmic events were markedly reduced by amiodarone ($p < 0.01$). Mortality for individually treated patients was 10%, for amiodarone-treated patients 5.1% and for untreated patients 13.2%. 1-year mortality was significantly lower for amiodarone-treated patients with LV ejection fraction $\geq 40\%$ than for patients with LV ejection fraction $< 40\%$ ($p < 0.03$). The probability of death after 84 months was 30% in the amiodarone group and 45% in the untreated group, and was significantly lower in the amiodarone group with respect to all deaths ($p = 0.024$) and cardiac deaths ($p = 0.027$). This mortality difference was due only to amiodarone treatment in the first year and the survival curves did not differ between the two groups during the late follow-up

BBB
Behandla Blodtryck Bättre
("Treat Blood Pressure Better")

Authors	**(a)** The BBB study group **(b)** Hansson L
Titles	**(a)** Rapid communication. The BBB study: a prospective randomized study of intensified antihypertensive treatment **(b)** The BBB study: The effect of intensified antihypertensive treatment on the level of blood pressure, side-effects, morbidity and mortality in "well-treated" hypertensive patients
References	**(a)** *J Hypertens* 1988;**6**:693–7 **(b)** *Blood Press* 1994;**3**:248–54
Disease	Hypertension
Purpose	To investigate whether a diastolic blood pressure of ≤ 80 mm Hg can be obtained in previously treated patients with hypertension through intensified antihypertensive treatment and to determine whether this can be achieved without increasing the incidence or the severity of side effects to unacceptable levels. Secondary objective: to see whether this further reduction in blood pressure would lead to a further reduction in hypertension-induced morbidity and mortality
Study design	Randomised, open, with blinded endpoint evaluation
Follow-up	5 years
Patients	2127 hypertensive patients, aged 45–67 years, with treated diastolic blood pressure in the range 90–100 mm Hg
Treatment regimen	Intensified antihypertensive treatment either by addition of pharmacological agents (not specified) or by non-pharmacological means, or unchanged therapy
Results	A difference in diastolic blood pressure of 7–7.5 mm Hg, between the group with intensified treatment and the group with unchanged treatment, was seen after 4 years. The adverse event score fell significantly in the group with intensified treatment and remained unchanged for the other group. There were no significant differences between the two groups with regard to cardiovascular morbidity and mortality

BCAPS
Beta-blocker Cholesterol-lowering Asymptomatic Plaque Study
Ongoing trial

Author	Hedblad B
Title	Beta-blocker Cholesterol-lowering Asymptomatic Plaque Study (BCAPS). Baseline results and intima-media thickness progression rate
Reference	66th Congress of the European Atherosclerosis Society. Florence, Italy: European Atherosclerosis Society, 1996:109
Disease	Hyperlipidaemia
Purpose	To investigate the effect of fluvastatin or metoprolol CR on the progression rate of signs of early carotid atherosclerotic lesions
Study design	Randomised, double-blind, placebo-controlled, parallel-group, factorial
Follow-up	3 years
Patients	799 subjects (54% women), mean age 61 $\pm$ 5 years, with discernible plaque in the right carotid artery
Treatment regimen	Fluvastatin, 40 mg, metoprolol CR, 25 mg, or their combination
Results	Not yet available

BEST
Beta-blocker Evaluation Survival Trial
Ongoing trial

Authors	The BEST Steering Committee
Title	Design of the Beta-blocker Evaluation Survival Trial (BEST)
Reference	*Am J Cardiol* 1995;**75**:1220–3
Disease	Congestive heart failure
Purpose	To assess the effect of bucindolol on total mortality when added to standard therapy for congestive heart failure
Study design	Randomised, placebo-controlled, stratified
Follow-up	≥ 18 months
Patients	Aim 2800 patients with compensated congestive heart failure due to idiopathic dilated cardiomyopathy or coronary disease with ejection fraction ≤ 0.35
Treatment regimen	Bucindolol, titrated 3–200 mg daily, or placebo
Concomitant therapy	Standard treatment for congestive heart failure
Results	Not yet available
Comments	Another study with the acronym BEST, the Beta-blocker Stroke Trial, can be found in the Appendix

BHAT
β-blocker Heart Attack Trial

Authors	**(a)** and **(b)** The BHAT research group **(c)** Viscoli CM, Horwitz RI, Singer BH
Titles	**(a)** A randomized trial of propranolol in patients with acute myocardial infarction. I. Mortality results **(b)** A randomized trial of propranolol in patients with acute myocardial infarction. II. Morbidity results **(c)** Beta-blockers after myocardial infarction: influence of first-year clinical course on long-term effectiveness
References	**(a)** *JAMA* 1982;**247**:1707–14 **(b)** *JAMA* 1983;**250**:2814–9 **(c)** *Ann Intern Med* 1993;**118**:99–105
Disease	AMI
Purpose	To determine whether daily administration of propranolol after MI results in a significant reduction in mortality from all causes during a 2-4-year follow-up period. Secondary objectives: to determine the effect of propranolol on coronary heart disease mortality, sudden cardiac death and coronary heart disease mortality plus definite nonfatal MI
Study design	Randomised, double-blind, placebo-controlled
Follow-up	Mean 25 months
Patients	3837 patients (1916 propranolol and 1921 placebo), mean age 54.8 years (range 30–69 years). Time since MI: 5–21 days
Treatment regimen	Propranolol hydrochloride, 60 or 80 mg tid
Results	Total mortality during the mean follow-up period was 7.2% in the propranolol group and 9.8% in the placebo group; this represents a mortality reduction of 26% in the propranolol group ($p < 0.005$). Sudden death was reduced by 28% ($p < 0.05$). Coronary incidence (ie, non-fatal reinfarction plus fatal coronary heart disease) was reduced by 23%. Serious side effects were uncommon. In 2914 low- and moderate-risk survivors at 1 year, survival curves by treatment were almost identical. In 383 high-risk patients, use of β-blockers was associated with a 43% proportional decline in the subsequent risk for death ($p = 0.01$)

BIP
Bezafibrate Infarction Prevention trial
Ongoing trial

Authors	**(a)** Goldbourt U, Behar S, Reicher-Reiss H, Agmon J, Kaplinsky E, Graff E *et al* **(b)** Barasch E, Benderly M, Graff E, Behar S, Reicher-Reiss H, Caspi A, Pelled B, Reisin L, Roguin N, Goldbourt U
Titles	**(a)** Rationale and design of a secondary prevention trial of increasing serum high-density lipoprotein cholesterol and reducing triglycerides in patients with clinically manifest atherosclerotic heart disease (the Bezafibrate Infarction Prevention trial) **(b)** Plasma fibrinogen levels and their correlates in 6457 coronary heart disease patients. The Bezafibrate Infarction Prevention (BIP) study
References	**(a)** *Am J Cardiol* 1993;**71**:909–15 **(b)** *J Clin Epidemiol* 1995;**48**:757–65
Disease	Atherosclerotic heart disease
Purpose	To determine whether elevation of high-density lipoprotein (HDL) cholesterol and reduction of triglycerides by bezafibrate can reverse the risk of coronary events attributable to atherosclerosis of the coronary arteries. Secondary, to investigate the effect of therapy on total mortality, anginal episodes, and heart failure
Study design	Randomised, double-blind, placebo-controlled
Follow-up	Minimum 5 years (mean 6.25 years)
Patients	Aim 3000 men and women, aged 45–74 years, with total serum cholesterol 180–250 mg/dl, HDL cholesterol ≤ 45 mg/dl, triglycerides ≤ 300 mg/dl and low-density lipoprotein cholesterol ≤ 180 mg/dl (≤ 160 mg/dl for patients aged < 50)
Treatment regimen	Bezafibrate, 400 mg/day, or placebo
Results	Results of the treatment trial not yet available. In 6457 patients screened for inclusion, fibrinogen levels were associated with body mass index, behavioural variables, and severity of coronary heart disease. Risk factors considered accounted for only 6% and 4%, respectively, of the fibrinogen variation in men and women

CABADAS
Prevention of Coronary Artery Bypass graft occlusion by Aspirin, Dipyridamole, and Acenocoumarol/ phenprocoumon Study

Authors	**(a)** van der Meer J, Hillege HL, Kootstra GJ, Ascoop CAPL, Pfisterer M, van Gilst WH, Lie KI **(b)** Mulder BJM, van der Doef RM, van der Wall EE, Tijssen JGP, Piek JJ, van der Meer J, Dunning AJ
Titles	**(a)** Prevention of one-year vein-graft occlusion after aortocoronary-bypass surgery: a comparison of low-dose aspirin, low-dose aspirin plus dipyridamole, and oral anticoagulants **(b)** Effect of various antithrombotic regimens (aspirin, aspirin plus dipyridamole, anticoagulants) on the functional status of patients and grafts one year after coronary artery bypass grafting
References	**(a)** *Lancet* 1993;**342**:257–64 **(b)** *Eur Heart J* 1994;**15**:1129–34
Disease	Angina pectoris
Purpose	To compare the efficacy and safety of low-dose aspirin, aspirin plus dipyridamole and oral anticoagulants in the prevention of vein-graft occlusion during the first year after aortocoronary bypass surgery
Study design	Randomised, double-blind, placebo-controlled for the aspirin groups, open for the oral anticoagulant group
Follow-up	1 year
Patients	948 patients, aged ≤ 70 years, with angina requiring aortocoronary bypass surgery with saphenous vein grafts
Treatment regimen	Aspirin, 50 mg/day, started after surgery, or dipyridamole, 5 mg/kg/24 h iv for 28 h from the day preceding surgery, followed by 200 mg/day bid plus aspirin, 50 mg/day, from midnight on the day of surgery, or either fixed dose of nicoumalone, 4 mg, or phenprocoumon, 6 mg, on the day before surgery and continued on the day following surgery, titrated to an international normalised ratio of 2.4–4.8
Results	Occlusion rate of distal anastomoses was 11 % in the aspirin plus dipyridamole group, 15% in the aspirin group and 13% in the oral anticoagulation group. Clinical events occurred in 20.3% of patients receiving aspirin plus dipyridamole, compared to 13.9% of the aspirin group and 16.9% of the oral anticoagulants group. Addition of dipyridamole to 50 mg/day aspirin did not significantly improve patency rates and increased the overall clinical events rate. Oral anticoagulants provided no benefit as compared to aspirin. In a subgroup of 127 patients, there were no differences in symptoms of angina pectoris or exercise capacity between the three groups

CAFA
Canadian Atrial Fibrillation Anticoagulation study

Authors	**(a)** Connolly SJ, Laupacis A, Gent M, Roberts RS, Cairns JA, Joyner C *et al* **(b)** Laupacis A, Sullivan K
Titles	**(a)** Canadian Atrial Fibrillation Anticoagulation (CAFA) study **(b)** Canadian Atrial Fibrillation Anticoagulation Study: were the patients subsequently treated with warfarin?
References	**(a)** *J Am Coll Cardiol* 1991;**18**:349–55 **(b)** *Can Med Assoc J* 1996;**154**:1669–74
Disease	Atrial fibrillation (non-rheumatic)
Purpose	To assess the efficacy of warfarin in reducing stroke and other systemic embolisms in non-valvular atrial fibrillation
Study design	Randomised, double-blind, placebo-controlled
Follow-up	Up to 2.75 years; mailed questionnaire 21 months after end of study
Patients	378 patients (original aim 630)
Treatment regimen	Warfarin titrated to an international normalised ratio of 2.0–3.0, or placebo
Results	The annual rate of primary outcome events (non-lacunar ischaemic stroke, other systemic embolism, intracranial or fatal haemorrhage) was 3.5% in the warfarin group and 5.2% in the placebo group ($p = 0.26$; risk reduction 37%). Fatal or major bleeding occurred at annual rates of 2.5% in warfarin-treated and 0.5% in placebo-treated patients. Minor bleeding occurred in 16% of patients receiving warfarin and 9% of those receiving placebo. After the end of the study, 60% of the patients continued warfarin, 6% continued warfarin but then stopped, 23% took aspirin, 2% took aspirin but then stopped, and 9% took neither drug. Patients were significantly more likely to take warfarin if they had received it during the trial than if they had received placebo
Comments	Results from the Copenhagen AFASAK study and the SPAF study led to the decision to stop this trial prematurely

CAMCAT
Canadian Multicenter Clentiazem Angina Trial

Authors	Waters D, Garceau D
Title	A dose-response study of clentiazem, a chloro-derivative of diltiazem, in patients with stable angina
Reference	*J Am Coll Cardiol* 1993;**21**:964–70
Disease	Stable angina pectoris
Purpose	To assess the efficacy and safety of clentiazem in stable angina
Study design	Randomised, double-blind, placebo-controlled
Follow-up	2 weeks
Patients	199 patients (175 men and 24 women), mean age 61 ± 8 years, with angina duration ≥ 1 year for 74% of patients
Treatment regimen	Dose titration of clentiazem from 20 mg/day to 120 mg/day, with a dose increase every 2 days (20, 40, 80, 120 mg/day). Final dose clentiazem 120 mg/day bid. Alternatively placebo
Concomitant therapy	Sublingual nitroglycerin
Results	A symptom-limited exercise test was performed 4 and 12 h after dosing at the end of treatment. At 4 h after dosing, exercise duration was significantly greater with clentiazem at doses of 40, 80 and 120 mg/day than with placebo. 80 and 120 mg/day clentiazem significantly increased the time to onset of angina and to ≥ 1 mm ST-segment depression compared to placebo. At 12 h after dosing, improvement of exercise duration was significantly greater with clentiazem at doses of 80 and 120 mg/day. The incidence of adverse events was similar for placebo (27%) and clentiazem (29%)

CAMIAT
Canadian Amiodarone Myocardial Infarction Arrhythmia Trial

Authors	Cairns JA, Connolly SJ, Roberts R, Gent M
Title	Randomised trial of outcome after myocardial infarction in patients with frequent or repetitive premature depolarisations: CAMIAT
Reference	*Lancet* 1997;**349**:675–82
Disease	AMI with ventricular premature depolarisations
Purpose	To investigate the effect of amiodarone on the risk of resuscitated ventricular fibrillation or arrhythmic death in survivors of MI with frequent or repetitive ventricular premature depolarisations (VPDs)($\geq$ 10 VPDs per h or $\geq$ 1 run of ventricular tachycardia)
Study design	Randomised, double-blind, placebo-controlled
Follow-up	2 years, mean 1.79 years
Patients	1202 patients (606 amiodarone and 596 placebo), aged >19 years, enrolled with AMI within past 6–45 days
Treatment regimen	Amiodarone, loading dose 10 mg/kg daily for 2 weeks, maintenance dose 300–400 mg daily for 3–5 months, 200–300 mg daily for 4 months, and 200 mg for 5–7 days per week for 16 months
Concomitant therapy	Aspirin, β-blocker, diltiazem, verapamil, other calcium antagonist, warfarin, digoxin, ACE inhibitor, thrombolytic
Results	Amiodarone therapy results in a relative-risk reduction of 48.5% in the occurrence of resuscitated ventricular fibrillation or arrhythmic death among survivors of MI with frequent or repetitive VPDs on ambulatory ECG monitoring. Death occurred in 31 patients (6.0%) in the placebo group and in 15 (3.3%) in the amiodarone group. Intention-to-treat analysis showed a corresponding reduction of 38.2% – primary outcome events occurred in 24 (6.9%) patients in the placebo group and in 15 (4.5%) in the amiodarone group
Comments	A pilot study with the same name was published in *Circulation* 1991;**84**:550–7

CAPE
Circadian Anti-ischemia Program in Europe

Authors	**(a)** Deanfield JE, Detry J-MRG, Lichtlen PR, Magnani B, Sellier P, Thaulow E **(b)** Detry J-MRG
Titles	**(a)** Amlodipine reduces transient myocardial ischemia in patients with coronary artery disease: double-blind Circadian Anti-ischemia Program in Europe (CAPE trial) **(b)** Amlodipine and the total ischemic burden: Circadian Anti-ischemia Program in Europe (CAPE) trial – methodology, safety and toleration
References	**(a)** *J Am Coll Cardiol* 1994;**24**:1460–7 **(b)** *Cardiology* 1994;**85**(suppl 2):24–30
Disease	Stable angina pectoris
Purpose	To determine the effect of amlodipine on the circadian pattern of myocardial ischaemia in patients with chronic stable angina
Study design	2:1 randomised, double-blind, placebo-controlled, parallel-group
Follow-up	8 weeks
Patients	315 patients (202 amlodipine and 113 placebo) with chronic angina pectoris and ≥ 3 angina attacks per week, and ≥ 4 ischaemic episodes or ≥ 20 min ST-segment depression during 48 h of Holter monitoring
Treatment regimen	Amlodipine, 5 mg once daily, or placebo for 4 weeks, then amlodipine, 10 mg once daily, or placebo
Concomitant therapy	Cardiovascular medications taken before inclusion in the study and sublingual glyceryl trinitrate for episodes of angina pectoris
Results	Compared to placebo, amlodipine significantly reduced both the frequency of ST-segment depression episodes (60% for amlodipine vs 44% for placebo, $p = 0.025$) and total integrated ST ischaemic area (62% vs 50%, $p = 0.042$). Amlodipine reduced ischaemia over the 24 h with the intrinsic circadian pattern maintained. In addition, there was a significant reduction in angina attack rate (70% for amlodipine vs 44% for placebo, $p = 0.0001$) and in glyceryl trinitrate consumption (67% vs 22%, respectively, $p = 0.0006$). Amlodipine and placebo demonstrated similar safety profiles (adverse events 17.3% for amlodipine and 13.3% for placebo). The withdrawal rate was low (amlodipine 2%, placebo 4%)

CAPPP
Captopril Prevention Project
Ongoing trial

Authors	**(a)** The CAPPP group **(b)** Hansson L
Titles	**(a)** The Captopril Prevention Project: a prospective intervention trial of angiotensin-converting enzyme inhibition in the treatment of hypertension **(b)** The Captopril Prevention Project (CAPPP): description and status
References	**(a)** *J Hypertens* 1990;**8**:985–90 **(b)** *Am J Hypertens* 1994;**7**(suppl):82S–3S
Disease	Hypertension
Purpose	To investigate whether antihypertensive treatment with captopril reduces cardiovascular mortality and morbidity more than a therapeutic regimen that does not include an ACE inhibitor. Secondary objective: to compare total mortality, the development or deterioration of ischaemic heart disease, left ventricular failure, atrial fibrillation, diabetes mellitus, and possible differences in renal function in the two groups
Study design	Randomised, open, parallel-group, blinded endpoint
Follow-up	5 years
Patients	Targeted 10,800 patients, aged 25–66 years, with a diastolic blood pressure of at least 100 mm Hg (no upper limit)
Treatment regimen	Captopril, 50 mg/day, increased to 100 mg/day if diastolic blood pressure > 90 mm Hg, and possibly combined with other antihypertensive drugs, preferably diuretics. In the non-ACE-inhibitor group, β-blockers or diuretics should be used as first-line therapy
Results	Not yet available
Comments	Initial name was CAPPHY: Captopril Primary Prevention in Hypertension

CAPRIE
Clopidogrel versus Aspirin in Patients at Risk of Ischaemic Events

Authors	CAPRIE Steering Committee
Title	A randomised, blinded trial of Clopidogrel versus Aspirin in Patients at Risk of Ischaemic Events (CAPRIE)
Reference	*Lancet* 1996;**348**:1329–39
Disease	Atherosclerotic vascular disease: recent AMI, stroke, or symptomatic peripheral arterial disease
Purpose	To assess the relative efficacy of clopidogrel and aspirin in reducing the risk of a composite outcome cluster of ischaemic stroke, MI, or vascular death; their relative safety was also assessed
Study design	Randomised, double-blind
Follow-up	1–3 years, mean 1.91 years
Patients	19,185 patients (9599 clopidogrel and 9586 aspirin), aged > 21 years
Treatment regimen	Clopidogrel, 75 mg once daily, or aspirin, 325 mg once daily
Results	There were 1960 first events which showed that patients treated with clopidogrel had an annual 5.32% risk of ischaemic stroke, MI, or vascular death compared to 5.83% with aspirin. These rates reflect a statistically significant (p = 0.043) relative-risk reduction of 8.7% in favour of clopidogrel. The overall safety profile of clopidogrel was at least as good as that of aspirin

CAPTURE
Chimeric 7E3 Antiplatelet Therapy in Unstable angina Refractory to standard treatment

Authors	**(a)** Ferguson III JJ **(b)** The CAPTURE investigators
Titles	**(a)** EPILOG and CAPTURE trials halted because of positive interim results **(b)** Randomised, placebo-controlled trial of abciximab before and during coronary intervention in refractory unstable angina: the CAPTURE study
References	**(a)** *Circulation* 1996;**93**:637 **(b)** *Lancet* 1997;**349**:1429–35
Disease	Refractory unstable angina pectoris
Purpose	To assess the effect of abciximab therapy in connection with percutaneous transluminal coronary angioplasty (PTCA) on mortality and incidence of AMI and urgent intervention for recurrent ischaemia
Study design	Randomised, placebo-controlled
Follow-up	30 days and 6 months
Patients	1265 patients with refractory unstable angina scheduled for PTCA (aim 1400 patients)
Treatment regimen	Bolus of abciximab, 0.25 mg/kg, plus an infusion, 10 mg/min, beginning 18–24 h before PTCA and continuing 1 h after PTCA, or placebo
Concomitant therapy	Aspirin, 50–250 mg daily, heparin from randomisation to 1 h after PTCA, and iv glyceryl trinitrate. Other cardiovascular drugs were allowed
Results	The primary endpoint (death, AMI, or urgent intervention within 30 days of enrolment) occurred in 15.9% of patients in the abciximab group and 11.3% of patients in the placebo group (p = 0.012). The difference was mainly due to reduction of the AMI incidence. Major bleeding complications occurred in 3.8% of the patients, although both major and minor bleeding events were more common during treatment with abciximab. Bleeding was more common in patients having received a high dose of heparin. At 6 months the difference was smaller. But the number of events per patient was lower after abciximab
Comments	Predefined stopping rules were met at a planned interim analysis of data for 1050 patients, and recruitment was stopped

CARE
Cholesterol And Recurrent Events trial
Ongoing trial

Authors	**(a)** Sacks FM, Pfeffer MA, Moyé L, Brown LE, Hamm P, Cole TG *et al* **(b)** Sacks FM, Pfeffer MA, Moye LA, Rouleau JL, Rutherford JD, Cole TG, Brown L, Warnica JW, Arnold JMO, Wun C-C, Davis BR, Braunwald E
Titles	**(a)** Rationale and design of a secondary prevention trial of lowering normal plasma cholesterol levels after acute myocardial infarction: the Cholesterol and Recurrent Events trial (CARE) **(b)** The effect of pravastatin on coronary events after myocardial infarction in patients with average cholesterol levels
References	**(a)** *Am J Cardiol* 1991;**68**:1436–46 **(b)** *N Engl J Med* 1996;**335**:1001–9
Disease	Previous AMI
Purpose	To assess whether pravastatin will reduce fatal coronary events and nonfatal AMI in patients with average cholesterol levels
Study design	Randomised, double-blind, placebo-controlled
Follow-up	≥ 5 years
Patients	4159 patients, aged 21–75 years, who have had AMI 3–20 months before randomisation, with plasma total cholesterol < 240 mg/dl, low-density lipoprotein (LDL) cholesterol 115–174 mg/dl and triglycerides ≤ 350 mg/dl
Treatment regimen	Pravastatin, 40 mg once daily, or placebo
Concomitant therapy	All previously prescribed medication continued. If LDL increased, dietary counselling was started, and if necessary also cholestyramine
Results	The frequency of fatal coronary events plus nonfatal infarctions was reduced by 24% in the pravastatin-treated patients (p = 0.003). The frequency of coronary artery bypass surgery (CABG) was reduced by 26% and the need for coronary angioplasty by 23% by pravastatin (p = 0.005 and p = 0.01, respectively). There was no reduction in coronary events among patients with baseline LDL cholesterol levels below 125 mg/dl

CARE
Clinical Altace Real-world Efficacy

Author	Kaplan NM
Title	The CARE study: a postmarketing evaluation of ramipril in 11,100 patients
Reference	*Clin Ther* 1996;**18**:658–70
Disease	Hypertension
Purpose	To confirm the efficacy and safety of ramipril at real-world conditions
Study design	Open
Follow-up	8 weeks
Patients	11,100 patients, aged 18–75 years (mean 55.7 years), with mild to moderate hypertension
Treatment regimen	Ramipril, 2.5–10 mg/day
Results	In patients with combined systolic and diastolic hypertension ramipril reduced mean blood pressure from 167/102 to 146/89 mm Hg (p < 0.0001). Elderly patients demonstrated the highest response rate, 87%, and black patients the lowest, 81%. In patients with isolated systolic blood pressure, ramipril reduced blood pressure from 167/85 to 149/82 mm Hg (p < 0.0001). These patients had a lower response rate, 72% for white and 64% for black patients. 13% of the patients experienced adverse events of which 81% were at least possibly related to the treatment. The most common adverse events were cough (3%), headache (2.4%) and dizziness (1.8%)

CARPORT
Coronary Artery Restenosis Prevention On Repeated Thromboxane A$_2$-receptor blockade study

Authors	Serruys PW, Rutsch W, Heyndrickx GR, Danchin N, Mast EG, Wijns W, Rensing BJ, Vos J, Stibbe J
Title	Prevention of restenosis after percutaneous transluminal coronary angioplasty with thromboxane A$_2$-receptor blockade. A randomised, double-blind, placebo-controlled trial
Reference	*Circulation* 1991;**84**:1568–80
Disease	Angina, coronary artery disease, restenosis
Purpose	To study the effect of thromboxane A$_2$-receptor blockade on restenosis rate 6 months after successful percutaneous transluminal coronary angioplasty (PTCA)
Study design	Randomised, double-blind, placebo-controlled, parallel-group
Follow-up	6 months
Patients	697 patients (follow-up angiography available in 575)
Treatment regimen	Thromboxane A$_2$-receptor antagonist (GR32191 B), 80 mg before PTCA and 40 mg orally for 6 months, or aspirin, 250 mg iv before PTCA and placebo for 6 months
Results	There were no significant differences between the placebo and treatment groups with respect to mean coronary artery diameter or severity of clinical events during follow-up. 6 months after PTCA, 75% of GR32191 B patients and 72% of control patients were symptom-free

CASCADE
Cardiac Arrest in Seattle: Conventional versus Amiodarone Drug Evaluation study

Authors	**(a)** The CASCADE investigators **(b)** Greene HL **(c)** The CASCADE investigators **(d)** Maynard C **(e)** Dolack GL
Titles	**(a)** Cardiac Arrest in Seattle: Conventional versus Amiodarone Drug Evaluation (the CASCADE study) **(b)** The CASCADE study: randomized antiarrhythmic drug therapy in survivors of cardiac arrest in Seattle **(c)** Randomized antiarrhythmic drug therapy in survivors of cardiac arrest (the CASCADE study) **(d)** Rehospitalization in surviving patients of out-of-hospital ventricular fibrillation (the CASCADE study) **(e)** Clinical predictors of implantable cardioverter-defibrillator shocks (results of the CASCADE trial)
References	**(a)** *Am J Cardiol* 1991;**67**:578–84 **(b)** *Am J Cardiol* 1993;**72**:70F–4F **(c)** *Am J Cardiol* 1993;**72**:280–7 **(d)** *Am J Cardiol* 1993;**72**:1295–300 **(e)** *Am J Cardiol* 1994;**73**:237–41
Disease	Ventricular fibrillation
Purpose	To assess the effect of amiodarone compared to other antiarrhythmic agents on cardiac mortality. Secondary, to compare the effects on the incidence of different arrhythmias
Study design	Randomised, open, controlled
Follow-up	1–3 years
Patients	228 patients. Patients enrolled up to 6 months after an episode of ventricular fibrillation, if they have a moderate to high risk of recurrence and either inducible ventricular tachycardia or ventricular fibrillation on electrophysiological study or complex arrhythmias on Holter monitoring, or both
Treatment regimen	Amiodarone, 1200 mg/day for up to 10 days and then 200–800 mg (mean 600 mg) orally once daily for 1–2 months. Doses then tapered off to a maintenance dose of 100–400 mg/day. Conventional therapy: procainamide, quinidine, disopyramide, tocainide, mexiletine, encainide, flecainide, propafenone, or combination therapy
Concomitant therapy	105 of the 228 patients (46%) also received an automatic implantable cardioverter/defibrillator
Results	Survival free of cardiac death, resuscitated ventricular fibrillation, or syncopal defibrillator shock for the entire population was 75% at 2 years (amiodarone 82%, conventional 69%), 59% at 4 years (amiodarone 66%,

conventional 52%) and 46% at 6 years (amiodarone 53%, conventional 40%). Survival free of cardiac death and sustained ventricular arrhythmias was 65% at 2 years (amiodarone 78%, conventional 52%), 43% at 4 years (amiodarone 52%, conventional 36%) and 30% at 6 years (amiodarone 41%, conventional 20%). Patients treated with amiodarone were less likely to receive a shock from an implanted defibrillator, and syncopal shock was less common in these patients. The annual rate of rehospitalisation after out-of-hospital ventricular fibrillation was 79/100 patients/year; more than 50% of these patients were rehospitalised in the first year. Independent predictors of syncopal shocks were low ejection fraction, female sex and conventional antiarrhythmic drug therapy

Comments   Due to the relatively high mortality, the investigators decided that all participating patients should have an automatic defibrillator implanted when possible

CASH
Cardiac Arrest Study Hamburg
Ongoing trial

Authors	**(a)** Siebels J, Cappato R, Roppel R, Schneider MAE, Kuck K-H **(b)** Siebels J, Kuck K-H and the CASH Investigators
Titles	**(a)** ICD versus drugs in cardiac arrest survivors: preliminary results of the Cardiac Arrest Study Hamburg **(b)** Implantable cardioverter defibrillator compared with antiarrhythmic drug treatment in cardiac arrest survivors (the Cardiac Arrest Study Hamburg)
References	**(a)** *Pacing Clin Electrophysiol* 1993;**16**:552–8 **(b)** *Am Heart J* 1994;**127**:1139–44
Disease	Cardiac arrest
Purpose	To compare the incidence of cardiac arrest, sudden cardiac death, cardiac mortality and total mortality among patients treated with antiarrhythmic drugs or an implantable cardioverter/defibrillator (ICD)
Study design	Randomised, controlled
Follow-up	Until the primary endpoints, total mortality and recurrence of cardiac arrest, are reached. For the propafenone arm, mean follow-up 11 months
Patients	230 patients (aim 400) enrolled within 3 months following cardiac arrest (propafenone 56, amiodarone 56, metoprolol 59, ICD 59)
Treatment regimen	Amiodarone, loading dose 1000 mg/day for 7 days followed by 400–600 mg/day, or metoprolol, titrated from 12.5–25 mg/day to maximally 300 mg/day over 10–20 days, or propafenone, titrated from 450 mg/day to maximally 900 mg/day over 8–14 days, or implantation of an ICD
Results	At 11 months, no sudden death or cardiac arrest occurred in the ICD group compared to 12% sudden death and 23% cardiac arrest recurrence or sudden death in the propafenone group (p < 0.05). The incidence of recurrent cardiac arrest alone is reduced by 23% with the ICD compared to propafenone
Comments	After a mean of 11 months of follow-up, the propafenone arm was stopped because total mortality and recurrence of cardiac arrest differed significantly from those of ICD-treated patients. The ICD, metoprolol and amiodarone arms are still ongoing. Another study with the acronym CASH, Cost Associated with Systolic Heart failure, has been published

CASS
Coronary Artery Surgery Study

Authors	**(a)** The CASS principal investigators and their associates **(b)** Weiner DA, Ryan TJ, Parsons L, Fisher LD, Chaitman BR, Sheffield LT, Tristani FE **(c)** Caracciolo EA, Davis KB, Sopko G, Kaiser GC, Corley SD, Schaff H, Taylor HA, Chaitman BR
Titles	**(a)** Myocardial infarction and mortality in the Coronary Artery Surgery Study (CASS) randomized trial **(b)** Prevalence and prognostic significance of silent and symptomatic ischemia after coronary bypass surgery: a report from the Coronary Artery Surgery Study (CASS) randomized population **(c)** Comparison of surgical and medical group survival in patients with left main equivalent coronary artery disease. Long-term CASS experience
References	**(a)** *N Engl J Med* 1984;**310**:750–8 **(b)** *J Am Coll Cardiol* 1991;**18**:343–8 **(c)** *Circulation* 1995;**91**:2335–44
Disease	Mild angina pectoris
Purpose	To determine whether coronary bypass surgery reduces the rate of mortality and MI in patients with mild angina and patients who are asymptomatic after infarction, but who have angiographically documented coronary disease
Study design	Randomised, open, parallel-group. Long-term follow-up: retrospective on the CASS registry
Follow-up	Randomised part: mean 6 years (range 4–8 years). Retrospective part: 15 years
Patients	780 patients (390 in each group), aged ≤ 65 years (mean 51 years) with coronary artery stenosis ≥ 70%. The retrospective part contains 912 patients (282 medical and 630 surgical) from the CASS registry with left main equivalent (LMEQ) coronary artery disease. 40 of these patients participated in the randomised part
Treatment regimen	Coronary artery bypass graft (CABG) or medical therapy
Concomitant therapy	All patients received medical care, including those assigned to the surgical group
Results	There was no significant difference in the survival rate or MI rate between the medical and the surgical therapy groups, when analysed according to initial group assignment, number of diseased vessels or ejection fraction. 174 patients were followed 12 years after bypass surgery. Survival was significantly better in the 112 patients with no ischaemia on exercise testing 6 months after surgery than in the 51 patients with silent ischaemia or the 11 patients with symptomatic

ischaemia. The 15-year follow-up on the patients with LMEQ coronary artery disease showed that cumulative survival estimates were 44% for the surgical group and 31% for the medical group. Median survival time in the surgical group was 13.1 years compared to 6.2 years in the medical group (p < 0.0001). CABG did not prolong median survival in the subgroups with normal or mildly abnormal left ventricular systolic function

Comments   All patients screened for this study, 24,959 persons, were entered into a registry. This serves as a repository for information on all patients undergoing CABG at each of the 15 CASS clinical sites. Several publications have been based on this registry

CASSIS
Czech And Slovak Spirapril Intervention Study

Authors	Widimsky J, Kremer HJ, Jerie P, Uhlir O
Title	Czech And Slovak Spirapril Intervention Study (CASSIS). A randomized, placebo and active-controlled, double-blind multicentre trial in patients with congestive heart failure
Reference	*Eur J Clin Pharmacol* 1995;**49**:95–102
Disease	Congestive heart failure, chronic
Purpose	To assess changes in exercise tolerance. Secondary, to assess cardiovascular signs and symptoms, quality of life, ejection fraction, and chest X-ray findings
Study design	Randomised, double-blind, placebo-controlled
Follow-up	12 weeks
Patients	248 patients
Treatment regimen	Spirapril, 1.5, 3 or 6 mg/day, enalapril 5–10 mg/day, or placebo
Concomitant therapy	For angina: nitrates and calcium antagonists. For heart failure: digitalis, diuretics, potassium-sparing diuretics and potassium supplements
Results	Exercise tolerance increased in all groups; no statistically significant differences were found between any of the groups. There was a statistically significant reduction in mortality in the pooled spirapril groups compared to placebo, and a trend for reduction in serious cardiovascular adverse events as well as duration of hospitalisation. These effects seemed to be dose-dependent. In patients with moderate to severe heart failure, combination with first-generation calcium antagonists had an unfavourable effect on exercise capacity and clinical parameters. 13 patients died from cardiovascular causes during the study, and one patient suffered a fatal road traffic accident. The overall as well as cardiovascular mortality was significantly different between all patients receiving ACE inhibitor and placebo ($p = 0.023$), between all patients receiving spirapril and placebo ($p = 0.025$), and between 3 mg spirapril and placebo ($p = 0.01$)

CAST
Cardiac Arrhythmia Suppression Trial

Authors	**(a)** The CAST investigators **(b)** Epstein AE, Bigger JT Jr, Wyse DG, Romhilt DW, Reynolds-Haertle RA, Hallstrom AP **(c)** Wyse DG, Hallstrom A, McBride R, Cohen JD, Steinberg JS, Mahmarian J **(d)** Anderson JL, Platia EV, Hallstrom A, Henthorn RW, Buckingham TA, Carlson MD, Carson PE **(e)** Goldstein S, Brooks MM, Ledingham R, Kennedy HL, Epstein AE, Pawitan Y, Bigger JT
Titles	**(a)** Preliminary report: effect of encainide and flecainide on mortality in a randomized trial of arrhythmia suppression after myocardial infarction **(b)** Events in the Cardiac Arrhythmia Suppression Trial (CAST): mortality in the entire population enrolled **(c)** Events in the Cardiac Arrhythmia Suppression Trial (CAST): mortality in patients surviving open label titration but not randomized to double-blind therapy **(d)** Interaction of baseline characteristics with the hazard of encainide, flecainide, and moricizine therapy in patients with myocardial infarction. A possible explanation for increased mortality in the Cardiac Arrhythmia Suppression Trial (CAST) **(e)** Association between ease of suppression of ventricular arrhythmia and survival
References	**(a)** *N Engl J Med* 1989;**321**:406–12 **(b)** *J Am Coll Cardiol* 1991;**18**:14–9 **(c)** *J Am Coll Cardiol* 1991;**18**:20–8 **(d)** *Circulation* 1994;**90**:2843–52 **(e)** *Circulation* 1995;**91**:79–83
Disease	Ventricular arrhythmia
Purpose	To determine whether the suppression of asymptomatic or mildly symptomatic ventricular arrhythmias after MI reduces the mortality rate in arrhythmia
Study design	Randomised, open (initial phase), double-blind (main phase), placebo-controlled
Follow-up	Mean 10 months
Patients	1727 patients (730 encainide or flecainide, 272 moricizine and 725 placebo) with 6 or more ventricular premature depolarisations/h on 24-h Holter recording and a left ventricular ejection fraction ≤ 0.55, if ≤ 90 days after MI, and ≤ 0.40 if > 90 days. Time since MI: 6 days to 2 years
Treatment regimen	Encainide, 35–50 mg tid, flecainide, 100–150 mg bid, or moricizine, 200–250 mg tid
Results	The number of deaths was greater with flecainide or encainide therapy (4.5%) than with placebo (1.2%); relative

risk (RR) was 3.6 (95% confidence interval, 1.7–8.5). Total mortality was also higher with encainide or flecainide therapy (7.7%) than with placebo (3.0%); RR was 2.5 (95% confidence interval, 1.6–4.5). The mortality of patients in the placebo group was lower than expected. Analysis showed the overall mortality rate to lie between 6.3% and 8.4%, which is similar to rates observed in other postinfarction studies. This implies that the low mortality in the placebo group is largely due to the process of selecting only those patients whose ventricular arrhythmias were suppressed in the prerandomisation open-label titration phase. Non-randomised patients had more extensive coronary heart disease and experienced higher mortality and resuscitated cardiac arrest rates than patients randomised to placebo. The adverse effects of flecainide and encainide were greater when ischaemic and electrical instability were present. Patients whose ventricular arrhythmias were easy to suppress had fewer arrhythmic deaths than those whose arrhythmias were hard to suppress ($p = 0.003$). Older age, lower frequency of prior heart disease and MI, higher incidence of anterior MI and ventricular premature depolarisation were associated with ease of suppression of ventricular arrhythmias; adjusting for these, easily suppressed ventricular arrhythmias were still significant predictors of arrhythmic death (RR 0.66, $p = 0.013$)

Comments	The CAST Data and Safety Monitoring Board, after reviewing the data in April 1989, recommended that encainide and flecainide be discontinued and the study be continued with moricizine. The continuing study design was slightly changed and called CAST II

CAST II
Cardiac Arrhythmia Suppression Trial II

Authors	**(a)** The Cardiac Arrhythmia Suppression Trial II investigators **(b)** Brooks MM, Gorkin L, Schron EB, Wiklund I, Campion J, Ledingham RB
Titles	**(a)** Effect of the antiarrhythmic agent moricizine on survival after myocardial infarction **(b)** Moricizine and quality of life in the cardiac arrhythmia suppression trial II
References	**(a)** *N Engl J Med* 1992;**327**:227–33 **(b)** *Control Clin Trials* 1994;**15**:437–49
Disease	Ventricular arrhythmia after AMI
Purpose	To determine whether the suppression of asymptomatic or mildly symptomatic arrhythmias after MI, by moricizine, reduces the mortality rate in arrhythmia
Study design	Randomised, double-blind, placebo-controlled
Follow-up	2 weeks (initial trial), mean 18 months (long-term trial)
Patients	1325 patients in the initial trial (665 moricizine and 660 placebo), 1155 patients in the long-term trial (581 moricizine and 574 placebo). Time since MI: < 90 days. The long-term trial included 1374 patients
Treatment regimen	Moricizine, 200 mg tid (initial trial), up to 900 mg tid (long-term trial), or placebo (both trials)
Results	During the initial 2-week trial, 17 patients (2.3%) died compared to 3 (0.3%) in the placebo group. The relative risk was 5.6 (95% confidence interval, 1.7–19.1). Adverse effects were also more common in the patients treated with moricizine. For the long-term trial there were 49 deaths (15%) as well as more frequent adverse events in the moricizine group compared to placebo (42 deaths, 12%). The differences were not significant for the long-term trial. The prospectively designed quality of life outcome measure was found to be sensitive for assessing pharmacological therapies in the treatment of heart disease, and showed that quality of life improved significantly in both the moricizine and placebo groups after entry into the trial
Comments	CAST II was stopped early because the first 2-week treatment period with moricizine was associated with excess mortality and morbidity. The likelihood of observing a significant benefit as calculated from the main study was only 0.078

CASTEL
Cardiovascular Study in the Elderly

Authors	Casiglia E, Spolaore P, Mazza A, Ginocchio G, Colangeli G, Onesto C, Di Menza G, Pegoraro L, Ambrosio GB
Title	Effect of two different approaches on total and cardiovascular mortality in a cardiovascular study in the elderly (CASTEL)
Reference	*Jpn Heart J* 1994;**35**:589–600
Disease	Hypertension
Purpose	To define whether or not antihypertensive treatment was able to reduce mortality in elderly hypertensive patients and if the effect on mortality was greater when a special therapy approach was used
Study design	Randomised, population-based
Follow-up	7 years
Patients	655 hypertensives (351 'special therapy' and 304 'free therapy') and 1404 normotensives (no therapy), all aged ≥ 65 years
Treatment regimen	'Special therapy' included: (1) clonidine, 0.15 mg/day, nifedipine, 20 mg/day, or a fixed combination of atenolol, 100 mg/day, and chlorthalidone, 25 mg/day; (2) periodic visits to the Hypertension Outpatients' Clinic; and (3) strict co-operation of the GPs. 'Free therapy' included conventional therapy freely decided by various physicians
Results	Overall 7-year mortality was 34.9% in the hypertensive patients receiving 'free therapy', 22.5% in those receiving special care, and 24.2% in the normotensives. Cardiovascular mortality was 23.7%, 12.2%, and 12.0%, respectively. Overall and cardiovascular annual cumulative mortality was significantly lower in the 'special therapy' group than in the 'free therapy' group. The fixed combination of atenolol and chlorthalidone reduced mortality below that of the normotensives, independent of other cardiovascular risk factors

CATS
Captopril And Thrombolysis Study

Authors	**(a)** Kingma JH, van Gilst WH, Peels CH **(b)** Kingma JH, van Gilst WH, Peels CH, Dambrink J-HE, Verheugt FWA, Wielenga RP **(c)** van Gilst WH, Kingma JH, Peels KH, Dambrink J-HE, St. John Sutton M
Titles	**(a)** Angiotensin-converting enzyme inhibition during thrombolytic therapy in acute myocardial infarction: the Captopril and Thrombolysis Study **(b)** Acute intervention with captopril during thrombolysis in patients with first anterior myocardial infarction. Results from the Captopril And Thrombolysis Study (CATS) **(c)** Which patient benefits from early angiotensin-converting enzyme inhibition after myocardial infarction? Results of one-year serial echocardiographic follow-up from the Captopril and Thrombolysis Study (CATS)
References	**(a)** *J Cardiovasc Pharmacol* 1992;**19**(suppl 4):S18–24 **(b)** *Eur Heart J* 1994;**15**:898–907 **(c)** *J Am Coll Cardiol* 1996;**28**:114–21
Disease	AMI
Purpose	To test the effect of angiotensin-converting enzyme inhibition, given with thrombolytic therapy, on evolving myocardial damage due to ischaemia and the consequences of early reperfusion following MI
Study design	Randomised, double-blind, placebo-controlled
Follow-up	1 year
Patients	298 patients (149 captopril and 149 placebo) with first anterior MI < 6 h after the onset of symptoms, and being candidates for thrombolysis
Treatment regimen	An initial oral dose of captopril, 6.25 mg, is given between 30 min and 1.5 h following the start of the streptokinase infusion if systolic blood pressure ≥ 100 mm Hg. Dose titration within 24 h to 25 mg tid if systolic blood pressure ≥ 95 mm Hg. Alternatively, no medication
Concomitant therapy	Premedication was streptokinase, 1.5 x 10^6 U over 30 min. Calcium channel blockers, β-blockers, or nitrates if specifically necessary. Aspirin, 80 mg/day, at the discretion of the investigator
Results	At discharge, 80% of patients in the captopril group were on study medication. Left ventricular volumes were significantly increased in both groups at 3 months and at 12 months, but there was no significant difference between the two groups. The incidence of arrhythmia was lower for the captopril group than for the placebo group (p < 0.05), paralleled by

lower noradrenaline levels upon thrombolysis. In addition, enzymatic infarct size was smaller in captopril patients, especially in larger infarcts (p < 0.05), but reinfarction tended to be more frequent in the captopril group. At 12 months the occurrence of left ventricular dilatation was significantly lower in captopril patients (p = 0.018), as was the incidence of heart failure (p < 0.03). The effect was most obvious in patients with medium-sized infarcts, and was not present in patients with large infarcts

| Comments | Another study with the acronym CATS, the Canadian American Ticlopidine Study, can be found in the Appendix |

CCAIT
Canadian Coronary Atherosclerosis Intervention Trial

Authors	**(a)** Waters D, Higginson L, Gladstone P *et al* **(b)** Waters D, Higginson L, Gladstone P, Boccuzzi SJ, Cook T, Lespérance J
Titles	**(a)** Effects of monotherapy with an HMG-CoA reductase inhibitor on the progression of coronary atherosclerosis as assessed by serial quantitative arteriography. The Canadian Coronary Atherosclerosis Intervention Trial **(b)** Effects of cholesterol lowering on the progression of coronary atherosclerosis in women: a Canadian Coronary Atherosclerosis Intervention Trial (CCAIT) substudy
References	**(a)** *Circulation* 1994;**89**:959–68 **(b)** *Circulation* 1995;**92**:2404–10
Disease	Coronary atherosclerosis
Purpose	To assess the effect of a hydroxymethylglutaryl coenzyme A (HMG-CoA) inhibitor, lovastatin, on the evolution of coronary atherosclerosis
Study design	Randomised, double-blind, placebo-controlled
Follow-up	2 years
Patients	331 patients, aged 21–50 years, with coronary atherosclerosis and fasting serum cholesterol 220–300 mg/dl
Treatment regimen	Lovastatin, 20 mg/day, titrated to 40 and 80 mg/day over 16 weeks to attain low-density lipoprotein (LDL) cholesterol ≤ 130 mg/dl, or placebo
Concomitant therapy	Dietary counselling
Results	Total and LDL cholesterol decreased by 21 ± 11 % and 29 ± 11%, respectively, in the lovastatin-treated group, but changed by < 2% in placebo patients. The coronary change score (the per-patient mean of the minimum lumen diameter changes for all lesions measured, excluding those < 25%) worsened by 0.09 ± 0.16 mm in the placebo group and by 0.05 ± 0.13 mm in the lovastatin group ($p = 0.01$). Progression with no regression at other sites occurred in 33% of lovastatin-treated and 50% of placebo-treated patients ($p = 0.003$). New coronary lesions developed in 23 lovastatin and 49 placebo patients ($p = 0.001$). Progression occurred in 7/25 lovastatin-treated women and in 17/29 placebo-treated women ($p = 0.03$). New coronary lesions developed in 1 lovastatin-treated woman and in 13 placebo-treated women ($p < 0.001$). There were no significant differences in angiographic endpoints between the women and the men who completed the trial

CCS-1
Chinese Cardiac Study – 1

Authors	Chinese Cardiac Study Collaborative Group
Title	Oral captopril versus placebo among 13 634 patients with suspected acute myocardial infarction: interim report from the Chinese Cardiac Study (CCS-1)
Reference	*Lancet* 1995;**345**:686–7
Disease	AMI, suspected or confirmed
Purpose	To assess the effect on mortality of captopril compared to placebo
Study design	Randomised, double-blind, placebo-controlled
Follow-up	4 weeks
Patients	13,634 patients (6814 captopril and 6820 placebo), admitted to 650 Chinese hospitals up to 36 h after the onset of suspected AMI
Treatment regimen	Captopril, 6.25 mg initially, 12.5 mg 2 h later, then 12.5 mg tid, or identical placebo
Concomitant therapy	Low-dose aspirin recommended
Results	Captopril was associated with a non-significant reduction in 4-week mortality (617 captopril vs 654 placebo, 2p = 0.3). There was a significant excess of hypotension, mostly early after the start of treatment, but no evidence of any adverse effect on early mortality, even among patients who were hypotensive on admission

CEDIM
L-Carnitine Ecocardiografia Digitalizzata Infarto Miocardico trial

Authors	Iliceto S, Scrutinio D, Bruzzi P, D'Ambrosio G, Boni L, Di Biase M, Biasco G, Hugenholtz PG, Rizzon P
Title	Effects of L-carnitine administration on left ventricular remodeling after acute anterior myocardial infarction: the L-Carnitine Ecocardiografia Digitalizzata Infarto Miocardico (CEDIM) trial
Reference	*J Am Coll Cardiol* 1995;**26**:380–7
Disease	Anterior AMI
Purpose	To evaluate the effects of L-carnitine administration on long-term left ventricular (LV) dilatation in patients with acute anterior myocardial infarction
Study design	Randomised, double-blind, placebo-controlled
Follow-up	12 months
Patients	472 patients (233 L-carnitine and 239 placebo), aged ≤ 80 years, with a first AMI within 24 h
Treatment regimen	L-carnitine, 9 g/day iv for the first 5 days and then 6 g/day orally for the next 12 months, or placebo
Concomitant therapy	Standard strategies for AMI adopted at each cardiac care unit, except for drugs with a direct effect on cardiac metabolism, which were not permitted
Results	A significant attenuation of LV dilatation was observed in patients treated with L-carnitine compared to placebo in the first year after AMI. The percentage increase in end-diastolic and end-systolic volumes from admission to 3, 6, and 12 months afterwards was significantly reduced in the L-carnitine group. There were no significant differences in LV ejection fraction between the two groups. The combined incidence of death and congestive heart failure after discharge was 14 (6%) in the L-carnitine group vs 23 (9.6%) in the placebo group (p = ns)

CELL
Cost Effectiveness of Lipid Lowering study

Authors	Lindholm LH, Ekbom T, Dash C, Isacsson Å, Scherstén B
Title	Changes in cardiovascular risk factors by combined pharmacological and nonpharmacological strategies: the main results of the CELL study
Reference	*J Intern Med* 1996;**240**:13–22
Disease	Hyperlipidaemia
Purpose	To evaluate the effect on overall cardiovascular risk of two types of health care advice ('usual' and 'intensive'), with or without medication, the target being a moderate decrease in cholesterol. Secondary, to evaluate the effect of the ritual of daily medication on compliance with the health care advice
Study design	Randomised, double-blind, controlled
Follow-up	18 months
Patients	681 patients (87% men), aged 30–59 years, with at least two cardiovascular risk factors in addition to moderate primary hyperlipidaemia
Treatment regimen	Half the subjects were randomised to 'intensive advice' given in group sessions led by doctors and nurses. The other half received 'usual advice'. In each of the two advice groups, one-third received an active lipid-lowering drug (pravastatin), one-third placebo, and one-third no drug at all. The initial dose was 10 mg in the evening and was titrated on a monthly basis up to a maximum of 40 mg per night to achieve a 15% reduction in cholesterol
Concomitant therapy	Antihypertensives, if necessary
Results	The change in the Framingham risk score was significantly reduced only in patients taking lipid-lowering medication (with intensive advice -0.13; 95% CI -0.20 to -0.06, and with usual advice -0.16; 95% CI -0.23 to -0.09). The other patients receiving intensive advice tended to fare better than those on usual advice. Lifestyle was not influenced significantly over the study period. The ritual of daily medication did not affect the outcome

CHAOS
Cambridge Heart Antioxidant Study

Authors	Stephens NG, Parsons A, Schofield PM, Kelly F, Cheeseman K, Mitchinson MJ, Brown MJ
Title	Randomised controlled trial of vitamin E in patients with coronary disease: Cambridge Heart Antioxidant Study (CHAOS)
Reference	*Lancet* 1996;**347**:781–6
Disease	Coronary atherosclerosis
Purpose	To test the hypothesis that treatment with a high dose of α-tocopherol would reduce subsequent risk of MI and cardiovascular death in patients with established ischaemic heart disease
Study design	Randomised, double-blind, placebo-controlled
Follow-up	Median 510 days (range 3–981)
Patients	2002 patients (1035 α-tocopherol and 967 placebo), mean age 61.8 years, with angiographically proven coronary atherosclerosis
Treatment regimen	α-tocopherol, capsules containing 800 IU daily or 400 IU daily, or identical placebo capsules
Results	Plasma tocopherol concentrations rose in the actively treated group from baseline mean 34.2 μmol/l to 51.1 μmol/l with 400 IU daily and to 64.5 μmol/l with 800 IU daily, but did not change in the placebo group. α-tocopherol treatment significantly reduced the risk of cardiovascular death and non-fatal MI (41 vs 64 events; relative risk 0.53 95% CI 0.34–0.83; p = 0.005). The beneficial effect was due to a significant reduction in the risk of non-fatal MI (14 vs 41; 0.23 (0.11–0.47); p = 0.005). However, there was a non-significant excess of cardiovascular deaths in the α-tocopherol group (27 vs 23; 1.18 (0.62–2.27); p = 0.61). All-cause mortality was 36 of 1035 α-tocopherol-treated patients and 27 of 967 placebo recipients

CHF STAT
Congestive Heart Failure: Survival Trial of Antiarrhythmic Therapy

Authors	**(a)** Singh S, Fletcher RD, Fisher S *et al* **(b)** Massie BM, Fisher SG, Deedwania PC, Singh BN, Fletcher RD, Singh SN
Titles	**(a)** Congestive Heart Failure: Survival Trial of Antiarrhythmic Therapy (CHF STAT) **(b)** Effect of amiodarone on clinical status and left ventricular function in patients with congestive heart failure
References	**(a)** *Control Clin Trials* 1992;**13**:339–50 **(b)** *Circulation* 1996;**93**:2128–34
Disease	Congestive heart failure and ventricular arrhythmia
Purpose	To determine the effect of antiarrhythmic therapy on mortality in patients with congestive heart failure and ventricular arrhythmia
Study design	Randomised, double-blind
Follow-up	2 years
Patients	674 patients with ejection fraction $\leq 40\%$
Treatment regimen	Amiodarone, 800 mg qid $\times$ 2 weeks, 400 mg qid $\times$ 50 weeks, 200 mg qid until the end of the study, or placebo
Concomitant therapy	Enalapril, 2.5–10 mg bid, or hydralazine, 25–75 mg qid plus isosorbide dinitrate, 30-40 mg tid or qid, or captopril, 25–50 mg tid
Results	Ejection fraction was significantly ($p < 0.001$) increased in the amiodarone group compared to the placebo group at 6, 12 and 24 months, but this was not associated with greater clinical improvement, lesser diuretic requirement, or fewer hospitalisations for heart failure. There was a trend towards reduction in hospitalisations and cardiac death combined (relative risk, RR, 0.82), which was significant in patients with non-ischaemic aetiology (RR 0.56, $p = 0.01$) and absent in the ischaemic group

CIBIS
Cardiac Insufficiency Bisoprolol Study

Authors	**(a)** Lechat P, Jaillon P, Boissel JP **(b)** CIBIS Investigators and Committees
Titles	**(a)** β-blockade treatment in heart failure: the Cardiac Insufficiency Bisoprolol Study (CIBIS) project **(b)** A randomized trial of β-blockade in heart failure. The Cardiac Insufficiency Bisoprolol Study (CIBIS)
References	**(a)** *J Cardiovasc Pharmacol* 1990;**16**(suppl 5):S158–63 **(b)** *Circulation* 1994;**90**:1765–73
Disease	Heart failure
Purpose	To evaluate the effects on mortality of treatment with bisoprolol in heart failure patients
Study design	Randomised, double-blind, placebo-controlled
Follow-up	2 years
Patients	641 patients, with chronic heart failure (NYHA classes III and IV) and left ventricular ejection fraction < 40%
Treatment regimen	Bisoprolol, 1.25 mg/day increasing to 5 mg/day over 1 month, or placebo
Concomitant therapy	All patients received a combination of diuretic and vasodilator (90% an angiotensin-converting enzyme inhibitor). Digitalis and amiodarone permitted, but not started within 6 weeks before to 2 months after inclusion. β-agonists or β-antagonists, calcium antagonists (except dihydropyridines) and phosphodiesterase inhibitors not permitted
Results	Significantly fewer patients receiving bisoprolol than receiving placebo required hospitalisation for cardiac decompensation (61 vs 90 patients, p < 0.01). In the bisoprolol group, 21% of patients gained at least one functional class at the end of the study compared to 15% of patients in the placebo group (p = 0.04). However, there was no significant reduction in mortality between the two groups, nor any significant difference in sudden death rate or death related to ventricular tachycardia or fibrillation

CIBIS II
Cardiac Insufficiency Bisoprolol Study II
Ongoing trial

Authors	The CIBIS II Scientific Committee
Title	Design of the Cardiac Insufficiency Bisoprolol Study II (CIBIS II)
Reference	*Fundam Clin Pharmacol* 1997;**11**:138–42
Disease	Congestive heart failure
Purpose	To evaluate the reduction in overall mortality in response to bisoprolol. Secondary, to determine the efficacy and safety of this compound in terms of cardiovascular death, hospitalisation, and definitive cessation of treatment
Study design	Randomised, placebo-controlled
Follow-up	At least 3 years
Patients	Aim at least 2500 patients
Treatment regimen	Bisoprolol, 1.25–10 mg/day, or placebo
Concomitant therapy	Conventional treatment for heart failure (diuretics, ACE inhibitors or other vasodilators)
Results	Not yet available

CIDS
Canadian Implantable Defibrillator Study
Ongoing trial

Authors	Connolly SJ, Gent M, Roberts RS *et al*
Title	Canadian Implantable Defibrillator Study (CIDS): study design and organization
Reference	*Am J Cardiol* 1993;**72**:103F–8F
Disease	Cardiac arrest or haemodynamically unstable ventricular tachycardia
Purpose	To compare implantable cardioverter defibrillator (ICD) therapy with amiodarone concerning effect on mortality and ventricular tachycardia and fibrillation
Study design	Randomised, stratified
Follow-up	At least 1 year
Patients	Aim 400 patients with documented: ventricular fibrillation or cardiac arrest requiring defibrillation or cardioversion, or sustained ventricular tachycardia causing syncope or at a rate of ≥ 150 beats/min causing pre-syncope or angina when left ventricular ejection fraction $\leq 35\%$, or profound syncope with subsequent evidence for either spontaneous ventricular tachycardia or sustained monomorphic ventricular tachycardia
Treatment regimen	ICD or amiodarone, ≥ 1200 mg/day for 1 week, then ≥ 400 mg/day for 10 weeks, followed by ≥ 300 mg/day for the rest of the study. The dose may be lowered to 200 mg/day, or other antiarrhythmic treatment, even ICD, given to patients with significant adverse events with amiodarone, ≥ 300 mg/day, for the rest of the study
Concomitant therapy	Other antiarrhythmic drugs, preferably not amiodarone
Results	Not yet available

CLAS-I
Cholesterol Lowering Atherosclerosis Study – I

Authors	**(a)** Blankenhorn DH, Nessim SA, Johnson RL, Sanmarco ME, Azen SP, Cashin-Hemphill L **(b)** Blankenhorn DH, Azen SP, Crawford DW *et al*
Titles	**(a)** Beneficial effects of combined colestipol-niacin therapy on coronary atherosclerosis and coronary venous bypass grafts **(b)** Effects of colestipol-niacin therapy on human femoral atherosclerosis
References	**(a)** *JAMA* 1987;**257**:3233–40 **(b)** *Circulation* 1991;**83**:438–47
Disease	Coronary atherosclerosis
Purpose	To determine whether combined therapy with colestipol hydrochloride plus niacin will produce clinically significant changes in coronary, carotid and femoral artery atherosclerosis, and coronary bypass grafts
Study design	Randomised, partly blinded, placebo-plus-diet-controlled
Follow-up	2 years
Patients	162 non-smoking men (80 colestipol plus niacin and 82 placebo), aged 40–59 years, with previous coronary venous bypass surgery and with fasting blood cholesterol levels of 4.81–9.10 mmol/l
Treatment regimen	Colestipol hydrochloride, 15 g bid, and niacin, 3–12 g/day (as three divided doses). Target diet for the active treatment group included less than 125 mg of cholesterol/day, while that of the placebo group included 250 mg of cholesterol/day
Concomitant therapy	Aspirin, 325 mg before breakfast for the first 14 days. No lipid-lowering agents except study medications were allowed, nor were anticoagulants or platelet-active drugs
Results	After 2 years, there was a 26% reduction in total blood cholesterol, a 43% reduction in low-density lipoprotein cholesterol and a 37% elevation in high-density lipoprotein cholesterol in the active treatment group. Deterioration in overall coronary status was significantly less in the active treatment group ($p < 0.001$). Atherosclerosis regression occurred in 16.2% of the colestipol plus niacin group vs 2.4% of the placebo group ($p = 0.002$). The percentages of patients with new lesions or adverse changes in bypass grafts were significantly reduced ($p < 0.04$ and $p < 0.03$, respectively) in the active treatment group. The effect of treatment on the femoral artery was significant but less marked than for the coronary arteries or bypass grafts. Skin-related or gastrointestinal side effects were significantly more common in the active treatment group

CLAS-II
Cholesterol Lowering Atherosclerosis Study – II

Authors	Cashin-Hemphill L, Mack WJ, Pogoda JM, Sanmarco ME, Azen SP, Blankenhorn DH
Title	Beneficial effects of colestipol-niacin on coronary athero-sclerosis. A 4-year follow-up
Reference	*JAMA* 1990;**264**:3013–7
Disease	Coronary atherosclerosis
Purpose	To determine whether combined therapy with colestipol hydrochloride plus niacin will produce clinically significant changes in coronary, carotid and femoral artery atherosclerosis, and coronary venous bypass grafts
Study design	Randomised, partly blinded, placebo-plus-diet-controlled
Follow-up	4 years
Patients	103 men continuing from CLAS-I
Treatment regimen	Colestipol hydrochloride, 15 g bid, and niacin, 3–12 g/day (as three divided doses). Target diet for the active treatment group included less than 125 mg of cholesterol/day, while that of the placebo group included 250 mg of cholesterol/day
Concomitant therapy	Aspirin, 325 mg before breakfast for the first 14 days. No lipid-lowering agents except study medications were allowed, nor were anticoagulants or platelet-active drugs
Results	At 4 years, significantly more patients in the colestipol plus niacin group than in the placebo group showed no progression (52% vs 15%, respectively) and regression (18% vs 6%, respectively) in native coronary artery lesions. Significantly fewer drug-treated than placebo-treated patients developed new lesions in native coronary arteries (14% vs 40%, respectively) and bypass grafts (16% vs 38%, respectively). There was a significant decrease in side effects in the active treatment group in CLAS-II compared to CLAS-I, though some were still significantly more common in the active treatment group than in the placebo group

CONSENSUS
Cooperative North Scandinavian Enalapril Survival Study

Authors	**(a)** The CONSENSUS trial study group **(b)** Swedberg K, Eneroth P, Kjekshus J, Wilhelmsen L **(c)** Swedberg K, Eneroth P, Kjekshus J, Snapinn S **(d)** Kjekshus J, Swedberg K, Snapinn S
Titles	**(a)** Effects of enalapril on mortality in severe congestive heart failure. Results of the Cooperative North Scandinavian Enalapril Survival Study (CONSENSUS) **(b)** Hormones regulating cardiovascular function in patients with severe congestive heart failure and their relation to mortality **(c)** Effects of enalapril and neuroendocrine activation on prognosis in severe congestive heart failure (follow-up of the CONSENSUS trial) **(d)** Effects of enalapril on long-term mortality in severe congestive heart failure
References	**(a)** *N Engl J Med* 1987;**316**:1429–35 **(b)** *Circulation* 1990;**82**:1730–6 **(c)** *Am J Cardiol* 1990;**66**:40D–5D **(d)** *Am J Cardiol* 1992;**69**:103–7
Disease	Congestive heart failure
Purpose	To investigate the effect of enalapril, in addition to conventional therapy, on mortality in severe congestive heart failure. To study the activation of hormones related to cardiovascular function and the effect of the overall hormone response to angiotensin-converting enzyme (ACE) inhibition
Study design	Randomised, double-blind, placebo-controlled
Follow-up	Average 188 days (range 1 day to 20 months)
Patients	253 patients (127 enalapril and 126 placebo: 194 in 6-month and 102 in 12-month follow-up), mean age 70 years, with symptoms at rest (NYHA class IV), and a heart size > 600 ml/m^2 body surface area in men and > 550 ml/m^2 in women. In 239 patients, hormone levels were measured at baseline and after 6 weeks
Treatment regimen	Enalapril, 2.5 mg/day up to 20 mg bid
Concomitant therapy	All patients received diuretics (frusemide), 94% digitalis, and 50% vasodilators, mainly isosorbide dinitrate. Other ACE inhibitors were not permitted
Results	At 6 months, crude mortality was reduced by 40% in the enalapril group compared to the placebo group (p = 0.002); at 1 year, it was reduced by 31% (p = 0.001) and at the end of the study it was reduced by 27% (p = 0.003). The entire reduction in total mortality was in patients with progressive

heart failure (a reduction of 50%). There was no difference in the incidence of sudden cardiac death between the two groups. A significant improvement in NYHA classification and a reduction in heart size was also observed in the enalapril group. A significant positive relationship was found between mortality and levels of angiotensin II ($p < 0.05$), aldosterone ($p = 0.003$), noradrenaline ($p < 0.001$), adrenaline ($p = 0.001$), and a trial natriuretic factor ($p = 0.003$). No similar relationship was observed among enalapril-treated patients. The difference between the original treatment groups remained at 2-year follow-up. Treatment with enalapril was, however, made available to all surviving patients

| Comments | The study was terminated prematurely on the recommendation of the Ethical Review Committee, because of the consistent difference in favour of enalapril |

CONSENSUS II
Cooperative New Scandinavian Enalapril Survival Study II

Authors	Swedberg K, Held P, Kjekshus J, Rasmussen K, Rydén L, Wedel H
Title	Effects of the early administration of enalapril on mortality in patients with acute myocardial infarction. Results of the Cooperative New Scandinavian Enalapril Survival Study II (CONSENSUS II)
Reference	*N Engl J Med* 1992;**327**:678–84
Disease	AMI
Purpose	To investigate the effect of early enalapril, in addition to conventional therapy, on mortality after AMI
Study design	Randomised, double-blind, placebo-controlled
Follow-up	6 months (see comments)
Patients	6090 patients (3044 enalapril and 3046 placebo) presenting within 24 h
Treatment regimen	Enalapril, 2.5 mg bid up to 20 mg/day, or placebo
Concomitant therapy	β-blockers, iv nitrates, aspirin or diuretics
Results	At 6 months, the mortality was 11% in the enalapril group and 9.9% in the placebo group. The results were consistent across all subgroups
Comments	The study was terminated in May 1991 on recommendation of the safety committee, because of no difference in favour of enalapril

CPHRP
Coronary Prevention and Hypertension Research Project
Ongoing trial

Authors	Brown MJ, Hopper RV, Dickerson C
Title	Coronary prevention and hypertension research clinic
Reference	*J Hum Hypertens* 1993;**7**:100
Disease	Hypertension
Purpose	To test whether 15 years of antihypertensive treatment reduces the incidence of MI with both older and newer drug groups and whether antithrombotic therapy can reduce the incidence of coronary artery disease irrespective of blood pressure control
Study design	Randomised
Follow-up	15 years
Patients	Aim 5000 hypertensive patients, so far 511 randomised
Treatment regimen	Either α-blockade, or β-blockade, or angiotensin-converting enzyme inhibitors, or diuretics, or no treatment (patients with diastolic blood pressure < 100 mm Hg, or aged < 45 years and diastolic blood pressure < 110 mm Hg). Secondary randomisation to Maxepa, or aspirin, or no treatment
Concomitant therapy	A calcium antagonist if required
Results	Not yet available

CRIS
Calcium antagonist Reinfarction Italian Study

Authors	Rengo F, Carbonin P, Pahor M, De Caprio L, Bernabei R, Ferrara N, Carosella L, Acanfora D, Parlati S, Vitale D, and the CRIS investigators
Title	A controlled trial of verapamil in patients after acute myocardial infarction: results of the Calcium antagonist Reinfarction Italian Study (CRIS)
Reference	*Am J Cardiol* 1996;**77**:365–9
Disease	AMI
Purpose	To assess the effects of verapamil on total mortality, cardiac mortality, reinfarction, and angina after an AMI
Study design	Randomised, double-blind, placebo-controlled
Follow-up	Mean 24 months
Patients	1073 patients (531 verapamil and 542 placebo; 91% men), aged 30–75 years, mean 55.5 years, who survived 5 days after admission. Time since MI: 7–21 days (mean 13.8)
Treatment regimen	Verapamil retard, 360 mg/day (120 mg every 8 h), or placebo
Concomitant therapy	Antiarrhythmics, digitalis, diuretic, antihypertensive, long-acting nitrates
Results	5.5% of the patients died during the follow-up period. There were no differences in between verapamil and placebo in total mortality (n = 30 and 29, respectively) and cardiac death (n = 21 and 22). The verapamil group had lower reinfarction rates (n = 39 vs 49, ns). Fewer patients developed angina in the verapamil group (n = 100 vs 132, RR = 0.8, 95% confidence interval 0.5–0.9). There were no differences in discontinuation of treatment owing to adverse reactions. This trial showed no effect of verapamil on mortality. The lower reinfarction rates in the verapamil group are in agreement with the results of other studies

CRISP
Cholesterol Reduction In Seniors Program pilot study

Authors	LaRosa JC, Applegate W, Crouse III JR *et al*
Title	Cholesterol lowering in the elderly. Results of the Cholesterol Reduction In Seniors Program (CRISP) pilot study
Reference	*Arch Intern Med* 1994;**154**:529–39
Disease	Hyperlipidaemia
Purpose	To test the feasibility of a study with lipid-lowering therapy in men and women over 65 years and to compare the effects of diet and active treatment on blood lipids
Study design	Randomised
Follow-up	1 year
Patients	431 subjects (71% women), aged > 65 years (mean 71 years), with low-density lipoprotein (LDL) cholesterol > 4.1 and < 5.7 mmol/l
Treatment regimen	Lipid-lowering diet and lovastatin, 20 mg or 40 mg once daily, or placebo
Results	In the 20 mg and 40 mg lovastatin groups, total cholesterol levels were reduced by 17% and 20%, respectively. LDL cholesterol was reduced by 24% and 28%, triglyceride levels were reduced by 4.4% and 9.9% and high-density lipoprotein cholesterol increased by 7.0% and 9.0%. Side-effects were low. No changes in lipid levels were observed in the placebo group. Gender, age and race did not significantly affect responses

DAVIT II
Danish Verapamil Infarction Trial II

Authors	**(a)** The Danish study group on verapamil in myocardial infarction **(b)** Jespersen CM, Fischer Hansen J
Titles	**(a)** Effect of verapamil on mortality and major events after acute myocardial infarction (The Danish Verapamil Infarction Trial II – DAVIT II) **(b)** Effect of verapamil on reinfarction and cardiovascular events in patients with arterial hypertension included in the Danish Verapamil Infarction Trial II
References	**(a)** *Am J Cardiol* 1990;**66**:779–85 **(b)** *Folha Med* 1995;**111**:229–33
Disease	AMI
Purpose	To examine whether treatment with verapamil from the second week after AMI and continued for 12–18 months might reduce total mortality and major events (ie, death or reinfarction)
Study design	Randomised, double-blind, placebo-controlled
Follow-up	Up to 18 months (mean 16 months)
Patients	1775 patients (878 verapamil and 897 placebo), aged < 76 years. Time after admission: 7–15 days
Treatment regimen	Verapamil, 120 mg tid (once daily or bid in case of adverse drug reactions)
Concomitant therapy	Treatment with calcium antagonists or β-blockers not permitted
Results	95 deaths and 146 major events occurred in the verapamil group and 119 deaths and 180 major events in the placebo group. The 18-month mortality rates were 11.1% and 13.8% ($p = 0.11$), and major event rates were 18.0% and 21.6% ($p = 0.03$), in the verapamil and placebo groups, respectively. In patients in the coronary care unit without heart failure, the mortality rates were 7.7% in the verapamil group and 11.8% in the placebo group ($p = 0.02$), and major event rates were 14.6% and 19.7%, respectively ($p = 0.01$). In patients with heart failure, the mortality rates were 17.9% in the verapamil group and 17.5% in the placebo group ($p = 0.79$), and major event rates were 24.9% and 24.9%, respectively ($p = 1.0$). In patients with arterial hypertension (149 on verapamil, 152 on placebo), the 18-month first reinfarction rates were 12.5% and 19.8% in the verapamil and placebo groups, respectively ($p = 0.04$). The first cardiovascular event rates in this group were 21.8% and 29.3%, respectively ($p = 0.07$)

DEFIANT
Doppler flow and Echocardiography in Functional cardiac Insufficiency: Assessment of Nisoldipine Therapy

Authors	**(a)** The DEFIANT research group **(b)** Lewis BS, Poole-Wilson PA
Titles	**(a)** Improved diastolic function with the calcium antagonist nisoldipine (coat-core) in patients post myocardial infarction: results of the DEFIANT study **(b)** The DEFIANT study of left ventricular function and exercise performance after acute myocardial infarction
References	**(a)** *Eur Heart J* 1992;**13**:1496–505 **(b)** *Cardiovasc Drugs Ther* 1994;**8**:407–18
Disease	Post-MI and mild left ventricular dysfunction
Purpose	To investigate whether nisoldipine could alter diastolic function in post-MI patients with mild left ventricular dysfunction
Study design	Randomised, double-blind, placebo-controlled, parallel-group
Follow-up	4 weeks
Patients	129 patients (66 nisoldipine-CC and 63 placebo), aged < 75 years, 7–35 days after MI and with left ventricular ejection fraction $\leq 50\%$
Treatment regimen	Nisoldipine-CC, 20 mg once daily
Concomitant therapy	Chronic treatment with β-blockers and aspirin at fixed dose. Sublingual nitrates for angina pectoris attacks
Results	Doppler echocardiography showed effects of nisoldipine on early diastolic peak velocity which was increased by 0.06 m/s (95% confidence interval, 0.01–0.11), on time velocity integral which was increased by 1.2 cm (95% confidence interval, 0.16–2.27) and on isovolumic relaxation time which was reduced by 14.7 ms (95% confidence interval, -22.5 to -6.9). Peak workload on exercise test was 12 watts higher in the nisoldipine group than the placebo group (95% confidence interval, 0.8–13.3). Exercise capacity in both groups was related to measurements of resting diastolic left ventricular function

DIAB-HYCAR
Hypertrophie Cardiaque et Ramipril chez des Diabétiques
Ongoing trial

Authors	Passa P, Chatellier G
Title	The DIAB-HYCAR study
Reference	*Diabetologia* 1996;**39**:1662–7
Disease	Non-insulin-dependent diabetes mellitus (NIDDM)
Purpose	To test the hypothesis that ACE inhibition with a low daily dose of ramipril, which has no significant effect on blood pressure, may reduce cardiovascular morbidity and/or mortality in normotensive or hypertensive NIDDM patients with persistent albuminuria
Study design	Randomised, double-blind, placebo-controlled
Follow-up	3 years
Patients	Aim 4000 patients, aged > 50 years, with NIDDM and persistent albuminuria
Treatment regimen	Ramipril, 1.25 mg/day, or placebo
Concomitant therapy	Usual oral antidiabetic treatment and antihypertensive treatment, if necessary (ACE inhibitors excluded)
Results	Not yet available

DIDI
Diltiazem in Dilated cardiomyopathy

Authors	Figulla HR, Gietzen F, Zeymer U, Raiber M, Hegselmann J, Soballa R, Hilgers R
Title	Diltiazem improves cardiac function and exercise capacity in patients with idiopathic dilated cardiomyopathy. Results of the diltiazem in dilated cardiomyopathy trial
Reference	*Circulation* 1996; **94**:346–52
Disease	Idiopathic dilated cardiomyopathy
Purpose	To evaluate the effect of diltiazem in idiopathic dilated cardiomyopathy patients with heart failure compensated by conventional treatment (ACE inhibitors, digitalis, diuretics, or nitrates)
Study design	Randomised, double-blind, placebo-controlled
Follow-up	24 months
Patients	186 patients (92 diltiazem and 94 placebo), aged between 18 and 70 years, with idiopathic dilated cardiomyopathy and a left ventricular ejection fraction < 0.50
Treatment regimen	Diltiazem or placebo. Diltiazem, 30 mg tid on days 1 and 2 and 60 mg tid on days 3 and 4. Patients weighing > 50 kg received 90 mg tid on day 5 and afterwards. Patients weighing ≤ 50 kg at entry received 60 mg diltiazem tid
Concomitant therapy	According to patient's needs (calcium antagonists and β-blockers excluded)
Results	33 patients dropped out; 153 patients finished the protocol. 27 patients died or were listed for heart transplantation: 16 in the placebo group and 11 in the diltiazem group. The transplant-listing-free survival rate was 85% for diltiazem and 80% for placebo ($p = 0.444$). After 24 months, only diltiazem significantly increased cardiac index at rest ($p = 0.1$) and under a workload ($p = 0.02$), systolic and diastolic blood pressure ($p = 0.003$ and $p = 0.004$), stroke volume index ($p = 0.003$), and stroke work index ($p = 0.000$) and decreased both pulmonary artery pressure under workload ($p = 0.007$) and heart rate ($p = 0.001$). Diltiazem also increased exercise capacity ($p = 0.002$) and subjective well-being ($p = 0.01$). Adverse reactions were minor and evenly distributed in the both groups, except for an increase in the PQ interval in the diltiazem group

DIG
Digitalis Investigation Group trial

Authors	**(a)** and **(b)** The Digitalis Investigation Group
Titles	**(a)** Rationale, design, implementation, and baseline characteristics of patients in the DIG trial: a large, simple, long-term trial to evaluate the effect of digitalis on mortality in heart failure **(b)** The effect of digoxin on mortality and morbidity in patients with heart failure
References	**(a)** *Control Clin Trials* 1996;**17**:77–97 **(b)** *N Engl J Med* 1997;**336**:525–33
Disease	Congestive heart failure with sinus rhythm
Purpose	To determine the effect of digoxin on all-cause mortality in patients with clinical heart failure who are in sinus rhythm and whose ejection fraction (EF) is ≤ 0.45. Ancillary study to examine the effect in those with an EF > 0.45
Study design	Randomised, double-blind, placebo-controlled
Follow-up	Maximum 5 years
Patients	Main study: 7788 patients (3397 digoxin and 3403 placebo) with EF ≤ 0.45. Ancillary study: 988 patients (492 digoxin and 496 placebo) with EF > 0.45
Treatment regimen	Digoxin, titrated, or placebo
Concomitant therapy	ACE inhibitors for patients with EF ≤ 0.45 and other drugs as decided by the investigator
Results	Digoxin did not reduce overall mortality (34.8% with digoxin vs 35.1% with placebo). However, digoxin reduced the rate of hospitalisation both overall and for worsening heart failure (p < 0.001). With regard to these parameters the results in the ancillary study were consistent with the findings of the main study

DIGAMI
Diabetes mellitus Insulin-Glucose infusion in Acute Myocardial Infarction

Authors	Malmberg K, Rydén L, Efendic S, Herlitz J, Nicol P, Waldenström A, Wedel H, Welin L
Title	Randomized trial of insulin-glucose infusion followed by subcutaneous insulin treatment in diabetic patients with acute myocardial infarction (DIGAMI study): effects on mortality at 1 year
Reference	*J Am Coll Cardiol* 1995;**26**:57–65
Disease	Diabetes mellitus, AMI
Purpose	To test the hypothesis that rapid improvement of metabolic control in diabetic patients with AMI by means of insulin-glucose infusion decreases the high initial mortality rate and that good metabolic control during the early postinfarction period improves the subsequent prognosis
Study design	Randomised, controlled
Follow-up	12 months
Patients	620 patients (306 insulin-glucose infusion and 314 conventional therapy) with suspected AMI combined with blood glucose > 11 mmol/l
Treatment regimen	Insulin-glucose infusion followed by multidose subcutaneous insulin for ≥ 3 months, or conventional therapy
Concomitant therapy	Standard coronary care, including thrombolysis, and iv and oral metoprolol
Results	The two groups' baseline characteristics were comparable. Blood glucose decreased from 15.4 ± 4.1 to 9.6 ± 3.3 mmol/l (mean ± SD) in the infusion group during the first 24 h, and from 15.7 ± 4.2 to 11.7 ± 4.1 among control patients (p = 0.0001). After 1 year, 57 patients (18.6%) in the infusion group and 82 (26.1%) in the control group had died (relative mortality reduction 29%, p = 0.027). The mortality reduction was particularly evident in patients with a low cardiovascular risk profile and no previous insulin treatment (3-month mortality rate 6.5% in the infusion group vs 13.5% in the control group; relative reduction 52%, p = 0.046; 1-year mortality rate 8.6% in the infusion group vs 18% in the control group; relative reduction 52%, p = 0.20)

DIMT
Dutch Ibopamine Multicenter Trial

Authors	**(a)** van Veldhuisen DJ, Man in 't Veld AJ, Dunselman PHJM, Lok DJA, Dohmen HJM, Poortermans JC, Withagen AJAM, Pasteuning WH, Brouwer J, Lie KI **(b)** van Veldhuisen DJ, Brouwer J, Man in 't Veld AJ, Dunselman PHJM, Boomsma F, Lie KI
Titles	**(a)** Double-blind placebo-controlled study of ibopamine and digoxin in patients with mild to moderate heart failure: results of the Dutch Ibopamine Multicenter Trial (DIMT) **(b)** Progression of mild untreated heart failure during six months follow-up and clinical and neurohumoral effects of ibopamine and digoxin as monotherapy
References	**(a)** *J Am Coll Cardiol* 1993;**22**:1564–73 **(b)** *Am J Cardiol* 1995;**75**:796–800
Disease	Mild to moderate heart failure
Purpose	To evaluate the efficacy and safety of ibopamine, and to compare it to digoxin and placebo in patients with mild to moderate heart failure
Study design	Randomised, double-blind, placebo-controlled
Follow-up	6 months
Patients	161 patients (53 ibopamine, 55 digoxin, 53 placebo), of whom 80% were in NYHA functional class II
Treatment regimen	Ibopamine, 100 mg tid, or digoxin, 0.25 mg once daily, or placebo
Concomitant therapy	Frusemide, up to 80 mg/day, short-acting nitrates and triamterene were allowed
Results	Digoxin preserved exercise capacity after 6 months compared to placebo (p = 0.008). Ibopamine was only effective in patients with relatively preserved left ventricular function, ejection fraction > 0.30 (p = 0.018 vs placebo). Plasma noradrenaline levels were decreased with digoxin and ibopamine therapy, but increased with placebo (both p < 0.05 vs placebo). Plasma aldosterone was unaffected, whereas plasma renin was decreased by digoxin and ibopamine. There were no significant changes in NYHA functional class between the three groups. Total mortality was 6 (ibopamine 1, digoxin 2, placebo 3). Among 64 patients who had received no medication at baseline, both ibopamine and digoxin significantly increased exercise capacity relative to placebo (p < 0.05). In these patients, plasma noradrenaline levels were increased significantly with placebo and decreased with ibopamine and digoxin (both p < 0.05 vs placebo), but plasma renin was decreased only by digoxin (p < 0.05 vs placebo)

DUCCS–I
Duke University Clinical Cardiology Study – I

Authors	O'Connor CM, Meese R, Carney R, Smith J, Conn E, Burks J et al
Title	A randomized trial of intravenous heparin in conjunction with anistreplase (anisoylated plasminogen streptokinase activator complex) in acute myocardial infarction: the Duke University Clinical Cardiology Study (DUCCS) 1
Reference	*J Am Coll Cardiol* 1994;**23**:11–8
Disease	AMI
Purpose	To test whether withholding heparin following anistreplase (APSAC) therapy reduces complications in patients with AMI
Study design	Randomised
Follow-up	Mean 5 days
Patients	250 patients (128 heparin), presenting within 6 h and 6–12 h of onset of symptoms
Treatment regimen	Either heparin, 15 U/kg body weight iv, 4 h after APSAC treatment, or no heparin
Concomitant therapy	APSAC, 30 U iv over 2–5 min, aspirin, 325 mg/day. β-blocking agent and nitrate therapy recommended
Results	The combined outcome of death, reinfarction, recurrent ischaemia and occlusion of the infarct-related artery occurred in 42% of the heparin-treated group vs 43% of the group without heparin (p = 0.94). A patent infarct-related artery was present in 80% of patients treated with heparin and in 73% of those not treated with heparin (p = 0.26). Left ventricular function was well preserved in both groups. Post-MI haemorrhagic complications were similar in both groups, but bleeding complications were twice as common in the heparin-treated group, 32% compared to 17.2% for the group not receiving heparin (p = 0.006). Moderate bleeding occurred in 18.8% of heparin-treated patients and in 10.7% of patients without heparin, severe bleeding in 8.6% receiving heparin and 5.7% without heparin. Life-threatening bleeds occurred in 4.7% of patients receiving heparin and 0.8% of patients not receiving heparin

DUCCS–II
Duke University Clinical Cardiology Group Study – II

Authors	O'Connor CM, Meese RB, McNulty S, Lucas K, Carney RJ, LeBoeuf RM, Maddox W, Bethea CF, Shadoff N, Trahey TF, Heinsimer JA, Burks JM, O'Donnell G, Krucoff MW, Califf RM
Title	A randomized factorial trial of reperfusion strategies and aspirin dosing in acute myocardial infarction
Reference	*Am J Cardiol* 1996;**77**:791–7
Disease	AMI
Purpose	To compare the thrombolytic regimens of accelerated alteplase (rt-PA) with iv heparin and anistreplase (APSAC) without heparin using surrogate measures of perfusion and left ventricular function and a composite clinical outcome scale to develop evidence relevant to the pursuit of a large clinical outcome trial using APSAC without heparin. Secondarily, to add to the information base about aspirin dose using a factorial design, since the dose of aspirin leading to the best clinical outcome remains unknown
Study design	Randomised, 2 x 2 factorial
Follow-up	Median 5 days
Patients	162 patients (83 APSAC and 79 rt-PA), aged > 18 years, with ST-segment elevation of at least 1 mV in ≥ 2 contiguous electrocardiographic leads or left bundle branch block
Treatment regimen	APSAC without heparin or rt-PA with heparin, aspirin, 81 mg/day or 325 mg/day
Results	Patients given rt-PA and heparin were better anticoagulated (p = 0.001), but APSAC-treated patients had more bleeding complications. In the electrocardiographic substudy, the rt-PA group achieved both 50% ST-segment recovery and steady-state recovery sooner than the APSAC group. Patients taking low-dose aspirin had lower in-hospital mortality and less recurrent ischaemia but more strokes than the standard-dose aspirin group

EAFT
European Atrial Fibrillation Trial

Authors	(a) EAFT study group (b) The European Atrial Fibrillation Trial study group
Titles	(a) Secondary prevention in non-rheumatic atrial fibrillation after transient ischaemic attack or minor stroke (b) Optimal oral anticoagulant therapy in patients with nonrheumatic atrial fibrillation and recent cerebral ischemia
References	(a) *Lancet* 1993;**342**:1255–62 (b) *N Engl J Med* 1995;**333**:5–10
Disease	Non-rheumatic atrial fibrillation, stroke
Purpose	To establish the preventive value of both anticoagulation and aspirin in patients with non-valvular atrial fibrillation and a transient ischaemic attack or minor stroke (secondary prevention trial)
Study design	Randomised, open oral anticoagulant treatment, double-blind aspirin treatment, placebo-controlled. Patients with contraindications to oral anticoagulants were randomised for aspirin and placebo
Follow-up	Minimum 1 year, maximum 4.6 years (mean 2.3 years)
Patients	1007 patients with non-rheumatic atrial fibrillation and recent transient ischaemic attack or minor stroke. 669 received oral anticoagulants
Treatment regimen	Oral anticoagulants to achieve a therapeutic international normalised ratio range 2.5–4.0 (aim 3.0). Aspirin, 300 mg/day, or placebo
Results	During mean follow-up the annual rate of outcome events was 8% in patients assigned to anticoagulants vs 17% in placebo-treated patients (relative risk, RR, 0.53). The risk of stroke was reduced from 12% to 4% per year (RR 0.34). The patients assigned to aspirin were grouped together whether they received anticoagulant treatment or not. These patients had an annual incidence of outcome events of 15% vs 19% in those on placebo (RR 0.83). Anticoagulation was significantly more effective than aspirin. Patients on anticoagulation suffered bleeding events significantly more often than patients on aspirin (p < 0.001) or placebo (p < 0.001), while patients on aspirin had more bleeding complications than patients on placebo (p = 0.39). The incidence of major bleeding events was low, both on anticoagulation (2.8% per year) and on aspirin (0.9% per year). The optimal level of anticoagulation with the lowest risk was with an international normalised ratio of 2–3.9. No treatment was effective with anticoagulation at international normalised ratio < 2, and most major bleeding complications occurred at values ≥ 5

ECASS
European Cooperative Acute Stroke Study

Authors	**(a)** Hacke W, Kaste M, Fieschi C, Toni D, Lesaffre E, von Kummer R, Boysen G, Bluhmki E, Höxter G, Mahagne M-H, Hennerici M **(b)** Fisher M, Pessin MS, Furian AJ
Titles	**(a)** Intravenous thrombolysis with recombinant tissue plasminogen activator for acute hemispheric stroke. The European Cooperative Acute Stroke Study ECASS **(b)** ECASS: lessons for future thrombolytic stroke trials
References	**(a)** *JAMA* 1995;**274**:1017–25 **(b)** *JAMA* 1995;**274**:1058–9
Disease	Acute stroke
Purpose	To evaluate the efficacy and safety of iv thrombolysis using recombinant tissue plasminogen activator (rt-PA) in patients with acute ischaemic stroke
Study design	Randomised, double-blind, placebo-controlled
Follow-up	90 ± 14 days
Patients	620 patients (313 rt-PA and 307 placebo), aged 18–80 years, with acute ischaemic hemispheric stroke and moderate to severe neurological deficit and without major early signs on initial computed tomography
Treatment regimen	rt-PA (alteplase), 1.1 mg/kg body weight, or placebo within 6 h from the onset of symptoms
Concomitant therapy	Acetylsalicylic acid, low-dose sc heparin, use of iv heparin after 24 h
Results	There was a significant difference in the RS (Rankin Scale) in favour of rt-PA-treated patients ($p = 0.035$). The combined BI (Barthel Index) and RS showed a difference in favour of rt-PA-treated patients in both analyses ($p < 0.001$). Neurological recovery at 90 days was significantly better for rt-PA-treated patients ($p = 0.03$). The speed of neurological recovery assessed by the SSS (Scandinavian Stroke Scale) was significantly better up to 30 days in the rt-PA treatment arm. In-hospital stay was significantly shorter in the rt-PA treatment arm. There were no statistically significant differences in mortality at 30 days or in the overall incidence of intracerebral haemorrhages between the rt-PA and placebo treatment arms. However, large parenchymal haemorrhages occurred significantly more frequently in the rt-PA-treated patients

ECSG-6
European Cooperative Study Group for recombinant tissue-type plasminogen activator

Authors	**(a)** de Bono DP, Simoons ML, Tijssen J *et al* **(b)** Simoons ML
Titles	**(a)** Effect of early intravenous heparin on coronary patency, infarct size, and bleeding complications after alteplase thrombolysis: results of a randomised double-blind European Cooperative Study Group trial **(b)** Retreatment with alteplase for early signs of reocclusion after thrombolysis
References	**(a)** *Br Heart J* 1992;**67**:122–8 **(b)** *Am J Cardiol* 1993;**71**:524–8
Disease	AMI
Purpose	To determine whether concomitant therapy with iv heparin affects coronary patency and outcome in patients treated with alteplase (rt-PA) thrombolysis for AMI, and whether retreatment with rt-PA can substitute for angioplasty in patients with early reocclusion after thrombolytic therapy
Study design	Randomised, double-blind, placebo-controlled
Patients	652 patients, aged 21–70 years. Time since onset of AMI: < 6 h
Treatment regimen	Heparin, 5000 U iv bolus, then 1000 U/h until angiography, or placebo. Immediately following the heparin or placebo bolus, rt-PA, 10 mg/h iv bolus, 50 mg/h for the first hour and 20 mg/h for the next 2 h. Repeated administration of rt-PA for reinfarction: within 24 h, 50 mg; > 24 h, 100 mg
Concomitant therapy	Analgesia as required. Aspirin, 250 mg iv bolus or 300 mg orally, followed by 75–125 mg orally on alternate days
Results	Patients treated with iv rt-PA and concomitant iv heparin had a higher coronary patency rate (83.7%) at 48–120 h than patients receiving placebo (75.1%). There was a non-significant trend towards reduced infarct size in patients receiving heparin. Bleeding complications occurred slightly more often in the heparin group (17.6%) than in the placebo group (15.1%). 26 patients (4%) showed signs of reinfarction and received a second dose of rt-PA. Patency for the infarct-related artery was 73% in the heparin group and 40% for those receiving placebo 2–120 h after the second dose of rt-PA

ELITE
Evaluation of Losartan In The Elderly study

Authors	Pitt B, Segal R, Martinez FA, Meurers G, Cowley AJ, Thomas I, Deedwania PC, Ney DE, Snavely DB, Chang PI
Title	Randomised trial of losartan versus captopril in patients over 65 with heart failure (Evaluation of Losartan In The Elderly study, ELITE)
Reference	*Lancet* 1997;**349**:747–52
Disease	Heart failure
Purpose	To determine whether specific angiotensin II receptor blockade with losartan offers safety and efficacy advantages in the treatment of heart failure over ACE inhibition with captopril in the elderly
Study design	Randomised, double-blind, controlled, parallel-group
Follow-up	48 weeks
Patients	722 patients (352 losartan and 370 captopril), aged ≥ 65 years with NYHA class II-IV heart failure and ejection fraction ≤ 40%, who had not previously had ACE inhibitors
Treatment regimen	Losartan titrated to 50 mg once daily, or captopril titrated to 50 mg tid
Concomitant therapy	All other cardiovascular therapies except open-label ACE inhibitors
Results	The frequency of persisting increases in serum creatinine was the same in both groups (10.5%). Fewer losartan patients discontinued therapy for adverse events (12.2% vs 20.8% for captopril, p = 0.002). No losartan-treated patients discontinued because of cough, compared to 14 in the captopril group. Death and/or hospital admission for heart failure occurred in 9.4% of the losartan and 13.2% of the captopril patients (risk reduction 32%; 95% CI -4% to +55%; p = 0.075). This risk reduction was primarily the result of a decrease in all-cause mortality (4.8% vs 8.7%; risk reduction 46%; 95% CI 5–69%; p = 0.035). Admissions with heart failure were the same in both groups (5.7%), as was improvement in NYHA class from baseline. Admission to hospital for any reason was less frequent with losartan than with captopril treatment (22.2% vs 29.7%)

ELSA
European Lacidipine Study on Atherosclerosis
Ongoing trial

Authors	**(a)** Bond MG, Mercuri M **(b)** First author of the respective article: Mercuri M / Hennig M / Zanchetti A / Mancia G / Giannattasio C / Agabiti Rosei E / Ruilope LM
Titles	**(a)** Potential modification of plaque behavior through the European lacidipine study on atherosclerosis **(b)** Several articles presenting the different aspects of ELSA
References	**(a)** *J Cardiovasc Pharmacol* 1995;**25**(suppl 3):S11–6 **(b)** *Blood Press* 1996;**5**(suppl 4):20–52
Disease	Hypertension, atherosclerosis
Purpose	To compare the effects of two antihypertensive agents, the calcium antagonist lacidipine and β-blocker atenolol on the development and progression of atherosclerosis in hypertensive patients
Study design	Randomised, double-blind, parallel-group
Follow-up	5 years
Patients	Aim 3600 patients, aged 45–75 years, with diastolic blood pressure 95–115 mm Hg and systolic blood pressure ≤ 210 mm Hg
Treatment regimen	Patients will be stratified into three groups according to a B-mode ultrasound analysis of the carotid wall morphology and after a 1-month run-in, patients will receive either lacidipine, 4–6 mg daily, or atenolol, 50–100 mg daily. Non-responders will be treated with hydrochlorothiazide (12.5 mg, titrated to 25 mg if necessary) on an open basis
Results	Not yet available

EMERAS
Estudio Multicéntrico Estreptoquinasa Repúblicas de América del Sur

Authors	EMERAS collaborative group
Title	Randomised trial of late thrombolysis in patients with suspected acute myocardial infarction
Reference	*Lancet* 1993;**342**:767–72
Disease	AMI
Purpose	To assess the effects of iv streptokinase on in-hospital and 1-year mortality. Secondary objective: to stratify in-hospital mortality according to the number of hours elapsed from the onset of pain
Study design	Randomised, double-blind, placebo-controlled
Follow-up	1 year
Patients	4534 patients, with no age limits. Time since onset of symptoms of suspected AMI: 6–24 h
Treatment regimen	Streptokinase, 1.5×10^6 U as a 1-h infusion, or placebo
Concomitant therapy	During follow-up, routine management at the discretion of the physician responsible. Low-dose aspirin was strongly recommended
Results	No significant differences in hospital mortality were observed between the streptokinase and placebo groups (11.9% vs 12.4%). A statistically non-significant reduction (12.7%) in the risk of death was observed in the streptokinase group from 7–12 h after symptom onset. The incidence of major clinical events was similar in the two groups. Streptokinase was associated with an excess of bleeding, which required transfusion, and with probable haemorrhagic strokes

EMIAT
European Myocardial Infarct Amiodarone Trial

Authors	**(a)** Camm AJ, Julian DG, Janse G *et al* **(b)** Schwartz PJ, Camm AJ, Frangin G, Janse MJ, Julian DG, Simon P **(c)** Julian DG, Camm AJ, Frangin G, Janse MJ, Munoz A, Schwartz PJ, Simon P
Titles	**(a)** The European Myocardial Infarct Amiodarone Trial (EMIAT) **(b)** Does amiodarone reduce sudden death and cardiac mortality after myocardial infarction? The European Myocardial Infarct Amiodarone Trial (EMIAT) **(c)** Randomised trial of effect of amiodarone on mortality in patients with left-ventricular dysfunction after recent myocardial infarction: EMIAT
References	**(a)** *Am J Cardiol* 1993;**72**:95F–8F **(b)** *Eur Heart J* 1994;**15**:620–4 **(c)** *Lancet* 1997;**349**:667–74
Disease	MI
Purpose	To evaluate the effect of amiodarone on mortality post-MI in patients with left ventricular ejection fraction $\leq 40\%$
Study design	Randomised, double-blind, placebo-controlled
Follow-up	Median 21 months
Patients	1486 patients (743 amiodarone and 743 placebo) enrolled between 5 and 21 days post-MI with a left ventricular ejection fraction $\leq 40\%$
Treatment regimen	Amiodarone, 800 mg/day for 2 weeks, followed by 400 mg/day for 3.5 months, and then 200 mg/day
Results	At mean of 16 months' follow-up, total mortality was 13.4%. 37% of the first 72 deaths occurred in patients without frequent or complex ventricular arrhythmias. At a median of 25 months of follow-up, all-cause mortality and cardiac mortality did not differ between the groups. In the amiodarone group there was a 35% risk reduction (95% confidence interval 0–58, $p = 0.05$) in arrhythmic deaths

EMIP
European Myocardial Infarction Project

Authors	The EMIP group
Title	Prehospital thrombolytic therapy in patients with suspected acute myocardial infarction
Reference	*N Engl J Med* 1993;**329**:383–9
Disease	AMI
Purpose	To evaluate the benefit:risk ratio of prehospital thrombolysis compared to in-hospital thrombolysis. Secondary objective: to evaluate the safety and feasibility of treatment
Study design	Randomised, double-blind, crossover, placebo-controlled
Follow-up	30 days
Patients	5469 patients (2750 prehospital group and 2719 hospital group) with suspected MI seen within 6 h of onset of symptoms
Treatment regimen	Anistreplase, 30 U iv, at home or on arrival in hospital, or placebo. Patients receiving anistreplase at home received placebo in hospital and vice versa
Concomitant therapy	Local standard care for MI
Results	Patients in the prehospital group received thrombolytic therapy 55 min earlier on average than those in the hospital group. There was no significant reduction in overall mortality in the prehospital group. However, death from cardiac causes was 16% lower in the prehospital group than in the hospital group ($p = 0.049$). Adverse events occurred more frequently in the prehospital group during the period before hospitalisation. These were offset by a higher incidence during the hospital period in the hospital group. There were no significant differences between the two groups in the number of fatal and nonfatal events
Comments	The trial was terminated early because it proved not possible to achieve the aim of 10,000 patients recruited within the 2-year study period

EMPAR
Enoxaparin MaxEPA Prevention of Angioplasty Restenosis

Authors	Cairns JA, Gill J, Morton B, Roberts R, Gent M, Hirsh J, Holder D, Finnie K, Marquis JF, Naqvi S, Cohen E
Title	Fish oils and low-molecular-weight heparin for the reduction of restenosis after percutaneous transluminal coronary angioplasty. The EMPAR study
Reference	*Circulation* 1996;**94**:1553–60
Disease	Coronary artery disease
Purpose	To investigate the ability of omega-3 polyunsaturated fatty acid (maxEPA) and low-molecular-weight heparin (enoxaparin) to reduce restenosis following successful coronary angioplasty
Study design	Randomised, blinded
Follow-up	16–20 weeks (target 18 weeks)
Patients	814 patients randomised; 653 patients eligible following percutaneous transluminal coronary angioplasty (PTCA)
Treatment regimen	Prior to PTCA, maxEPA, 18 caps/day, or placebo for 18 weeks. Following PTCA, either enoxaparin, 30 mg subcutaneously bid, or no treatment
Results	Restenosis rates/patient: 46.5% for fish oils, 44.7% for placebo, 45.8% for enoxaparin, 45.4% for control (no treatment). Restenosis rates/lesion: 39.7% for fish oils, 38.7% for placebo, 38.0% for enoxaparin, 40.4% for control (no treatment). There were no differences in mean minimal luminal diameter at follow-up coronary angiography, and no significant differences in the occurrence of ischaemic events

ENTICES
Enoxaparin and Ticlopidine after Elective Stenting

Authors	Kruse KR, Greenberg CS, Tanguay J-F, Gammon RS, Muhlestein JB, Krucoff MW, Matar FA, Morrison LA, Sawchak SR, Berkowitz SD, Phillips HR, Stack RS, Califf RM, Zidar JP
Title	Thrombin and fibrin activity in patients treated with enoxaparin, ticlopidine and aspirin versus the conventional coumadin regimen after eclective stenting: the ENTICES trial
Reference	*J Am Coll Cardiol* 1996;**27**:334A
Disease	Cardiovascular disease
Purpose	To determine if treatment with enoxaparin + ticlopidine is superior to conventional therapy in influencing haematological factors and complications after stenting
Study design	Randomised
Follow-up	30 days
Patients	122 patients (79 study group and 43 control group) receiving Palmer-Schatz stent placement for restenotic lesions, lesions that would take up two stents, or post-MI lesions of at least 48 h duration
Treatment regimen	Study group: post-stent therapy with enoxaparin, 30-60 mg (0.5 mg/kg) bid sc for 10 days, oral ticlopidine, 250 mg bid for 30 days and aspirin, 325 mg once daily for life. Control group: standard post-stent therapy with heparin, aspirin, dipyridamole, dextran and warfarin
Results	Objective success rates were 93% in the control group and 97% in the study group. Hospitalisation after stenting was 5 days in the control group and 3 days in the study group. Treatment with enoxaparin + ticlopidine led to a significant reduction in adverse clinical events and in bleeding complications. For these two groups respectively the events rates at 30 days were: stent thrombosis 0% vs 7%; death 0% vs 5%; MI 4% vs 12%; CABG 0% vs 9%; repeat PTCA 1% vs 7%; total adverse clinical events 5% vs 21%. In addition, a composite endpoint gave bleeding and/or vascular complications in 5% vs 17% of patients

ENTIM
Etude des Nouveaux Thrombolytiques dans l'Infarctus du Myocarde

Authors	Lusson J-R, Anguenot T, Wolf J-E, Maublant J, Bertrand B, Schiele F
Title	Comparative effects of APSAC and rt-PA on infarct size and left ventricular function in acute myocardial infarction. A multicentre randomized study
Reference	*Circulation* 1991;**84**:1107–17
Disease	AMI
Purpose	To compare the efficacy and safety (patency rates, myocardial salvage, short-term and 1-year mortality) of alteplase and anistreplase in AMI
Study design	Randomised, double-blind, parallel-group
Follow-up	1 year
Patients	183 patients, aged ≤ 70 years, with first episode of AMI. Time since onset of symptoms: < 4 h
Treatment regimen	Anistreplase (APSAC), 30 mg iv over 5 min, or alteplase (rt-PA), 10 mg bolus injection and 90 mg iv over 180 min
Results	In-hospital mortality was 5 patients in the APSAC group and 7 in the rt-PA group (p = ns). The fibrinogen level fell from 3.45 g/l to 0.65 g/l with APSAC treatment and to 2.00 g/l with rt-PA treatment (p < 0.0001), but the occurrence of bleeding problems was the same in the two groups (11 and 9 patients, respectively). The achievement of patency (72% vs 76%), first week left ventricular ejection fraction (LVEF) (0.50 vs 0.52), third week LVEF (0.48 vs 0.47), and infarct size (11% vs 9%), for APSAC and rt-PA, respectively, were similar in both groups

EPAMSA
Estudio Piloto Argentino de Muerte Súbita y Amiodarone

Authors	Garguichevich JJ, Ramos JL, Gambarte A, Gentile A, Hauad S, Scapin O, Sirena J, Tibaldi M, Toplikar J
Title	Effect of amiodarone therapy on mortality in patients with left ventricular dysfunction and asymptomatic complex ventricular arrhythmias: Argentine pilot study of sudden death and amiodarone (EPAMSA)
Reference	*Am Heart J* 1995;**130**:494–500
Disease	Left ventricular dysfunction, asymptomatic ventricular arrhythmias
Purpose	To investigate the efficacy of prophylactic antiarrhythmic treatment with amiodarone in reducing 1-year mortality in patients with reduced left ventricular ejection fraction ($< 35\%$) and asymptomatic ventricular arrhythmias
Study design	Randomised, controlled
Follow-up	12 months
Patients	127 patients (66 amiodarone and 61 controls), aged 40–75 years, with left ventricular ejection fraction at rest $< 35\%$ and asymptomatic complex ventricular arrhythmias without clinical heart failure or electrolyte abnormalities
Treatment regimen	Amiodarone, 800 mg/day for 2 weeks followed by 400 mg/day thereafter, or no antiarrhythmic therapy
Results	Amiodarone reduced the overall mortality rate, which was 10.5% in the amiodarone group vs 28.6% in the control group (odds ratio 0.29; 95% CI 0.10–0.84; log-rank test 0.02) and sudden death rate, which was 7.0% in the amiodarone group and 20.4% in the control group (odds ratio 0.29%; 95% CI 0.08–1.00; log-rank test 0.04). Side-effects were rare and amiodarone had to be discontinued only in 3 patients

EPIC
Evaluation of c7E3 Fab in the Prevention of Ischemic Complications

Authors	**(a)** Moliterno DJ, Califf RM, Aguirre FV, Anderson K, Sigmon KN, Weisman HF, Topol EJ **(b)** Califf RM, Lincoff AM, Tcheng JE, Topol EJ **(c)** Lefkovits J, Ivanhore RJ, Califf RM, Bergelson BA, Anderson KM, Stoner GL, Weisman HF, Topol EJ **(d)** Lefkovits J, Blankenship JC, Anderson KM, Stoner GL, Talley JD, Worley SJ, Weisman HF, Califf RM, Topol EJ
Titles	**(a)** Effect of platelet glycoprotein IIb/IIIa integrin blockade on activated clotting time during percutaneous transluminal coronary angioplasty or directional atherectomy (the EPIC trial) **(b)** An overview of the results of the EPIC trial **(c)** Effects of platelet glycoprotein IIb/IIIa receptor blockade by a chimeric monoclonal antibody (abciximab) on acute and six-month outcomes after percutaneous transluminal coronary angioplasty for acute myocardial infarction **(d)** Increased risk of non-Q wave myocardial infarction after directional atherectomy is platelet dependent: evidence from the EPIC trial
References	**(a)** *Am J Cardiol* 1995;**75**:559–62 **(b)** *Eur Heart J* 1995;**16**(suppl L):43–9 **(c)** *Am J Cardiol* 1996;**77**:1045–51 **(d)** *J Am Coll Cardiol* 1996;**28**:849–55
Disease	Ischaemic heart disease, MI
Purpose	To determine whether abciximab (c7E3 Fab) treatment improves outcomes in patients undergoing direct coronary angioplasty (PTCA)
Study design	Randomised, double-blind, placebo-controlled
Follow-up	6 months
Patients	2038 high-risk patients, aged < 80 years, undergoing coronary intervention
Treatment regimen	Abciximab, a bolus of 0.25 mg/kg body weight, followed by a 12-h infusion (10 μg/min) of abciximab or placebo, or placebo bolus plus infusion
Concomitant therapy	PTCA or directional atherectomy. Aspirin and heparin before the intervention and heparin iv for at least 12 h after the procedure
Results	Patients undergoing directional atherectomy had a lower baseline risk of acute complications but a higher incidence of any MI (10.7% vs 6.3%, p = 0.021) and non-Q-wave MI (9.6% vs 4.9%, p = 0.006). Bolus and infusion of abciximab reduced non-Q-wave MI rates after atherectomy by 71% (15.4% for placebo vs 4.5% for bolus and infusion,

p = 0.046). Non-Q-wave MI rates after PTCA were not affected by abciximab, although Q-wave MI were reduced from 2.6% to 0.8% (p = 0.017)

Comments	Other studies with the acronym EPIC have been performed, eg, Echo Persantine Italian Cooperative and European Prevalence of Infection in intensive Care

EPILOG
Evaluation in PTCA to Improve Long-term Outcome with abciximab GP IIb/IIIa blockade

Authors	The EPILOG investigators
Title	Platelet glycoprotein IIb/IIIa receptor blockade and low-dose heparin during percutaneous coronary revascularization
Reference	N Engl J Med 1997;**336**:1689–96
Disease	Coronary artery disease, scheduled for coronary angioplasty (PTCA)
Purpose	To evaluate the effects of cF7E3 glycoprotein receptor blockade (abciximab) during coronary interventions on mortality and morbidity
Study design	Randomised, double-blind, placebo-controlled
Follow-up	30 days
Patients	2792 patients (aim 4800), undergoing PTCA
Treatment regimen	Control arm: standard dose heparin (100 U/kg bolus, titrated to an activated clotting time of ≥ 300 s) plus placebo. Experimental arms: standard-dose heparin plus abciximab (0.25 mg/kg bolus plus 0.125 µg/kg/min infusion for 12 h), or low-dose heparin (70 U/kg bolus, to achieve an activated clotting time of ≥ 200 s) plus abciximab
Concomitant therapy	Aspirin, 325 mg/day, starting 2 h before PTCA
Results	At 30 days, the composite event rate was 11.7% in the group with placebo and standard-dose heparin, 5.2% in the group with abciximab plus low-dose heparin ($p < 0.001$), and 5.4% in the group with abciximab plus standard-dose heparin ($p < 0.001$). There were no significant differences between the groups in the risk of major bleeding. Minor bleeding was more frequent in the patients receiving abciximab plus standard-dose heparin
Comments	After the first interim analysis in 1500 patients a highly significant reduction in the incidence of death and AMI was observed in patients receiving abciximab. This exceeded the predetermined stopping level and after recommendation from the Safety and Efficacy Monitoring Committee the study was stopped

ERA
Enoxaparin Restenosis after Angioplasty trial

Authors	Faxon DP, Spiro TE, Minor S, Coté G, Douglas J, Gottlieb R, Califf R, Dorosti K, Topol E, Gordon JB, Ohmen M
Title	Low-molecular-weight heparin in prevention of restenosis after angioplasty. Results of enoxaparin restenosis (ERA) trial
Reference	*Circulation* 1994;**90**:908–14
Disease	Coronary artery disease
Purpose	To determine whether treatment with enoxaparin after coronary angioplasty (PTCA) would reduce the incidence of restenosis
Study design	Randomised, double-blind
Follow-up	6 months
Patients	458 patients (227 enoxaparin and 231 placebo), aged ≥ 21 years, scheduled for PTCA
Treatment regimen	Enoxaparin, 40 mg/day sc for 1 month, or placebo, after successful PTCA
Concomitant therapy	Acetylsalicylic acid, 325 mg/day
Results	Restenosis occurred in 51% of the placebo group and 52% of the enoxaparin group (relative risk 1.07, $p = 0.625$). Adverse clinical events were infrequent and did not differ between the groups, with the exception of minor bleeding complications, which were more common in the enoxaparin group

ERICA
European Risk and Incidence, a Coordinated Analysis
Ongoing trial

Authors	**(a)** and **(b)** ERICA research group
Titles	**(a)** The CHD risk-map of Europe **(b)** Prediction of coronary heart disease in Europe. The 2nd report of the WHO-ERICA Project
References	**(a)** *Eur Heart J* 1988;**9**(suppl 1):1–36 **(b)** *Eur Heart J* 1991;**12**:291–7
Disease	Coronary heart disease (CHD)
Purpose	To establish, through uniform analysis, the distribution of CHD risk factors in Europe, to compute on this basis a risk-map of Europe and finally, by using available follow-up data, to devise European coefficients for the multiple logistic function (MLF) prediction of future CHD events
Study design	Collection of all existing cardiovascular disease epidemiological studies in Europe and central analysis of the data
Follow-up	Started in 1982 and still continuing
Patients	151,923 subjects from 35 studies and 17 countries
Results	There have been adequate 6-year follow-up data so far from 18,931 of 84,609 men in the 40–59 year age group, making it possible to assess CHD mortality in relation to five risk factors (age, serum cholesterol, systolic blood pressure, body mass index and cigarette smoking). Except for body mass index, all appear as significant contributors to multiple risk. Age and cholesterol in the South and systolic blood pressure in the West do not reach the level of significance. Body mass index does not seem to contribute significantly to the risk of CHD in Europe, except in the South. By applying the MLF analysis, coefficients for the prediction of observed CHD deaths in the four regions (North, South, East and West) were computed. Application of these coefficients showed that > 50% of all deaths occurred in the highest quintile (20%) of the initial multiple risk distribution

ESPIRAL
Effects of antihypertensive treatment on progression of renal insufficiency
Ongoing trial

Authors	Marín R, Ruilope LM, Aljama P, Aranda P, Díez Martinez J
Title	Effect of antihypertensive treatment on progression of renal insufficiency in non-diabetic patients (ESPIRAL trial)
Reference	*Nefrologia* 1995;**15**:464–75
Disease	Renal failure, hypertension
Purpose	To study the influence of fosinopril and nifedipine slow-release on the progression of chronic renal failure in non-diabetic patients
Study design	Randomised, open
Follow-up	3 years
Patients	Aim 250 patients, with progressively failing renal function shown by an increase in serum creatinine (SCr) of at least 25% in the previous 2 years and SCr levels between 1.5 and 4.0 mg/dl, and blood pressure $\geq$ 140/90 mm Hg
Treatment regimen	Fosinopril, 10–30 mg/day, or nifedipine, slow release 30-60 mg/day. If blood pressure control is insufficient, frusemide, 20–100 mg/day, will be added first and then atenolol, 25–100 mg/day, and/or doxazosin, 1–12 mg/day
Concomitant therapy	Diet with 4–5 g/day salt content and protein content of 0.9–1 g/kg body weight
Results	Not yet available

ESPRIM
European Study of Prevention of Infarct with Molsidomine

Authors	European Study of Prevention of Infarct with Molsidomine (ESPRIM) group
Title	The ESPRIM trial: short-term treatment of acute myocardial infarction with molsidomine
Reference	*Lancet* 1994;**344**:91–7
Disease	AMI
Purpose	To assess whether linsidomine and molsidomine can reduce mortality in patients with recent MI
Study design	Randomised, double-blind, placebo-controlled
Follow-up	Mean 13 months
Patients	4017 patients (2007 linsidomine/molsidomine and 2010 placebo) with suspected AMI without signs of overt heart failure (Killip III/IV)
Treatment regimen	Linsidomine, 1 mg/h iv for 48 h, followed by molsidomine, 16 mg per os daily for 12 days, or placebo
Concomitant therapy	Vasodilators not permitted
Results	The molsidomine and placebo groups showed similar all-cause 35-day mortality: 168 deaths (8.4%) vs 176 (8.8%), p = 0.66. There was similarly no difference in long-term mortality: at an average of 13 months, 294 (14.7%) vs 285 (14.2%) deaths, p = 0.67. The two groups showed similar frequencies of major and minor adverse events, but headache was significantly more common in the molsidomine group

ESPRIT
European Study of the Prevention of Reocclusion after Initial Thrombolysis

Authors	Malcolm AD, Keltai M, Walsh MJ
Title	ESPRIT: a European study of the prevention of reocclusion after initial thrombolysis with duteplase in acute myocardial infarction
Reference	*Eur Heart J* 1996;**17**:1522–31
Disease	AMI
Purpose	To evaluate the efficacy and safety of duteplase, a double-chain recombinant tissue-type plasminogen activator, in patients with AMI treated within 4 h of onset of chest pain
Study design	Open
Follow-up	72 h
Patients	273 patients, aged ≤ 75 years, with suspected AMI with onset 4 h earlier
Treatment regimen	Duteplase, 0.4 MU/kg iv in the first hour, with 10% injected as a bolus in the first 60 s. A maintenance iv infusion of duteplase, 0.20 MU/kg, was then given over the next 3 h
Concomitant therapy	Oral aspirin and iv heparin
Results	TIMI grade 2 or 3 patency of the infarct-associated coronary artery was achieved at 90 min in 70% of the patients and 7% of these patent infarct-associated coronary arteries had reoccluded by 20–36 h. Clinical reinfarction during the 72-h period was observed in 7%. Total in-hospital mortality was 8%. Serious or life-threatening bleeding occurred in 4% of the patients. There was one haemorrhagic stroke, with fatal outcome

ESSENCE
Efficacy and Safety of Subcutaneous Enoxaparin in unstable angina and Non-Q-wave myocardial infarction
Ongoing trial

Authors	Cohen M, Blaber R, Demers C, Gurfinkel EP, Langer A, Fromell G, Turpie AGG, Premmereur J
Title	The Essence trial: efficacy and safety of subcutaneous enoxaparin in unstable angina and non-Q-wave MI: a double-blind, randomized, parallel-group, multicenter study comparing enoxaparin and intravenous unfractionated heparin: methods and design
Reference	*J Thromb Thrombolysis* 1997;**4**:271–4
Disease	Unstable angina or non-Q-wave MI
Purpose	To evaluate the efficacy of enoxaparin (low-molecular-weight heparin) vs unfractionated heparin, plus aspirin, in patients with unstable angina or non-Q-wave infarction
Study design	Randomised, double-blind, placebo-controlled, parallel-group
Follow-up	30 days
Patients	At least 3180 patients, aged ≥ 18 years with recent onset of unstable angina and evidence of underlying ischaemic heart disease, or non-Q-wave MI. So far 3019 patients (33% women) have been randomised, mean age 64 years, 46% with prior MI
Treatment regimen	Enoxaparin, 1 mg/kg sc every 12 h, or bolus unfractionated heparin, 5000 IU iv followed by a continuous heparin infusion to maintain the aPTT at 2 x control, or placebo
Concomitant therapy	Aspirin, 100–325 mg/day
Results	Interim results for 3019 patients: overall event rates at 14 days are 1.7% mortality, 5.9% subsequent reinfarction, and 17% recurrent angina. The composite rate is 23.6%

ESTIC
Estudio Supervivencia en el Tratamiento de la Insufficiencia Cardiaca
Ongoing trial

Authors	The ESTIC investigators
Title	Study on survival and treatment of congestive heart failure in Spain (ESTIC)
Reference	*J Heart Failure* 1993;**1**(abstract suppl):abstract 187
Disease	Congestive heart failure
Purpose	To compare the effect of captopril with that of digoxin, when added to diuretics, on mortality and quality of life for patients with moderate congestive heart failure
Study design	Randomised, open, controlled
Follow-up	3 years
Patients	Aim 548 patients, aged < 80 years, in NYHA classes II and III with an AMI < 3 months earlier
Treatment regimen	Captopril, 50 mg/day, or digoxin, 0.25 mg/day
Concomitant therapy	Frusemide, 20 mg/day
Results	Preliminary results for 111 patients show no significant differences in 1-year mortality for the captopril group (5.9%) compared to the digoxin group (9.8%)

ESVEM
Electrophysiologic Study Versus
Electrocardiographic Monitoring

Authors	**(a)** and **(b)** Mason JW **(c)** Lazzara R **(d)** Reiter MJ, Mann D, Reiffel JE, Hahn E, Hartz V, and the ESVEM Investigators **(e)** Mason JW, Marcus FI, Bigger JT, Lazzara R, Reiffel JA, Reiter MJ, Mann D **(f)** Reiffel JA, Reiter MJ, Freedman RA, Mann D, Huang SKS, Hahn E, Hartz V, Mason J, and the ESVEM Investigators
Titles	**(a)** A comparison of electrophysiologic testing with Holter monitoring to predict antiarrhythmic-drug efficacy for ventricular tachyarrhythmias **(b)** A comparison of seven antiarrhythmic drugs in patients with ventricular tachyarrhythmias **(c)** Clinical implications of the ESVEM trial **(d)** Significance and incidence of concordance of drug efficacy predictions by Holter monitoring and electrophysiological study in the ESVEM trial **(e)** A summary and assessment of the findings and conclusions of the ESVEM trial **(f)** Influence of Holter monitor and electrophysiological study methods and efficacy criteria on the outcome of patients with ventricular tachycardia and ventricular fibrillation in the ESVEM trial
References	**(a)** *N Engl J Med* 1993;**329**:445–51 **(b)** *N Engl J Med* 1993;**329**:452–8 **(c)** *N Trends Arrhythmias* 1994;**9**:1183–5 **(d)** *Circulation* 1995;**91**:1988–95 **(e)** *Prog Cardiovasc Dis* 1996;**38**:347–58 **(f)** *Prog Cardiovasc Dis* 1996;**38**:359–70
Disease	Ventricular tachycardia
Purpose	To determine whether electrophysiological study or ECG Holter monitoring is more accurate in predicting antiarrhythmic drug efficacy in patients with aborted sudden death or sustained ventricular tachyarrhythmias
Study design	Randomised, open, parallel-group
Follow-up	Up to 6.2 years
Patients	486 patients (242 electrophysiological and 244 Holter) with ventricular tachyarrhythmias that were inducible during electrophysiological study or 10 or more premature ventricular complexes/h during Holter monitoring
Treatment regimen	Electrophysiological study or ECG Holter monitoring. Mean doses of antiarrhythmic drugs: imipramine, 2.75 mg/kg/day, mexiletine, 11.37 mg/kg/day, pirmenol, 4.92 mg/kg/day, procainamide, 56.96 mg/kg/day, propafenone, 10.83 mg/

kg/day, quinidine, 27.28 mg/kg/day and sotalol, 5.59 mg/kg/day. Mean long-term doses generally slightly lower

Results

45% of patients in the electrophysiological study group and 77% in the Holter group received a prediction of efficacy (p < 0.001). Holter monitoring in those patients randomised to the electrophysiological group showed concordance of efficacy prediction in only 46% of patients. There was no significant difference between study groups in the distribution of mortality and types of recurrence of arrhythmia. A total of 296 patients were identified as receiving effective treatment; among these there were 46 deaths and 150 recurrences of arrhythmia over a 6-year period. Of these 296 patients, those in the electrophysiological study group had a higher prediction of efficacy with sotalol (35%) than with the other drugs (16%, p < 0.001). There was no significant difference among the drugs in the Holter-monitoring group. Sotalol was shown to be more effective than the other antiarrhythmic drugs in preventing death and recurrence of arrhythmia. The percentage of patients with adverse drug effects, requiring discontinuation of the drug, was lowest with sotalol (16%) compared to the other drugs (23–43%). Neither excess non-coronary disease in the electrophysiological study group nor excess β-blocker use in the Holter group influenced the results of the trial. Discrepancies were observed between the actual and the predicted modes of initiation of ventricular tachycardias and between spontaneous and induced rhythms. Suppression of both spontaneous ventricular ectopy and inducible ventricular tachyarrhythmias did not improve outcome compared to the Holter monitoring group

Comments

The ESVEM trial has been criticised on grounds related to its enrolment, methods and efficacy criteria. Some of the criticisms have been accepted and some refuted by the trial investigators

EURAMIC
European community multicenter study on Antioxidants, Myocardial Infarction and breast Cancer

Authors	Kardinaal AFM, Kok FJ, Ringstad J, Gomez-Aracena J, Mazaev VP, Kohlmeier L, Martin BC, Aro A, Kark JD, Delgado-Rodriguez M, Riemersma RA, van 't Veer P, Huttunen JK, Martin-Moreno JM
Title	Antioxidants in adipose tissue and risk of myocardial infarction: the EURAMIC study
Reference	*Lancet* 1993;**342**:1379–84
Disease	Coronary heart disease, MI
Purpose	To compare concentrations of α-tocopherol and β-carotene in adipose-tissue samples from people with AMI and controls
Study design	Case-control
Follow-up	2 years
Patients	1410 men (683 AMI and 727 controls), aged < 70 years, with stable dietary patterns and no weight loss > 5 kg in the previous year
Treatment regimen	Subcutaneous adipose tissue was collected from the volunteers by needle aspiration and a non-fasting blood sample was collected no later than 24 h after onset of symptoms
Results	Mean adipose-tissue β-carotene concentration was 0.35 µg/g in cases and 0.42 µg/g in controls, with age-adjusted and centre-adjusted mean difference 0.07 µg/g (95% CI 0.04–0.10). Mean α-tocopherol concentrations were 193 µg/g and 192 µg/g respectively for cases and controls. The age-adjusted and centre-adjusted quintile of β-carotene as compared to the highest was 2.62 (95% CI 1.79–3.83). Additional control for body mass index and smoking reduced the odds ratio to 1.78 (95% CI 1.17–2.71); other established risk factors did not substantially alter this ratio. The increased risk was mainly confined to current smokers: the multivariate odds ratio in the lowest β-carotene quintile in smokers was 2.39 (95% CI 1.35–4.25), whereas it was 1.07 for people who had never smoked. A low α-tocopherol concentration was not associated with risk of MI

EVA
Epidemiological study on Vascular and cognitive Aging

Authors	Bizbiz L, Bonithon-Kopp C, Ducimetiere P, Berr C, Alperovitch A, Robert L
Title	Relation of serum elastase activity to ultrasonographically assessed carotid artery wall lesions and cardiovascular risk factors. The EVA study
Reference	*Atherosclerosis* 1996;**120**:47–55
Disease	Atherosclerosis
Purpose	To study the potential interest of serum elastase activity (SEA) as a marker of vascular ageing and atherosclerosis as part of an epidemiological study on vascular and cognitive ageing
Study design	Epidemiological
Follow-up	4 years
Patients	555 men and 774 women, volunteers, aged 59–71 years
Results	The distribution of SEA values was skewed to the right in men and women, the mean value being 0.52 ± 0.55 U/ml in men and 0.43 ± 0.52 U/ml in women. This difference could be entirely explained by alcohol consumption. SEA increased strongly with alcohol consumption in men and women. It was also positively and significantly correlated with body mass index and systolic blood pressure. SEA significantly decreased with age in men and was not influenced by smoking in either sex. SEA was significantly increased in diabetic compared to non-diabetic men; the increase was not significant in women. For both sexes together, the association between diabetes and SEA was independent of other clinical risk factors. No significant associations were observed with intima-media thickness or atherosclerotic plaques assessed by B-mode carotid ultrasound. Among biological risk factors, triglycerides in both sexes and glucose in men appeared the strongest correlates of increase in SEA. In multivariate analysis, independent determinants of an increased SEA were age, alcohol, triglycerides, and glucose in men, and alcohol and triglycerides in women

EWPHE
European Working Party on High blood pressure in the Elderly trial

Authors	Amery A, Birkenhäger WH, Bulpitt CJ, Dollery CT (eds)
Title	The European Working Party on High blood pressure in the Elderly. Proceedings of a symposium held in Rome, 19–20 November 1989
Reference	*Am J Med* 1991;**90**(suppl 3A):3A-1S–64S and addenda
Disease	Hypertension
Purpose	To assess the effects of antihypertensive drug therapy in patients over 60 years of age
Study design	Randomised, double-blind, placebo-controlled
Follow-up	Average 4.7 years (maximum 11 years)
Patients	840 patients (416 active treatment and 424 placebo; 70% women), aged ≥ 60 years (mean 72 years). Diastolic blood pressure (DBP) at entry: 90–119 mm Hg
Treatment regimen	1st phase: hydrochlorothiazide, 25 mg/day, and triamterene, 50 mg/day. 2nd phase: methyldopa, 250–2000 mg/day
Concomitant therapy	Any appropriate treatment allowed
Results	There was no significant reduction in total mortality rate, but there was a significant reduction in cardiovascular mortality rate ($p < 0.05$). Deaths from MI were also reduced ($p < 0.05$). Fatal cardiovascular events and nonfatal cerebrovascular events were reduced during active treatment ($p < 0.01$ and $p < 0.05$, respectively), but nonfatal cardiac events were not. In treated patients, a U-shaped relationship was seen between mortality and systolic blood pressure (SBP), while in the placebo group, this relationship was apparent between mortality and DBP. In treated patients, the highest mortality occurred in those with the lowest DBP. After 3 months, the decrease (in mm Hg) in SBP and DBP was more pronounced in those aged > 70 years in both treated and placebo groups. Major changes in ECG indicative of reduction in left ventricular hypertrophy occurred during the first year of treatment, and were irrespective of the type of treatment. ECG changes were not correlated with changes in SBP. Serum creatinine and serum uric acid increased significantly in treated patients, but not in the placebo group. Total, cardiovascular and non-cardiovascular mortality rates were unrelated to initial serum uric acid. Symptoms more common in treated patients than in the placebo group were dry mouth (42% vs 27%), nasal congestion (27% vs 21%) and diarrhoea (25% vs 18%)

EXCEL
Expanded Clinical Evaluation of Lovastatin study

Authors	**(a)** Bradford RH, Shear CL, Chremos AN, Dujovne C, Franklin FA, Hesney M, Higgins J, Langendörfer A, Pool JL, Schnaper H, Stephenson WP
	(b) Bradford RH, Shear CL, Chremos AN, Dujovne C, Downton M, Franklin FA, Gould AL, Hesney M, Higgins J, Hurley DP, Langendorfer A, Nash DT, Pool JL, Schnaper H
	(c) Bradford RH, Shear CL, Chremos AN, Franklin FA, Nash DT, Hurley DP, Dujovne CA, Pool JL, Schnaper H, Hesney M, Langendörfer A
	(d) Pool JL, Shear CL, Downton M, Schnaper H, Stinnett S, Dujovne C, Bradford RH, Chremos AN
	(e) Shear CL, Franklin FA, Stinnett S, Hurley DP, Bradford RH, Chremos AN, Nash DT, Langendorfer A
	(f) Bradford RH, Downton M, Chremos AN, Langendörfer A, Stinnett S, Nash DT, Mantell G, Shear CL
	(g) Bradford RH, Shear CL, Chremos AN, Dujovne CA, Franklin FA, Grillo RB, Higgins J, Langendorfer A, Nash DT, Pool JL, Schnaper H

Titles	**(a)** Expanded Clinical Evaluation of Lovastatin (EXCEL) study: design and patient characteristics of a double-blind, placebo-controlled study in patients with moderate hypercholesterolemia
	(b) Expanded Clinical Evaluation of Lovastatin (EXCEL) study results. I. Efficacy in modifying plasma lipoproteins and adverse event profile in 8245 patients with moderate hypercholesterolemia
	(c) Expanded Clinical Evaluation of Lovastatin (EXCEL) study results: III. Efficacy in modifying lipoproteins and implications for managing patients with moderate hypercholesterolemia
	(d) Lovastatin and coadministered antihypertensive/cardiovascular agents
	(e) Expanded Clinical Evaluation of Lovastatin (EXCEL) study results. Effect of patient characteristics on lovastatin-induced changes in plasma concentrations of lipids and lipoproteins
	(f) Efficacy and tolerability of lovastatin in 3390 women with moderate hypercholesterolemia
	(g) Expanded Clinical Evaluation of Lovastatin (EXCEL) study results: two-year efficacy and safety follow-up

References	**(a)** *Am J Cardiol* 1990;**66**:44B–55B
	(b) *Arch Intern Med* 1991;**151**:43–9
	(c) *Am J Med* 1991;**91**(suppl 1B):1B-18S–24S
	(d) *Hypertension* 1992;**19**:242–8
	(e) *Circulation* 1992;**85**:1293–303
	(f) *Ann Intern Med* 1993;**118**:850–5
	(g) *Am J Cardiol* 1994;**74**:667–73

Disease	Moderate hypercholesterolaemia

Purpose	To clarify dose-response relationship of lovastatin therapy to its lipid/lipoprotein-modifying efficacy and treatment-related adverse events in a population with moderately elevated plasma low-density lipoprotein (LDL) and total cholesterol levels
Study design	Randomised, double-blind, diet- and placebo-controlled
Follow-up	48 weeks, then 2 years
Patients	8245 patients (1642 lovastatin, 20 mg/day; 1645 lovastatin, 40 mg/day; 1646 lovastatin, 20 mg bid; 1649 lovastatin, 40 mg bid, and 1663 placebo), aged 18–70 years, with primary type 2 hyperlipoproteinaemia (hypercholesterolaemia), defined as fasting plasma total cholesterol level of 240–300 mg/dl, LDL cholesterol level $\geq$ 160 mg/dl and triglyceride level < 350 mg/dl. 997 patients followed for 2 years
Treatment regimen	Lovastatin, 20 or 40 mg with the evening meal, or 20 or 40 mg bid
Concomitant therapy	American Heart Association phase 1 diet or a more restrictive diet. Other lipid-lowering agents or investigational drugs not permitted
Results	Lovastatin produced a dose-dependent lowering of LDL cholesterol of 24–40% ($p < 0.001$). High-density lipoprotein (HDL) cholesterol was raised by 7–9% by lovastatin. Furthermore, a dose-dependent reduction of 10–19% in triglycerides was produced by lovastatin. Results were similar in the subgroup of 3390 women. No significant variation was found in total mortality, death due to coronary heart disease, nonfatal MI or cancer. The incidence of clinical and laboratory adverse events requiring discontinuation was 6% in the placebo group and 7–9% in the lovastatin groups. No new types of adverse experiences related to lovastatin were reported. There was no evidence that the lovastatin-induced changes were attenuated by co-administration with any commonly used antihypertensives. Patient characteristics had little clinically important effect on dose-dependent LDL cholesterol lowering by lovastatin, but in patients with initially high triglycerides and low HDL cholesterol, lovastatin elevation of HDL cholesterol was enhanced. 82–95% of women achieved the National Cholesterol Education Program goal for LDL cholesterol; oestrogen replacement therapy did not alter the efficacy or safety profile of lovastatin. At 2 years, the LDL cholesterol response to lovastatin was maintained, triglyceride reductions were somewhat less, and increases in HDL cholesterol were moderately greater than after 48 weeks. The incidence of clinical adverse events requiring discontinuation in the second year was 4% in the placebo group and 2–6% in the lovastatin groups

FACET
Flosequinan-ACE inhibitor Trial

Authors	Massie BM, Berk MR, Brozena SC *et al*
Title	Can further benefit be achieved by adding flosequinan to patients with congestive heart failure who remain symptomatic on diuretic, digoxin, and an angiotensin converting enzyme inhibitor? Results of the Flosequinan-ACE inhibitor Trial (FACET)
Reference	*Circulation* 1993;**88**:492–501
Disease	Congestive heart failure
Purpose	To test whether flosequinan improves exercise tolerance and quality of life in patients with congestive heart failure when added to treatment with diuretics, digoxin and angiotensin-converting enzyme inhibitors
Study design	Randomised, double-blind, placebo-controlled
Follow-up	4 months
Patients	322 patients with NYHA class II and III coronary heart failure and left ventricular ejection fraction $\leq 35\%$
Treatment regimen	Oral flosequinan, 100 mg once daily, or 75 mg bid, or placebo
Concomitant therapy	Diuretics (96% loop diuretics), captopril or enalapril, digoxin (90%)
Results	At 4 months, exercise time increased by 64 s in the 100 mg flosequinan group, compared to 5 s in the placebo group (p < 0.05). For the 75 mg bid group the improvement was insignificant. Compared to placebo, quality of life improved in the 100 mg group and worsened in the 75 mg bid group. Adverse events were reported in most of patients in all treatment groups. There was no significant difference in mortality between treatment groups
Comments	The PROFILE study, evaluating the effect of flosequinan on survival, was terminated early because of excess mortality in patients treated with flosequinan, 100 mg once daily

FAPIS
Flecainide And Propafenone Italian Study

Authors	Chimienti M, Cullen MT Jr, Casadei G
Title	Safety of long-term flecainide and propafenone in the management of patients with symptomatic paroxysmal atrial fibrillation: report from the Flecainide And Propafenone Italian Study investigators
Reference	*Am J Cardiol* 1996;**77**:60A–5A
Disease	Symptomatic paroxysmal atrial fibrillation (AF)
Purpose	To compare the relative safety of 2 class Ic antiarrhythmic agents, flecainide acetate and propafenone HCl during long-term treatment of paroxysmal AF
Study design	Randomised, open, controlled, parallel-group
Follow-up	12 months
Patients	200 patients (97 flecainide and 103 propafenone), aged 18–70 years, with at least 2 ECG-documented episodes of paroxysmal AF in the previous 4 months requiring drug treatment
Treatment regimen	Flecainide, initially 200 mg/day, or propafenone, initially 450 mg/day. Dose increases up to maximum flecainide, 300 mg/day, or propafenone, 900 mg/day, were permitted after ≥ 2 attacks of paroxysmal AF
Results	140 patients completed the study. 10 patients receiving flecainide reported 14 adverse cardiac experiences and 4 discontinued flecainide. 7 patients receiving propafenone reported 8 adverse cardiac experiences and 5 discontinued propafenone. 1 propafenone patient developed ventricular tachycardia and 2 flecainide patients experienced AF with a rapid ventricular response. The intention-to-treat analysis showed that the probability of safe and effective treatment after 12 months was 77% for flecainide and 75% for propafenone. There was an acceptable risk-benefit profile in patients with paroxysmal AF and no evidence of clinically significant heart disease in those treated with either drug for 12 months. There was no statistically significant difference in safety or efficacy between flecainide and propafenone in this study

FAPS
Felodipine Atherosclerosis Prevention Study
Ongoing trial

Authors	Wong ND, Teng W, Abrahamson D, Willner R, Henein N, Franklin SS, Kashyap ML, Rosenzweig B, Kukes G, Detrano RC
Title	Noninvasive tracking of coronary atherosclerosis by electron beam computed tomography: rationale and design of the Felodipine Atherosclerosis Prevention Study (FAPS)
Reference	*Am J Cardiol* 1995;**76**:1239–42
Disease	Coronary atherosclerosis
Purpose	To evaluate the efficacy of felodipine ER to stabilise the progression of atherosclerosis, estimated by serial changes in coronary calcium evaluated by non-invasive electron beam computed tomography
Study design	Randomised, double-blind, placebo-controlled
Follow-up	2 years
Patients	180 patients, men aged 40–69 years and women aged 50–69 years, with moderate type IIa dyslipidaemia and cardiovascular disease with cardiovascular risk factors
Treatment regimen	Felodipine ER, 5 mg/day (titrated to 10 mg/day after first month, as tolerated), or placebo
Concomitant therapy	Simvastatin, 10 mg/day titrated to 40 mg/day in 10 mg increments to maintain a low-density lipoprotein cholesterol of < 130 mg/dl or < 100 mg/dl in those with previous cardiovascular disease
Results	Not yet available

FATS
Familial Atherosclerosis Treatment Study

Authors	**(a)** Brown G, Albers JJ, Fisher LD *et al* **(b)** Brown BG, Hillger L, Zhao X-Q, Poulin D, Albers JJ
Titles	**(a)** Regression of coronary artery disease as a result of intensive lipid-lowering therapy in men with high levels of apolipoprotein B **(b)** Types of change in coronary stenosis severity and their relative importance in overall progression and regression of coronary disease. Observations from the FATS trial
References	**(a)** *N Engl J Med* 1990;**323**:1289–98 **(b)** *Ann NY Acad Sci* 1995;**748**:407–18
Disease	Coronary heart disease
Purpose	To compare two intensive strategies for modification of lipid levels with a more conventional approach, in men at particularly high risk of cardiovascular events as a result of established coronary atherosclerosis
Study design	Randomised, double-blind, placebo-controlled (or colestipol-controlled)
Follow-up	30 months
Patients	146 men, aged ≤ 62 years, with elevated apolipoprotein B levels and family history of coronary artery disease. All had evidence of coronary atherosclerosis with at least one lesion causing at least 50% stenosis or three lesions causing at least 30% stenosis. 120 patients completed the 32-month protocol (46 conventional therapy, 38 lovastatin plus colestipol, 36 niacin plus colestipol)
Treatment regimen	**(1)** Lovastatin, 20 mg bid (if necessary increased to 40 mg bid), plus colestipol, 5 g tid for 10 days and then increased to 10 g tid **(2)** Niacin, 125 mg bid, gradually increased to 1 g qid at 2 months, plus colestipol as in (1) **(3)** Conventional therapy with placebos for colestipol and lovastatin (if necessary, colestipol was given instead of its placebo even to these patients)
Concomitant therapy	Dietary goals keyed to the American Heart Association's target levels 1 and 2 were set up (same for all three groups). Aspirin, β-blockers, diuretic agents, calcium antagonists, long-acting nitrates and angiotensin-converting enzyme inhibitors were used
Results	Levels of low-density lipoprotein and high-density lipoprotein cholesterol changed by a mean of -7% and +5%, respectively (conventional therapy) compared to -46% and +15% (lovastatin plus colestipol) and -32% and +43% (niacin plus colestipol). On conventional therapy, 46% of patients had definite lesion progression (and no regression)

in at least one of nine proximal coronary segments; regression was the only change in 11%. With lovastatin plus colestipol the corresponding figures were 21% and 32%, respectively; with niacin plus colestipol they were 25% and 39%. Death, MI, or revascularisation for worsening symptoms occurred in 10 of 52 patients on conventional therapy, compared to 3 of 46 on lovastatin plus colestipol and 2 of 48 on niacin plus colestipol. Several side-effects appeared in patients on lipid-lowering drugs and led to the withdrawal of 9 patients. The major therapeutic benefit of intensive lipid-lowering therapy was preventing incremental change in non-occluded lesions, with less striking benefits on recanalisation of occluded lesions and late regression of previously dilated lesions

FEST
Fosinopril Efficacy/Safety Trial

Authors	Erhardt L, MacLean A, Ilgenfritz J, Gelperin K, Blumenthal M
Title	Fosinopril attenuates clinical deterioration and improves exercise tolerance in patients with heart failure
Reference	*Eur Heart J* 1995;**16**:1892–9
Disease	Heart failure
Purpose	To determine the effects of the phosphinic acid ACE inhibitor fosinopril on exercise tolerance and the characteristic symptoms and clinical deterioration in patients with mild to moderately severe heart failure
Study design	Randomised, double-blind, placebo-controlled
Follow-up	12 weeks
Patients	308 patients (155 fosinopril and 153 placebo), aged 18–75 years, with NYHA class II or III heart failure
Treatment regimen	Fosinopril, 10 mg/day (level I), titrated over 4 weeks to 20 mg/day (level II), then to the target maintenance dose of 40 mg/day (level III), as tolerated, or placebo
Concomitant therapy	Diuretics plus digoxin and/or nitrates as needed
Results	245 patients completed the study (fosinopril 127 and placebo 118). 63 patients discontinued (fosinopril 28, placebo 35), including 8 patients who died (fosinopril 5, placebo 3). 135 fosinopril patients (87.1%) reached the dose of 40 mg/day. By the end of the study bicycle exercise time increased more with fosinopril (38.1 s) than with placebo (23.5 s) (p = 0.101 (ANCOVA); 0.010). More fosinopril patients than placebo patients remained free of clinical deterioration (89% vs 75%) and the worst events in fosinopril patients tended to be less severe than those in placebo patients (p = 0.001). Fosinopril reduced the need for supplementary diuretic (8% vs 20%, p < 0.002), hospitalisations (3% vs 12%, p = 0.002), and discontinuation owing to deterioration (2% vs 12%, p < 0.001). Mortality was similar in both groups (fosinopril 3%, placebo 2%, p = 0.723). Dyspnoea (p = 0.017), fatigue (p = 0.019), and NYHA class (p = 0.008) improved under fosinopril compared to placebo

FIPS
Frankfurt Isoptin Progression Study

Authors	Schneider W, Kober G, Roebruck P *et al*
Title	Retardation of development and progression of coronary atherosclerosis: a new indication for calcium antagonists?
Reference	*Eur J Clin Pharmacol* 1990;**39**(suppl 1):S17–23
Disease	Coronary artery disease
Purpose	To evaluate the influence of verapamil (Isoptin) on progression of coronary atherosclerosis after coronary artery bypass grafting
Study design	Randomised, double-blind, placebo-controlled
Follow-up	3 years
Patients	162 patients (82 verapamil and 80 placebo)
Treatment regimen	Verapamil, 120 mg tid, or placebo
Concomitant therapy	Aspirin in 86% of patients; isosorbide dinitrate or isosorbide mononitrate in 44% of patients; diuretics in 34% of patients. Other drugs were taken occasionally
Results	1-year follow-up was completed by 162 patients. There was a homogeneous distribution in the two groups for all clinical variables, graft patency rates and the incidence of clinical events (cardiac death, MI, need for cardiac surgery or percutaneous transluminal coronary angioplasty)

FIRST
Flolan International Randomised Survival Trial

Authors	Califf RM, Adams KF, Armstrong PW, Darius H, Gheorghiade M, Handberg E, Harrell FE Jr, McKenna WJ, McNulty SE, Schulman K, Soler-Soler J, Swedberg K, Uretsky B, Wheeler WS, Zannad F
Title	Flolan International Randomized Survival Trial (FIRST): final results
Reference	*J Am Coll Cardiol* 1996;**27**:141A
Disease	End-stage heart failure
Purpose	To evaluate the effect of epoprostenol on mortality and morbidity in patients with end-stage heart failure
Study design	Randomised, controlled
Follow-up	Aim 12 months, the results are from 6 months' estimates
Patients	471 patients (aim 875), mean age 65 ± 10 years, with left ventricular ejection fraction < 25%, congestive heart failure with NYHA class III or IV, pulmonary capillary wedge pressure > 15 mm Hg, and cardiac index < 2.5 l/min/m^2
Treatment regimen	Standard care with or without continuous iv infusion of epoprostenol
Results	Mortality in the patients treated with epoprostenol was significantly higher than in those on placebo (53% vs 41%). The need for iv vasoactive drugs was also higher (51% vs 42%). Other variables were similar in the two groups
Comments	The trial was interrupted in July 1993 due to the increased mortality in the patients treated with epoprostenol

FISH
Finnish Isradipine Study in Hypertension

Authors	Luomanmäki K, Inkovaara J, Hartikainen M *et al*
Title	Efficacy and tolerability of isradipine and metoprolol in treatment of hypertension: the Finnish Isradipine Study in Hypertension (FISH)
Reference	*J Cardiovasc Pharmacol* 1992;**20**:296–303
Disease	Mild to moderate hypertension
Purpose	To compare the efficacy of, tolerability of, and metabolic changes induced by isradipine and metoprolol as monotherapy or combined therapy
Study design	Randomised, double-blind, controlled
Follow-up	24 weeks
Patients	797 men and women (398 isradipine and 399 metoprolol) with diastolic blood pressure (DBP) ≥ 95 and < 115 mm Hg
Treatment regimen	Isradipine, 1.25 mg bid, or metoprolol, 50 mg bid. Dose titration at 4 weeks if DBP > 90 mm Hg, then isradipine, 2.5 mg bid, or metoprolol, 100 mg bid. At 8 weeks, patients on doubled dose with DBP > 90 mm Hg also received the other drug at the lower dose (metoprolol, 50 mg bid, or isradipine, 1.25 mg bid, respectively). Patients on single dose with DBP > 90 mm Hg at 8 weeks doubled their dose
Results	At 8 weeks, monotherapy with isradipine normalised DBP in 52% of patients with a mean daily dose of 4.26 mg. Metoprolol monotherapy normalised DBP in 58% of patients with a mean daily dose of 155 mg. At 24 weeks, including combined therapy, normotension was seen for 68% in the isradipine group and 66% in the metoprolol group. 38% of patients in the isradipine group and 33% in the metoprolol group had transient side effects. There were more discontinuations because of adverse effects in the isradipine group than in the metoprolol group ($p < 0.05$). There were no changes in serum lipids during isradipine monotherapy. Metoprolol monotherapy induced a significant increase in mean triglyceride level and a decrease in high-density lipoprotein cholesterol level

FLARE
Fluvastatin Angioplasty Restenosis trial
Ongoing trial

Authors	Foley DP, Bonnier H, Jackson G, Macaya C, Shepherd J, Vrolix M, Serruys PW
Title	Prevention of restenosis after coronary balloon angioplasty: rationale and design of the FLuvastatin Angioplasty REstenosis (FLARE) trial
Reference	*Am J Cardiol* 1994;**73**:50D–61D
Disease	Obstructive coronary artery disease
Purpose	To evaluate the ability of fluvastatin to prevent restenosis after successful single-lesion coronary angioplasty (PTCA)
Study design	Randomised, double-blind, placebo-controlled
Follow-up	7 months
Patients	Aim 830 patients undergoing PTCA
Treatment regimen	Fluvastatin, 40 mg bid, or placebo
Results	Not yet available

FLUENT
Fluvastatin long-term Extension Trial

Author	Davidson MH
Title	Fluvastatin long-term Extension Trial (FLUENT): summary of efficacy and safety
Reference	*Am J Med* 1994;**96**(suppl 6A):6A-41S–4S
Disease	Hypercholesterolaemia
Purpose	To evaluate the efficacy and safety of fluvastatin over a period of 48 weeks
Study design	Open
Follow-up	48 weeks
Patients	918 patients with hypercholesterolaemia, low-density lipoprotein (LDL) cholesterol ≥ 227 mg/dl, having completed a previous short-term study of fluvastatin
Treatment regimen	Fluvastatin, 20–40 mg once daily, to achieve LDL cholesterol < 130 mg/dl
Concomitant therapy	Cholestyramine if needed to obtain the desired LDL cholesterol level
Results	The mean percentage change from baseline was statistically significant for LDL cholesterol (-30.7%, $p < 0.001$), total cholesterol (-21.9%, $p < 0.001$) and high-density lipoprotein cholesterol (+3.5%, $p < 0.001$). Only 4 patients (0.5%) withdrew because of drug-related adverse events

FRAMINGHAM STUDY

Authors	Kannel W, Larson M
Title	Long-term epidemiologic prediction of coronary disease. The Framingham experience
Reference	*Cardiology* 1993;**82**:137–52
Disease	Cardiovascular disease
Purpose	To define precursive factors and the natural history of cardiovascular disease
Follow-up	Ongoing (started 1948), up to 36 years of follow-up reported
Patients	5209 men and women, living in Framingham, aged 30–62 years at entry. Children of the subjects studied and their spouses have been included in later examinations
Treatment regimen	Biennial follow-up with standardised examinations, including complete history, physical examination, chest radiography, ECG and various blood chemistry parameters
Results	Several aspects of cardiovascular disease have been studied, such as the epidemiology and relationships between different symptoms, events and risk factors
Comments	This study has been the basis for a vast number of publications over the years. A small selection of references is listed below.

Epidemiology of heart failure
– Kannel WS, *Am Heart J* 1991;**121**:951–7
– Ho KK, *J Am Coll Cardiol* 1993;**22**(suppl A):6A–13A

Atrial fibrillation
– Benjamin EJ, *JAMA* 1994;**271**:840–4
– Wolf PA, *Am Heart J* 1996;**131**:790–5

Smoking
– Freund KM, *Ann Epidemiol* 1993;**3**:417–24
– D'Agostino RB, *Am J Epidemiol* 1995;**141**:822–7

Risk factors for hypertension
– Kannel WB, *Am Heart J* 1993;**125**:1154–8
– Kannel WB, *JAMA* 1996;**275**:1571–6

Left ventricular geometric patterns
– Krumholz HM, *J Am Coll Cardiol* 1995;**25**:879–84

Risk factors for MI
Wong ND, *Ann Intern Med* 1991;**115**:687–93

Risk factors for stroke
– Wolf PA, *Ann Epidemiol* 1993;**3**:471–5
– D'Agostino RB, *Stroke* 1994;**25**:40–3
– Kannel WB, *JAMA* 1996;**276**:1269–78

Risk factors for sudden death
– Cupples LA, *Circulation* 1992;**85**(suppl I):I-11–8

Angina pectoris
– Brand FN, *Am Heart J* 1996;**132**:174–8

Risk factors for coronary artery disease
– Wilson PW, *Am J Hypertens* 1994;**7**:7S–12S

Risk factors for cardiovascular disease
– Kannel WB, *Cardiology* 1992;**81**:291–8
– Kannel WB, *Eur Heart J* 1992;**13**(suppl D):82–8
– Sytkowski PA, *Am J Epidemiol* 1996;**143**:338–50

Risk factors for cardiovascular death
– Cupples LA, *Am Heart J* 1993;**125**:863–72
– Gillman MW, *Am Heart J* 1993;**125**:1148–54

Risk factors in the elderly
– Larson MG, *Stat Med* 1995;**14**:1745–56
– Goldberg RJ, *Arch Intern Med* 1996;**156**:505–9

FRISC
Fragmin during Instability in Coronary artery disease

Authors	Fragmin during Instability in Coronary Artery Disease (FRISC) study group
Title	Low-molecular-weight heparin during instability in coronary artery disease
Reference	*Lancet* 1996;**347**:561–8
Disease	Unstable coronary artery disease
Purpose	To investigate whether subcutaneous low-molecular-weight heparin in addition to aspirin and antianginal drugs protects against recurrence of cardiac events in unstable coronary artery disease
Study design	Randomised, double-blind, placebo-controlled, parallel-group
Follow-up	5–7 months
Patients	1506 patients, of which 963 men (median age 69 years) and 543 women (median age 71 years), with unstable coronary artery disease (total 1506), hospitalised for chest pain within the previous 72 h
Treatment regimen	Dalteparin (Fragmin), approximately 120 U/kg body weight (maximum 10,000 U) every 12 h for the first 6 days, then 7500 U daily for the next 35–45 days, or placebo
Concomitant therapy	Aspirin, 75 mg/day (initially 300 mg), and β-blockers; calcium antagonists and organic nitrates as needed. Glyceryl trinitrate acutely at the discretion of the physician
Results	Mortality and reinfarction in the first 6 days were lower with dalteparin (1.8% vs 4.8%; risk ratio 0.37: 95% CI 0.20–0.68), as was the need for iv heparin (3.8% vs 7.7%; 0.49: 0.32–0.75) and for revascularisation (0.4% vs 1.2%; 0.33: 0.10–1.10). The difference in the composite endpoint (death, MI, revascularisation, iv heparin) was significant in favour of dalteparin (5.4% vs 10.3%; 0.52: 0.37–0.75). The differences in death and reinfarction rates and in the composite endpoint persisted at 40 days, the effect being confined to non-smokers (80% of sample). Survival analysis showed a risk of reactivation and reinfarction when the dose was decreased, more pronounced in smokers. 4–5 months after the end of treatment there were no significant differences in the rates of death, reinfarction, or revascularisation. The regimen was safe and compliance was adequate

GESIC
Grupo Español para el Seguimiento
del Injerto Coronario

Authors	Sanz G, Pajarón A, Alegría E *et al*
Title	Prevention of early aortocoronary bypass occlusion by low-dose aspirin and dipyridamole
Reference	*Circulation* 1990;**82**:765–73
Disease	Coronary artery occlusion
Purpose	To assess the efficacy of low-dose aspirin alone or in combination with dipyridamole in improving early (< 1 month) saphenous vein graft patency
Study design	Randomised, double-blind, placebo-controlled
Follow-up	1 month
Patients	927 patients
Treatment regimen	Aortocoronary bypass surgery. Aspirin, 50 mg tid, and/or dipyridamole, 75 mg tid, both started 7 h after operation
Concomitant therapy	Preoperation: dipyridamole, 100 mg 6-hourly for 48 h
Results	The occlusion rate of distal anastomosis was 14.2% with aspirin (p = 0.05), 12.9% with aspirin plus dipyridamole (p = 0.005) and 18% with placebo. Occlusion of grafts occurred in 27.1% of patients in the aspirin group (p = ns), in 24.3% of patients in the aspirin plus dipyridamole group (p = 0.01) and in 33% of patients in the placebo group

GESICA
Grupo de Estudio de la Sobrevida en la Insuficiencia Cardiaca en Argentina

Authors	Doval HC, Nul DR, Grancelli HO, Perrone SV, Bortman GR, Curiel R
Title	Randomised trial of low-dose amiodarone in severe congestive heart failure
Reference	*Lancet* 1994;**344**:493–8
Disease	Severe congestive heart failure
Purpose	To evaluate the effect of low-dose amiodarone on the mortality of patients with severe chronic heart failure without symptomatic ventricular arrhythmias
Study design	Randomised, open, controlled, parallel-group, stratified
Follow-up	2 years
Patients	516 patients with advanced chronic heart failure who were stable in functional capacity and did not need antiarrhythmic treatment
Treatment regimen	Standard treatment and amiodarone, 600 mg/day for 14 days and then 300 mg/day for 2 years, or standard treatment only (diuretics, digitalis, and ACE inhibitors)
Results	There were 87 deaths in the amiodarone group (33.5%) compared to 106 in the control group (41.4%) (risk reduction 28%; 95% CI 4%–45%; log rank test p = 0.024). There were reductions in sudden death (risk reduction 27%; p = 0.16) and death from progressive heart failure (risk reduction 23%; p = 0.16). Fewer patients receiving amiodarone died or were hospitalised for worsening heart failure (119 vs 149; risk reduction 31%; 95% CI 13–46%; p = 0.0024). The decrease in mortality and hospitalisation was present in all examined subgroups and independent of the presence of non-sustained ventricular tachycardia. Side effects were reported in 17 patients (6.1%); amiodarone was withdrawn in 12 patients

GISSI-1
Gruppo Italiano per lo Studio della Streptochinasi nell'Infarto miocardico

Authors	**(a)** and **(b)** GISSI
Titles	**(a)** Effectiveness of intravenous thrombolytic treatment in acute myocardial infarction **(b)** Long-term effects of intravenous thrombolysis in acute myocardial infarction: final report of the GISSI study
References	**(a)** *Lancet* 1986;**i**:397–402 **(b)** *Lancet* 1987;**ii**:871–4
Disease	AMI
Purpose	To determine whether iv streptokinase is clinically beneficial in terms of reduction of in-hospital and 1-year mortality, whether the effect, if present, is dependent on the interval between onset of pain and treatment, and whether the risks associated with the treatment are acceptable
Study design	Randomised, unblinded, parallel-group
Follow-up	1 year (11,521 patients)
Patients	11,712 patients (5860 streptokinase and 5852 control), all ages accepted (65% aged ≤ 65 years and 10% > 75 years)
Treatment regimen	Streptokinase, 1.5 x 10^6 U iv, infused over 1 h
Concomitant therapy	Other drugs, including heparin, nitrates, calcium antagonists, antiplatelet agents, antiarrhythmic agents and β-blockers, administered according to normal practice
Results	At 21 days, overall hospital mortality was 10.7% in the streptokinase group and 13% in the control group, representing an 18% reduction in the streptokinase group (relative risk, 0.81; p = 0.0002). In those treated within 3 h, overall mortality was reduced by 23% (p = 0.0005). At 12 months, total mortality in the streptokinase group was 17.2% vs 19.0% in the control group (relative risk: 0.90; p = 0.0008)

GISSI-2
Gruppo Italiano per lo Studio della Sopravvivenza nell'Infarto miocardico

Authors	**(a)** Gruppo Italiano per lo Studio della Sopravvivenza nell'Infarto miocardico **(b)** The International Study Group **(c)** Maggioni AP, Franzosi MG, Santoro E, White H, Van de Werf F, Tognoni G, the Gruppo Italiano per lo Studio della Sopravvivenza nell'Infarto miocardico II (GISSI-2), the International Study Group **(d)** GISSI-2 and International Study Group **(e)** Fresco C, Avanzini F, Bosi S, Franzosi MG, Maggioni AP, Santoro L, Bellanti G
Titles	**(a)** GISSI-2: a factorial randomised trial of alteplase versus streptokinase and heparin versus no heparin among 12 490 patients with acute myocardial infarction **(b)** In-hospital mortality and clinical course of 20 891 patients with suspected acute myocardial infarction randomised between alteplase and streptokinase with or without heparin **(c)** The risk of stroke in patients with acute myocardial infarction after thrombolytic and antithrombotic treatment **(d)** Six-month survival in 20 891 patients with acute myocardial infarction randomized between alteplase and streptokinase with or without heparin **(e)** Prognostic value of a history of hypertension in 11,483 patients with acute myocardial infarction treated with thrombolysis
References	**(a)** *Lancet* 1990;**336**:65–71 **(b)** *Lancet* 1990;**336**:71–5 **(c)** *N Engl J Med* 1992;**327**:1–6 **(d)** *Eur Heart J* 1992;**13**:1692–7 **(e)** *J Hypertens* 1996;**14**:743–50
Disease	AMI
Purpose	To compare the benefits and risks of streptokinase and alteplase (rt-PA) in patients with AMI and to study the effects of heparin, given after thrombolytic treatment, on the incidence of early postinfarction ischaemic events in patients already receiving aspirin
Study design	Randomised, open, controlled, factorial 2 × 2
Follow-up	15 days (in-hospital period), 1 and 6 months
Patients	12,490 patients. Time since onset of AMI: 6 h. Extended group for mortality analysis 20,891 patients (12,490 from GISSI-2 and 8401 recruited elsewhere)
Treatment regimen	Streptokinase, 1.5 x 10^6 U iv, infused over 30–60 min, or alteplase, 100 mg iv, infused over 3 h, plus heparin, 12,000 U subcutaneously bid, or no heparin

Concomitant therapy	Recommended in all patients, aspirin, 300–325 mg/day, and atenolol, 5–10 mg iv by slow injection, as soon as evolving MI was diagnosed
Results	There were no specific differences in combined endpoint 'death plus severe left ventricular damage' (alteplase: 23.1%; streptokinase: 22.5%; relative risk, RR: 1.04; 95% confidence interval: 0.95–1.13), nor after addition of heparin (heparin: 22.7%; no heparin: 22.9%; RR: 0.99; 95% confidence interval: 0.91–1.08). Rates of major in-hospital cardiac complications were similar. Incidence of major bleeding was significantly higher in streptokinase plus heparin-treated patients, whereas overall incidence of stroke was similar in all groups. Patients with AMI who receive thrombolytic therapy have a small risk of stroke (1.14%). Treatment with alteplase resulted in a small but significant excess of stroke, while more major bleeds occurred with streptokinase than with alteplase. 6-month mortality rates were similar for patients randomised to alteplase or streptokinase, and for patients randomised to heparin or no heparin. Reinfarction and cardiovascular accidents were similar in all treatment groups. Patients with a history of hypertension had significantly higher mortality both during hospital stay and the next 6 months

GISSI-3
Gruppo Italiano per lo Studio della Sopravvivenza nell'Infarto miocardico

Authors	**(a)**, **(b)** and **(c)** GISSI-3 study group
Titles	**(a)** GISSI-3 study protocol on the effects of lisinopril, of nitrates, and of their association in patients with AMI **(b)** GISSI-3: effects of lisinopril and transdermal glyceryl trinitrate singly and together on 6-week mortality and ventricular function after acute myocardial infarction **(c)** Six-month effects of early treatment with lisinopril and transdermal glyceryl trinitrate singly and together withdrawn six weeks after acute myocardial infarction: the GISSI-3 trial
References	**(a)** *Am J Cardiol* 1992;**70**:62C–9C **(b)** *Lancet* 1994;**343**:1115–22 **(c)** *J Am Coll Cardiol* 1996;**27**:337–44
Disease	AMI
Purpose	To study the effects of lisinopril and nitrates, used alone or in combination, on survival and ventricular function after AMI
Study design	Randomised, open, controlled, factorial
Follow-up	6 weeks and 6 months
Patients	18,895 patients (4731 nitrates, 4713 lisinopril, 4722 lisinopril plus nitrates, 4729 controls) enrolled within 24 h of MI
Treatment regimen	Glyceryl trinitrate, 5 µg/min iv, increased by 5–20 µg/min during the first 30 min, or until systolic blood pressure decreased by 10%. At 24 h after AMI, transdermal glyceryl trinitrate, 10 mg, or a 50 mg oral dose of isosorbide-5-mononitrate. Oral lisinopril, 2.5–5 mg/day, increased to 10 mg/day at 24 h post-MI. In case of hypotension, 5 or 2.5 mg/day maintenance dose. Alternatively, lisinopril and transdermal glyceryl trinitrate. Controls, no trial therapy. Trial therapy was continued for 6 weeks
Concomitant therapy	Routine clinical practice for AMI: thrombolysis, oral aspirin and iv β-blockers
Results	At 6 weeks, overall mortality was 6.7%. Lisinopril produced significant reductions in overall mortality and in the combined outcome measure of mortality and severe ventricular dysfunction. The systemic administration of glyceryl trinitrate did not show any independent effect on the same outcome measures. Systemic combined administration of lisinopril and glyceryl trinitrate produced a significant reduction in overall mortality and in the combined endpoint. At 6 months, 18.1% of patients randomised to lisinopril died or developed severe ventricular dysfunction compared to 19.3% of those randomised to no lisinopril (2p = 0.03). No difference in mortality was found between patients with and without glyceryl trinitrate (18.4% vs 18.9%, 2p = 0.39)

GLANT
Study Group on Long-term Antihypertensive Therapy

Authors	The GLANT study group
Title	A 12-month comparison of ACE inhibitor and Ca antagonist therapy in mild to moderate essential hypertension – The GLANT study
Reference	*Hypertens Res* 1995;**18**:235–44
Disease	Mild to moderate hypertension
Purpose	To investigate the long-term effects of delapril and calcium antagonist therapy in a large number of patients with hypertension
Study design	Comparative
Follow-up	12 months
Patients	1936 patients (980 delapril and 956 calcium antagonist), average age 60 years, with mild to moderate hypertension and no history of cerebrovascular disease, MI, angina pectoris, or renal impairment
Treatment regimen	Delapril, 30–60 mg/day, increased if necessary up to 120 mg/day, or manidipine, nifedipine, nisoldipine, nicardipine, nilvadipine, nitrendipine, or others
Concomitant therapy	If antihypertensive effect insufficient, β-blocker, a diuretic, or both
Results	Blood pressure decreased significantly from 1 month of treatment onwards, the reduction being greater under calcium antagonists ($p < 0.001$). Vascular events occurred in 11 out of 980 delapril patients and in 18 out of 956 receiving calcium antagonist ($p = ns$). Cerebrovascular disease developed in 5 delapril patients and 11 calcium antagonist patients and heart disease developed in 5 and 7 patients, respectively. Delapril was discontinued owing to side effects significantly more frequently than the calcium antagonist ($p < 0.001$). There was no significant difference in the incidence of vascular events and it seemed that blood pressure reduction in itself did not necessarily lead to a parallel decrease in vascular complications

GMT
Göteborg Metoprolol Trial

Authors	**(a)** Hjalmarson A, Elmfeldt D, Herlitz J *et al* **(b)** Several consecutive articles, most having Herlitz J as first author **(c)** Rydén L, Ariniego R, Arnman K *et al*
Titles	**(a)** Effect on mortality of metoprolol in acute myocardial infarction. A double-blind randomised trial **(b)** The Göteborg Metoprolol Trial in acute myocardial infarction **(c)** A double-blind trial of metoprolol in acute myocardial infarction. Effects on ventricular tachyarrhythmias
References	**(a)** *Lancet* 1981;**ii**:823–7 **(b)** *Am J Cardiol* 1984;**53**:1D–50D **(c)** *N Engl J Med* 1983;**308**:614–8
Disease	AMI
Purpose	To investigate the effects of metoprolol on mortality 3 months after AMI and its effects on infarct size and arrhythmias
Study design	Randomised, double-blind, placebo-controlled
Follow-up	3 months
Patients	1395 patients (262 withdrawals), aged 40–74 years
Treatment regimen	Metoprolol, 15 mg iv, within 48 h of onset of suspected AMI, followed by 200 mg/day orally given as 50 mg 6-hourly on days 0–2 and 100 mg 12-hourly thereafter
Results	There was a significant reduction (36%) in mortality with metoprolol compared to placebo: 40 deaths (5.7%) vs 62 deaths (8.9%), respectively ($p < 0.03$). Infarct size was significantly reduced in patients treated within 12 h ($p < 0.01$). Ventricular fibrillation occurred in 6 patients given metoprolol (6 episodes) and in 17 patients given placebo (41 episodes) ($p < 0.01$). Metoprolol did not influence the occurrence of premature ventricular contractions or short bursts of ventricular tachycardia. Ventricular fibrillation occurred in 17 patients with placebo, but in only 6 with metoprolol ($p < 0.05$). During the hospital stay, significantly fewer patients receiving metoprolol than placebo required lignocaine ($p < 0.01$)

GREAT
Grampian Region Early Anistreplase Trial

Authors	**(a)** GREAT group **(b)** and **(c)** Rawles J
Titles	**(a)** Feasibility, safety, and efficacy of domiciliary thrombolysis by general practitioners: Grampian Region Early Anistreplase Trial **(b)** Halving of mortality at 1 year by domiciliary thrombolysis in the Grampian Region Early Anistreplase Trial (GREAT) **(c)** Magnitude of benefit from earlier thrombolytic treatment in acute myocardial infarction: new evidence from Grampian Region Early Anistreplase Trial (GREAT)
References	**(a)** *BMJ* 1992;**305**:548–53 **(b)** *J Am Coll Cardiol* 1994;**23**:1–5 **(c)** *BMJ* 1996;**312**:212–5
Disease	AMI
Purpose	To assess the feasibility, safety and efficacy of domiciliary thrombolysis by general practitioners compared to hospital thrombolysis
Study design	Randomised, double-blind, parallel-group
Follow-up	1 year, extended to 30 months
Patients	311 patients with suspected AMI seen at home between 20 min and 4 h after the onset of symptoms
Treatment regimen	Anistreplase, 30 U iv over 5 min, at home or on arrival at hospital. Patients receiving placebo at home were given anistreplase in hospital
Concomitant therapy	Opiate analgesic (81%) or nitrate. Aspirin was given to 84% of patients. 12 patients received antiarrhythmic therapy
Results	The average time to administration of anistreplase at home was 101 min (61% within 2 h of the onset of symptoms) and in hospital 240 min. 3 months after trial entry, 7.6% fewer patients had died in the group given thrombolytic therapy at home compared to the hospital group (p = 0.04). Full thickness Q-wave infarction was less common in patients with confirmed infarction treated at home (difference 14.6%, p = 0.02). 1 year after trial entry 10.4% of patients given anistreplase at home died compared to 21.6% of those given anistreplase in hospital. The benefits of thrombolytic therapy at home were most marked when treatment was administered within 2 h of the onset of symptoms. Death within 30 months was positively related to age (p < 0.0001) and to delay between start of symptoms and thrombolytic treatment (p = 0.0004). In patients presenting 2 h after start of symptoms, each hour's delay in receiving thrombolysis led to loss of 21 lives/1000 within 30 days (p = 0.03) and 69 lives/1000 within 30 months (p = 0.0004)

GUSTO-I
Global Utilization of Streptokinase and t-PA for Occluded coronary arteries – I

Authors	**(a)** The GUSTO investigators **(b)** Califf RM, White HD, Van de Werf F, Sadowski Z, Armstrong PW, Vahanian A, Simoons ML, Simes RJ, Lee KL, Topol EJ **(c)** White HD, Barbash GI, Califf RM, Simes RJ, Granger CB, Weaver WD, Kleiman NS, Aylward PE, Gore JM, Vahanian A, Lee KL, Ross AM, Topol EJ **(d)** Lesnefsky EJ, Lundergan CF, Hodgson JMcB, Nair R, Reiner JS, Greenhouse SW, Califf RM, Ross AM
Titles	**(a)** An international randomized trial comparing four thrombolytic strategies for acute myocardial infarction **(b)** One-year results from the global utilization of streptokinase and TPA for occluded coronary arteries (GUSTO-I) trial **(c)** Age and outcome with contemporary thrombolytic therapy. Results from the GUSTO-I trial **(d)** Increased left ventricular dysfunction in elderly patients despite successful thrombolysis: The GUSTO-I angiographic experience
References	**(a)** *N Engl J Med* 1993;**329**:673–82 **(b)** *Circulation* 1996;**94**:1233–8 **(c)** *Circulation* 1996;**94**:1826–33 **(d)** *J Am Coll Cardiol* 1996;**28**:331–7
Disease	AMI
Purpose	To compare aggressive thrombolytic strategies with standard thrombolytic regimens in the treatment of AMI
Study design	Randomised, parallel-group
Follow-up	30 days and 1 year
Patients	41,021 patients with AMI < 6 h after onset of symptoms
Treatment regimen	**(1)** Streptokinase, 1.5 x 10^6 U over 60 min, plus subcutaneous (sc) heparin, 12,500 U bid; or **(2)** streptokinase, 1.5 x 10^6 U over 60 min, plus iv heparin as a bolus of 5000 U, then 1000–1200 U/h adjusted to an activated partial thromboplastin time of 60–85 s; or **(3)** accelerated tissue plasminogen activator (rt-PA) as a 15 mg bolus, then 0.75 mg/kg up to 50 mg over 30 min, and 0.5 mg/kg up to 35 mg over the next 60 min, with iv heparin as above; or **(4)** rt-PA, 1.0 mg/kg iv over 60 min, up to 90 mg, and streptokinase, 1.9 x 10^6 U over 60 min given simultaneously, and iv heparin as above
Concomitant therapy	Aspirin, 160–325 mg/day. Atenolol, 5 mg iv in two divided doses, then oral atenolol, 50–100 mg once daily. Other medication or treatment at the discretion of the physician

Results   Mortality at 30 days was 7.2% in the streptokinase and sc heparin group, 7.4% for streptokinase and iv heparin, 6.3% for accelerated rt-PA and iv heparin, and 7% for the combination of rt-PA and streptokinase plus iv heparin. This corresponds to a 14% reduction in mortality for accelerated rt-PA compared to the two streptokinase only regimens ($p = 0.001$). 1-year mortality rates remained in favour of accelerated rt-PA (9.1%) over streptokinase with sc heparin (10.1%, $p = 0.011$) and streptokinase with iv heparin (10.1%, $p = 0.009$). Combination therapy showed an intermediate 1-year mortality of 9.9%, which was statistically indistinguishable from streptokinase ($p = 0.47$) but was marginally different from accelerated rt-PA ($p = 0.05$). There was a significant excess of haemorrhagic strokes at 30 days in the accelerated rt-PA group ($p = 0.03$) and for the combination group ($p < 0.001$), compared to streptokinase only. However, a consistent pattern of fewer complications was seen in the accelerated rt-PA group. The combined endpoint of death or disabling stroke was significantly lower in the accelerated rt-PA group (6.9%) than in the streptokinase only groups (7.8%, $p = 0.006$). Accelerated rt-PA treatment resulted in a lower 1-year mortality in all but the oldest patients (47% rt-PA vs 40.3% streptokinase). Patients > 75 years had higher mortality rate at 30 days than patients ≤ 75 years, but absolute net benefit was still greater with accelerated rt-PA. Older patients had a higher baseline risk profile for both clinical and angiographic characteristics. 30-day mortality increased markedly with age (3.0% in patients aged < 65, 9.5% in those aged 65–74, 19.6% in those aged 75–85, and 30.3% in patients aged > 85), as did stroke, cardiogenic shock, bleeding, and reinfarction. Despite patency at 90 min, 30-day mortality in the elderly remained elevated (17.8% vs 4% in adults) ($p ≤ 0.0001$). Elderly patients were mainly female and showed more hypertension, multivessel coronary artery disease, previous MI, anterior MI, and later time to treatment (3–6 h). Combined death or disabling stroke occurred less often with accelerated rt-PA in all but the oldest patients who showed a weak trend towards a lower incidence with streptokinase and heparin (odds ratio 1.13, 95% CI 0.6–2.1)

GUSTO II
Global Use of Strategies To open Occluded coronary arteries II

Authors	**(a)** The Global Use of Strategies to Open Occluded Coronary Arteries (GUSTO) IIa investigators **(b)** The Global Use of Strategies to Open Occluded Coronary Arteries (GUSTO) IIb investigators
Titles	**(a)** Randomized trial of intravenous heparin versus recombinant hirudin for acute coronary syndromes **(b)** A comparison of recombinant hirudin with heparin for the treatment of acute coronary syndromes
References	**(a)** *Circulation* 1994;**90**:1631–7 **(b)** *N Engl J Med* 1996;**335**:775–82
Disease	AMI
Purpose	To compare the therapeutic efficacy of direct antithrombin therapy with hirudin and anticoagulant therapy with heparin in patients with probable AMI
Study design	Randomised, double-blind, double-dummy, controlled
Follow-up	30 days
Patients	**IIa:** 2564 patients (aim 12,000) within 12 h of probable AMI **IIb:** 12,142 patients as above
Treatment regimen	**IIa:** heparin, 5000 U iv bolus followed by 1000–1300 U/h, or hirudin, 0.6 mg/kg iv bolus followed by 0.2 mg/kg/h **IIb:** heparin, 5000 U iv bolus followed by 1000 U/h, or hirudin, 0.1 mg/kg iv bolus followed by 0.1 mg/kg/h
Concomitant therapy	If ST segment was elevated, thrombolytic therapy (streptokinase or tissue-type plasminogen activator, rt-PA)
Results	**IIa:** The incidence of haemorrhagic stroke was greater in patients receiving hirudin than in those receiving heparin, and the difference was greater in patients additionally given thrombolytic therapy. The activated partial thromboplastin time (aPTT) appears to be a useful index for predicting haemorrhagic stroke in patients receiving thrombolytic therapy **IIb:** At 24 h, the risk of death or MI was significantly lower in the hirudin group than in the heparin group (p = 0.001). At 30 days the difference in the incidence of death or MI was no longer significant
Comments	The IIa trial was interrupted due to excess intracerebral haemorrhagic events, after the enrollment of 2564 patients. On the basis of the findings, the trial was reinitiated with lower doses of heparin and hirudin and exclusion of patients with prior stroke, uncontrolled hypertension, and renal dysfunction, GUSTO IIb A substudy was GUSTO IIb angioplasty, which is reported in *N Engl J Med* 1997;**336**:1621–8

HALT
Hypertension And Lipid Trial

Authors	Levy D, Walmsley P, Levenstein M
Title	Principal results of the Hypertension and Lipid Trial (HALT): A multicenter study of doxazosin in patients with hypertension
Reference	*Am Heart J* 1996;**131**:966–73
Disease	Hypertension
Purpose	To assess the efficacy and safety of the selective α_1-adrenergic blocker doxazosin
Study design	Open
Follow-up	16 weeks
Patients	842 patients (507 men and 335 women), > 35 years of age (mean 54.7 ± 12.5 years), with a diastolic blood pressure of 96–100 mm Hg
Treatment regimen	Doxazosin, starting at 1 mg/day and increasing at weekly intervals if required. Final mean dose was 7.8 mg/day
Results	Doxazosin therapy led to a significant reduction of systolic and diastolic blood pressure with no significant effect on heart rate. Blood levels of total cholesterol, low-density lipoprotein cholesterol and triglycerides were reduced, with no change in high-density lipoprotein cholesterol. The mean predicted 5-year coronary disease risk was significantly reduced by the treatment

HAPPHY
Heart Attack Primary Prevention in Hypertension trial

Authors	Wilhelmsen L, Berglund G, Elmfeldt D *et al*
Title	Beta-blockers versus diuretics in hypertensive men: main results from the HAPPHY trial
Reference	*J Hypertens* 1987;**5**:561–72
Disease	Mild to moderate hypertension
Purpose	To compare antihypertensive therapy with β-blockers and thiazide diuretic treatment with respect to the incidence of nonfatal MI, mortality from coronary heart disease and total mortality in men with mild to moderate hypertension. A prerequisite was an equal reduction in blood pressure in both treatment groups
Study design	Randomised, open, parallel-group
Follow-up	Mean 45.1 months
Patients	6569 men (3272 diuretic and 3297 β-blocker), aged 40–64 years. Diastolic blood pressure at entry was 100–130 mm Hg
Treatment regimen	Initial diuretic treatment: bendroflumethiazide, 5 mg/day, or hydrochlorothiazide, 50 mg/day. β-blocker: atenolol, 100 mg/day, or metoprolol, 200 mg/day. Additional treatment: hydralazine, 75–100 mg/day, spironolactone, 75–150 mg/day, or other
Results	There were no significant differences between the two groups. Although the total mortality was lower, the incidence of fatal and nonfatal coronary heart disease events was slightly higher and the incidence of fatal and nonfatal stroke slightly lower in the β-blocker group

HART
Heparin-Aspirin Reperfusion Trial

Authors	Hsia J, Hamilton WP, Kleiman N, Roberts R, Chaitman BR, Ross AM
Title	A comparison between heparin and low-dose aspirin as adjunctive therapy with tissue plasminogen activator for acute myocardial infarction
Reference	*N Engl J Med* 1990;**323**:1433–7
Disease	AMI
Purpose	To compare the effect of heparin and aspirin on the patency of the infarct-related artery after administration of recombinant tissue plasminogen activator (rt-PA)
Study design	Randomised, open, parallel-group
Follow-up	7–24 h and 7 days
Patients	205 patients (106 heparin and 99 aspirin), aged < 76 years (mean age 56 years). Time since onset of AMI: < 6 h
Treatment regimen	rt-PA, 100 mg iv, infused over 6 h, plus either aspirin, 80 mg/day orally, or heparin, 5000 U iv bolus, followed by an infusion of 1000 U/h
Results	7 h after beginning medical treatment, 82% of the infarct-related arteries in the patients given heparin were patent, compared to only 52% in those given aspirin (p < 0.0001). Of the initially patent vessels, 88% remained patent after 7 days in the heparin group, compared to 95% in the aspirin group (p = ns). 18 haemorrhagic events occurred in the heparin group and 15 in the aspirin group. 8 and 2 ischaemic events recurred in the two groups, respectively. Total mortality was 1.9% in the heparin group and 4% in the aspirin group

HDFP
Hypertension Detection and Follow-up Program

Authors	**(a)** and **(b)** The HDFP cooperative group
	(c) Comberg H-U, Heyden S, Knowles M, Tyroler HA, Hames CG
	(d) Tyroler HA, Ford CE
Titles	**(a)** Five-year findings of the Hypertension Detection and Follow-up Program. I. Reduction in mortality of persons with high blood pressure, including mild hypertension
	(b) Persistence of reduction in blood pressure and mortality of participants in the Hypertension Detection and Follow-up Program
	(c) Long-term survey of 450 hypertensives of the HDFP
	(d) Serum cholesterol and coronary heart disease risk in female and older hypertensives. The experience under usual community care in the Hypertension Detection and Follow-up Program
References	**(a)** *JAMA* 1979;**242**:2562–71
	(b) *JAMA* 1988;**259**:2113–22
	(c) *Munch Med Wochenschr* 1991;**133**:32–8
	(d) *Ann Epidemiol* 1992;**2**:155–60
Disease	Hypertension
Purpose	To compare the effects of a systematic antihypertensive treatment programme (stepped-care) and community medical therapy (referred care) on 5-year mortality in patients with hypertension
Study design	Randomised, open, controlled
Follow-up	**(a)** and **(d)** 5 years
	(b) 8 years
	(c) 12 years
Patients	10,940 patients, aged 30–69 years. Diastolic blood pressure at entry was > 90 mm Hg
Treatment regimen	1st step: chlorthalidone, 25–100 mg/day, and/or triamterene, 50–300 mg/day, or spironolactone, 25–100 mg/day
	2nd step: reserpine, 0.1–0.25 mg/day, or methyldopa, 500–2000 mg/day
	3rd step: hydralazine, 30–200 mg/day
	4th step: guanethidine sulphate, 10–200 mg/day, with or without steps 2 and 3
	5th step: addition or substitution of other drugs
Results	**(a)** 5-year mortality was reduced by 17% in the stepped-care group compared to the referred-care group (6.4% vs 7.7%; $p < 0.1$) and was reduced by 20% in the subgroups with diastolic blood pressure of 90–104 mm Hg at entry (5.9% stepped-care group vs 7.4% referred-care group; $p < 0.1$). In the subgroups with diastolic blood pressure of 105–114 mm Hg and > 115 mm Hg at entry, the differences in 5-year

mortality between the two groups were 13% and 7%, respectively (p = ns). The net difference of the changes in diastolic blood pressure after treatment between the two groups (ie, stepped-care change minus referred-care change) for all participants ranged from 6.3 mm Hg in the first year to 4.9 mm Hg in the fifth year

(b) In the stepped-care group there was a decline in the antihypertensive medication being taken in the post-trial period, the opposite was seen in the referred-care group. Mean diastolic blood pressure increased in the stepped-care group but was still 1.1 mm Hg lower than in the referred-care group, where mean blood pressure had decreased. Total mortality was still 15% lower in the stepped-care group compared to the referred-care group

(c) After 12 years, blood pressure levels were still higher in the referred-care than in the stepped-care group, despite greater use of medication. The incidence of left ventricular hypertrophy was lower in the stepped-care than in the referred-care group

(d) In referred-care patients, the risk of fatal coronary heart disease in relation to serum cholesterol level was as strong in women as in men < 65 years. In younger and older women, there was no association of serum cholesterol level with combined fatal plus nonfatal coronary events. In both younger and older men, serum cholesterol level was strongly predictive of fatal plus nonfatal coronary events

HDS
Hypertension in Diabetes Study
Ongoing trial

Authors	(a) Turner R, Holman R, Stratton I, Manley S, Frighi V (b) Hypertension in Diabetes Study group
Titles	(a) Hypertension in diabetes study III. Prospective study of therapy of hypertension in type 2 diabetic patients: efficacy of ACE inhibition and β-blockade (b) Hypertension in Diabetes Study IV. Therapeutic requirements to maintain tight blood pressure control
References	(a) *Diabetic Med* 1994;**11**:773–82 (b) *Diabetologia* 1995;**39**:1554–61
Disease	Hypertension
Purpose	To determine the efficacy and safety of captopril and atenolol in the management of hypertension in diabetic patients, and the effect of this therapy on the development of diabetic complications
Study design	Randomised, controlled
Follow-up	5 years
Patients	758 patients completing 5 years of the study (with a total recruitment of 1148 patients at present). All with type 2 diabetes and borderline to mild hypertension
Treatment regimen	Captopril (ACE inhibitor), starting at 25 mg bid and increasing to 50 mg bid if required, or atenolol (β-blocker), starting at 50 mg daily and increasing to a maximum of 100 mg if required. Some patients were dosed to produce tight control of blood pressure (< 150 mm Hg systolic, < 85 mm Hg diastolic), and other patients were dosed to produce looser blood pressure control (< 180 mm Hg systolic, < 105 mm Hg diastolic)
Concomitant therapy	Diabetic therapy with diet, sulphonylurea, insulin or metformin. If necessary, additional antihypertensive therapy with frusemide, slow-release nifedipine, methyldopa or prazosin
Results	Captopril and atenolol were equally effective in reducing blood pressure and led to similar incidence of side effects and hypoglycaemic episodes. Patients allocated to atenolol increased their body weight by a mean of 2.3 kg compared to 0.5 kg in those allocated to captopril ($p < 0.01$). Allocation to atenolol was also associated with small increases in triglyceride, and decreases in low- and high-density lipoprotein. The ongoing trial is expected to assess the effect of antihypertensive strategies on the development of diabetic complications

HEART
Healing and Early Afterload Reducing Therapy

Authors	**(a)** Pfeffer MA, Hennekens CH **(b)** Pfeffer MA, Greaves SC, Arnold JMO, Glynn RJ, LaMotte FS, Lee RT, Menapace FJ Jr, Rapaport E, Ridker PM, Rouleau J-L, Solomon SD, Hennekens CH
Titles	**(a)** When a question has an answer: rationale for our early termination of the HEART trial **(b)** Early versus delayed angiotensin-converting enzyme inhibition therapy in acute myocardial infarction. The Healing and Early Afterload Reducing Therapy trial
References	**(a)** *Am J Cardiol* 1995;**75**:1173–5 **(b)** *Circulation* 1997;**95**:2643–51
Disease	AMI
Purpose	To assess the clinical value of early ACE-inhibitor therapy in the acute and chronic management of patients with AMI
Study design	Randomised, double-blind, placebo-controlled
Follow-up	14 days and 90 days
Patients	352 patients (aim 600) with anterior AMI
Treatment regimen	Group I: placebo, day 1–13, and ramipril, 10 mg/day, day 14–90 Group II: ramipril, 0.625 mg/day, day 1–90 Group III: ramipril, 10 mg/day, day 1–90 (increased from 1.25 mg/day)
Concomitant therapy	Nitroglycerin preparations discontinued. Other therapy at the discretion of the physician
Results	Due to the reduced number of patients, the statistical analysis mostly showed trends and not differences. There were no significant differences in the frequency of death, congestive heart failure, and reinfarction between the groups during the first 14 days. Left ventricular ejection fraction (EF) increased in all groups during the first 14 days, and the increase was greatest in the full-dose ramipril group. Patients with the lowest baseline EF had the greatest ramipril effect. The risk for hypotension was also greatest in the full-dose ramipril group. During the late phase (day 14–90) all groups were on active therapy and no statistically significant differences were observed. The trend of improvement of left ventricular function was, however, greatest in the group starting ramipril on day 14
Comments	During the trial, results from GISSI-3 and ISIS-4 made it clear that the therapy should be started early, since the benefits, particularly a reduction in mortality, are mainly achieved during the first few weeks after AMI

HELVETICA

Hirudin in a European restenosis prevention trial Versus heparin Treatment In PTCA patients

Authors	Serruys PW, Herrman J-PR, Simon R, Rutsch W, Bode C, Laarman G-J, van Dijk R, van den Bos AA, Umans VAWM, Fox KAA, Close P, Deckers JW
Title	A comparison of hirudin with heparin in the prevention of restenosis after coronary angioplasty
Reference	*N Engl J Med* 1995;**333**:757–63
Disease	Unstable angina pectoris
Purpose	To assess the ability of hirudin and heparin to prevent cardiovascular events after coronary angioplasty (PTCA)
Study design	Randomised, double-blind, parallel-group, controlled
Follow-up	7 months
Patients	1154 patients (894 men and 260 women), mean age about 58 ± 9 years, undergoing PTCA for unstable angina
Treatment regimen	**(1)** Heparin, 10,000 U iv bolus, followed by iv infusion at 15 U/kg/h for 24 h, with sc placebo **(2)** Hirudin, 40 mg iv bolus followed by iv infusion at 0.2 mg/kg/h for 24 h, with sc placebo **(3)** As (2), plus hirudin, 40 mg sc bid for 3 consecutive days
Concomitant therapy	Aspirin, 100–500 mg/day, for at least 14 days
Results	The administration of hirudin led to a significant reduction in early cardiac events, which occurred in 11.0%, 7.9% and 5.6% of patients in treatment groups (1), (2) and (3), respectively. However, at 7 months, the event-free survival was similar in all 3 treatment groups (63.5–68.0%), with the poorest result in the iv hirudin + sc placebo group and the best result in the iv + sc hirudin group

HERS
Heart and oestrogen/progestin Replacement Study
Ongoing trial

Author	Bush TL
Title	Evidence for primary and secondary prevention of coronary artery disease in women taking oestrogen replacement therapy
Reference	*Eur Heart J* 1996;**17**(suppl D):9–14
Disease	Coronary artery disease
Purpose	To assess the cardioprotective effect of combined hormonal therapy with oestrogen and progestin in women with documented coronary artery disease, and to assess the safety of this therapy with particular reference to the risk of endometrial cancer
Study design	Randomised
Follow-up	Up to 6 years
Patients	Approx. 3000 women enrolled so far
Treatment regimen	Combined hormonal replacement with oestrogen/progestin
Results	To be expected in 1999

HHS
Helsinki Heart Study

Authors	**(a)** Frick MH, Elo O, Haapa K *et al* **(b)** Heinonen OP, Huttunen JK, Manninen V *et al*
Titles	**(a)** Helsinki Heart Study: primary-prevention trial with gemfibrozil in middle-aged men with dyslipidemia **(b)** The Helsinki Heart Study: coronary heart disease incidence during an extended follow-up
References	**(a)** *N Engl J Med* 1987;**317**:1237–45 **(b)** *J Intern Med* 1994:**235**:41–9
Disease	Coronary heart disease
Purpose	To investigate the effect of gemfibrozil on the incidence of coronary heart disease in asymptomatic middle-aged men at high risk because of abnormal concentrations of blood lipids
Study design	**(a)** Randomised, double-blind, placebo-controlled **(b)** Open
Follow-up	Mean, 60.4 months, post-trial period 3.5 years
Patients	**(a)** 4081 men (2051 gemfibrozil and 2030 placebo; 2859 completed the study), aged 40–55 years, with serum non-high-density lipoprotein (non-HDL) cholesterol level (total cholesterol minus HDL cholesterol) $\geq$ 200 mg/dl **(b)** 3889 men of whom 67% chose gemfibrozil treatment
Treatment regimen	Gemfibrozil, 600 mg bid
Results	**(a)** Gemfibrozil initially increased the HDL-cholesterol level by more than 10%, followed by a small decline with time. It reduced the total cholesterol level by 11%, the low-density lipoprotein cholesterol level by 10%, the non-HDL cholesterol level by 14% and the triglyceride level by 43%, though this last level increased slightly during the final years of the trial. The overall reduction in cardiac endpoints in the gemfibrozil group was 34.0% (95% confidence interval, 8.2–52.6). Total mortality was 2.19% with gemfibrozil vs 2.07% with placebo (p = ns). Gastrointestinal problems were more common with gemfibrozil **(b)** Cardiovascular mortality over the entire study period was similar, but all-cause mortality was slightly higher among men of the original gemfibrozil group compared to the placebo group (p = 0.19)

HINT
Holland Interuniversity Nifedipine/metoprolol Trial

Authors	**(a)** The HINT research group **(b)** Tijssen JGP, Lubsen J
Titles	**(a)** Early treatment of unstable angina in the coronary care unit: a randomised, double blind, placebo controlled comparison of recurrent ischaemia in patients treated with nifedipine or metoprolol or both **(b)** Early treatment of unstable angina with nifedipine and metoprolol – the HINT trial
References	**(a)** *Br Heart J* 1986;**56**:400–13 **(b)** *J Cardiovasc Pharmacol* 1988;**12**(suppl 1):S71–7
Disease	Unstable angina pectoris
Purpose	To determine whether nifedipine and metoprolol, alone or in combination, prevent recurrence of ischaemia or progression to MI in patients with unstable angina
Study design	Randomised, double-blind, placebo-controlled
Follow-up	48 h
Patients	515 patients, aged ≤ 70 years
Treatment regimen	Nifedipine, 60 mg/day in 6 divided doses, and/or metoprolol, 100 mg bid
Concomitant therapy	Routine care for at least 48 h. Sedatives and anticoagulants according to normal practice. Nitrates, antiarrhythmics, digitalis and antihypertensive agents other than β-blockers permitted
Results	In patients not pretreated with β-blockers, trial medication effects, expressed as ratios of event rates relative to placebo were 1.15 with nifedipine, 0.76 with metoprolol and 0.80 with nifedipine plus metoprolol. In these patients, the nifedipine:placebo ratio for the rate of infarction was 1.5 (0.87–2.74). In patients pretreated with β-blockers, nifedipine was beneficial, with a ratio of event rates relative to placebo of 0.68. Equal numbers of patients developed MI and reversible ischaemia. Most infarctions occurred early, within 6 h of randomisation
Comments	The study was discontinued on 27 October 1984 as interim analysis showed an increased risk for MI in patients assigned to nifedipine alone

HIT
High-density lipoprotein Intervention Trial
Ongoing trial

Authors	Bloomfield Rubins H, Robins SJ, Iwane MK *et al*
Title	Rationale and design of the department of Veterans Affairs High-density lipoprotein cholesterol Intervention Trial (HIT) for secondary prevention of coronary artery disease in men with low high-density lipoprotein cholesterol and desirable low-density lipoprotein cholesterol
Reference	*Am J Cardiol* 1993;**71**:45–52
Disease	Coronary artery disease
Purpose	To determine whether lipid-lowering therapy reduces the combined incidence of death due to coronary artery disease and nonfatal MI in men with established coronary artery disease, low levels of high-density lipoprotein (HDL) cholesterol and satisfactory levels of low-density lipoprotein (LDL) cholesterol
Study design	Randomised, double-blind, placebo-controlled
Follow-up	5–7 years
Patients	2500 men, aged ≤ 73 years, with coronary artery disease, HDL cholesterol ≤ 40 mg/dl, LDL cholesterol ≤ 140 mg/dl and triglycerides ≤ 300 mg/dl
Treatment regimen	Gemfibrozil, 1200 mg once daily, or placebo
Concomitant therapy	Health counselling and the American Heart Association Step 1 diet
Results	Not yet available

HIT-III
Hirudin for the Improvement of Thrombolysis phase III study

Authors	Neuhaus K-L, von Essen R, Tebbe U, Jessel A, Heinrichs H, Mäurer W, Döring W, Harmjanz D, Kötter V, Kalhammer E, Simon H, Horacek T
Title	Safety observations from the pilot phase of the randomized r-Hirudin for Improvement of Thrombolysis (HIT-III) Study. A study of the Arbeitsgemeinschaft Leitender Kardiologischer Krankenhausärzte (ALKK)
Reference	*Circulation* 1994;**90**:1638–42
Disease	AMI
Purpose	To compare the efficacy of treatment with heparin and recombinant hirudin in preventing death or reinfarction after AMI
Study design	Randomised, double-blind
Follow-up	30 days
Patients	302 patients, mean age about 61 ± 11 years. Further safety data assessed for an additional 246 patients. Aim 1000 patients
Treatment regimen	Aspirin, 250 mg, followed by hirudin, 0.4 mg/kg iv bolus, or heparin, 70 U/kg iv bolus. After thrombolytic therapy was started (alteplase, 15 mg iv bolus, followed by 50 mg over 30 min and another 35 mg over the next 60 min), the patients were given hirudin, 0.15 mg/kg/h, or heparin, 15 U/kg/h, iv for 48–72 h
Concomitant therapy	Aspirin, 100–500 mg/day
Results	The incidence of intracranial bleeding in the hirudin group was 3.4% compared to 0% in the heparin group. Treatment with hirudin was also associated with increased incidences of major bleeding, ventricular rupture and in-hospital deaths. Lower doses of hirudin may be safer
Comments	The trial was stopped due to an increased incidence of intracranial bleeding in the hirudin group. A pilot study to HIT-III with the acronym HIT-I was published in *Eur Heart J* 1996;**17**:(suppl D):22–7 Another study with the acronym HIT, Head Injury Treatment, has been published

HOPE
Heart Outcomes Prevention Evaluation study
Ongoing trial

Authors	The HOPE study investigators
Title	The HOPE (Heart Outcomes Prevention Evaluation) study: the design of a large, simple randomized trial of an angiotensin-converting enzyme inhibitor (ramipril) and vitamin E in patients at high risk of cardiovascular events
Reference	*Can J Cardiol* 1996;**12**:127–37
Disease	Cardiovascular disease
Purpose	To evaluate whether ramipril and/or vitamin E reduce the incidence of cardiovascular morbidity and mortality in a high-risk population. The primary endpoints are MI, cardiovascular death or stroke. The secondary endpoints include acute cardiac ischaemia, arterial stenosis or overt nephropathy
Study design	Randomised, double-blind, parallel-group, placebo-controlled, factorial
Follow-up	Mean 3.5 years
Patients	9541 patients (2543 women and 6998 men), > 55 years, with one of the following: previous MI, angina pectoris, multivessel percutaneous transluminal coronary angioplasty (PTCA) or coronary artery bypass grafting (CABG), multivessel coronary artery disease, peripheral vascular disease, cerebrovascular disease, diabetes mellitus with an additional risk factor
Treatment regimen	Ramipril, 2.5 mg once daily for 1 week, then 5 mg for 3 weeks, then 10 mg and daily vitamin E, 400 U, or placebo plus vitamin E, 400 U, or placebo daily
Results	Not yet available
Comments	Several substudies of HOPE have been published, see MICRO-HOPE (Microalbuminuria, Cardiovascular and Renal Outcomes) and SECURE (Study to Evaluate Carotid Ultrasound changes in patients treated with Ramipril and vitamin E). Another substudy of HOPE, MORE (Mechanisms Of Reduced Events), will assess biochemical markers and include a pharmacoeconomic evaluation

HOT
Hypertension Optimal Treatment Study

Authors	**(a)** Hansson L **(b)** Hansson L, Zanchetti A **(c)** Hansson L, Zanchetti A **(d)** Julius S **(e)** Ruilope LM, Hansson L, Zanchetti A **(f)** Hansson L, Zanchetti A, Carruthers SG, Dahlöf B, Elmfeldt D, Julius S, Ménard J, Rahn KH, Wedel H, Westerling S
Titles	**(a)** The Hypertension Optimal Treatment study (the HOT Study) **(b)** The Hypertension Optimal Treatment (HOT) Study – patient characteristics: randomization, risk profiles, and early blood pressure results **(c)** The Hypertension Optimal Treatment (HOT) Study: 12-month data on blood pressure and tolerability. With special reference to age and gender **(d)** The Hypertension Optimal Treatment (HOT) Study in the United States **(e)** Renal aspects of the Hypertension Optimal Treatment (HOT) Study **(f)** Effects of intensive blood-pressure lowering and low-dose aspirin in patients with hypertension: principal results of the Hypertension Optimal Treatment (HOT) randomised trial
References	**(a)** *Blood Press* 1993;**2**:62–8 **(b)** *Blood Press* 1994;**3**:322–7 **(c)** *Blood Press* 1995;**4**:313–9 **(d)** *Am J Hypertens* 1996;**9**:41S–4S **(e)** *J Nephrol* 1996;**9**:147–51 **(f)** *Lancet* 1998;**351**:1755–62
Disease	Hypertension
Purpose	To assess the relationship of major cardiovascular events (nonfatal, acute and silent MI, nonfatal stroke, and all cardiovascular causes of death) with three target diastolic blood pressures (≤ 90, ≤ 85, and ≤ 80 mm Hg) as well as with achieved diastolic blood pressure (DBP) during active antihypertensive therapy. Secondary, to assess whether low-dose aspirin, in addition to antihypertensive therapy, reduces the incidence of major cardiovascular events
Study design	Randomised, open, single-blind (antihypertensive treatment) and double-blind (aspirin)
Follow-up	Mean 3.8 years (range 3.3–4.9)
Patients	18,790 men and women, aged 50–80 years
Treatment regimen	Felodipine, 5 mg once daily. If necessary low-dose ACE inhibitor or β-blocker was added, and dosages were titrated as necessary. Hydrochlorothiazide could be added or high-

dose ACE inhibitor combined with low-dose β-blocker or vice-versa. Patients were randomised to three target DBP groups, ≤ 90, ≤ 85, or ≤ 80 mm Hg. In each group patients were randomised to low-dose aspirin or placebo

Results   The DBP was reduced to 85.2, 83.2 and 81.1 mm Hg in the target groups ≤ 90, ≤ 85 and ≤ 80 mm Hg, respectively. This means that a reduction of DBP of 20.3, 22.3, and 24.3 mm Hg was achieved in the respective groups. The proportion of patients reaching the target blood pressures increased gradually up to 36 months. At 1 year the percentage of patients at target in the elderly subgroup was higher in all three groups. The three blood pressure target groups were comparable for serum creatinine levels at 1 year, and renal function at baseline did not influence achievement of blood pressure target, though patients with renal failure needed more therapy to attain similar falls in DBP. There were no differences in achieved blood pressure between patients randomised to aspirin or placebo. The lowest incidence of major cardiovascular events occurred at a mean achieved blood pressure of 82.6 mm Hg diastolic and 138.5 mm Hg systolic, and the lowest risk of cardiovascular mortality at 86.5 mm Hg diastolic and 138.8 mm Hg systolic. Reduction below these levels did not cause any untoward changes, that is, there was no J-formed relation between blood pressure and event incidence. In the 1501 patients with diabetes mellitus at baseline there was a 51% reduction in major cardiovascular events in target group ≤ 80 mm Hg compared to the ≤ 90 mm Hg group. Aspirin reduced major cardiovascular events by 15% and all MI by 36%. There was no effect on the incidence of stroke or fatal bleeds by aspirin, but nonfatal major bleeds were twice as common with aspirin

Hy-C
Hydralazine Captopril trial

Authors	Fonarow GC, Chelimsky-Fallick C, Warner Stevenson L *et al*
Title	Effect of direct vasodilation with hydralazine versus angiotensin-converting enzyme inhibition with captopril on mortality in advanced heart failure: the Hy-C trial
Reference	*J Am Coll Cardiol* 1992;**19**:842–50
Disease	Advanced heart failure
Purpose	To compare angiotensin-converting enzyme inhibition and direct vasodilatation on the prognosis of advanced heart failure
Study design	Randomised
Follow-up	8 ± 7 months
Patients	117 patients evaluated for cardiac transplantation with congestive heart failure, NYHA class III or IV, and abnormal haemodynamic status at rest
Treatment regimen	Captopril, 6.25 mg, titrated up to 100 mg qid, or hydralazine, titrated up to 150 mg qid. These treatments were exchanged if acceptable haemodynamic status was not obtained (44% patients on captopril, 22% on hydralazine)
Concomitant therapy	Isosorbide dinitrate, 10 mg, titrated up to 80 mg qid as therapy needed, in patients receiving hydralazine and in patients receiving captopril with coronary artery disease or with pulmonary wedge pressure > 20 mm Hg after 24 h with captopril. Class I antiarrhythmic agents or amiodarone for ventricular arrhythmias, digoxin, loop diuretics, intermittent metolazone
Results	The actuarial 1-year survival rate was 81% in the captopril group and 51% in the hydralazine group (p = 0.05). This was mainly due to a reduction in sudden death in the captopril group. Actuarial rates: 5% for captopril, 37% for hydralazine (p = 0.01). Therapy with captopril, low capillary wedge pressure during therapy and serum sodium ≤ 135 mg/dl were each an independent predictor of survival

HYCAR
Hypertrophie Cardiaque et Ramipril

Authors	**(a)** Lièvre M, Guéret P, Gayet C, Roudaut R, Haugh MC, Delair S, Boissel J-P **(b)** Lièvre M, Guéret P, Gayet C, Roudaut R, Delair S, Boissel JP
Titles	**(a)** Ramipril-induced regression of left ventricular hypertrophy in treated hypertensive individuals **(b)** Regression of left ventricular hypertrophy with ramipril, independently of blood pressure reduction: the HYCAR study
References	**(a)** *Hypertension* 1995;**25**:92–7 **(b)** *Arch Mal Coeur Vaiss* 1995;**88**(special issue 2):35–42
Disease	Hypertension and left ventricular hypertrophy
Purpose	To assess the effect of ramipril on left ventricular hypertrophy and blood pressure in hypertensive patients given frusemide
Study design	Randomised, double-blind, parallel-group, placebo-controlled
Follow-up	6 months
Patients	115 patients (75 ramipril, 40 placebo) with hypertension and left ventricular mass (LVM) > 120 g/m^2 (men) or > 98 g/m^2 (women)
Treatment regimen	Ramipril, 1.25 mg or 5 mg once daily, or placebo
Concomitant therapy	Frusemide, 20 mg once daily
Results	After 6 months, LVM increased by 9 ± 8 g in the placebo group, and decreased by 13 ± 8 g (p = 0.04 vs placebo) and 20 ± 7 g (p = 0.004 vs placebo) in the groups receiving 1.25 and 5 mg ramipril, respectively. Similar changes were observed for LVM index, but the change in the 1.25 mg group reached only borderline significance. These changes were correlated with treatment (1.25 mg ramipril, p = 0.03; 5 mg ramipril, p = 0.01) and the baseline value of LVM index (p = 0.005). No significant differences in casual or ambulatory blood pressure were found between the 3 groups, and changes in casual or ambulatory systolic and diastolic blood pressures were not predictive of changes in LVM

HYVET
Hypertension in the Very Elderly Trial
Ongoing trial

Authors	Bulpitt CJ, Fletcher AE, Amery A, Coope J, Evans JG, Lightowlers S, O'Malley K, Palmer A, Potter J, Sever P, Staessen J, Swift C
Title	The Hypertension in the Very Elderly Trial (HYVET)
Reference	*J Hum Hypertens* 1994;**8**:631–2
Disease	Hypertension
Purpose	To determine whether active treatment of hypertension in patients over the age of 80 years reduced the incidence of total stroke events by 40%
Study design	Randomised, open
Follow-up	5 years
Patients	Aim 2100 patients, aged > 80 years
Treatment regimen	Either ACE inhibitor (lisinopril, 2.5 mg) or diuretic (bendrofluazide, 2.5 mg) or no treatment. In the active treatment groups, the doses may be doubled if necessary, and a calcium antagonist (diltiazem SR, 120–240 mg) may be added if necessary
Results	Not yet available

IMAGE
International Multicenter Angina Exercise study

Authors	Savonitto S, Ardissino D, Egstrup K, Rasmussen K, Bae EA, Omland T, Schjelerup-Mathiesen PM, Marraccini P, Wahlqvist I, Merlini PA, Rehnqvist N
Title	Combination therapy with metoprolol and nifedipine versus monotherapy in patients with stable angina pectoris. Results of the International Multicenter Angina Exercise (IMAGE) study
Reference	*J Am Coll Cardiol* 1996;**27**:311–6
Disease	Angina pectoris
Purpose	To assess whether combination therapy with metoprolol and nifedipine provides a greater anti-ischaemic effect than monotherapy
Study design	Randomised, double-blind, parallel-group
Follow-up	10 weeks
Patients	280 patients, aged ≤ 75 years, with stable angina pectoris
Treatment regimen	Metoprolol CR, 200 mg/day, or nifedipine retard, 20 mg bid. At week 6, all patients were blindly randomised to continue the same treatment plus placebo or to add the alternative drug
Results	At week 6, metoprolol and nifedipine increased mean exercise time to 1 mm ST-segment depression compared to week 1 ($p < 0.01$); metoprolol was more effective than nifedipine ($p < 0.05$). At week 10, the groups on combination therapy had a further increase in time to 1 mm ST-segment depression ($p < 0.05$ vs placebo). 11% of patients adding nifedipine to metoprolol and 29% of patients adding metoprolol to nifedipine ($p < 0.0001$) had an increase in exercise tolerance greater than the 90th percentile of the distribution of changes in the corresponding monotherapy plus placebo groups

IMPACT-II
Integrilin to Minimise Platelet Aggregation and Coronary Thrombosis – II

Authors	The IMPACT-II investigators
Title	Randomised placebo-controlled trial of effect of eptifibatide on complications of percutaneous coronary intervention: IMPACT-II
Reference	*Lancet* 1997;**349**:1422–8
Disease	Coronary artery disease
Purpose	To assess whether treatment with eptifibatide (Integrilin) during and after percutaneous coronary intervention can reduce the incidence of death, MI, unplanned surgical or repeat percutaneous revascularisation, or coronary stent implantation for abrupt closure (composite endpoint) within 30 days after the intervention
Study design	Randomised, double-blind, placebo-controlled
Follow-up	30 days
Patients	4010 patients (1328 placebo, 1349 eptifibatide low-dose, 1333 eptifibatide high-dose)
Treatment regimen	Eptifibatide, 135 µg/kg bolus before the angioplasty plus 0.5 or 75 µg/kg/min infusion during 20–24 h, or placebo
Concomitant therapy	Aspirin, 325 mg, and heparin, 100 U/kg, before study drug and further heparin if needed
Results	By 30 days, the composite endpoint had occurred in 151 (11.4%) patients in the placebo group, 124 (9.2%, p = 0.035) in the low-dose eptifibatide group, and 132 (9.9%, p = 0.18) in the high-dose eptifibatide group. Rates of major bleeding or transfusion were not increased by eptifibatide
Comments	Another study with the acronym IMPACT, International Mexiletine and Placebo Antiarrhythmic Coronary Trial, has been published – see Appendix

INJECT
International Joint Efficacy Comparison of Thrombolytics

Authors	International Joint Efficacy Comparison of Thrombolytics
Title	Randomised, double-blind comparison of reteplase double-bolus administration with streptokinase in acute myocardial infarction (INJECT): trial to investigate equivalence
Reference	*Lancet* 1995;**346**:329–36
Disease	AMI
Purpose	To compare the efficacy of reteplase and streptokinase in patients with AMI, with the primary aim of demonstrating equivalence of the two treatments
Study design	Randomised, double-blind, double-dummy, controlled
Follow-up	6 months
Patients	6010 patients, seen within 12 h of the onset of AMI
Treatment regimen	Streptokinase, 1.5 MU infused iv over 60 min, or reteplase, two 10 MU bolus injections given 30 min apart
Concomitant therapy	Aspirin and heparin
Results	At 35 days, there were 270 deaths (9.02%) in the reteplase group and 285 (9.53%) in the streptokinase group; the 6-month mortality rates were 11.02% and 12.05%, respectively. Statistical evaluation showed that reteplase was at least as effective as streptokinase with regard to mortality rate and the incidences of in-hospital stroke, bleeding events and recurrent MI. There were significantly fewer cases of atrial fibrillation, asystole, cardiac shock, heart failure and hypotension in the reteplase group

INSIGHT

International Nifedipine GITS Study Intervention as a Goal in Hypertension Treatment

Ongoing trial

Authors	Brown MJ, Castaigne A, Ruilope LM, Mancia G, Rosenthal T, de Leeuw PW, Ebner F
Title	INSIGHT: International Nifedipine GITS Study Intervention as a Goal in Hypertension Treatment
Reference	*J Hum Hypertens* 1996;**10**(suppl 3):S157–60
Disease	Hypertension
Purpose	To compare cardiovascular and cerebrovascular morbidity and mortality in high-risk hypertensive patients treated with nifedipine GITS or amiloride plus hydrochlorothiazide
Study design	Randomised, double-blind, controlled
Follow-up	3 years
Patients	Aim 6600 patients (3300 per group), aged 55–80 years, with blood pressure ≥ 150/95 mm Hg or a systolic value of ≥ 160 mm Hg regardless of diastolic pressure
Treatment regimen	Nifedipine GITS, 30–60 mg/day, or amiloride plus hydrochlorothiazide, 2.5/25–5/50 mg/day
Concomitant therapy	Add-on therapy allowed with atenolol, 25–50 mg, or enalapril, 5–10 mg, and additional antihypertensive drug at the discretion of the physician
Results	Not yet available

INTACT
International Nifedipine Trial on Antiatherosclerotic Therapy

Authors	**(a)** Jost S, Deckers JW, Nellessen U *et al* **(b)** Lichtlen PR, Hugenholtz PG, Rafflenbeul W, Hecker H, Jost S, Deckers JW **(c)** Jost S, Deckers JW, Nikutta P, Wiese B, Rafflenbeul W, Hecker H, Lippolt P, Lichtlen PR
Titles	**(a)** Clinical application of quantitative coronary angiography using the CAAS system: preliminary results of the INTACT study (International Nifedipine Trial on Antiatherosclerotic Therapy) **(b)** Retardation of angiographic progression of coronary artery disease by nifedipine. Results of the International Nifedipine Trial on Antiatherosclerotic Therapy (INTACT) **(c)** Evolution of coronary stenoses is related to baseline severity – a prospective quantitative angiographic analysis in patients with moderate coronary disease
References	**(a)** *Int J Cardiac Imaging* 1988;**3**:75–86 **(b)** *Lancet* 1990;**335**:1109–13 **(c)** *Eur Heart J* 1994;**15**:648–53
Disease	Mild coronary artery disease
Purpose	To show retardation of the anatomical progression of coronary artery disease over 3 years and to determine whether the formation of new coronary lesions could be prevented by treatment with nifedipine
Study design	Randomised, double-blind, placebo-controlled
Follow-up	3 years
Patients	425 patients (214 nifedipine and 211 placebo), aged < 65 years and with at least one cardiac risk factor. 348 had two angiograms 3 years apart
Treatment regimen	Nifedipine started at 5 mg tid orally, gradually increased to 20 mg qid at week 17, or placebo
Concomitant therapy	Oral nitrates, β-blockers, antiplatelet agents, anticoagulants and lipid-lowering drugs permitted
Results	The number of new lesions was 0.59/patient with nifedipine and 0.82/patient with placebo (28% reduction; p = 0.034). Side effects occurred in 16 patients given placebo and in 55 given nifedipine (p = 0.003). There were 8 cardiac and 4 non-cardiac deaths with nifedipine, and 2 cardiac deaths with placebo. Progression of atherosclerosis in the patients who had repeat angiograms occurred predominantly in mild preexisting coronary stenoses and developed at previously angiographically normal sites. Conventional angiographic parameters failed to identify arterial sites with an increased risk for progression

INTERCEPT

Incomplete infarction Trial of European Research Collaborators Evaluating Prognosis post-Thrombolysis

Ongoing trial

Authors	Boden WE, Scheldewaert R, Walters EG, Whitehead A, Coltart DJ, Santoni J-P, Belgrave G, Starkey IR
Title	Design of a placebo-controlled clinical trial of long-acting diltiazem and aspirin versus aspirin alone in patients receiving thrombolysis with a first acute myocardial infarction
Reference	*Am J Cardiol* 1995;**75**:1120–3
Disease	AMI
Purpose	To assess the therapeutic benefit of adding diltiazem to aspirin treatment in AMI patients undergoing thrombolysis
Study design	Randomised, double-blind, placebo-controlled, parallel-group
Follow-up	6 months
Patients	Patients with evolving first AMI who are eligible for thrombolysis and who are able to enter the trial within 96 h after the onset of AMI
Treatment regimen	Aspirin, 160 mg once daily, plus either placebo or diltiazem LA, 300 mg once daily
Concomitant therapy	Intravenous thrombolysis with tissue plasminogen activator or streptokinase
Results	Not yet available

IPO-V2

Indagine Policentrica Ospedaliera con Vessel – 2

Authors	Condorelli M, Chiariello M, Dagianti A, Penco M, Dalla Volta S, Pengo V, Schivazappa L, Mattioli G, Mattioli AV, Brusoni B, Trotta E, Bignamini A
Title	IPO-V2: a prospective, multicentre, randomized, comparative clinical investigation of the effects of sulodexide in preventing cardiovascular accidents in the first year after acute myocardial infarction
Reference	*J Am Coll Cardiol* 1994;**23**:27–34
Disease	AMI
Purpose	To assess the efficacy of the antithrombotic agent sulodexide in preventing death and thromboembolic events after AMI
Study design	Randomised, controlled, parallel-group
Follow-up	Minimum 12 months
Patients	3986 patients (3280 men and 706 women), mean age approx. 60 ± 10 years, discharged from the coronary care unit following recovery from AMI
Treatment regimen	Standard therapy, with or without sulodexide as a single im injection of 600 LRU daily (LRU = lipoprotein-lipase-releasing unit) for 1 month, followed by oral capsules of 500 LRU bid
Concomitant therapy	Standard therapy as prescribed by cardiologist; however, patients receiving heparin, oral anticoagulants, antiplatelet agents or fibrinolytics were excluded from the study
Results	The mortality rate was 7.1% in the control group and 4.8% in the sulodexide group ($p = 0.0022$). Treatment with sulodexide was also associated with significant decreases in the incidences of further infarction (4.6% vs 3.3%) and left ventricular thrombus formation (1.3% vs 0.6%). There were only a few minor adverse events associated with the treatment

IRS II
Invasive Reperfusion Study II

Authors	Pacouret G, Charbonnier B, Curien ND *et al*
Title	Invasive reperfusion study II. Multicentre European randomized trial of anistreplase vs streptokinase in acute myocardial infarction
Reference	*Eur Heart J* 1991;**12**:179–85
Disease	AMI
Purpose	To compare the early coronary patency rate, safety and biological effects of anistreplase and streptokinase
Study design	Randomised, open, parallel-group
Follow-up	The hospitalisation period
Patients	116 men and women (58 in each group), aged < 70 years. Time since onset of symptoms: < 6 h
Treatment regimen	Anistreplase, 30 U iv in 2-5 min, or streptokinase, 1.5×10^6 U over 1 h
Concomitant therapy	Routine treatment of AMI, plus heparin, 5000 U iv, and hydrocortisone, 100 mg iv. Continuous heparin infusion, 1000 U/h, was started 6 h after beginning thrombolytic treatment and continued for 5–10 days. Aspirin and other antiaggregant drugs not permitted during the first 24 h
Results	90-min coronary patency rate assessed in 107 patients was significantly higher with anistreplase (70% vs 51%; $p < 0.05$). 50 patients had assessable coronary angiograms at 90 min and 24 h. The 24-h patency rate was 92.35% (24/26) with anistreplase vs 87.5% (21/24) with streptokinase. No early reocclusion occurred with anistreplase vs 15.4% (2/13) with streptokinase ($p = ns$). Bleeding complications occurred in 12% of the anistreplase group and in 21% of the streptokinase group. Major systemic fibrinolysis was observed in both groups

ISAM
Intravenous Streptokinase in Acute Myocardial infarction

Authors	**(a)** The ISAM study group
	(b) Schröder R, Neuhaus K-L, Leizorovicz A, Linderer T, Tebbe U
	(c) Schröder R, Neuhaus K-L, Linderer T, Brüggemann T, Tebbe U, Wegscheider K
	(d) Voth E, Tebbe U, Schicha H, Neumann P, Schröder R, Neuhaus KL, Emrich D
	(e) Schröder R, Linderer T, Brüggemann T, Neuhaus K-L, Tebbe U, Wegscheider K, for the ISAM Study Group
	(f) Voth E, Tebbe U, Schicha H, Neuhaus K-L, Schröder R
Titles	**(a)** A prospective trial of Intravenous Streptokinase in Acute Myocardial infarction (ISAM). Mortality, morbidity and infarct size at 21 days
	(b) A prospective placebo-controlled double-blind multi-center trial of Intravenous Streptokinase in Acute Myocardial infarction (ISAM): long-term mortality and morbidity
	(c) Impact of late coronary artery reperfusion on left ventricular function one month after acute myocardial infarction (results from the ISAM study)
	(d) Intravenous streptokinase in acute myocardial infarction (ISAM): assessment of left ventricular function 1 and 7 months after infarction by radionuclide ventriculography
	(e) Rationale for thrombolysis: later than 4–6 h from symptom onset, and in patients with smaller myocardial infarctions
	(f) Intravenous Streptokinase in Acute Myocardial infarction (ISAM) trial: serial evaluation of left ventricular function up to 3 years after infarction estimated by radionuclide ventriculography
References	**(a)** *N Engl J Med* 1986;**314**:1465–71
	(b) *J Am Coll Cardiol* 1987;**9**:197–203
	(c) *Am J Cardiol* 1989;**64**:878–84
	(d) *Eur Heart J* 1990;**11**:885–96
	(e) *Eur Heart J* 1990;**11**(suppl F):19–28
	(f) *J Am Coll Cardiol* 1991;**18**:1610–6
Disease	AMI
Purpose	To assess the effects of iv streptokinase on mortality at 21days following AMI and to compare the results in patients treated within 3 h to those treated 3–6 h after onset of symptoms
Study design	Randomised, double-blind, placebo-controlled
Follow-up	21 days, 1 month, 4–7 months and 31 months (mean)
Patients	1741 patients (859 streptokinase and 882 placebo), aged ≤ 75 years (mean 58 years). Time since AMI: < 6 h

Treatment regimen	Streptokinase, 1.5×10^6 U infused over 1 h, within 6 h of onset of symptoms, or placebo
Concomitant therapy	Immediately after randomisation: heparin, 5000 U, aspirin, 500 mg, and methylprednisolone, 250 mg iv. After administration of streptokinase: heparin, 800–1000 U/h for 72–96 h, and phenprocoumon, 15 mg, on the first day and 12 mg for the next 20 days. 40% received β-blockers
Results	In 21 days, 54 patients (6.3%) given streptokinase and 63 (7.1%) given placebo died (p = ns). Of those treated within 3 h of onset of symptoms, 25 (5.2%) patients in the streptokinase group and 30 (6.5%) patients in the placebo group died (p = ns). There was no difference in mortality between the two groups after 7 and 31 months, whereas there was a significantly higher rate of reinfarction in the streptokinase group (p = 0.02). Coronary artery patency at 1 month after AMI was similar in the streptokinase and placebo groups (64% vs 56%). The time to peak serum levels of creatine kinase of myocardial origin (CK-MB) after the onset of symptoms was significantly shorter (13.9 h vs 19.2 h) and the CK-MB infarct size was significantly smaller with streptokinase than with placebo. After 1 month, patients with anterior AMI in the streptokinase group had higher left ventricular ejection fractions (LVEF) than the placebo group (50% vs 42%; p = 0.013); this difference was greater in patients treated within 3 h (p = 0.004) and minimal in those treated at 3–6 h. The difference in ejection fraction between the streptokinase and placebo groups persisted during the 3-year follow-up period. Exercise-induced increase in LVEF was greater in streptokinase-treated patients at both 1 and 7 months (p = 0.015). The absence of ST-segment resolution was a powerful independent predictor of early mortality (p = 0.0001), and in subgroups with an overall higher risk of dying mortality was strongly determined by the extent of early ST-segment resolution. Significantly better left ventricular function was associated with patency of infarct artery at 1 month. Bleeding occurred in 51 patients (5.9%) and in 13 (1.5%) patients, respectively (p < 0.0001)
Comments	Several substudies have been made retrospectively on the information from this study

ISIS-1
First International Study of Infarct Survival

Authors	**(a)** and **(b)** ISIS-1 (First International Study of Infarct Survival) Collaborative Group
Titles	**(a)** Randomised trial of intravenous atenolol among 16027 cases of suspected acute myocardial infarction: ISIS-1 **(b)** Mechanisms for the early mortality reduction produced by beta-blockade started early in acute myocardial infarction: ISIS-1
References	**(a)** *Lancet* 1986;**ii**:57–66 **(b)** *Lancet* 1988;**i**:921–3
Disease	AMI
Purpose	To assess the effects of early β-blockade on vascular mortality during the first week following AMI and after long-term follow-up
Study design	Randomised, open, parallel-group
Follow-up	Mean 20 months
Patients	16,027 patients (8037 atenolol and 7990 control), mean age 58 years. Time since AMI: < 12 h
Treatment regimen	Atenolol, 5–10 mg iv over 5 min, followed by 100 mg/day orally for 7 days
Concomitant therapy	Physicians free to use any other additional therapy considered appropriate, but β-blockers avoided in the control group
Results	During days 0–7 of the study, there were 313 vascular deaths (3.89%) with atenolol and 365 (4.57%) in the control group, representing a 15% reduction with atenolol ($2p < 0.04$; 95% confidence interval: 1–27%). During days 7–365, there were an additional 512 vascular deaths (6.4%) with atenolol and 558 (7.0%) in the control group ($2p = 0.09$). After day 365, there was a non-significant excess of vascular deaths with atenolol (179 vs 145 in the placebo group; $2p = 0.07$). Immediate β-blockade increased the extent of inotropic drug use (5.0% vs 3.4% in the placebo group; $2p < 0.0001$), mainly on days 0 and 1 when the largest mortality benefit was observed (121 vs 171 deaths). The observed difference in early mortality was mainly due to a reduction in electromechanical dissociation (reflecting acute rupture) with atenolol

ISIS-2
Second International Study of Infarct Survival

Authors	**(a)** The ISIS-2 collaborative group **(b)** Bourke JP, Young AA, Richards DAB, Uther JB
Titles	**(a)** Randomised trial of intravenous streptokinase, oral aspirin, both, or neither among 17187 cases of suspected acute myocardial infarction: ISIS-2 **(b)** Reduction in incidence of inducible ventricular tachycardia after myocardial infarction by treatment with streptokinase during infarct evolution
References	**(a)** *Lancet* 1988;**ii**:349–60 **(b)** *J Am Coll Cardiol* 1990;**16**:1703–10
Disease	AMI
Purpose	To assess the effects of iv streptokinase and oral aspirin either alone or in combination in patients with suspected AMI
Study design	Randomised, double-blind, placebo-controlled
Follow-up	Maximum 34 months (median 15 months)
Patients	17,187 patients, all ages accepted. Time since suspected AMI: ≤ 24 h (median 5 h)
Treatment regimen	Streptokinase, 1.5×10^6 U iv over 1 h, and/or aspirin, 162.5 mg/day orally for 1 month, or placebo
Concomitant therapy	Physicians free to use any other additional therapy considered appropriate
Results	There was a reduction in 5-week vascular mortality with streptokinase alone or aspirin alone. There were 791 deaths (9.2%) with streptokinase vs 1029 (12.0%) with placebo (25% odds reduction; SD = 4; $2p < 0.00001$) and 804 deaths (9.4%) with aspirin vs 1016 (11.8%) with placebo (23% odds reduction; SD = 4; $2p < 0.00001$). There were 343 vascular deaths (8.0%) with streptokinase plus aspirin vs 568 (13.2%) with placebo (42% odds reduction; SD = 5; 95% confidence limit, 34–50%). Streptokinase was associated with an excess of bleeds requiring transfusion (0.5% vs 0.2% in the placebo group), but with fewer strokes (0.6% vs 0.8%). Aspirin significantly reduced nonfatal reinfarction (1.0% vs 2.0% in the placebo group) and nonfatal stroke (0.3% vs 0.6%)

ISIS-3
Third International Study of Infarct Survival

Authors	The ISIS-3 (Third International Study of Infarct Survival) collaborative group
Title	ISIS-3: a randomised comparison of streptokinase vs tissue plasminogen activator vs anistreplase and of aspirin plus heparin vs aspirin alone among 41 299 cases of suspected acute myocardial infarction
Reference	*Lancet* 1992;**339**:753–70
Disease	AMI
Purpose	To compare the three clot-dissolving drugs streptokinase, tissue plasminogen activator (rt-PA) and anisoylated plasminogen streptokinase activator complex (APSAC), and to compare heparin plus aspirin with aspirin alone in patients with definite or suspected AMI
Study design	Randomised, double-blind, parallel-group, factorial
Follow-up	6 months
Patients	41,299 patients (13,780 streptokinase, 13,746 rt-PA and 13,773 APSAC; 20,643 aspirin alone and 20,656 aspirin plus heparin). Time since onset of symptoms: ≤ 24 h
Treatment regimen	Streptokinase, 1.5×10^6 U iv over 1 h, rt-PA, 0.6×10^6 U/kg iv over 4 h, or APSAC, 30 U iv over 3 min. All patients received aspirin, 162.5 mg/day, or aspirin (same dose) plus heparin, 12,500 U bid subcutaneously for 7 days
Results	The addition of heparin to aspirin was associated with an excess of major non-cerebral bleeds and with definite or probable cerebral haemorrhage, but there was no significant difference with respect to total stroke. During the heparin treatment period, there were slightly fewer deaths in the aspirin plus heparin group. Some of this early benefit may, however, be lost when heparin treatment ceases; no significant mortality advantage was observed in days 0–35 or during 2 months' follow-up. There was a greater number of reports of allergy and a slight excess of strokes, with much of this excess attributed to cerebral haemorrhage in the APSAC group compared to the streptokinase group. There was no significant difference between the two groups in the rate of reinfarction or mortality during days 0–35. The survival rate after 6 months was also similar in the two groups. There was a significant excess of strokes in the rt-PA group compared to the streptokinase group, many of which were reported soon after treatment started and were attributed to cerebral haemorrhage. Fewer reinfarctions were observed in the rt-PA group than in the streptokinase group. There was no significant difference in mortality between day 0 and day 35 and no difference in 6-month survival between the streptokinase and rt-PA groups

ISIS-4
Fourth International Study of Infarct Survival

Authors	**(a)** ISIS-4 Collaborative Group **(b)** ISIS-4 (Fourth International Study of Infarct Survival) Collaborative Group
Titles	**(a)** Fourth International Study of Infarct Survival: protocol for a large simple study of the effects of oral mononitrate, of oral captopril, and of intravenous magnesium **(b)** ISIS-4: a randomised factorial trial assessing early oral captopril, oral mononitrate, and intravenous magnesium sulphate in 58 050 patients with suspected acute myocardial infarction
References	**(a)** *Am J Cardiol* 1991;**68**:87D–100D **(b)** *Lancet* 1995;**345**:669–85
Disease	AMI
Purpose	To assess reliably the separate and combined effects on 5-week mortality of adding oral controlled-release isosorbide mononitrate, oral captopril, or iv magnesium, to current standard treatments for a wide range of types of patients with definite or suspected AMI
Study design	Randomised, partly placebo-controlled, partly open, 2×2×2 factorial
Follow-up	5 weeks
Patients	58,050 patients with suspected AMI. Time since onset of symptoms: ≤ 24 h
Treatment regimen	Oral captopril, 6.25 mg titrated to 50 mg bid, for 1 month, or placebo; and/or oral controlled-release isosorbide mononitrate (Imdur®), 30 mg titrated to 60 mg once daily, for 1 month, or placebo; and/or iv magnesium, 8 mmol bolus followed by 72 mmol over 24 h or open control
Concomitant therapy	Aspirin was recommended as was fibrinolytic therapy, when needed. Non-trial nitrates, non-trial angiotensin-converting enzyme (ACE) inhibitors, or non-trial magnesium used only if a clear indication developed. Use of other concomitant drugs not restricted
Results	For patients receiving captopril there was a small but significant reduction in 5-week mortality compared to placebo. The survival advantage appeared to be maintained for at least 1 year. The survival advantage was greatest for high-risk patients. Neither mononitrate nor magnesium had significant effects on mortality at 5 weeks. Mononitrate therapy, when started early in AMI, was well-tolerated in all groups of patients

ISLAND
Infarct Size Limitation:
Acute N-acetylcysteine Defense trial
Ongoing trial

Authors	Šochman J, Vrbská J, Musilová B, Roček M
Title	Infarct Size Limitation: Acute N-acetylcysteine Defense (ISLAND trial): preliminary analysis and report after the first 30 patients
Reference	*Clin Cardiol* 1996;**19**:94–100
Disease	AMI
Purpose	To assess the efficacy of N-acetylcysteine in reducing infarct size in AMI patients
Study design	Randomised, controlled
Follow-up	Minimum 2 weeks
Patients	30 patients having suffered their first anterior wall AMI. Group A (n = 10) patients had successful recanalisation of the infarct-related coronary artery with streptokinase; Group B (n = 10) patients had failed infarct-related recanalisation; Group C (n = 10) patients had successful recanalisation and additionally received the study treatment
Treatment regimen	N-acetylcysteine, 100 mg/kg
Results	Treatment with N-acetylcysteine was associated with a considerable improvement in left ventricular ejection fraction and significant myocardial salvage (of 26.2 ± 8.1% jeopardised myocardium, infarct size was reduced to 10.8 ± 7.1% = 58.8% salvage). It is hoped to recruit additional patients in this pilot stage of the ISLAND trial

IST
International Stroke Trial

Authors	International Stroke Trial Pilot Study Collaborative Group
Title	Study design of the International Stroke Trial (IST), baseline data, and outcome in 984 randomised patients in the pilot study
Reference	*J Neurol Neurosurg Psychiatry* 1996;**60**:371–6
Disease	Acute stroke
Purpose	To test the feasibility of a very large trial assessing the efficacy and safety of two antithrombotic regimens, aspirin and heparin, started within 48 h of symptom onset
Study design	Randomised, controlled, open, factorial
Follow-up	6 months
Patients	984 patients
Treatment regimen	Aspirin, 300 mg/day, vs no aspirin; subcutaneous heparin, either 5000 U bid or 12,500 U bid, vs no heparin
Concomitant therapy	Other treatment at the discretion of the physician
Results	Within 14 days, 97 patients (10%) died, 30 (3%) had a fatal or nonfatal recurrent ischaemic stroke, 9 (0.9%) had a fatal or nonfatal stroke due to intracranial haemorrhage, 8 (0.8%) had a fatal or nonfatal pulmonary embolus. At 6 months, 22% of patients were dead, 38% were alive but dependent, 23% were independent but not fully recovered. Based on these findings, 20,000 patients might need to be recruited to show a benefit of antithrombotic therapy
Comments	The large IST study with 19,435 patients has been published in *Lancet* 1997;**349**:1569–81

JETS-1
Japanese E5510 TIA Study – 1

Authors	Maruyama S, Uchiyama S, Tohgi H, Hirai S, Ikeda Y, Shinohara Y, Matsuda T, Fujishima M, Kameyama M
Title	A randomized trial of E5510 versus aspirin in patients with transient ischaemic attacks
Reference	*Angiology* 1995;**46**:999–1007
Disease	Transient ischaemic attacks (TIA)
Purpose	To compare the efficacy of the novel antiplatelet agent E5510 and aspirin in preventing the recurrence of TIA
Study design	Randomised, double-blind, parallel-group
Follow-up	24 weeks
Patients	227 patients who had at least one TIA in the 12 weeks prior to the study
Treatment regimen	E5510, 4 mg/day, E5510, 2 mg/day, or aspirin, 324 mg/day, for 12–24 weeks
Results	The incidence of recurrent TIA or stroke was significantly reduced by treatment with E5510, ie was 8.5% in the 4 mg group, 11.7% in the 2 mg group and 21.5% in the aspirin group. Only minor adverse events were reported, and there tended to be fewer in the E5510 groups than in the aspirin group

KAMIT
Kentucky Acute Myocardial Infarction Trial

Authors	Grines CL, Nissen SE, Booth DC *et al*
Title	A prospective, randomized trial comparing combination half-dose tissue-type plasminogen activator and streptokinase with full-dose tissue-type plasminogen activator
Reference	*Circulation* 1991;**84**:540–9
Disease	AMI
Purpose	To compare the effects of half-dose tissue plasminogen activator (rt-PA) plus streptokinase to that of full-dose rt-PA in patients with AMI
Study design	Randomised, open, parallel-group
Follow-up	7 days
Patients	216 patients, aged 18–75, presenting within 6 h of onset of symptoms
Treatment regimen	rt-PA, 10 mg iv bolus then 40 mg/h, plus streptokinase, 1.5 x 10^6 U iv over 1 h, or rt-PA, 10 mg iv bolus, then 50 mg/h over 1 h and 20 mg/h over 2 h
Concomitant therapy	Lignocaine, 2 mg/min during the first 24 h. Aspirin, 325 mg/day, diltiazem, 240 mg/day, and iv heparin, adjusted to partial thromboplastin times 1.5–2 times normal, until follow-up catheterisation at day 7. Temporary interruption of heparin if fibrinogen levels < 100 mg/dl
Results	Acute patency, at 90 min, was significantly greater after the combined therapy (79%) than after rt-PA alone (64%, $p < 0.05$). A marked depletion of fibrinogen levels occurred after the combined therapy compared to rt-PA treatment ($p < 0.0001$); this effect persisted for 24 h. Reocclusion was 3% for the rt-PA/streptokinase group and 10% for the rt-PA group. At day 7, greater myocardial salvage was seen for the group receiving combined therapy compared to the group receiving rt-PA alone ($p < 0.05$). In-hospital mortality and serious bleeding were similar between the two groups

KAPS
Kuopio Atherosclerosis Prevention Study

Authors	Salonen R, Nyyssönen K, Porkkala-Sarataho E, Salonen JT
Title	The Kuopio Atherosclerosis Prevention Study (KAPS): effect of pravastatin treatment on lipids, oxidation resistance of lipoproteins, and atherosclerotic progression
Reference	*Am J Cardiol* 1995;**76**:34C–9C
Disease	Atherosclerosis
Purpose	To analyse the effect of lowering low-density lipoprotein (LDL) cholesterol on the progression and regression of carotid and femoral atherosclerosis in hypercholesterolaemic men
Study design	Randomised, double-blind, placebo-controlled
Follow-up	3 years
Patients	447 men with serum LDL cholesterol ≥ 4 mmol/l and total serum cholesterol < 7.5 mmol/l despite 2.5 months of dietary counselling and placebo
Treatment regimen	Pravastatin, 40 mg/day, or placebo
Concomitant therapy	Dietary advice and placebo (557 men) during 2.5 months pretrial
Results	Pravastatin reduced the rate of progression by 45% (p = 0.005) in carotid arteries and by 66% (p = 0.002) in common carotid arteries. The treatment effect was greater in subjects with thick arterial walls at baseline, in smokers, and in subjects with low plasma α-tocopherol. Subjects who received pravastatin had a higher antioxidative capacity of LDL, a longer oxidation lag of VLDL plus LDL, and a reduced oxidation rate of VLDL plus LDL in vitro

LATE
Late Assessment of Thrombolytic Efficacy study

Authors	**(a)** LATE study group **(b)** Becker RC, Charlesworth A, Wilcox RG, Hampton J, Skene A, Gore JM, Topol EJ
Titles	**(a)** Late Assessment of Thrombolytic Efficacy (LATE) study with alteplase 6–24 hours after onset of acute myocardial infarction **(b)** Cardiac rupture associated with thrombolytic therapy: impact of time to treatment in the Late Assessment of Thrombolytic Efficacy (LATE) study
References	**(a)** *Lancet* 1993;**342**:759–66 **(b)** *J Am Coll Cardiol* 1995;**25**:1063–8
Disease	AMI
Purpose	To compare the effect on survival of recombinant human tissue plasminogen activator (alteplase) and placebo, with treatment starting 6–24 h after the onset of symptoms of AMI
Study design	Randomised, double-blind, placebo-controlled
Follow-up	Minimum 6 months, 73% of patients 1 year
Patients	5711 patients (2836 alteplase and 2875 placebo)
Treatment regimen	Alteplase, 10 mg iv bolus, then 50 mg/h over 1 h and 20 mg/h over 2 h, or placebo
Concomitant therapy	Immediate oral aspirin, then 75–300 mg/day. Heparin recommended, an initial iv bolus of 5000 U then either a further bolus of 5000 U and 1000 U/h or 1000 U/h
Results	Intention-to-treat analysis of survival revealed a non-significant reduction in the alteplase group compared to placebo. However, for treatment within 12 h of onset of symptoms there was a significant reduction of mortality at 35 days with alteplase. Relative reduction of mortality was 25.6% (p = 0.002). The difference for patients treated at 12–24 h after symptom onset was less, though some patients may benefit even when treated after 12 h. Treatment with alteplase resulted in an excess of haemorrhagic strokes, but at 6 months the number of disabled survivors was the same in both groups. In patients treated with alteplase within 12 h there was a non-significant increase in the proportion of deaths due to cardiac rupture, but for those treated after 12 h the proportion of rupture deaths was lower than with placebo. Alteplase appeared to accelerate rupture events, typically to within 24 h of treatment

LCAS
Lipoprotein and Coronary Atherosclerosis Study

Authors	**(a)** Herd JA, West MS, Ballantyne C, Farmer J, Gotto AM Jr **(b)** Herd JA, Ballantyne CM, Farmer JA, Ferguson III JJ, Gould KL, Jones PH, West MS, Gotto AM Jr
Titles	**(a)** Baseline characteristics of subjects in the Lipoprotein and Coronary Atherosclerosis Study (LCAS) with fluvastatin **(b)** The effect of fluvastatin on coronary atherosclerosis: the Lipoprotein and Coronary Atherosclerosis Study (LCAS)
References	**(a)** *Am J Cardiol* 1994;**73**:42D–9D **(b)** *Circulation* 1996;**94**(suppl I):I-597
Disease	Hyperlipidaemia
Purpose	To evaluate the effect of fluvastatin on the progression of coronary artery disease in patients with low to moderate hypercholesterolaemia
Study design	Randomised, blinded, placebo-controlled
Follow-up	2.5 years
Patients	429 patients with at least 1 coronary artery stenosis 30–75% untreated by PTCA, and low-density lipoprotein (LDL) cholesterol 115–190 mg/dl
Treatment regimen	Fluvastatin, 20 mg bid, or placebo
Concomitant therapy	To ensure that placebo patients received adequate care, adjunctive cholestyramin was prescribed in all patients whose LDL cholesterol remained $\geq$ 160 mg/dl after 10 weeks of AHA Step I diet prior to randomisation
Results	Fluvastatin after 10 weeks lowered total cholesterol by 26.5%, LDL cholesterol by 26.5% and triglycerides by 10.1%, and raised high-density lipoprotein cholesterol by 5.5%. Average minimum lumen diameter was increased by 0.100 mm in patients receiving fluvastatin (p > 0.0051). There was a 32.8% (20 vs 31) reduction of 'any cardiac morbid or any fatal event' in the monotherapy groups
Comments	Complete results published in *Am J Cardiol* 1997;**80**:278–86

LIFE
Losartan Intervention For Endpoint
reduction in hypertension
Ongoing trial

Authors	(a) Dahlöf B (b) Kjeldsen SE, Omvik P
Titles	(a) Effect of angiotensin II blockade on cardiac hypertrophy and remodelling: a review (b) Losartan and the LIFE-study. Antihypertensive treatment with AT_1-receptor antagonist
References	(a) *J Hum Hypertens* 1995;**9**(suppl 5):S37–44 (b) *Tidsskr Nor Laegeforen* 1996;**116**:504–7
Disease	Hypertension with left ventricular hypertrophy
Purpose	To compare the long-term effects of losartan and atenolol on cardiovascular mortality and morbidity in hypertensive patients with left ventricular hypertrophy. Secondary, also regression of left ventricular hypertrophy
Study design	Randomised, triple-blind, controlled, parallel-group, double-dummy
Follow-up	5 years
Patients	Aim 8300 patients, aged 55–88 years, with hypertension and left ventricular hypertrophy documented by ECG. Exclusion criteria include prior MI, heart failure or stroke
Treatment regimen	Losartan, 50–100 mg/day, or atenolol, 50–100 mg/day
Concomitant therapy	Hydrochlorothiazide and other agents may be added if required to control blood pressure
Results	Not yet available

LIMIT-2
Second Leicester Intravenous Magnesium Intervention Trial

Authors	**(a)** Woods KL, Fletcher S, Roffe C, Haider Y **(b)** Woods KL, Fletcher S
Titles	**(a)** Intravenous magnesium sulphate in suspected acute myocardial infarction: results of the second Leicester Intravenous Magnesium Intervention Trial (LIMIT-2) **(b)** Long-term outcome after intravenous magnesium sulphate in suspected acute myocardial infarction: the second Leicester Intravenous Magnesium Intervention Trial (LIMIT-2)
References	**(a)** *Lancet* 1992;**339**:1553–8 **(b)** *Lancet* 1994;**343**:816–9
Disease	AMI
Purpose	To assess the effect of iv magnesium salts on mortality in suspected AMI
Study design	Randomised, double-blind, placebo-controlled
Follow-up	1–5.5 years (mean 2.7 years)
Patients	2316 patients with suspected AMI
Treatment regimen	Magnesium sulphate iv, 8 mmol over 5 min, then 65 mmol over 24 h, or physiological saline
Concomitant therapy	Thrombolysis and/or aspirin
Results	The mortality rate from ischaemic heart disease was reduced by 21% (p = 0.001) and all-cause mortality by 16% (p = 0.03) in magnesium-treated patients. Within the coronary care unit the incidence of left ventricular failure was reduced by 25% in the magnesium group (p = 0.009). Adverse events of magnesium treatment were transient flushing and an increased incidence of sinus bradycardia

LIMITS
Liquemin In Myocardial Infarction during Thrombolysis with Saruplase study

Authors	Tebbe U, Windeler J, Boesl I, Hoffmann H, Wojcik J, Ashmawy M, Schwarz ER, von Loewis of Menar P, Rosemeyer P, Hopkins G, Barth H
Title	Thrombolysis with recombinant unglycosylated single-chain urokinase-type plasminogen activator (saruplase) in acute myocardial infarction: influence of heparin on early patency rate (LIMITS Study)
Reference	*J Am Coll Cardiol* 1995;**26**:365–73
Disease	AMI
Purpose	To evaluate the effect of a bolus dose of heparin on the efficacy and safety of saruplase for thrombolysis in patients with AMI
Study design	Randomised, double-blind, parallel-group
Follow-up	1 year
Patients	118 patients (84% men), mean age approx. 59 ± 9 years. Aim 200 patients
Treatment regimen	Within 6 h of onset of symptoms a bolus of heparin, 5000 U, or placebo, prior to thrombolysis with saruplase, 20 mg bolus followed by infusion of 60 mg over 60 min. Starting 30 min after completion of thrombolysis, an iv heparin infusion was given for 5 days. All patients also received an additional bolus of heparin, 5000 U, before performing coronary angiography 6–12 h after the start of thrombolysis
Results	The addition of a heparin bolus prior to thrombolysis with saruplase increased the proportion of patients with a patent infarct-related vessel from 56.5% to 78.6% when assessed 6–12 h after the start of thrombolysis. There were fewer in-hospital deaths in the group given pre-thrombolysis heparin than in the reference group (5.4% vs 14.5%), but more bleeding complications (14.3% vs 8.1%). There were no cerebrovascular events or allergic reactions. The 1-year reinfarction rate was 1.9% in both groups, and health status was comparable in both groups at that time
Comments	After inclusion of the first 100 patients, the results of the interim analysis caused the central ethics and advisory board to terminate the study

LIPID
Long-term Intervention with Pravastatin in Ischemic Disease
Ongoing trial

Authors	The LIPID study group
Title	Design features and baseline characteristics of the LIPID (Long-term Intervention with Pravastatin in Ischemic Disease) study: a randomized trial in patients with previous acute myocardial infarction and/or unstable angina pectoris
Reference	*Am J Cardiol* 1995;**76**:474–9
Disease	AMI and/or unstable angina pectoris
Purpose	To determine whether treatment with pravastatin will reduce coronary mortality and morbidity in patients with a history of AMI or unstable angina pectoris and a baseline cholesterol level of 4.0–7.0 mmol/l
Study design	Randomised, double-blind, placebo-controlled
Follow-up	At least 5 years
Patients	9014 patients (1511 women and 7503 men), aged 31–75 years, were randomised, including 5754 after AMI and 3260 after hospitalisation for unstable angina pectoris
Treatment regimen	Pravastatin, 40 mg, or placebo each evening
Concomitant therapy	Dietary advice
Results	Interim analysis characterises the baseline features of the patients, but results relating to the effects of treatment are awaited
Comments	The study incorporates several substudies, eg on cost-effectiveness, quality of life, diet, and carotid ultrasound

LOMIR-MCT-IL
Lomir – Multicenter study – Israel

Authors	**(a)** Amir M, Cristal N, Bar-On D, Loidl A **(b)** Yodfat Y, Bar-On D, Amir M, Cristal N
Titles	**(a)** Does the combination of ACE inhibitor and calcium antagonist control hypertension and improve quality of life? The LOMIR-MCT-IL study experience **(b)** Quality of life in normotensives compared to hypertensive men treated with isradipine or methyldopa as monotherapy or in combination with captopril: the LOMIR-MCT-IL study
References	**(a)** *Blood Press* 1994;**3**(suppl 1):40–2 **(b)** *J Hum Hypertens* 1996;**10**:117–22
Disease	Mild to moderate hypertension
Purpose	To evaluate the therapeutic efficacy and influence on quality of life of methyldopa and isradipine, and to assess the further benefit of additional captopril medication
Study design	Double-blind, parallel-group, placebo-controlled
Follow-up	1 year
Patients	368 men (29 isradipine, 40 methyldopa, 44 placebo), aged 40–65 years, with mild to moderate hypertension but no other chronic disease
Treatment regimen	Isradipine, 2.5–5 mg, methyldopa, 500–1000 mg, or placebo. Doses were adjusted according to the blood pressure response. If blood pressure was not normalised, captopril, 25–50 mg, was added
Results	Diastolic blood pressure was normalised in 36% of patients in the placebo group, 50% of patients in the methyldopa group and 64% in the isradipine group. The addition of captopril increased these percentages by 39%, 34% and 26%, respectively. Quality-of-life assessment after 1 year showed significantly improved scores in the isradipine plus captopril group

MAAS
Multicentre Anti-Atheroma Study

Authors	MAAS investigators
Title	Effect of simvastatin on coronary atheroma: the Multicentre Anti-Atheroma Study (MAAS)
Reference	*Lancet* 1994;**344**:633–8
Disease	Hyperlipidaemia and coronary artery disease
Purpose	To test whether, and to what extent and how quickly, a substantial reduction of plasma lipids will lead to retardation of diffuse and focal coronary atheroma
Study design	Randomised, double-blind, placebo-controlled
Follow-up	4 years
Patients	381 patients, aged 30-67 years, with at least 2 coronary artery segments arteriographically atheromatous, a mean serum cholesterol concentration of 5.5–8.0 mmol/l and triglycerides < 4.0 mmol/l
Treatment regimen	Diet and simvastatin, 20 mg once daily, or placebo
Concomitant therapy	Antiplatelet agents and/or anticoagulants. Medications other than lipid-lowering drugs permitted
Results	Patients on simvastatin had a 23% reduction in serum cholesterol, a 31% reduction in low-density lipoprotein, and a 9% increase in high-density lipoprotein compared to placebo. In the placebo group there were reductions in mean and minimum lumen diameter, whereas these increased in the simvastatin group (combined p = 0.006). Patients receiving placebo had an increase in mean diameter stenosis of 3.6%, whereas patients receiving simvastatin had a reduction in mean diameter stenosis of 2.6%. With simvastatin, treatment effects were seen regardless of diameter stenosis at baseline. Angiographic progression occurred less often in the simvastatin group, 41 vs 54 patients; and regression was more frequent, 33 vs 20 patients (combined p = 0.02). Significantly more new lesions and new total occlusions developed in the placebo group compared to the simvastatin group, 48 vs 28, and 18 vs 8, respectively. There was no difference in clinical outcome between the two groups

MADIT
Multicenter Automatic Defibrillator Implantation Trial

Authors	**(a)** MADIT executive committee **(b)** Moss AJ
Titles	**(a)** Multicenter Automatic Defibrillator Implantation Trial (MADIT): design and clinical protocol **(b)** Update on MADIT: the Multicenter Automatic Defibrillator Implantation Trial
References	**(a)** *Pacing Clin Electrophysiol* 1991;**14**:920–7 **(b)** *Am J Cardiol* 1997;**79**(suppl 6A):16–7
Disease	Ventricular tachycardia and previous Q-wave AMI
Purpose	To determine whether implantation of an automatic implantable cardioverter/defibrillator (AICD), in patients at high risk for sudden death, will reduce mortality compared to conventional pharmacological treatment
Study design	Randomised
Follow-up	Average 27 months
Patients	Aim 300 patients, aged 25–75 years, with a previous Q-wave infarction (> 1 month), ventricular tachycardia, left ventricular ejection fraction ≤ 0.35 and in NYHA classes I–III
Treatment regimen	AICD or conventional drug therapy
Results	There was a 54% reduction in all-cause mortality in the AICD group relative to conventional treatment (p = 0.009). The major drug used in the non-device arm was amiodarone (74% of the patients)
Comments	In 1996, as a consequence of the AICD positive effect, the safety committee recommended the trial be terminated, with 196 patients randomised

MAPHY
Metoprolol Atherosclerosis Prevention in Hypertensives study

Authors	**(a)** Wikstrand J, Warnold I, Olsson G, Tuomilehto J, Elmfeldt D, Berglund G **(b)** Wikstrand J, Warnold I, Tuomilehto J, Olsson G, Barber HJ, Eliasson K, Elmfeldt D, Jastrup B, Karatzas NB, Leer J, Marchetta F, Ragnarsson J, Robitaille N-M, Valkova L, Wesseling H, Berglund G **(c)** Olsson G, Tuomilehto J, Berglund G *et al*
Titles	**(a)** Primary prevention with metoprolol in patients with hypertension. Mortality results from the MAPHY study **(b)** Metoprolol versus thiazide diuretics in hypertension. Morbidity results from the MAPHY study **(c)** Primary prevention of sudden cardiovascular death in hypertensive patients. Mortality results from the MAPHY study
References	**(a)** *JAMA* 1988;**259**:1976–82 **(b)** *Hypertension* 1991;**17**:579–88 **(c)** *Am J Hypertens* 1991;**4**:151–8
Disease	Hypertension
Purpose	To compare the effects of metoprolol, given as initial antihypertensive treatment, and thiazide diuretics in reducing cardiovascular complications of high blood pressure
Study design	Randomised, open, parallel-group
Follow-up	842 days to 10.8 years (mean 5 years)
Patients	3234 men (1609 metoprolol and 1625 placebo), aged 40–64 years. Diastolic blood pressure at entry: 100–130 mm Hg
Treatment regimen	Metoprolol, 200 mg/day maximum (mean 174 mg/day), hydrochlorothiazide, 50 mg/day maximum (mean 46 mg/day), or bendroflumethiazide, 5 mg/day maximum (mean 4.4 mg/day)
Concomitant therapy	Additional drugs (eg hydralazine, spironolactone) given, if necessary, to reduce diastolic blood pressure to < 95 mm Hg
Results	The risk of cardiovascular events was significantly lower in the metoprolol group than in the diuretic group (p = 0.001). Total mortality was significantly lower with metoprolol than with diuretics; 65 patients in the metoprolol group died compared to 83 patients in the diuretic group (p = 0.028). Significantly lower cardiovascular mortality (p = 0.012), coronary heart disease mortality (p = 0.048) and stroke mortality (p = 0.043) were observed in the metoprolol group. In smokers, both total mortality and coronary heart disease mortality were significantly lower in those receiving metoprolol than in those receiving diuretics

MARCATOR
Multicenter American Research trial with Cilazapril after Angioplasty to prevent Transluminal coronary Obstruction and Restenosis

Authors	**(a)** Faxon DP **(b)** Berger PB, Holmes DR Jr, Ohman EM, O'Hanesian MA, Murphy JG, Schwartz RS, Serruys PW, Faxon DP
Titles	**(a)** Effect of high dose angiotensin-converting enzyme inhibition on restenosis: final results of the MARCATOR study, a multicenter, double-blind, placebo-controlled trial of cilazapril **(b)** Restenosis, reocclusion and adverse cardiovascular events after successful balloon angioplasty of occluded versus nonoccluded coronary arteries. Results from the Multicenter American Research trial with Cilazapril after Angioplasty to prevent Transluminal coronary Obstruction and Restenosis (MARCATOR)
References	**(a)** *J Am Coll Cardiol* 1995;**25**:362–9 **(b)** *J Am Coll Cardiol* 1996;**27**:1–7
Disease	Coronary artery disease
Purpose	To assess the effect of low- and high-dose ACE inhibition with cilazapril in the prevention of restenosis after percutaneous transluminal coronary angioplasty (PTCA)
Study design	Randomised, double-blind, placebo-controlled, parallel-group
Follow-up	6 months
Patients	1436 patients (1153 men and 283 women), aged 27–83 years, following successful PTCA
Treatment regimen	Treatment was started within 6 h of successful PTCA and consisted of either placebo or cilazapril, 1 mg bid, 5 mg bid or 10 mg bid
Concomitant therapy	Aspirin
Results	The mean minimal coronary lumen diameter decreased between the immediate post-PTCA period and the 6-month control in all treatment groups, with no significant differences between the groups. Clinical events during follow-up were also similar in all four treatment groups. Cilazapril therefore did not prevent restenosis or exert a beneficial effect on the outcome after coronary angioplasty. In an analysis of 139 patients with successful angioplasty of complete coronary occlusion compared to 1295 patients with successful angioplasty of subtotal stenosis, the frequency of restenosis was slightly but not significantly greater in the group with previous complete stenosis

MARS
Monitored Atherosclerosis Regression Study

Authors	**(a)** Blankenhorn DH, Azen SP, Kramsch DM *et al* **(b)** Alaupovic P, Hodis HN, Knight-Gibson C, Mack WJ, LaBree L, Cashin-Hemphill L, Corder CN, Kramsch DM, Blankenhorn DH **(c)** Mack WJ, Krauss RM, Hodis HN
Titles	**(a)** Coronary angiographic changes with lovastatin therapy. The Monitored Atherosclerosis Regression Study (MARS) **(b)** Effects of lovastatin on apoA- and apoB-containing lipoproteins. Families in a subpopulation of patients participating in the Monitored Atherosclerosis Regression Study (MARS) **(c)** Lipoprotein subclasses in the Monitored Atherosclerosis Regression Study (MARS). Treatment effects and relation to coronary angiographic progression
References	**(a)** *Ann Intern Med* 1993;**119**:969–76 **(b)** *Arterioscler Thromb* 1994;**14**:1906–14 **(c)** *Arterioscler Thromb Vasc Biol* 1996;**16**:697–704
Disease	Coronary artery disease
Purpose	To assess the effects of lovastatin on coronary angiographic findings in patients with coronary artery disease
Study design	Randomised, double-blind, placebo-controlled
Follow-up	0.6–2.7 years (mean 2.2 years)
Patients	270 patients, aged 37–67 years, with total cholesterol ranging 4.92–7.64 mmol/l
Treatment regimen	A cholesterol-lowering diet and either lovastatin, 40 mg bid, or placebo
Results	Lovastatin lowered total cholesterol level by 32%, low-density lipoprotein (LDL) cholesterol by 38% and apolipoprotein B by 26%, and raised high-density lipoprotein (HDL) cholesterol by 8.5% (p = 0.001). All LDL, intermediate-density lipoprotein and VLDL masses were significantly decreased, and all HDL masses significantly raised with lovastatin compared to placebo. Small VLDL and HDL_3 mass were the most important correlates of coronary artery lesion progression. Mean percentage diameter of stenosis increased by 2.2% in patients receiving placebo and by 1.6% in patients receiving lovastatin (p > 0.20). For lesions of 50% or greater, the mean percentage diameter of stenosis increased by 0.9% after placebo but decreased by 4.1% after lovastatin treatment (p = 0.005). Lovastatin significantly lowered apoB, apoC-III, apoE, and slightly increased apoA-I. The reducing effect of lovastatin on apoB-containing lipoproteins was mediated through a selective decrease in cholesterol-rich lipoprotein B particles

MAST-E
Multicenter Acute Stroke Trial – Europe

Authors	**(a)** The MAST group **(b)** Hommel M, Boissel JP, Cornu C, Boutitie F, Lees KR, Besson G, Leys D, Amarenco P, Bogaert M **(c)** The Multicenter Acute Stroke Trial – Europe study group
Titles	**(a)** Protocol for the Multicenter Acute Stroke Trial – thrombolysis study **(b)** Termination of trial of streptokinase in severe acute ischaemic stroke **(c)** Thrombolytic therapy with streptokinase in acute ischemic stroke
References	**(a)** *Clin Trials Meta-Analysis* 1993;**28**:329–44 **(b)** *Lancet* 1994;**345**:57 **(c)** *N Engl J Med* 1996;**335**:145–50
Disease	Acute ischaemic stroke
Purpose	To assess the efficacy of thrombolysis by streptokinase in patients with acute ischaemic stroke in the middle cerebral artery territory. Primary variable: death plus severe disability
Study design	Randomised, double-blind, placebo-controlled
Follow-up	6 months
Patients	300 patients (aim 600), hospitalised within 6 h from the sudden onset of a focal neurological deficit attributable to an ischaemia in the middle cerebral artery
Treatment regimen	Streptokinase, 1.5×10^6 U iv over 1 h, or placebo
Concomitant therapy	Best medical treatment according to local practice. Heparin was authorised and antithrombotic or antiplatelet treatment was recommended after the acute phase
Results	At 10 days the mortality rate was significantly higher in the streptokinase group than in the placebo group (34.0% vs 18.2%, p = 0.002), mainly due to haemorrhagic transformation of ischaemic cerebral infarcts. At 6 months, the combined endpoint of mortality rate and severe disability was similar in the 2 groups, but the mortality was still higher in the streptokinase group
Comments	Recruitment was stopped in September 1994 because of a significantly higher incidence of symptomatic haemorrhage and mortality at 10 days in the streptokinase group compared to the placebo group

MAST-I
Multicenter Acute Stroke Trial – Italy

Authors	**(a)** MAST-I collaborative group **(b)** Multicentre Acute Stroke Trial – Italy (MAST-I) group **(c)** Tognoni G, Roncaglioni MC
Titles	**(a)** Thrombolytic and antithrombotic therapy in acute ischemic stroke. Multicenter Acute Stroke Trial – Italy (MAST-I) **(b)** Randomised controlled trial of streptokinase, aspirin, and combination of both in treatment of acute ischaemic stroke **(c)** Dissent: an alternative interpretation of MAST-I
References	**(a)** In: Del Zoppo GJ, Mori E, Hacke W, eds. Thrombolytic therapy in acute ischemic stroke II. Berlin: Springer, 1993:86–94 **(b)** *Lancet* 1995;**346**:1509–14 **(c)** *Lancet* 1995;**346**:1515
Disease	Acute ischaemic stroke
Purpose	To determine whether there is a favourable risk-to-benefit ratio for thrombolytic and antiplatelet treatment in acute ischaemic stroke and to demonstrate a reduction in 6-month mortality and disability by both streptokinase and aspirin
Study design	Randomised, open, controlled
Follow-up	6 months
Patients	622 patients, $\leq$ 6 h of acute ischaemic stroke
Treatment regimen	Streptokinase, 1.5×10^6 U iv over 1 h, and/or aspirin, 300 mg orally once daily, or 100 mg iv, for 10 days, or standard treatment
Concomitant therapy	Subcutaneous heparin for patients at risk of deep venous thrombosis. After 10 days, aspirin, ticlopidine or anticoagulants according to local practice
Results	Streptokinase was associated with an excess of 10-day case fatality ($2p < 0.00001$). Of the 4 groups, only patients receiving streptokinase plus aspirin had a significantly higher risk of early death than those who received neither drug ($2p < 0.00001$). Streptokinase (alone or with aspirin) and aspirin alone non-significantly reduced the incidence of combined 6-month case fatality and severe disability
Comments	MAST-I was stopped prematurely when the excess case fatality with streptokinase became evident. The interpretation of the results of this study was challenged by 2 members of the Collaborative Group, on the grounds that too much emphasis was placed on *post-hoc* subgroup analysis, rather than on the excess risk of thrombolysis revealed by analysis of the predefined subgroup and outcome events

MATH
Modern Approach to the Treatment of Hypertension

Authors	(a) Krakoff LR, Bravo EL, Tuck ML, Friedman CP (b) Bravo EL, Krakoff LR, Tuck ML, Friedman CP (c) Krakoff LR
Titles	(a) Nifedipine gastrointestinal therapeutic system in the treatment of hypertension. Results of a multicenter trial (b) Antihypertensive effectiveness of nifedipine gastrointestinal therapeutic system in the elderly (c) Effectiveness of nifedipine gastrointestinal therapeutic system for treatment of hypertension: results of the MATH trial
References	(a) *Am J Hypertens* 1990;**3**:318S–25S (b) *Am J Hypertens* 1990;**3**:326S–32S (c) *J Cardiovasc Pharmacol* 1993;**21**(suppl 2):S14–7
Disease	Mild to moderate hypertension
Purpose	To test the efficacy and safety of a new formulation of nifedipine, the gastrointestinal therapeutic system (GITS)
Study design	Open
Follow-up	12 weeks after desired blood pressure was reached
Patients	1155 patients with diastolic blood pressure between 95 and 110 mm Hg
Treatment regimen	Nifedipine GITS, 30 mg once daily, titrated to a maximum of 180 mg once daily, in 30 mg increments over 6 weeks to achieve diastolic blood pressure < 90 mm Hg
Results	76% of patients achieved a blood pressure < 90 mm Hg during titration ($p < 0.0001$). For more than 50% of patients, doses of 30–60 mg/day were sufficient. The response rate for elderly patients ($\geq$ 65 years) was 85%; these also required the lowest average daily dose (67 ± 42 mg/day compared to 87 ± 48 mg/day). Response rates were similar in black and white patients, in diabetic and non-diabetic patients, and in normal-weight, overweight and obese patients. There were no significant changes in the metabolic risk factors, such as serum glucose and cholesterol levels. There was a significant reduction in serum uric acid (-0.5 mg/dl, $p < 0.001$). The most common adverse events were leg and foot oedema and headache. A total of 14.4% withdrew because of adverse events, 8.6% due to oedema

McSPI
Multicenter Study of Perioperative Ischemia

Author	Mangano DT
Title	Multicenter outcome research
Reference	*J Cardiothorac Vasc Anesth* 1994;**8**(suppl 1):10–2
Disease	Coronary artery disease
Purpose	About 350,000 coronary artery bypass grafts (CABG) are performed annually in the USA and 50,000 of these patients experience morbid complications after the surgery. Furthermore, about 8 million patients who undergo other surgeries have risk factors for coronary disease and more than 1 million of these patients suffer postsurgical cardio-vascular morbidity.
	In 1984 a multidisciplinary study group was formed and named the Study of Perioperative Ischemia Research Group (SPI). This was later transformed to a permanent group named the Multicenter SPI Research Group (McSPI). Several centres are connected to the group and these centres perform studies in connection mainly with CABG. Major areas within the interest of McSPI are newer anti-ischaemics, perioperative sympathetic modulators, and new approaches to postoperative analgesia and sedation. The group is expanding into Canada, Europe, Japan, New Zealand, and Australia. Besides making studies the association trains the research skills of the participating investigators. Major areas within the interest of McSPI are newer anti-ischaemics, eg adenosine-regulating agents, perioperative sympathetic modulators, and new approaches to postoperative analgesia and sedation

MDC
Metoprolol in Dilated Cardiomyopathy trial

Authors	(a) Waagstein F, Bristow MR, Swedberg K *et al* (b) Andersson B, Hamm C, Persson S, Wikström G, Sinagra G, Hjalmarson Å, Waagstein F (c) Wiklund I, Waagstein F, Swedberg K, Hjalmarsson Å
Titles	(a) Beneficial effects of metoprolol in idiopathic dilated cardiomyopathy (b) Improved exercise hemodynamic status in dilated cardiomyopathy after beta-adrenergic blockade treatment (c) Quality of life on treatment with metoprolol in dilated cardiomyopathy: results from the MDC trial
References	(a) *Lancet* 1993;**342**:1441–6 (b) *J Am Coll Cardiol* 1994;**23**:1397–404 (c) *Cardiovasc Drugs Ther* 1996;**10**:361–8
Disease	Heart failure from idiopathic dilated cardiomyopathy
Purpose	To evaluate the effect of metoprolol vs placebo on mortality and need for heart transplantation. The secondary objectives were to assess the effects of metoprolol on cardiac function, exercise capacity, quality of life, and hospital readmission
Study design	Randomised, double-blind, placebo-controlled, parallel-group
Follow-up	12–18 months
Patients	383 patients (189 placebo and 194 metoprolol), aged 16–75 years, with ejection fraction < 0.40
Treatment regimen	During 6–7 weeks a slow increase of study drug from 10 mg/day to 100–150 mg/day. The highest dose tolerated was given as maintenance dose (mean dose 108 mg metoprolol)
Concomitant therapy	Conventional heart failure treatment such as digitalis, diuretics, angiotensin-converting enzyme inhibitors, or nitrates
Results	38 patients in the placebo group reached a primary endpoint (death or need for heart transplantation) compared to 25 in the metoprolol group (a risk reduction of 34%, p = 0.058). There was a significantly greater increase in ejection fraction in the metoprolol group than in the placebo group both at 6 and at 12 months of follow-up. Compared to placebo, metoprolol significantly improved exercise cardiac index and stroke work index (p ≤ 0.0001), exercise systolic arterial pressure (p = 0.0003) and exercise oxygen consumption index (p = 0.045). Exercise capacity improved at 6 months compared to baseline for both metoprolol and placebo, but at 12 months only for metoprolol. Quality of life analysis showed that, from baseline to 18 months, the

metoprolol-treated patients had a significant improvement in life satisfaction, physical activity, and total score, whereas the placebo group did not change at all. NYHA class improved significantly more from baseline to 12 months' follow-up in the metoprolol group. The number of readmissions to a hospital or emergency department was significantly lower in the metoprolol group

MDPIT
Multicenter Diltiazem Post-Infarction Trial

Authors	(a) The MDPIT research group (b) Goldstein RE, Boccuzzi SJ, Cruess D, Nattel S
Titles	(a) The effect of diltiazem on mortality and reinfarction after myocardial infarction (b) Diltiazem increases late-onset congestive heart failure in postinfarction patients with early reduction in ejection fraction
References	(a) *N Engl J Med* 1988;**319**:385–92 (b) *Circulation* 1991;**83**:52–60
Disease	AMI
Purpose	To determine the effects of long-term therapy with diltiazem on mortality and reinfarction rates in patients with previous MI
Study design	Randomised, double-blind, placebo-controlled
Follow-up	12–52 months (mean 25 months)
Patients	2466 patients (1234 diltiazem and 1232 placebo), aged 25–75 years (mean 58 years). Time since onset of AMI: 3–15 days
Treatment regimen	Diltiazem, 60 mg bid or qid, or placebo
Results	Total mortality was 166 patients in the diltiazem group and 167 patients in the placebo group. There were 11% fewer first recurrent cardiac events (death from cardiac cause or nonfatal reinfarction) with diltiazem (202 events) than with placebo (226 events) (Cox hazard ratio 0.90; 95% confidence limits, 0.74–1.08). Adverse events were reported by 662 patients in the diltiazem group and 607 patients in the placebo group; the difference was mainly due to an excess of atrioventricular block, atrial bradycardia and hypotension in the diltiazem group. Patients in the diltiazem group with left ventricular dysfunction had more cardiac events than patients on placebo. This was a tendency for patients with pulmonary congestion (p = ns) and borderline significant for patients with anterolateral Q-wave infarction (p = 0.041). For patients with an ejection fraction < 0.40 late congestive heart failure appeared in 12% (39/326) receiving placebo and 21% (61/297) receiving diltiazem (p = 0.004)

MEHP
Metoprolol in Elderly Hypertension Patients study

Authors	Wikstrand J, Westergren G, Berglund G *et al*
Title	Antihypertensive treatment with metoprolol or hydrochlorothiazide in patients aged 60 to 75 years. Report from a double-blind international multicenter study
Reference	*JAMA* 1986;**255**:1304–10
Disease	Hypertension
Purpose	To compare traditional treatment for hypertension with a regimen comprising a β_1-selective blocker (metoprolol) initially and then, if the patient's response was unsatisfactory after 4 weeks, the addition of a small dose of a diuretic (hydrochlorothiazide)
Study design	Randomised, double-blind, parallel-group
Follow-up	8 weeks
Patients	562 patients (281 in each group), aged 60–75 years. Diastolic blood pressure at entry: 100–130 mm Hg
Treatment regimen	1st step: metoprolol, 100 mg/day 2nd step: hydrochlorothiazide, 12.5 mg/day, in addition to metoprolol, 100 mg/day *or* 1st step: hydrochlorothiazide, 25 mg/day 2nd step: hydrochlorothiazide, 25 mg/day, in addition to hydrochlorothiazide, 25 mg/day
Results	Systolic and diastolic blood pressures were significantly reduced with both regimens. A diastolic blood pressure ≤ 95 mm Hg after 4 weeks of treatment was found in 50% of patients in the metoprolol group and in 47% of patients in the hydrochlorothiazide group, and after 8 weeks of treatment in 65% and 61%, respectively. There were no significant differences in total symptom score or single symptoms between the two groups, but hypokalaemia and hyperuricaemia occurred in significantly more patients in the hydrochlorothiazide group

MERCATOR
Multicenter European Research trial with Cilazapril after Angioplasty to prevent Transluminal coronary Obstruction and Restenosis

Authors	**(a)** The MERCATOR study group **(b)** Hermans WRM, Foley DP, Rensing BJ, Serruys PW
Titles	**(a)** Does the new angiotensin converting enzyme inhibitor cilazapril prevent restenosis after percutaneous transluminal coronary angioplasty? Results of the MERCATOR study: a multicenter, randomized, double-blind placebo-controlled trial **(b)** Morphologic changes during follow-up after successful percutaneous transluminal coronary balloon angioplasty: quantitative angiographic analysis in 778 lesions — further evidence for the restenosis paradox
References	**(a)** *Circulation* 1992;**86**:100–10 **(b)** *Am Heart J* 1994;**127**:483–94
Disease	Coronary artery stenosis
Purpose	To assess the effect of cilazapril in angiographic restenosis prevention after percutaneous transluminal coronary angioplasty (PTCA)
Study design	Randomised, double-blind, placebo-controlled
Follow-up	6 months
Patients	693 patients with significant narrowing of one or more major coronary arteries, scheduled for PTCA
Treatment regimen	Cilazapril, 2.5 mg, after successful PTCA, followed by 5 mg bid, or placebo
Concomitant therapy	Aspirin, 75–125 mg bid
Results	There were no significant differences at follow-up angiography between the placebo or cilazapril groups. 64% of patients in the control group and 62% in the treated group were event-free at 6 months of follow-up. Clinical events, on an intention-to-treat basis, included death, nonfatal MI, coronary revascularisation and recurrent angina requiring medical therapy. There were no significant differences between the two groups for these events. 26 patients in the cilazapril group and 14 patients in the placebo group stopped treatment because of adverse experiences (hypotension, cough, rash, dizziness or gastrointestinal problems). More severe stenosis before angioplasty was a typical feature for restenosis. No differences between the groups were observed for lesion length, balloon-inflated vessel segment, or roughness index

MERIT-HF
Metoprolol CR/XL Randomized Intervention Trial in Heart Failure
Ongoing trial

Authors	The International Steering Committee on behalf of the MERIT-HF Study Group
Title	Rationale, design and organization of Metoprolol CR/XL Randomized Intervention Trial in Heart Failure (MERIT-HF)
Reference	*Am J Cardiol* 1997;**80**(suppl 9B):54J–8J
Disease	Congestive heart failure
Purpose	To investigate the effect of metoprolol succinate controlled-release on total mortality when added to standard therapy in congestive heart failure. Secondary, the effects on mortality, hospitalisations, and other clinical events. In two substudies, the impact on quality of life and healthcare costs will be evaluated
Study design	Randomised, double-blind, placebo-controlled
Follow-up	2.4 years
Patients	Aim 3200 patients, aged 40–80 years, with left ventricular ejection fraction ≤ 0.40 and NYHA class II–IV
Treatment regimen	Metoprolol, 200 mg once daily after a slow titration from 12.5 or 25 mg once daily, or placebo
Results	Not yet available. The study is expected to be completed in 2000

MEXIS
Metoprolol and Xamoterol Infarction Study

Authors	**(a)** Persson H, Rythén-Alder E, Melcher A, Erhardt L **(b)** Persson H, Eriksson SV, Erhardt L
Titles	**(a)** Effects of β receptor antagonists in patients with clinical evidence of heart failure after myocardial infarction: double blind comparison of metoprolol and xamoterol **(b)** Effects of beta receptor antagonists on left ventricular function in patients with clinical evidence of heart failure after myocardial infarction. A double-blind comparison of metoprolol and xamoterol
References	**(a)** *Br Heart J* 1995;**74**:140–8 **(b)** *Eur Heart J* 1996;**17**:741–9
Disease	AMI and mild to moderate heart failure
Purpose	To assess the effects of xamoterol and metoprolol on exercise capacity, echocardiography and quality of life, in patients with mild to moderate heart failure after AMI
Study design	Randomised, double-blind, parallel-group
Follow-up	1 year
Patients	210 patients (106 metoprolol and 104 xamoterol) with signs of heart failure 5–7 days after AMI
Treatment regimen	Xamoterol, 100–200 mg bid, or metoprolol, 50–100 mg bid
Results	Exercise time at 3 months was increased by 22% in the metoprolol group and by 29% in the xamoterol group (non-significant). After 1 year, the exercise time increased from 391 ± 162 s to 506 ± 209 s for patients receiving metoprolol, and from 387 ± 138 s to 528 ± 200 s for patients receiving xamoterol. The difference between the two drugs was non-significant. Mortality was 4.7% for patients on metoprolol and 5.8% for patients on xamoterol. Nonfatal reinfarction occurred in 6.6% of patients on metoprolol and 5.8% on xamoterol. There were 17% withdrawals among patients receiving metoprolol and 22% among those receiving xamoterol. Heart rates at rest and during exercise were higher for patients receiving xamoterol. Improvements in quality of life, clinical signs of heart failure and NYHA functional class occurred in both treatment groups over 1 year, with minor benefits of xamoterol on breathlessness, peripheral oedema and functional class. Compared to metoprolol, xamoterol impaired left ventricular systolic function in patients with clinical evidence of heart failure after AMI

M-HEART
Multi-Hospital Eastern Atlantic Restenosis Trial

Authors	Pepine CJ, Hirshfeld JW, Macdonald RG *et al*
Title	A controlled trial of corticosteroids to prevent restenosis after coronary angioplasty
Reference	*Circulation* 1990;**81**:1753–61
Disease	Coronary artery stenosis
Purpose	To evaluate the role of corticosteroids in reducing the rate of restenosis in patients after successful percutaneous transluminal coronary angioplasty (PTCA) and to identify factors predictive of restenosis
Study design	Randomised, double-blind, placebo-controlled
Follow-up	6 ± 2 months
Patients	915 patients (457 methylprednisolone and 458 placebo) with PTCA performed on at least one stenosis, with a ≥ 60% reduction in luminal diameter within 2–24 h of completion of study drug infusion
Treatment regimen	Methylprednisolone, 1 g iv in 200 ml of 5% dextrose and water, or placebo, 5% dextrose and water alone, 200 ml iv given over 30–45 min, 2–24 h before PTCA
Concomitant therapy	Usual antianginal medication. Before PTCA, aspirin, 325 mg, and heparin, 10,000 U iv bolus and 1000 U/h. Glyceryl trinitrate given iv just before the pre-PTCA (baseline) angiogram. After the procedure, aspirin was continued, but an attempt was made to withdraw antianginal drugs
Results	The mean PTCA success rate was 87%. There were no differences in clinical or angiographic baseline variables between the two groups. Endpoint analysis (death, angiographic stenosis, recurrent ischaemia necessitating early restudy, and coronary artery bypass graft surgery) showed no significant difference between placebo and corticosteroid treatment. Angiographic restudy showed a restenosis rate of 39% in the placebo group and 40% in the methylprednisolone group (p = ns)

M-HEART II
Multi-Hospital Eastern Atlantic Restenosis Trial II

Authors	**(a)** Savage MP, Goldberg S, Macdonald RG *et al* **(b)** Savage MP, Goldberg S, Bove AA, Deutsch E, Vetrovec G, Macdonald RG, Bass T, Margolis JR, Whitworth HB, Taussig A, Hirshfeld JW, Cowley M, Hill JA, Marks RG, Fischman DL, Handberg E, Herrmann H, Pepine CJ
Titles	**(a)** Multi-Hospital Eastern Atlantic Restenosis Trial II: a placebo-controlled trial of thromboxane blockade in the prevention of restenosis following coronary angioplasty **(b)** Effect of thromboxane A_2 blockade on clinical outcome and restenosis after successful coronary angioplasty: Multi-Hospital Eastern Atlantic Restenosis Trial (M-HEART II)
References	**(a)** *Am Heart J* 1991;**122**:1239–44 **(b)** *Circulation* 1995;**92**:3194–200
Disease	Coronary artery stenosis
Purpose	To study the effect of thromboxane blockade by antiplatelet therapy in the prevention of clinical failure, ie restenosis, death or AMI, following successful coronary angioplasty
Study design	Randomised, double-blind, placebo-controlled, double-dummy
Follow-up	6 months
Patients	752 patients undergoing planned percutaneous transluminal coronary angioplasty (PTCA) for at least 1 coronary artery with $\geq 60\%$ diameter reduction
Treatment regimen	Aspirin, 325 mg/day, or sulotroban, 800 mg qid, or placebo. Treatment started 1 h prior to PTCA
Concomitant therapy	PTCA, all patients received aspirin on the day preceding PTCA, heparin 10,000 U iv bolus and 1000 U/h during angioplasty
Results	Neither active treatment differed significantly from placebo in the rate of angiographic restenosis (39% aspirin, 53% sulotroban, 43% placebo). Aspirin significantly improved clinical outcome compared to placebo ($p = 0.046$) and sulotroban ($p = 0.006$). Clinical failure occurred in 30% (aspirin group), 44% (sulotroban group) and 41% (placebo group). MI was significantly reduced by aspirin and sulotroban compared to placebo (1.2%, 1.8% and 5.7%, respectively, $p = 0.03$)

MHFT
Munich Mild Heart Failure Trial

Authors	Kleber FX, Niemöller L, Doering W
Title	Impact of converting enzyme inhibition on progression of chronic heart failure: results of the Munich Mild Heart Failure Trial
Reference	*Br Heart J* 1992;**67**:289-96
Disease	Heart failure
Purpose	To test whether interference with the renin-angiotensin system by angiotensin-converting enzyme inhibition favourably influences the progression of heart failure
Study design	Randomised, double-blind, placebo-controlled
Follow-up	Mean 2.7 years
Patients	170 patients, aged > 18 years, with heart failure in NYHA classes I, II or III
Treatment regimen	Captopril, 25 mg bid, or placebo
Concomitant therapy	Standard treatment according to the patient's need
Results	Heart failure progressed to class IV in 9 patients (10.8%) treated with captopril and in 23 patients (26.4%) treated with placebo (p = 0.01). The mean time until this deterioration was 223 days longer in the captopril group than in the placebo group (p = 0.02). Progression of heart failure to class IV was a powerful predictor of death. In both groups 22 patients died, with 81.1 % of deaths being due to heart failure: 34.1% to progressive heart failure and 47.7% to sudden death. Half the deaths in the placebo group were due to progressive heart failure, but only 18.2% of those in the captopril group (p = 0.10). The therapeutic efficacy of captopril was better in NYHA classes I and II than in class III

MIAMI
Metoprolol In Acute Myocardial Infarction trial

Authors	**(a)** The MIAMI trial research group **(b)** Herlitz J, Karlson BW, Hjalmarson Å **(c)** Herlitz J, Hjalmarson Å, Karlson BW **(d)** The MIAMI Trial Research Group
Titles	**(a)** Metoprolol in acute myocardial infarction (MIAMI). A randomised placebo-controlled international trial **(b)** Mortality and morbidity during one year of follow-up in suspected acute myocardial infarction in relation to early diagnosis: experiences from the MIAMI trial **(c)** Prognosis during one year for patients with myocardial infarction in relation to the development of Q waves: experiences from the Miami trial **(d)** Long-term prognosis after early intervention with metoprolol in suspected acute myocardial infarction: experiences from the MIAMI trial
References	**(a)** *Eur Heart J* 1985;**6**:199–211 **(b)** *J Intern Med* 1990;**228**:125–31 **(c)** *Clin Cardiol* 1990;**13**:261–4 **(d)** *J Intern Med* 1991;**230**:233–8
Disease	AMI
Purpose	To evaluate the effects of early intervention with metoprolol on short-term mortality (15 days) after AMI
Study design	Randomised, double-blind, placebo-controlled
Follow-up	**(a)** 15 days **(b-d)** 1 year
Patients	5778 patients (2877 metoprolol and 2901 placebo), aged < 75 years (median 60 years). Time since onset of AMI: < 24 h
Treatment regimen	Metoprolol, 15 mg iv within 24 h of onset of suspected AMI, followed by 200 mg/day orally, given as 50 mg every 6 h on days 0–2 and 100 mg every 12 h on days 3–16 (at least)
Results	There were 142 deaths (4.9%) in the placebo group and 123 (4.3%) in the metoprolol group (p = ns). In the high mortality risk group (2038 patients), metoprolol was associated with a 29% lower mortality. In patients treated within 7 h of onset of AMI, the incidence of definite AMI was lower in patients receiving metoprolol (70.1%) than in controls (74.0%); maximum serum aspartate aminotransferase (ASAT) activity was 4.7 U in the metoprolol group and 5.3 U in the placebo group. These differences were not observed in patients treated later. Patients who developed a confirmed infarction had a 1-year mortality rate of 12.8%, significantly higher than the mortality rate in patients with possible infarction (6.3%, p < 0.001) and in those with no infarction

(5.0%, p < 0.001). Among those patients with a confirmed infarction, mortality at 1 year was 14.3% in those who developed Q waves compared to 9.0% of those who did not develop Q waves (p < 0.001). Reinfarction during the first year occurred in 8.2% of those with and 12.5% of those without Q waves (p < 0.001). Other morbidity aspects were relatively independent of the original presence of Q waves. Overall mortality over 1 year was 10.6% in patients who received early metoprolol compared to 10.7% for placebo patients (p = ns)

MICRO-HOPE

Microalbuminuria, Cardiovascular and Renal Outcomes in the Heart Outcomes Prevention Evaluation

Ongoing trial

Authors	Gerstein HC, Bosch J, Pogue J, Taylor DW, Zinman B, Yusuf S, and the HOPE study investigators
Title	Rationale and design of a large study to evaluate the renal and cardiovascular effects of an ACE inhibitor and vitamin E in high-risk patients with diabetes. The MICRO-HOPE study
Reference	*Diabetes Care* 1996;**19**:1225–8
Disease	Diabetes and microalbuminuria; prevention of cardiovascular disease and diabetic nephropathy
Purpose	To assess the value of the ACE inhibitor and vitamin E in preventing major cardiovascular events in patients at high risk for cardiovascular disease (HOPE study). In the MICRO-HOPE part of the study, a specific subset of patients with diabetes is investigated. Primary variables: the development of diabetic nephropathy in patients with micro-albuminuria or the development of microalbuminuria in patients not presenting this condition at baseline
Study design	Randomised, double-blind, placebo-controlled
Follow-up	4 years
Patients	3657 diabetic subjects, aged ≥ 55 years, including 1129 with microalbuminuria (a subset of 9541 subjects enrolled in the HOPE study)
Treatment regimen	The patients are randomised to receive placebo, ramipril, 2.5 mg/day for 1 week, 5 mg/day for 3 weeks, then 10 mg/day thereafter, vitamin E, 400 U/day, or combined ramipril and vitamin E
Results	Not yet available

MIDAS
Multicenter Isradipine/Diuretic Atherosclerosis Study

Authors	**(a)** Applegate WB, Byington RP **(b)** Borhani NO **(c)** Borhani NO, Mercuri M, Borhani PA, Buckalew VM, Canossa-Terris M, Carr AA, Kappagoda T, Rocco MV, Schnaper HW, Sowers JR, Bond MG
Titles	**(a)** MIDAS, the Multicenter Isradipine/Diuretic Atherosclerosis Study. Design features and baseline data **(b)** MIDAS: rationale, design and descriptive data of trial patients **(c)** Final outcome results of the Multicenter Isradipine Diuretic Atherosclerosis Study (MIDAS). A randomized controlled trial
References	**(a)** *Am J Hypertens* 1991;**4**:114S–7S **(b)** *Blood Press* 1994;**3**(suppl 1):29–35 **(c)** *JAMA* 1996;**276**:785–91
Disease	Atherosclerosis and hypertension
Purpose	To determine whether isradipine is more effective than hydrochlorothiazide in retarding the rate of progression of carotid artery atherosclerosis in patients with hypertension
Study design	Randomised, double-blind, controlled, parallel-group
Follow-up	3 years
Patients	883 patients, aged > 40 years, with an atherosclerotic lesion in the extracranial carotid artery, a mean sitting diastolic blood pressure of 90–115 mm Hg, low-density lipoprotein levels of 130–189 mg/dl, total serum cholesterol of ≤ 240 mg/dl and triglyceride levels of ≤ 300 mg/dl
Treatment regimen	Isradipine, 2.5 or 5 mg bid, or hydrochlorothiazide, 12.5 or 25 mg bid
Concomitant therapy	If necessary enalapril, 2.5–10 mg bid, was added
Results	There was no difference in the rate of progression of mean maximum intimal-medial thickness between isradipine and hydrochlorothiazide over 3 years (p = 0.68). There was a nonsignificant higher incidence of major vascular events (eg AMI, stroke, congestive heart failure, angina, and sudden death) in the isradipine group vs the hydrochlorothiazide group (5.65% vs 3.17%, p = 0.07). Nonmajor vascular events and procedures were significantly more in the isradipine group vs the hydrochlorothiazide group (9.05% vs 5.22%, p = 0.02)

MIRSA
Multicenter International Randomized Study of Angina pectoris

Authors	de Muinck ED, Buchner-Moell D, van de Ven LLM, Lie KI
Title	Comparison of the safety and efficacy of bisoprolol versus atenolol in stable exercise-induced angina pectoris: a Multicenter International Randomized Study of Angina pectoris (MIRSA)
Reference	*J Cardiovasc Pharmacol* 1992;**19**:870–5
Disease	Angina pectoris
Purpose	To compare the efficacy and safety of bisoprolol with atenolol
Study design	Randomised, double-blind, controlled, parallel-group
Follow-up	3 months
Patients	147 patients (76 bisoprolol and 71 atenolol), aged 21–80 years, with stable exercise-induced angina pectoris
Treatment regimen	Bisoprolol, 10 mg once daily, or atenolol, 100 mg once daily
Concomitant therapy	Sublingual nitroglycerin as required
Results	After 3 months, the weekly angina attack rate was reduced significantly for both bisoprolol and atenolol. There was no significant difference between the two groups in attack rate and nitroglycerin consumption. Peak exercise capacity increased significantly with bisoprolol and with atenolol. Adverse events were experienced by 52% of patients in the bisoprolol group and 45% in the atenolol group, with no significant differences between the two groups

MITI
Myocardial Infarction Triage and Intervention project

Authors	Weaver WD, Cerqueira M, Hallstrom AP, Litwin PE, Martin JS, Kudenchuk PJ, Eisenberg M
Title	Prehospital-initiated vs hospital-initiated thrombolytic therapy. The Myocardial Infarction Triage and Intervention Trial
Reference	*JAMA* 1993;**270**:1211–6
Disease	AMI
Purpose	The project was started to evaluate new treatment strategies, including paramedic therapy, for patients with an AMI and includes a registry of all patients admitted for suspected AMI in the Seattle metropolitan area. The pharmaceutical part was planned to compare the effect of prehospital and hospital initiation of thrombolytic therapy in patients with chest pain and ST-segment elevation on combined death, stroke, serious bleeding, and infarct size
Study design	The first diagnosis of AMI was made by paramedics with the aid of a portable ECG system and a telephone link to an emergency department physician. From this diagnosis thrombolytic therapy with alteplase (rt-PA) was decided and the selected patients were randomised for open paramedic or hospital administration of alteplase. All information on patients with chest pain was collected in the registry
Follow-up	Study endpoints during hospital stay, infarct size and left ventricular function at 30 days
Patients	The registry collected reports on 14,283 persons admitted to a coronary care unit with chest pain. Of these, 360 paramedic-selected patients, aged < 75 years, alert and cooperative and with continuing chest pain since < 6 h, were included in the thrombolysis study
Treatment regimen	Prehospital or hospital administration of alteplase, 100 mg over 3 h, plus aspirin, 325 mg
Concomitant therapy	Heparin, 5000 U iv bolus, followed by continuous infusion for at least 48 h
Results	Initiating treatment before hospital arrival decreased the interval from symptom onset to treatment from 110 to 77 min (p < 0.001). Although more patients whose therapy was initiated before hospital arrival had resolution of pain by admission (23% vs 7%; p < 0.001), there were no significant differences in the composite score (p = 0.64), mortality (5.7% vs 8.1%), ejection fraction (53% vs 54%), or infarct size (6.1% vs 6.5%). A secondary analysis of time to treatment and outcome owed that treatment initiated within 70 min of symptom onset was associated with better outcome (composite score, p = 0.009; mortality 1.2% vs

8.7%, p < 0.04; infarct size 4.9% vs 11.2%, p < 0.001; and ejection fraction 53% vs 49%, p = 0.03) than later treatment. Identification of patients eligible for thrombolysis by paramedics reduced the hospital treatment time from 60 min (for patients not in the study) to 20 min (for study patients allocated to begin treatment in the hospital)

Comments	Several publications have now appeared based on the MITI project registry, including the following:

Length of hospital stay after AMI
– Every NR, *J Am Coll Cardiol* 1996;**28**:287–93

Presentation, treatment and outcome in men and women
– Kudenchuk PJ, *Am J Cardiol* 1996;**78**:9–14

MOCHA
Multicenter Oral Carvedilol Heart failure Assessment

Authors	Bristow MR, Gilbert EM, Abraham WT, Adams KF, Fowler MB, Hershberger RE, Kubo SH, Narahara KA, Ingersoll H, Krueger S, Young S, Schusterman N
Title	Congestive heart failure/myocardial disease: carvedilol produces dose-related improvements in left ventricular function and survival in subjects with chronic heart failure. Clinical investigation and reports
Reference	*Circulation* 1996;**94**:2807–16
Disease	Congestive heart failure
Purpose	To assess the effect of carvedilol in addition to standard therapy on submaximal exercise. Secondary, to assess the effect on quality of life and changes in clinical status defined by NYHA class, ejection fraction, cardiovascular events causing hospitalisation and changes in heart failure signs
Study design	Randomised, double-blind, placebo-controlled
Follow-up	6 months
Patients	345 patients with symptomatic, stable heart failure able to walk 15–450 m in 6 min and ejection fraction $\leq 35\%$
Treatment regimen	Carvedilol, 6.25, 12.5 or 25 mg bid, or placebo
Concomitant therapy	Standard therapy with diuretics, digoxin and ACE inhibitors
Results	Carvedilol had no detectable effect on submaximal exercise, neither according to 6-min corridor walk test nor to 9-min self-powered treadmill test. However, carvedilol was associated with dose-related improvements in left ventricular function and survival. When the three carvedilol groups were combined, the all-cause mortality risk was reduced by 73% compared to placebo-treated patients ($p < 0.001$). Carvedilol also reduced the hospitalisation rate ($p = 0.01$)

MONICA
Monitoring trends and determinants in Cardiovascular disease
Ongoing trial

Authors	**(a)** The WHO MONICA project principal investigators **(b)** Tunstall-Pedoe H, Kuulasmaa K, Amouyel P, Arveiler D, Rajakangas A-M, Pajak A **(c)** WHO MONICA Project
Titles	**(a)** The World Health Organization MONICA Project (monitoring trends and determinants in cardiovascular disease): a major international collaboration **(b)** Myocardial infarction and coronary deaths in the World Health Organization MONICA project. Registration procedures, event rates, and case-fatality rates in 38 populations from 21 countries in four continents **(c)** Stroke incidence and mortality correlated to stroke risk factors in the WHO MONICA project. An ecological study of 18 populations
References	**(a)** *J Clin Epidemiol* 1988;**41**:105–14 **(b)** *Circulation* 1994;**90**:583–612 **(c)** *Stroke* 1997;**28**:1367–74
Disease	Cardiovascular disease
Purpose	To evaluate the trends and determinants in cardiovascular mortality and coronary heart disease, and cerebrovascular disease morbidity, and to assess their relationship with known risk factors (eg, lifestyle, health care and socio-economic status) and cardiovascular risk factors (eg, blood pressure, smoking, serum cholesterol) in 41 collaborative centres using a standardised protocol
Study design	Open
Follow-up	10 years
Patients	Approximately 15 million subjects, aged 25–64 years, grouped according to sex and age (10-year age groups), with at least 200 subjects in each group
Results	Age-standardised annual rates of AMI and coronary death for the main diagnostic group in men aged 35–64 covered a 12-fold range, from 915 per 100,000 for North Karelia, Finland, to 76 per 100,000 for Beijing, China. For women, rates covered an 8.5-fold range from 256 per 100,000 for Glasgow, UK, to 30 per 100,000 for Catalonia, Spain. Case-fatality rates at 28 days ranged from 37% to 81% for men (mean 48%) and from 31% to 91% for women (mean 54%). There was no significant correlation across populations for men between coronary event and case-fatality rates. For women, there was a significant inverse correlation between event and case-fatality rates. Unclassifiable deaths averaged 22% across the 38 populations but represented half of all registered deaths in 2 populations and a third or more of all deaths in 15 populations. Stroke incidence has

been reported for 18 populations. The highest stroke attack rates were found in Novosibirsk in Siberia, Russia, and in Finland, with a more than 3-fold higher incidence than in Friuli, Italy. The presence of conventional cardiovascular risk factors (ie smoking and elevated blood pressure) explained 21% of the variation in stroke incidence among the populations in men and 42% in women

| Comments | Over 500 publications exist, describing the results for specific areas, with emphasis on particular risk factors and their influence on cardiovascular morbidity and mortality |

MRC
Medical Research Council study

Authors	**(a)** The MRC working party **(b)** Peart S **(c)** Medical Research Council Working Party on mild hypertension
Titles	**(a)** MRC trial of treatment of mild hypertension: principal results **(b)** Results of the MRC (UK) trial of drug therapy for mild hypertension **(c)** Coronary heart disease in the Medical Research Council trial of treatment of mild hypertension
References	**(a)** *BMJ* 1985;**291**:97–104 **(b)** *Clin Invest Med* 1987;**10**:616–20 **(c)** *Br Heart J* 1988;**59**:364–78
Disease	Mild hypertension
Purpose	To determine whether drug treatment of mild hypertension reduced the rates of stroke, coronary events and death due to hypertension. Secondary objective: to compare the effects of bendrofluazide and propranolol on blood pressure and the incidence of adverse reactions
Study design	Randomised, single-blind, placebo-controlled, parallel-group
Follow-up	5.5 years
Patients	17,354 patients (bendrofluazide, 2238 men and 2059 women; propranolol, 2285 men and 2118 women; and placebo, 4525 men and 4129 women), aged 35–64 years (mean 51 years in men and 53 years in women). Diastolic blood pressure at entry: 90–109 mm Hg
Treatment regimen	Bendrofluazide, 10 mg/day, or propranolol, up to 240 mg/day
Concomitant therapy	Supplementary treatment (mainly methyldopa) was added if blood pressure did not respond satisfactorily to the primary drug
Results	After 1 year, diastolic blood pressure of < 90 mm Hg was seen in 66% of men and 71% of women in the bendrofluazide group, 60% of men and 64% of women in the propranolol group, and 38% of men and 42% of women in the placebo group, and after 5 years, in 72% of men and 78% of women in the bendrofluazide group, 71% of men and 76% of women in the propranolol group, and 43% of men and 50% of women in the placebo group. The stroke rate was 1.4/1000 patient-years in the treatment group vs 2.6/1000 patient-years in the placebo group (p < 0.01 on sequential analysis). The stroke rate was reduced in both

smokers and non-smokers taking bendrofluazide, but only in non-smokers taking propranolol; this difference between the drugs was significant ($p = 0.03$). The rates of all cardiovascular events were 6.7/1000 patient-years in the treatment group vs 8.2/1000 patient-years in the placebo group ($p < 0.05$ on sequential analysis). Treatment made no difference to the overall rates of coronary events or to overall mortality rates. The coronary event rate was lower in non-smokers than in smokers on placebo, and also lower in non-smoking men on propranolol than in non-smokers on placebo. All-cause mortality was increased in women on treatment but reduced in men on treatment; the difference between the sexes was significant ($p = 0.05$). With bendrofluazide, there was a significant increase in the incidence of impaired glucose tolerance, lethargy, constipation, nausea, dizziness and headache in both men and women, and of gout and impotence in men. Propranolol treatment was associated with an increase in the incidence of Raynaud's phenomenon, dyspnoea, rashes, lethargy, nausea, dizziness and headache

Comments   Further analysis of the data suggests that benefit from reduction of stroke was underestimated (*J Hum Hypertens* 1995;**9**:409–12)

MRC
Medical Research Council trial of treatment of hypertension in older adults

Authors	**(a)** The MRC working party **(b)** Lever AF, Brennan PJ
Titles	**(a)** Medical Research Council trial of treatment of hypertension in older adults: principal results **(b)** MRC trial of treatment in elderly hypertensives
References	**(a)** *BMJ* 1992;**304**:405–12 **(b)** *Clin Exp Hypertens* 1993;**15**:941–2
Disease	Hypertension
Purpose	To establish whether antihypertensive treatment in patients aged 65–74 years reduces mortality and morbidity due to stroke and coronary heart disease and mortality from all causes. Secondary objective: to compare the effects of amiloride and atenolol and to see whether responses to treatment differed between men and women
Study design	Randomised, single-blind, placebo-controlled, parallel-group
Follow-up	Mean 5.8 years
Patients	4396 patients (amiloride, 454 men and 627 women; atenolol, 456 men and 646 women; placebo, 926 men and 1287 women), aged 65–74 years. Systolic blood pressure (SBP) at entry: 160–209 mm Hg
Treatment regimen	Amiloride, 2.5 mg/day, plus hydrochlorothiazide, 25 mg/day, or atenolol, 50 mg once daily, or placebo
Concomitant therapy	If target SBP of 150 or 160 mm Hg (depending on therapy initial SBP) was not reached after 6 months, the dose was doubled and, if further control was necessary, the other test drug was added
Results	Both treatments reduced blood pressure below the level in the placebo group. Patients in the active treatment groups had a 25% reduction in stroke, a 19% reduction in coronary events and a 17% reduction in all cardiovascular events, compared to the placebo groups. The diuretic group had significantly reduced risks of stroke, coronary events and all cardiovascular events compared to the placebo group. The β-blocker group showed no significant reduction in these end-points

MRFIT
Multiple Risk Factor Intervention Trial

Authors	The MRFIT research group
Title	Multiple Risk Factor Intervention Trial. Risk factor changes and mortality results
Reference	*JAMA* 1982;**248**:1465-77
Disease	Coronary heart disease, hypertension
Purpose	To test the efficacy of a multifactor intervention programme in coronary heart disease
Study design	Randomised, open, usual care controlled
Follow-up	6–8 years, 10.5 years, 16 years
Patients	12,866 men (6428 special intervention and 6438 usual care), aged 35–57 years (mean 46 years)
Treatment regimen	Special intervention treatment for hypertension with hydrochlorothiazide or chlorthalidone as first drug. Reserpine, hydralazine, guanethidine, or certain alternative drugs were added sequentially if goal blood pressure not achieved. Counselling on cigarette smoking and dietary advice about lowering blood cholesterol levels were given
Results	Mortality from coronary heart disease was 17.9 deaths/1000 in the special intervention group and 19.3 deaths/1000 in the group receiving usual care. Total mortality rates were 41.2 deaths/1000 in the special intervention group and 40.4 deaths/1000 in the group receiving usual care. At 10.5 years, coronary heart disease mortality was still 10.6% lower in the special intervention group compared to the usual care group, and the AMI rate was 24.3% lower. At 16 years, the differences remained about the same. Only the differences in AMI rate were statistically significant
Comments	The study has been the basis for many publications over the years. A small selection of the references are listed below: *Circulation* 1990;**82**:1616–28 *Prev Med* 1991;**20**:183–96 *Am J Cardiol* 1992;**70**:14F–8F *Arch Intern Med* 1992;**152**:56–64 *Cardiology* 1993;**82**:191–222 (118 refs) *Circulation* 1995;**92**:2437–45 *Circulation* 1996;**94**:946–51 *Am J Clin Nutr* 1997;**65**(suppl):191S–5S *Am J Clin Nutr* 1997;**65**(suppl):196S–210S

MUSTT
Multicenter Unsustained Tachycardia Trial
Ongoing trial

Authors	**(a)** Buxton AE, Fisher JD, Josephson ME *et al* **(b)** Buxton AE
Titles	**(a)** Prevention of sudden death in patients with coronary artery disease: the Multicenter Unsustained Tachycardia Trial (MUSTT) **(b)** Ongoing risk stratification trials: the primary prevention of sudden death
References	**(a)** *Prog Cardiovasc Dis* 1993;**36**:215–26 **(b)** *Control Clin Trials* 1995;**17**:47–51S
Disease	Ventricular tachycardia
Purpose	To identify, by signal-averaged ECG and electrophysiology, in untreated patients, those at greatest risk for sudden death. To use these studies to optimise antiarrhythmic treatment to reduce sudden death and total mortality
Study design	Randomised
Follow-up	2 years
Patients	Aim 900 patients with coronary artery disease or MI > 4 days before enrolment, and a left ventricular ejection fraction ≤ 0.40, and symptom-free, non-sustained ventricular tachycardia
Treatment regimen	Either electrophysiologically guided therapy or no therapy. Drugs to be used are procainamide, quinidine, disopyramide, propafenone, sotalol, amiodarone as monotherapy, or the combinations of quinidine or disopyramide plus mexiletine and procainamide or quinidine plus acebutolol
Results	Not yet available

NASCET

North American Symptomatic Carotid Endarterectomy Trial

Authors	**(a)** North American Symptomatic Carotid Endarterectomy Trial (NASCET) steering committee **(b)** North American Symptomatic Carotid Endarterectomy Trial collaborators **(c)** Gasecki AP, Eliasziw M, Ferguson GG, Hachinski V, Barnett HJM
Titles	**(a)** North American Symptomatic Carotid Endarterectomy Trial. Methods, patient characteristics, and progress **(b)** Beneficial effect of carotid endarterectomy in symptomatic patients with high-grade carotid stenosis **(c)** Long-term prognosis and effect of endarterectomy in patients with symptomatic severe carotid stenosis and contralateral carotid stenosis or occlusion: results from NASCET
References	**(a)** *Stroke* 1991;**22**:711–20 **(b)** *N Engl J Med* 1991;**325**:445–53 **(c)** *J Neurosurg* 1995;**83**:778–82
Disease	Transient ischaemic attack or minor stroke with ipsilateral carotid artery stenosis
Purpose	Evaluation of the effect of carotid endarterectomy on non-fatal and fatal stroke or death
Study design	Randomised, stratified
Follow-up	30 days, 1 year and 2 years
Patients	1212 patients (596 medical care and 616 medical care plus carotid endarterectomy) with transient ischaemic attacks or minor stroke within the previous 120 days. Patients were stratified according to severity of carotid stenosis: 30–69% or 70–99%
Treatment regimen	Carotid endarterectomy and best available medical therapy, including aspirin, 1300 mg/day
Results	Results are available for the 659 patients with the most severe stenosis. Life-table estimates of the cumulative risk of any ipsilateral stroke at 2 years were 26% in the 331 medical care patients and 9% in the 328 surgical care patients (p < 0.001). For major fatal ipsilateral stroke, the corresponding estimates were 13.1% and 2.5%, respectively (p < 0.001). Endarterectomy was still found to be beneficial when all strokes and deaths were included in the analysis (p < 0.001). An occluded contralateral carotid artery significantly increased the risk of stroke within 2 years associated with a severely stenosed ipsilateral carotid artery. Despite higher perioperative (30 days) morbidity in the presence of an occluded contralateral artery, the 2-year prognosis was better for patients with endarterectomy than for those with medical therapy

Comments   As a significant benefit with surgical care was evident for patients with a 70–99% ipsilateral carotid artery stenosis, the monitoring committee stopped the trial for these patients in February 1991

N-CAP
Nifedipine GITS Circadian Anti-ischemia Program

Authors	Parmley WW, Nesto RW, Singh BN *et al*
Title	Attenuation of the circadian patterns of myocardial ischemia with nifedipine GITS in patients with chronic stable angina
Reference	*J Am Coll Cardiol* 1992;**19**:1380–9
Disease	Stable angina pectoris
Purpose	To test the effect of nifedipine gastrointestinal therapeutic system (GITS) as monotherapy or combined with a β-blocker on the circadian pattern of angina and silent ischaemia in patients with chronic stable angina
Study design	Single-blind
Follow-up	7–10 weeks
Patients	207 patients with chronic stable angina pectoris, relieved by nitroglycerin, with at least 2 episodes of symptomatic myocardial ischaemia a week and 2 episodes of silent ischaemia on a 48-h Holter ECG
Treatment regimen	Nifedipine GITS, 30 mg/day for 1 week, titrated at increments of 30 mg/week up to a maximum dose of 180 mg/day, or to a dose level above that at which symptomatic angina was abolished and maintained for 4 weeks on this dose, followed by a washout period
Concomitant therapy	Those patients taking β-blockers at study entry continued taking them at a stable dosage
Results	Nifedipine GITS significantly reduced the weekly number of angina episodes from 5.7 to 1.8 ($p = 0.0001$) and the number of ischaemic events from 7.3 to 4 ($p = 0.0001$) and reduced the duration of the events. There was a significant increase in these during the placebo withdrawal period. A similar effect was seen when nifedipine GITS was combined with β-blocker treatment. Nifedipine GITS was given either as a morning or evening dose, the two regimens resulted in equal anti-ischaemic benefit. The principal adverse event was oedema, which was dose-related

NORDIL
The Nordic Diltiazem study
Ongoing trial

Authors	The NORDIL group
Title	The Nordic Diltiazem Study (NORDIL). A prospective intervention trial of calcium antagonist therapy in hypertension
Reference	*Blood Press* 1993;**2**:312–21
Disease	Hypertension
Purpose	To evaluate the potential preventive effects of diltiazem on cardiovascular morbidity and mortality compared to conventional antihypertensive agents used in the treatment of hypertension
Study design	Randomised, open, blinded-endpoint, parallel-group
Follow-up	5 years
Patients	Aim 12,000 men and women, aged 50–69 years, with primary hypertension
Treatment regimen	Diltiazem or β-blockers or diuretics
Results	Not yet available

PACE
Prevention by low dose Aspirin of Cardiovascular disease in the Elderly
Ongoing trial

Authors	**(a)** Silagy CA, McNeil JJ, Bulpitt CJ, Donnan GA, Tonkin AM, Worsam B **(b)** Silagy CA, McNeil JJ, Donnan GA, Tonkin AM, Worsam B, Campion K **(c)** Silagy CA, McNeil JJ, Donnan GA, Tonkin AM, Worsam B, Campion K
Titles	**(a)** Rationale for a primary prevention study using low-dose aspirin to prevent coronary and cerebrovascular disease in the elderly **(b)** Adverse effects of low-dose aspirin in a healthy elderly population **(c)** The Pace pilot study: 12-month results and implications for future primary prevention trials in the elderly
References	**(a)** *J Am Geriatr Soc* 1991;**39**:484–91 **(b)** *Clin Pharmacol Ther* 1993;**54**:84–9 **(c)** *J Am Geriatr Soc* 1994;**42**:643–7
Disease	Cardiovascular and cerebrovascular disease
Purpose	To test the effect of low-dose aspirin in the primary prevention of cardiovascular and cerebrovascular disease in the elderly
Study design	Randomised, double-blind, placebo-controlled
Follow-up	4 years
Patients	Aim 15,000 healthy subjects, aged $\geq$ 70 years, with no evidence of pre-existing cardiovascular or cerebrovascular disease
Treatment regimen	Aspirin, 100 mg/day, or placebo
Results	Results from a pilot phase with 400 subjects (aspirin 200, placebo 200) followed for 1 year show that gastrointestinal symptoms occurred in 18% of subjects receiving aspirin vs 13% receiving placebo. Aspirin-treated subjects had a significant decrease in mean haemoglobin levels. Two fatal cardiovascular events, 3 nonfatal cardiovascular events and 8 nonfatal cerebrovascular events occurred during 1 year, which were 15%, 15% and 40%, respectively, of the incidences in age- and sex-matched general population. Compliance with medication was 87%
Comments	Secondary 'soft' endpoints (eg transient ischaemic attack and unstable angina) required withdrawal from the study and possibly contributed to the small number of primary 'hard' endpoints

PACK
Prevention of Atherosclerotic Complications with Ketanserin

Authors	**(a)** The PACK trial group **(b)** Verstraete M
Titles	**(a)** Prevention of atherosclerotic complications: controlled trial of ketanserin **(b)** The PACK trial: morbidity and mortality effects of ketanserin
References	**(a)** *BMJ* 1989;**298**:424–30 **(b)** *Vasc Med* 1996;**1**:135–40
Disease	Claudication
Purpose	To determine whether ketanserin prevents important vascular events, such as death, MI, major stroke and leg amputation, in patients with claudication
Study design	Randomised, double-blind, placebo-controlled
Follow-up	12 months
Patients	3899 patients (1930 ketanserin and 1969 placebo), aged > 40 years (mean 63 years). Ankle/arm systolic blood pressure ratio (in both arteries of at least one foot) ≤ 0.85
Treatment regimen	Ketanserin, 20 mg tid for 1 month, then 40 mg tid
Concomitant therapy	Diuretics permitted. Dipyridamole, β-blockers, ticlopidine and aspirin not permitted
Results	There were 104 deaths with ketanserin and 92 with placebo. There were 136 study endpoints (fatal and nonfatal) with ketanserin and 132 with placebo: definite MI, major stroke, amputation above the ankle, excision of ischaemic viscera, or other vascular causes of death. These results were due to a harmful interaction between ketanserin and potassium-losing diuretics. Secondary analysis, excluding patients taking potassium-losing diuretics or antiarrhythmic agents, showed that there were 65 endpoints in 1514 patients in the ketanserin group and 87 in 1557 patients in the placebo group, representing a reduction of 23% in the ketanserin group. Pain-free treadmill walking distance was not increased by ketanserin. Ankle systolic pressure did not change in either group, but brachial systolic pressure decreased with ketanserin, which therefore increased the ankle/arm systolic pressure ratio
Comments	9 months after the study start, the ethics and safety committee recommended that all patients taking diuretics should stop receiving trial treatment (167 on ketanserin, 144 on placebo)

PAMI
Primary Angioplasty in Myocardial Infarction trial

Authors	**(a)** Grines CL, Browne KF, Marco J *et al* **(b)** Stone GW, Grines CL, Browne KF, Marco J, Rothbaum D, O'Keefe J, Hartzler GO, Overlie P, Donohue B, Chelliah N, Timmis GC, Vlietstra R, Strezelecki M, Puchrowicz-Ochocki S, O'Neill WW
Titles	**(a)** A comparison of immediate angioplasty with thrombolytic therapy for acute myocardial infarction **(b)** Predictors of in-hospital and 6-month outcome after acute myocardial infarction in the perfusion era: the Primary Angioplasty in Myocardial Infarction (PAMI) trial
References	**(a)** *N Engl J Med* 1993;**328**:673–9 **(b)** *J Am Coll Cardiol* 1995;**25**:370–7
Disease	AMI
Purpose	To compare percutaneous transluminal coronary angioplasty (PTCA) and thrombolytic therapy in AMI
Study design	Randomised
Follow-up	6 months
Patients	395 patients. Time after onset of MI: < 12 h
Treatment regimen	PTCA, or tissue plasminogen activator (rt-PA), 100 mg iv or 1.25 mg/kg over 3 h for patients weighing < 65 kg
Concomitant therapy	Before randomisation: oxygen, iv glyceryl trinitrate, oral aspirin, 325 mg, and a 10,000 U iv bolus of heparin. Patients assigned to PTCA: heparin, 5000–10,000 U iv. All patients received iv heparin for 3–5 days to achieve a partial thromboplastin time 1.5–2 times the control, oral aspirin, 325 mg/day, and oral diltiazem, 30–60 mg qid. β-blockers and iv lignocaine at the discretion of the investigator
Results	The success rate was 97% for patients undergoing PTCA. The in-hospital mortality rates were 6.5% for the rt-PA group and 2.6% for the PTCA group (p = 0.06). Intracranial bleeding occurred more commonly among patients who received rt-PA (2%) compared to those who underwent PTCA (0%, p = 0.05). At 6 weeks, the mean ejection fraction during exercise and at rest were similar for the two groups. By 6 months, reinfarction or death had occurred in 16.8% of patients in the rt-PA group and 8.5% of patients in the PTCA group (p = 0.02). Advanced age and treatment with rt-PA vs PTCA were independently correlated with increased in-hospital mortality, and with in-hospital mortality or nonfatal reinfarction. The reduction in in-hospital death or reinfarction was most marked in patients > 65 years (p = 0.048). The beneficial effect of PTCA vs rt-PA was maintained to 6 months

PASS
Practical Applicability of Saruplase Study

Authors	Vermeer F, Bär F, Windeler J, Schenkel W
Title	Saruplase, a new fibrin specific thrombolytic agent; final results of the PASS study (1698 patients)
Reference	*Circulation* 1993;**88**:I-292
Disease	AMI
Purpose	To test the efficacy of saruplase (unglycosylated recombinant single-chain urokinase-type plasminogen activator) in AMI
Study design	Open
Patients	1698 patients. Time since onset of symptoms: < 6 h
Treatment regimen	Saruplase, 80 mg iv
Concomitant therapy	Heparin, 5000 U bolus prior to saruplase, then heparin iv over 24 h
Results	In-hospital mortality was 5.4% and reinfarction 3.8% following saruplase. Bleeding complications occurred in 5.3% of patients

PATAF
Primary prevention of Arterial Thromboembolism in patients with Atrial Fibrillation
Ongoing trial

Principal investigators	Knottnerus JA, Lodder J, Vermeer F, van Ree J
Title	Primary preventive effects of anticoagulants and acetyl-salicylic acid on arterial thromboembolism in patients with nonvalvular atrial fibrillation in general practice (PATAF)
Reference	*Stroke* 1994;**25**:1318
Disease	Non-valvular atrial fibrillation
Purpose	To compare the efficacy of warfarin in two different dosages and aspirin for the primary prevention of ischaemic stroke and systemic thromboembolism in patients with non-valvular atrial fibrillation
Study design	Randomised
Follow-up	1–4.5 years
Patients	Aim 800 patients, aged > 60 years, with sustained or intermittent atrial fibrillation
Treatment regimen	Oral anticoagulants, to achieve an international normalised ratio 2.5–3.5, or 1.1–1.6, or aspirin, 150 mg/ day
Results	Not yet available

PATENT
Pro-urokinase And t-PA Enhancement of Thrombolysis trial

Authors	Zarich SW, Kowalchuk GJ, Weaver WD, Loscalzo J, Sassower M, Manzo K, Byrnes C, Muller JE, Gurewich V
Title	Sequential combination thrombolytic therapy for acute myocardial infarction: results of the Pro-urokinase and t-PA Enhancement of Thrombolysis (PATENT) trial
Reference	*J Am Coll Cardiol* 1995;**26**:374–9
Disease	AMI
Purpose	To examine the efficacy and safety of a sequential combination of recombinant tissue-type plasminogen activator (rt-PA) and pro-urokinase in patients with AMI
Study design	Open
Follow-up	24 h
Patients	101 patients (86 men and 15 women). Time since onset of symptoms: < 6 h
Treatment regimen	All patients received premedication with heparin, 5000 IU iv, and aspirin, 160 mg po. Thrombolysis was undertaken with a single iv bolus injection of rt-PA (alteplase), 5 or 10 mg over 1 min, followed immediately by an infusion of nonglycosylated recombinant pro-urokinase, 40 mg/h, for 90 min. Coronary angiography was performed at 90 min, and in some cases was repeated at 24 h
Concomitant therapy	Aspirin daily. Optional β-blocker and/or nitroglycerin
Results	The higher dose of rt-PA (10 mg) seemed to promote major bleeding complications and was used only in the first 10 patients; the next 91 patients received a dose of 5 mg. Angiography at 90 min showed that the infarct-related artery was patent in 77% of patients, with TIMI grade 3 flow in 60% of cases. Angiography was repeated at 24 h in 28 patients and showed that the artery remained patent at that time. There were 10 major bleeding episodes, including 9 cases of groin haematoma at the catheterisation site. There were 26 minor bleeding episodes that were confined to the catheterisation sites. There were no cerebrovascular accidents

PEPI
Postmenopausal Estrogen/Progestin Interventions

Authors	The Writing Group for the PEPI trial
Title	Effects of estrogen or estrogen/progestin regimens on heart disease risk factors in postmenopausal women. The Postmenopausal Estrogen/Progestin Interventions (PEPI) trial
Reference	*JAMA* 1995;**273**:199–208
Disease	Cardiovascular disease (risk factors)
Purpose	To assess the effects of various oestrogen and oestrogen-progestin regimens on selected heart disease risk factors in healthy postmenopausal women
Study design	Randomised, double-blind, placebo-controlled
Follow-up	3 years
Patients	875 healthy postmenopausal women, aged 45–64 years
Treatment regimen	(1) Conjugated equine oestrogen (CEE), 0.625 mg/day, (2) CEE, 0.625 mg/day plus cyclic medroxyprogesterone acetate (MPA), 10 mg/day for the first 12 days each month, (3) CEE, 0.625 mg/day plus consecutive MPA, 2.5 mg/day, (4) CEE, 0.625 mg/day plus cyclic micronised progesterone (MP), 200 mg/day for the first 12 days each month, or (5) placebo
Results	Compared to placebo, the active treatments led to increased serum levels of high-density lipoprotein (HDL) cholesterol and triglycerides, with reduced levels of low-density lipoprotein cholesterol, fibrinogen and post-challenge insulin, and no significant effect on blood pressure. Oestrogen by itself had the best effect on HDL cholesterol, but was associated with an increased rate of endometrial hyperplasia and need for hysterectomy. In women with a uterus, CEE with cyclic MP had the next most favourable effect on HDL cholesterol with no excess risk of endometrial hyperplasia

PHYLLIS
Plaque Hypertension Lipid-Lowering Italian Study
Ongoing trial

Authors	The PHYLLIS project group
Title	Plaque Hypertension Lipid-Lowering Italian Study (PHYLLIS): a protocol for non-invasive evaluation of carotid atherosclerosis in hypercholesterolaemic hypertensive subjects
Reference	*J Hypertens* 1993;**11**(suppl 5):S314–5
Disease	Carotid artery atherosclerosis
Purpose	To determine whether fosinopril (compared to hydrochlorothiazide), pravastatin (compared to diet) or pravastatin plus fosinopril can slow the rate of carotid artery atherosclerosis progression in hypertensive patients with hypercholesterolaemia
Study design	Randomised, double-blind, double-dummy, controlled, factorial
Follow-up	At least 3 years
Patients	Aim 800 outpatients (200 in each treatment group), aged 45–70 years, with mild to moderate hypertension, moderate hypercholesterolaemia and early carotid atherosclerosis
Treatment regimen	Hydrochlorothiazide, 25 mg/day; fosinopril, 20 mg/day; hydrochlorothiazide, 25 mg/day, plus pravastatin, 40 mg/day; or fosinopril, 20 mg/day, plus pravastatin, 40 mg/day
Concomitant therapy	Diet in all cases
Results	Not yet available

PLAC I
Pravastatin Limitation of Atherosclerosis in the Coronary arteries

Authors	**(a)** Pitt B, Ellis SG, Mancini GBJ, Rosman HS, McGovern ME **(b)** Pitt B, Mancini GBJ, Ellis SG, Rosman HS, Park J-S, McGovern ME
Titles	**(a)** Design and recruitment in the United States of a multicenter quantitative angiographic trial of pravastatin to limit atherosclerosis in the coronary arteries (PLAC I) **(b)** Pravastatin limitation of atherosclerosis in the coronary arteries (PLAC I): reduction in atherosclerosis progression and clinical events
References	**(a)** *Am J Cardiol* 1993;**72**:31–5 **(b)** *J Am Coll Cardiol* 1995;**26**:1133–9
Disease	Coronary artery disease with hypercholesterolaemia
Purpose	To test the effect of pravastatin on the progression of coronary artery disease in patients with moderate hypercholesterolaemia
Study design	Randomised, double-blind, placebo-controlled
Follow-up	3 years
Patients	408 patients with at least 1 stenosis $\geq$ 50% in a major epicardial coronary artery and low-density lipoprotein (LDL) cholesterol between 3.36 and 4.91 mmol/l
Treatment regimen	Pravastatin, 40 mg once daily, or placebo
Concomitant therapy	For patients with LDL cholesterol levels $\geq$ 4.91 mmol/l after inclusion, dietary advice followed by cholestyramine, 1 packet/day titrated up to 6 packets/day. For LDL cholesterol levels still $\geq$ 4.91 mmol/l, open-label pravastatin, 5–10 mg, or placebo
Results	Results obtained at 90 days showed 18% and 26% reduction in serum triglycerides and LDL cholesterol, respectively, and an 8% increase in high-density lipoprotein (HDL) cholesterol in the pravastatin-treated group. There were 17 MIs in the placebo group and 5 in the pravastatin group. After 3 years of follow-up, pravastatin decreased total and LDL cholesterol and triglyceride levels by 19%, 28% and 8%, and increased HDL cholesterol by 7% (p $\leq$ 0.001 vs placebo for all lipid variables). Progression of atherosclerosis was reduced by 40% for minimal vessel diameter (p = 0.04), and there was a consistent but non-significant effect on mean diameter and percentage diameter stenosis. There were fewer new lesions in the pravastatin group (p $\leq$ 0.03). There were 8 MIs in the pravastatin group and 17 in the placebo group (p $\leq$ 0.05, 60% risk reduction), with the benefit beginning to emerge at 1 year

PLAC-II
Pravastatin, Lipids, and Atherosclerosis in the Carotid arteries – II

Authors	**(a)** Crouse III JR, Byington RP, Bond MG, Espeland MA, Craven TE, Sprinkle JW, McGovern ME, Furberg CD **(b)** Byington RP, Furberg CD, Crouse III JR, Espeland MA, Bond MG
Titles	**(a)** Pravastatin, Lipids, and Atherosclerosis in the Carotid arteries (PLAC-II) **(b)** Pravastatin, Lipids and Atherosclerosis in the Carotid arteries (PLAC-II)
References	**(a)** *Am J Cardiol* 1995;**75**:455–9 **(b)** *Am J Cardiol* 1995;**76**:54C–9C
Disease	Coronary disease, atherosclerosis
Purpose	To determine whether the reduction in low-density lipoprotein (LDL) cholesterol obtained with pravastatin leads to retardation of atherosclerosis progression as measured by the carotid intimal-medial thickness
Study design	Randomised, double-blind, placebo-controlled
Follow-up	3 years
Patients	151 coronary patients with moderately elevated LDL cholesterol levels and coronary artery disease
Treatment regimen	Pravastatin, at an initial dose of 20 mg/day, taken 3–4 h after the evening meal. The dose was increased to 40 mg/day or reduced to 10 mg/day as necessary to achieve an LDL cholesterol target range of 90–110 mg/dl
Results	Treatment with pravastatin led to reduced plasma levels of total cholesterol and LDL cholesterol, and increased high-density lipoprotein cholesterol. This treatment also led to a 12% (not significant) decrease in the mean yearly progression of intimal-medial thickness in the carotid arteries as a whole (common, bifurcation, internal); the reduction in this progression was more marked (35%, significant) in the common carotid artery. Treatment with pravastatin was also associated with considerable (60–80%) and significant reductions in the incidences of clinical coronary artery disease events

PLUR

Praxisblutdruckmessung versus Langzeit-blutdruckmessung Unter der therapie mit Ramipril

Ongoing trial

Authors	Lüders S, Gerdes M, Scholz M, Heydenbluth R, Schoel G, Haupt A, Eckardt R, Züchner C, Schrader J
Title	First results of a long-term study comparing office blood pressure measurement (OBP) vs. ambulatory blood pressure measurement (ABPM) in patients on ramipril therapy (PLUR-study)
Reference	*Nieren-Hochdruckkr* 1995;**24**:118–20
Disease	Hypertension
Purpose	To determine whether 24-h ambulatory blood pressure measurements (ABPM) really are higher than office blood pressure measurements (OBP) and whether this difference is reflected in the mortality figures
Study design	Randomised, parallel-group, comparative
Follow-up	5 years. The 1-year results are presented here
Patients	So far 1250 patients (648 men and 602 women), aged 35–65 years, with blood pressure > 140/90 mm Hg
Treatment regimen	Ramipril, starting at 1.25–2.5 mg daily and adjusted according to the clinical response (max. 5 mg). If necessary, combination with hydrochlorothiazide, felodipin, metoprolol or nifedipine retard was allowed
Results	22% of the patients assigned to the ABPM group on the basis of hypertensive OBP values were found to have normotensive ABPM values and were not enrolled in the study; these patients clearly exhibited 'white coat hypertension'. Conversely, 15.5% of patients had lower ABPM values than OBP values (reverse white-coat hypertension). After 1 year, significantly more patients in the OBP group were receiving the maximum ramipril dose (5 mg) and significantly more patients in the ABPM group were receiving the minimum ramipril dose (1.25 mg). The proportion of patients receiving the middle ramipril dose (2.5 mg) was the same in both groups, and the frequency of use of combination therapy was also the same in both groups. The 2 groups were also comparable with regard to side-effects

PQRST
Probucol Quantitative Regression Swedish Trial

Authors	**(a)** Walldius G, Regnström J, Nilsson J *et al* **(b)** Walldius G, Erikson U, Olsson AG, Bergstrand L, Hådell K, Johansson J, Kaijser L, Lassvik C, Mölgaard J, Nilsson S, Schäfer-Elinder L, Stenport G, Holme I **(c)** Johansson J, Olsson AG, Bergstrand L, Schäfer-Elinder L, Nilsson S, Erikson U, Mölgaard J, Holme I, Walldius G
Titles	**(a)** The role of lipids and antioxidative factors for development of atherosclerosis. The Probucol Quantitative Regression Swedish Trial (PQRST) **(b)** The effect of probucol on femoral atherosclerosis: the Probucol Quantitative Regression Swedish Trial (PQRST) **(c)** Lowering of HDL$_{2b}$ by probucol partly explains the failure of the drug to affect femoral atherosclerosis in subjects with hypercholesterolemia. A Probucol Quantitative Regression Swedish Trial (PQRST) report
References	**(a)** *Am J Cardiol* 1993;**71**:15B–9B **(b)** *Am J Cardiol* 1994;**74**:875–83 **(c)** *Arterioscler Thromb Vasc Biol* 1995;**15**:1049–56
Disease	Atherosclerosis, hypercholesterolaemia
Purpose	To determine whether development of atherosclerosis in the femoral artery can be retarded, or regression induced, by altering serum lipoproteins with probucol, cholestyramine and dietary management
Study design	Randomised, double-blind, placebo-controlled
Follow-up	3 years
Patients	274 patients (138 probucol and 136 placebo), aged < 71 years, with mean total cholesterol levels > 9 mmol/l, low-density lipoprotein (LDL) cholesterol levels > 6 mmol/l and total triglyceride levels = 2 mmol/l
Treatment regimen	After 3 months' diet, patients received cholestyramine, 8–16 g/day. After a further 2 months, patients responding to cholestyramine received probucol, 500 mg bid. Responders to probucol continued the study for 3 years
Concomitant therapy	Diet aimed to increase intake of polyunsaturated fatty acids
Results	Results from the open phase of the trial indicate that dietary intervention reduced the total cholesterol level by 4% and addition of cholestyramine reduced this level by a further 20%. Similar effects were seen for LDL cholesterol. Addition of probucol reduced total cholesterol by a further 17% and LDL cholesterol by 10%. Probucol also reduced the levels

of high-density lipoprotein (HDL) cholesterol by 31%. These reductions were significant. At 3 years, probucol-treated patients had 17% lower serum cholesterol, 12% lower LDL cholesterol, 24% lower total HDL cholesterol, and 34% lower HDL_2 cholesterol than control subjects; lipoprotein differences were significant throughout the trial. Lumen volume, extent of atherosclerosis, ST-segment depression on exercise testing and ankle/arm blood pressure did not differ between groups. The change in lumen volume in a subgroup of 72 subjects was correlated with lowering of HDL_2 cholesterol and more specifically to the HDL_{2b} concentration

PRACTICAL
Placebo-controlled, Randomized, ACE inhibitor, Comparative Trial In Cardiac infarction and LV function

Authors	Foy SG, Crozier IG, Turner JG, Richards AM, Frampton CM, Nicholls MG, Ikram H
Title	Comparison of enalapril versus captopril on left ventricular function and survival three months after acute myocardial infarction (the "PRACTICAL" study)
Reference	*Am J Cardiol* 1994;**73**:1180–6
Disease	AMI
Purpose	To determine the effects of early ACE inhibition with enalapril and captopril on mortality rates and left ventricular performance in AMI patients
Study design	Randomised, double-blind, placebo-controlled, parallel-group
Follow-up	12 months
Patients	225 patients (173 men and 52 women), mean age 63–64 years, seen and treated within 24 h of the onset of symptoms
Treatment regimen	(1) oral captopril, 6.25 mg at 2-h intervals for 3 doses, followed by 25 mg tid, starting 6 h after the initial dose; (2) oral enalapril, 1.25 mg at 2-h intervals for 3 doses, followed by 5 mg tid, starting 6 h after the initial dose; or (3) placebo, at the same times as in groups 1 and 2
Concomitant therapy	Standard therapy as indicated in each case
Results	42 patients were withdrawn from treatment, mainly for hypotension, rash or withdrawal of consent, and another 12 required dose reduction due to intolerable adverse effects at the target dose. Treatment with either of the tested ACE inhibitors led to a significant increase in left ventricular ejection fraction and a significant attenuation of left ventricular dilatation. The beneficial effects of ACE-inhibitor treatment did not depend on the initial degree of left ventricular dysfunction and were similar with both drugs. However, survival at 90 days and 12 months was significantly improved only in the enalapril group

PRAISE
Prospective Randomized Amlodipine Survival Evaluation

Authors	Packer M, O'Connor M, Ghali JK, Pressler ML, Carson PE, Belkin RN, Miller AB, Neuberg GW, Frid D, Wertheimer JH, Cropp AB, DeMets DL
Title	Effect of amlodipine on morbidity and mortality in severe chronic heart failure
Reference	*N Engl J Med* 1996;**335**:1107–14
Disease	Chronic heart failure
Purpose	To assess the efficacy and safety of a calcium antagonist, amlodipine, in patients with severe chronic heart failure
Study design	Randomised, double-blind, placebo-controlled, parallel-group
Follow-up	6–33 months (median 13.8 months)
Patients	1153 patients with severe chronic heart failure and ejection fraction < 30%. The heart failure was associated with ischaemic heart disease in 732 cases and non-ischaemic cardiomyopathy in 421 cases
Treatment regimen	Amlodipine, at an initial dose of 5 mg once daily for 2 weeks, then increased (if tolerated) to 10 mg, or placebo. The dosage could be reduced later if side-effects occurred
Results	A primary fatal or nonfatal event occurred in 42% of patients in the placebo group and 39% in the amlodipine group. The mortality rate was 38% in the placebo group and 33% in the amlodipine group. However, there was no difference in these rates between the amlodipine and placebo treatments in patients with ischaemic conditions; the risk of death and the combined risk of fatal and nonfatal events were reduced only in patients with non-ischaemic dilated cardiomyopathy. The number of withdrawals and side-effects was comparable in both groups, but oedema and orthostatic hypotension were more frequent in the amlodipine group

PRECISE
Prospective Randomized Evaluation of Carvedilol on Symptoms and Exercise

Authors	Packer M, Colucci WS, Sackner-Bernstein JD, Liang C-s, Goldscher DA, Freeman I, Kukin ML, Kinhal V, Udelson JE, Klapholz M, Gottlieb SS, Pearle D, Cody RJ, Gregory JJ, Kantrowitz NE, LeJemtel TH, Young ST, Lukas MA, Shusterman NH
Title	Double-blind, placebo-controlled study of the effects of carvedilol in patients with moderate to severe heart failure. The PRECISE Trial
Reference	*Circulation* 1996;**94**:2793–9
Disease	Heart failure
Purpose	To assess the clinical effects of carvedilol in a large population of patients with moderate to severe heart failure
Study design	Randomised, double-blind, placebo-controlled
Follow-up	6 months
Patients	278 patients (204 men and 74 women), mean age approx. 60 ± 12 years, with moderate to severe chronic heart failure
Treatment regimen	Carvedilol, 6.25 mg bid for 2 weeks during an open-label run-in period. Patients who tolerated this dose were randomly assigned to long-term treatment with carvedilol or placebo. The initial dosage was 12.5 mg bid and was increased to 25 or 50 mg bid, if tolerated
Concomitant therapy	Digoxin, diuretics and/or ACE inhibitor, as required and kept constant during the trial
Results	Compared to the placebo group, patients treated with carvedilol had a greater frequency of symptomatic improvement and lower risk of subjective and objective deterioration. Treatment with carvedilol was also associated with a significant increase in ejection fraction and a significant decrease in combined risk of morbidity and mortality, but had little effect on exercise tolerance or quality of life scores. The effects of treatment were similar in patients with ischaemic heart disease or idiopathic dilated cardiomyopathy. Adverse effects were mainly dizziness and fatigue, but generally disappeared after dosage adjustment

PRIMI
Pro-urokinase In Myocardial Infarction trial

Authors	**(a)** PRIMI trial study group **(b)** Ostermann H, Schmitz-Huebner U, Windeler J, Bär F, Meyer J, van de Loo J
Titles	**(a)** Randomised double-blind trial of recombinant pro-urokinase against streptokinase in acute myocardial infarction **(b)** Rate of fibrinogen breakdown related to coronary patency and bleeding complications in patients with thrombolysis in acute myocardial infarction – results from the PRIMI trial
References	**(a)** *Lancet* 1989;**i**:863–8 **(b)** *Eur Heart J* 1992;**13**:1225–32
Disease	AMI
Purpose	To compare the therapeutic value of recombinant single-chain urokinase plasminogen activator (saruplase) with that of streptokinase, when given to patients with a first AMI within 4 h of onset of symptoms
Study design	Randomised, double-blind, placebo-controlled
Follow-up	72 h
Patients	401 patients (198 saruplase and 203 streptokinase; 383 with confirmed AMI), aged 21–75 years (mean 58 years). Time since onset of AMI: < 4 h
Treatment regimen	Saruplase, 20 mg iv bolus followed by 60 mg iv over 60 min, or streptokinase, 1.5×10^6 U iv over 60 min, plus dexamethasone, 40 mg
Concomitant therapy	Premedication with heparin, 5000 U, and glyceryl trinitrate, 3–6 mg/h iv. After thrombolytic infusion, heparin, 20 U/kg/h for 72 h, and coumarin were given. Other medication as necessary
Results	At 60 min, patency was achieved in 71.8% of patients in the saruplase group and 48.0% of patients in the streptokinase group (p < 0.001), at 90 min, in 71.2% and 63.9%, respectively (p = 0.15), and at 24–36 h, in 84.7% and 88.4%, respectively. At 24–36 h, 6 of 121 patients receiving saruplase and 5 of 114 receiving streptokinase showed reocclusion of the vessel. At the end of the thrombolytic infusion, fibrinogen concentration had decreased to 0.44 g/l with saruplase and to 0.17 g/l with streptokinase (p < 0.001). Lower fibrinogen levels and a faster rate of fibrinogen breakdown were associated with higher patency rates at 90 min (p < 0.05), irrespective of the drug used. Bleeding complications were less common in the saruplase group than in the control group (p < 0.01)

PROCAM
Prospective Cardiovascular Münster study

Authors	**(a)**, **(b)** and **(c)** Assmann G, Schulte H
Titles	**(a)** The Prospective Cardiovascular Münster Study: prevalence and prognostic significance of hyperlipidemia in men with systemic hypertension **(b)** The Prospective Cardiovascular Münster (PROCAM) study: prevalence of hyperlipidemia in persons with hypertension and/or diabetes mellitus and the relationship to coronary heart disease **(c)** Relation of high-density lipoprotein cholesterol and triglycerides to incidence of atherosclerotic coronary artery disease (the PROCAM experience)
References	**(a)** *Am J Cardiol* 1987;**59**:9G–17G **(b)** *Am Heart J* 1988;**116**:1713–24 **(c)** *Am J Cardiol* 1992;**70**:733–7
Disease	Coronary heart disease
Purpose	To determine the prevalence of coronary heart disease risk factors in the German population, to improve the prediction and early recognition of coronary heart disease, and to derive recommendations for the primary prevention of vascular diseases
Study design	All participants completed a standardised questionnaire concerning individual and family history, including lifestyle data. Blood pressure, weight and height were measured, an ECG was recorded at rest, and a 12-h fasting blood sample was obtained for determination of > 20 laboratory parameters
Follow-up	Started 1979
Patients	Company employees and members of the civil service in Westphalia. 14,799 men and 6507 women participated in the entry examination of the trial
Results	Predictive criteria for identifying people at risk for developing coronary heart disease were determined as: plasma total cholesterol/high-density lipoprotein (HDL) cholesterol ratio ≥ 6.5; plasma total cholesterol ≥ 300 mg/dl, or cholesterol > 200 mg/dl and HDL cholesterol < 35 mg/dl (high risk); and the upper 20% risk computed by means of a multiple logistic function based on statistics for age, plasma total cholesterol and HDL cholesterol levels, systolic blood pressure, angina pectoris, diabetes mellitus, cigarette smoking and family history of MI. In men aged 40–65 years, followed up for 4 years, longitudinal data analysis showed that hypertension, diabetes mellitus, and hyperlipidaemia are independent risk factors for coronary heart disease, and that hyperlipidaemia is the most significant of the three. Furthermore, hypertriglyceridaemia is a powerful additional coronary risk factor when excessive triglycerides coincide with a high ratio

(> 5.0) of plasma low-density lipoprotein cholesterol to HDL cholesterol. The prevalence of this subgroup was only 3.7%, but it included a quarter of all atherosclerotic coronary artery events

| Comments | Many publications have now appeared on the importance of different predictors of coronary heart disease, including the following: |

Triglycerides
– Assmann G, *Eur J Epidemiol* 1992;**8**(suppl 1):99–103

HDL cholesterol
– Assmann G, *Cardiovasc Risk Factors* 1993;**3**:297–304
– Assmann G, *Atherosclerosis* 1996;**124**(suppl):S11–20

Haemostatic variables
– Heinrich J, *Arterioscler Thromb* 1994;**14**:54–9 (erratum **14**:1392)
– Assmann G, *Isr J Med Sci* 1996;**32**:364–70

PROMISE
Prospective Randomized Milrinone Survival Evaluation trial

Authors	**(a)** Packer M **(b)** Packer M, Carver JR, Rodeheffer RJ *et al*
Titles	**(a)** Effect of phosphodiesterase inhibitors on survival of patients with chronic congestive heart failure **(b)** Effect of oral milrinone on mortality in severe chronic heart failure
References	**(a)** *Am J Cardiol* 1989;**63**(suppl A):41A–5A **(b)** *N Engl J Med* 1991;**325**:1468–75
Disease	Chronic congestive heart failure
Purpose	To evaluate the effect of the phosphodiesterase inhibitor, milrinone, on the survival of patients with severe chronic congestive heart failure
Study design	Randomised, double-blind, placebo-controlled
Follow-up	1 day to 20 months (mean 6.1 months)
Patients	1088 patients (561 milrinone and 527 placebo) with NYHA class III or IV heart failure symptoms and a left ventricular ejection fraction < 0.35
Treatment regimen	Milrinone, 40 mg/day
Concomitant therapy	Digitalis, diuretics and an angiotensin-converting enzyme inhibitor
Results	Milrinone treatment was associated with a 28% increase in all-cause mortality compared to placebo (p = 0.038), and a 34% increase in cardiovascular mortality (p = 0.016). Milrinone was also associated with a 69% increase in the risk of sudden cardiac death (p = 0.005), but no increase in the risk of death due to progressive heart failure. Survival in all sub-groups of patients was adversely affected by milrinone
Comments	The study was stopped prematurely on 4 October 1990, 5 months before its scheduled completion, due to the adverse effects of milrinone on survival

PROTECT
Perindopril Regression Of vascular Thickening European Community Trial
Ongoing trial

Authors	**(a)** Ludwig M, Stumpe KO, Heagerty AM *et al* **(b)** Stumpe KO, Ludwig M, Heagerty AM, Kolloch RE, Mancia G, Safar M, Zanchetti A
Titles	**(a)** Vascular wall thickness in hypertension: the Perindopril Regression of Vascular Thickening European Community Trial (PROTECT) **(b)** Vascular wall thickness in hypertension: the Perindopril Regression of Vascular Thickening European Community Trial: PROTECT
References	**(a)** *J Hypertens* 1993;**11**(suppl 5):S316–7 **(b)** *Am J Cardiol* 1995;**76**:50E–4E
Disease	Hypertension
Purpose	To compare the effects of perindopril and hydrochloro-thiazide in slowing or reversing progression of increased intimal-medial thickness of carotid and femoral arteries in hypertensive patients. Secondary, to compare the effect of study drugs on left ventricular mass, posterior wall thickness, interventricular septal thickness, and left ventricular end-diastolic diameter
Study design	Randomised, double-blind, controlled
Follow-up	2 years
Patients	800 patients, aged 35–55 years, with diastolic blood pressure 95–110 mm Hg and ultrasonographically proven intimal-medial thickness ≥ 0.8 mm of the common carotid artery
Treatment regimen	Perindopril, 4 mg/day increased to 8 mg/day at 1 month if diastolic blood pressure not < 95 mm Hg, or hydrochlorothiazide, 12.5 mg/day or 25 mg/day at 1 month if diastolic blood pressure not < 95 mm Hg
Results	Not yet available

PURSUIT
Platelet IIb/IIIa Underpinning the Receptor for Suppression of Unstable Ischemia Trial

Authors	Schulman SP, Goldschmidt-Clermont PJ, Topol EJ, Califf RM, Navetta FI, Willerson JT, Chandra NC, Guerci AD, Ferguson JJ, Harrington RA, Lincoff AM, Yakubov SJ, Bray PF, Bahr RD, Wolfe CL, Yock PG, Anderson HV, Nygaard TW, Mason SJ, Effron MB, Fatterpacker A, Raskin S, Smith J, Brashears L, Gottdiener P, du Mee C, Kitt MM, Gerstenblith G
Title	Effects of integrelin, a platelet glycoprotein IIb/IIIa receptor antagonist, in unstable angina. A randomized multicenter trial
Reference	*Circulation* 1996;**94**:2083–9
Disease	Unstable angina pectoris
Purpose	To assess the effects of treatment with integrelin on the frequency and duration of ischaemia in patients with unstable angina
Study design	Randomised, double-blind, placebo-controlled, double-dummy
Follow-up	72 h
Patients	227 patients (142 men and 85 women), aged 21–80 years, with unstable angina
Treatment regimen	Oral aspirin, 325 mg/day, plus placebo iv integrelin, or placebo oral aspirin plus iv integrelin in one of two doses for 24–72 h. The low-dose integrelin group received a bolus of 45 µg/kg over 3 min followed by a continuous infusion at 0.5 µg/kg/min, and the high-dose group received a bolus of 90 mg/kg followed by infusion at 1.0 µg/kg/min
Concomitant therapy	All patients received standard medical therapy for unstable angina, including intravenous heparin infusion to maintain activated partial thromboplastin time between 1.5 and 2.5 times control
Results	Holter monitoring of ischaemic episodes during treatment showed that the number of ischaemic episodes and their duration were reduced in a dose-dependent manner by the administration of integrelin compared to aspirin. There was no rebound after withdrawal of the study drug. There were few adverse events, with no difference between the groups with regard to bleeding events. There were fewer cases of refractory ischaemia or MI in the integrelin groups than in the aspirin group

PUTS
Perindopril Therapeutic Safety study

Authors	Stumpe KO, Overlack A
Title	A new trial of the efficacy, tolerability, and safety of angiotensin-converting enzyme inhibition in mild systemic hypertension with concomitant diseases and therapies
Reference	*Am J Cardiol* 1993;**71**:32E–7E
Disease	Mild hypertension
Purpose	To assess the interaction between angiotensin-converting enzyme inhibition and the diseases and therapies commonly found associated with mild hypertension
Study design	Randomised, double-blind, placebo-controlled
Follow-up	6 weeks
Patients	480 men and women, aged 30–70 years, with diastolic blood pressure (DBP) 90–104 mm Hg, and any of the following: hyperlipidaemia, type II diabetes, ischaemic heart disease, cardiac arrhythmia, peripheral arterial occlusive disease, nephropathy with proteinuria, chronic obstructive lung disease or treatment with non-steroidal anti-inflammatory drugs (NSAIDs)
Treatment regimen	Perindopril, 4 mg once daily, or placebo
Results	Results are available for 269 patients so far, divided into 5 disease groups. For all these patients, DBP decreased significantly more than in the placebo group, 65% achieving 90 mm Hg compared to 30% on placebo. Perindopril had no unfavourable effects on serum lipid and apolipoprotein concentrations in patients with hyperlipidaemia. Glycaemic control was not affected by perindopril in type II diabetes patients. For patients with ischaemic heart disease, ST-segment depression after 6 weeks was significantly less than with placebo ($p < 0.001$), and angina attack rate was reduced. Urinary albumin excretion was reduced by perindopril for patients with nephropathy. Prostaglandin E_2 was stimulated, in NSAID-treated patients, by perindopril

QUIET
Quinapril Ischemic Event Trial

Authors	**(a)** Texter M, Lees RS, Pitt B, Dinsmore RE, Uprichard ACG **(b)** Lees RS, Pitt B, Chan RC, Holmvang G, Dinsmore RE, Campbell LW, Haber HE, Klibaner MI, Cashin-Hemphill L **(c)** and **(d)** Cashin-Hemphill L, Dinsmore RE, Chan RC, Williams SN, Holmvang G, Haber HE, Lees RS
Titles	**(a)** The Quinapril Ischemic Event Trial (QUIET) design and methods: evaluation of chronic ACE inhibitor therapy after coronary artery intervention **(b)** Baseline clinical and angiographic data in the Quinapril Ischemic Event (QUIET) trial **(c)** LDL cholesterol and angiographic progression in the QUIET trial **(d)** Atherosclerosis progression in subjects with and without post-angioplasty restenosis in QUIET
References	**(a)** *Cardiovasc Drugs Ther* 1993;**7**:273–82 **(b)** *Am J Cardiol* 1996;**78**:1011–6 **(c)** *J Am Coll Cardiol* 1997;**29**(suppl A):85A **(d)** *J Am Coll Cardiol* 1997;**29**(suppl A):418A
Disease	Coronary artery atherosclerosis and cardiac ischaemia
Purpose	To assess the efficacy of quinapril in reducing severe ischaemia and to slow or prevent the development of coronary artery atherosclerosis
Study design	Randomised, double-blind, placebo-controlled
Follow-up	3 years
Patients	1750 normotensive patients, aged ≤ 75 years, having undergone successful single-vessel or double-vessel coronary angioplasty (PTCA) or atherectomy 12–72 h previously, with low-density lipoprotein cholesterol ≤ 4.27 mmol/l and with left ventricular ejection fraction ≥ 40%
Treatment regimen	Quinapril, 10 mg on day 1, then 20 mg once daily, or placebo
Results	453 patients were included in an angiographic substudy. There was no difference in restenosis rate between quinapril- and placebo-treated patients. However, in patients with high low-density lipoprotein cholesterol levels the patients treated with placebo showed a more rapid progression of coronary atherosclerosis than those treated with quinapril

RAAMI
Rapid Administration of Alteplase (r-PA) in Myocardial Infarction trial

Authors	Carney RJ, Murphy GA, Brandt TR *et al*
Title	Randomized angiographic trial of recombinant tissue-type plasminogen activator (alteplase) in myocardial infarction
Reference	*J Am Coll Cardiol* 1992;**20**:17–23
Disease	AMI
Purpose	To evaluate whether 'front-loaded' alteplase (rt-PA) (larger dose in the first 60 min) in patients with AMI will enhance the angiographic patency rate
Study design	Randomised, open, parallel-group
Follow-up	90 min
Patients	281 patients. Time since onset of AMI: ≤ 6 h
Treatment regimen	rt-PA, 100 mg (58 x 10^6 U), given either front-loaded over 90 min (15 mg bolus plus 50 mg over 30 min plus 35 mg over 60 min) or over the standard 180 min (10 mg bolus plus 50 mg over 60 min plus 40 mg over 120 min)
Results	Infarct-related artery patency at 60 min was 76% of the front-loaded group and 63% of the control group, and at 90 min, it was 81% and 77%, respectively. Recurrent ischaemia, reinfarction, reocclusion and death occurred equally in both groups, as did bleeding, transfusions and stroke. Overall, of patients with occluded arteries at 60 min and patent arteries at 90 min, 33% had recurrent ischaemia vs 15% of patients with patent arteries at 60 min

RAAS
Randomized Angiotensin receptor antagonist – ACE inhibitor Study
Ongoing trial

Authors	Pitt B, Chang P, Grossman W, Dunlay M, Timmermans PBMWM
Title	Rationale, background, and design of the Randomized Angiotensin receptor antagonist–Angiotensin-converting enzyme inhibitor Study (RAAS)
Reference	*Am J Cardiol* 1996;**78**:1129–31
Disease	Heart failure with left ventricular systolic dysfunction
Purpose	To test the hypothesis that the addition of an angiotensin II type 1 receptor blocker (losartan) to an ACE inhibitor (enalapril) will provide better blockade of activation of the renin-angiotensin-aldosterone system in patients with heart failure and left ventricular systolic dysfunction, and to assess the safety of this therapy
Study design	Randomised, double-blind, placebo-controlled, double-dummy
Follow-up	6–48 weeks
Patients	Aim 120 patients (3 treatment groups of 40 patients each) with heart failure and left ventricular systolic dysfunction
Treatment regimen	Enalapril, 10 mg bid, plus either one of enalapril, 2.5–10 mg bid, losartan, 12.5–50 mg, or placebo
Results	Not yet available

RACE
Ramipril Cardioprotective Evaluation

Authors	Agabiti-Rosei E, Ambrosioni E, Dal Palù C, Muiesan ML, Zanchetti A
Title	ACE inhibitor ramipril is more effective than the β-blocker atenolol in reducing left ventricular mass in hypertension. Results of the RACE (RAmipril Cardioprotective Evaluation) study
Reference	*J Hypertens* 1995;**13**:1325–34
Disease	Hypertension
Purpose	To compare the effects of ramipril and atenolol on left ventricular hypertrophy and blood pressure in patients with hypertension
Study design	Randomised, open, blinded endpoint
Follow-up	6 months
Patients	193 patients (115 men and 78 women), aged 27–70 years, with mild to moderate hypertension
Treatment regimen	Ramipril, 2.5 mg once daily, or atenolol, 50 mg once daily. If blood pressure control was unsatisfactory, the initial dose was doubled after 2 weeks. If needed, a diuretic was added after a further 2 weeks
Results	Systolic and diastolic blood pressures were reduced significantly and to similar degrees by both treatments. Heart rate was significantly reduced only in the atenolol group. Left ventricular mass was reduced only slightly in the atenolol group but was reduced significantly in the ramipril group (-11% at 6 months). Side-effects were reported by 6 patients in the ramipril group and 8 in the atenolol group

RADIANCE
Randomized Assessment of the effect of Digoxin on Inhibitors of the Angiotensin-Converting Enzyme study

Authors	Packer M, Gheorghiade M, Young JB *et al*
Title	Withdrawal of digoxin from patients with chronic heart failure treated with angiotensin-converting-enzyme inhibitors
Reference	*N Engl J Med* 1993;**329**:1–7
Disease	Heart failure
Purpose	To evaluate the effect of withdrawal of digoxin from patients with chronic heart failure who were clinically stable while receiving digoxin, diuretics and captopril or enalapril
Study design	Randomised, double-blind
Follow-up	12 weeks
Patients	178 patients (85 digoxin and 93 placebo) with NYHA class II or III heart failure and left ventricular ejection fraction ≤ 35% and clinically stable
Treatment regimen	Continued digoxin adjusted to give a serum concentration of 0.9–2.0 mg/ml, or placebo
Concomitant therapy	Diuretics to give optimal fluid balance, captopril, 25 mg, or enalapril, 5 mg
Results	Worsening heart failure necessitating withdrawal from the study developed in 23 patients on placebo, but only in 4 on digoxin ($p < 0.001$). The relative risk of worsening heart failure in the placebo group compared to the digoxin group was 5.9. All measure of functional capacity deteriorated significantly in patients receiving placebo compared to those continuing to receive digoxin. In addition, the patients switched from digoxin to placebo had significantly lower quality of life scores, decreased ejection fractions and increases in heart rate and body weight

RALES
Randomized Aldactone Evaluation Study

Author	Pitt B
Title	ACE inhibitor co-therapy in patients with heart failure: rationale for the Randomized Aldactone Evaluation Study (RALES)
Reference	*Eur Heart J* 1995;**16**(suppl N):107–10
Disease	Heart failure
Purpose	To explore the benefit of adding spironolactone to therapy with ACE inhibitors in heart failure patients
Study design	Randomised, double-blind, placebo-controlled, parallel dose-finding
Follow-up	12 weeks
Patients	200 patients with heart failure and left ventricular ejection fraction $\leq$ 40% already receiving therapy with an ACE inhibitor, a loop diuretic and, possibly, digoxin
Treatment regimen	Additional spironolactone, 12.5, 25, 50 or 75 mg/day, or placebo
Concomitant therapy	ACE inhibitor, a loop diuretic and, possibly, digoxin
Results	The addition of spironolactone to the therapy of these patients led to a dose-dependent pharmacological effect which was significant even with the lowest dose. The effect comprised a decrease in plasma N-terminal pro-atrial natriuretic factor and increased levels of plasma renin and urinary aldosterone. The incidence of hyperkalaemia was increased at spironolactone doses of 50 and 75 mg daily. A dose of 25 mg daily may be recommended. However, if spironolactone is used for symptomatic therapy of patients with refractory or severe heart failure, doses up to 100 mg bid may be required
Comments	A RALES Mortality Trial is planned to determine the effects of added spironolactone 25 mg/day on heart failure mortality and morbidity in 1400 patients followed up for 3 years

RaMI
Ravenna Myocardial Infarction trial

Authors	Coccolini S, Berti G, Bosi S, Pretolani M, Tumiotto G
Title	Prehospital thrombolysis in rural emergency room and subsequent transport to a coronary care unit: Ravenna Myocardial Infarction (RaMI) trial
Reference	*Int J Cardiol* 1995;**49**(suppl):S47–58
Disease	AMI
Purpose	To assess the feasibility, safety and efficacy of thrombolysis in the emergency room of a rural hospital with no coronary care unit prior to transfer to the coronary care unit of a city hospital
Study design	Open, parallel-group
Follow-up	5 weeks
Patients	280 consecutive patients (211 men and 69 women; 102 group 1 and 178 group 2), mean age about 63 years, with suspected AMI, seen within 6 h of onset of symptoms and with no contraindications to fibrinolysis
Treatment regimen	Anistreplase (APSAC), 30 U iv bolus injection in 4 min, either in a rural emergency room (group 1) or in a coronary care unit (group 2)
Concomitant therapy	Basic standard medical care in all cases
Results	The accuracy of diagnosis of AMI was 91% in group 1 and 100% in group 2. The patients in group 1 received treatment faster than those in group 2; they also had lower creatine phosphokinase peak values and lower echocardiographic wall motion abnormality score index values. Complications were rare and none occurred during transfer to the coronary care unit. Mortality at 35 days was 7.5% in group 1 and 10.7% in group 2. Early thrombolytic treatment is therefore beneficial even when performed outside of a coronary care unit

RAPID 1
Recombinant plasminogen activator Angiographic Phase II International Dose-finding study

Authors	**(a)** Smalling RW, Bode C, Kalbfleisch J, Sen S, Limbourg P, Forycki F, Habib G, Feldman R, Hohnloser S, Seals A, and the RAPID investigators **(b)** Weaver WD
Titles	**(a)** More rapid, complete, and stable coronary thrombolysis with bolus administration of reteplase compared with alteplase infusion in acute myocardial infarction **(b)** Results of the RAPID 1 and RAPID 2 thrombolytic trials in acute myocardial infarction
References	**(a)** *Circulation* 1995;**91**:2725–32 **(b)** *Eur Heart J* 1996;**17**(suppl E):14–20
Disease	AMI
Purpose	To determine whether bolus administration of the recombinant plasminogen activator reteplase is superior to standard infusion of alteplase in obtaining infarct-related artery patency in AMI patients
Study design	Randomised, open, parallel-group
Follow-up	To hospital discharge (5–14 days)
Patients	606 patients, aged 18–75 years. Time since onset of symptoms: < 6 h
Treatment regimen	The patients were randomised to one of four treatments: (1) reteplase, 15 MU as a single bolus (2) reteplase, 10 MU bolus followed after 30 min by a 5 MU bolus (3) reteplase, 10 MU bolus followed after 30 min by a 10 MU bolus (4) alteplase, 6–10 mg bolus followed by infusion to give a total dose of 60 mg over the first hour, then infusion at 20 mg/h for another 2 h to give a final total dose of 100 mg in 3 h
Concomitant therapy	Standard therapy
Results	The effects of treatment were primarily assessed by coronary angiography at 30, 60 and 90 min after the start of treatment and again on discharge from hospital. The best results in terms of infarct-related artery patency, global ejection fraction and regional wall motion values were obtained in the group treated with reteplase, 10 + 10 MU. The results in the other three groups were all significantly poorer than in this group. The incidence of bleeding complications was similar in all treatment groups

RAPID 2
Reteplase (r-PA) vs Alteplase Patency Investigation During myocardial infarction

Author	Weaver WD
Title	Results of the RAPID 1 and RAPID 2 thrombolytic trials in acute myocardial infarction
Reference	*Eur Heart J* 1996;**17**(suppl E):14–20
Disease	AMI
Purpose	To compare the early thrombolytic efficacy of the bolus regimen of reteplase with an acceleratd infusion of alteplase in obtaining infarct-related artery patency in AMI patients
Study design	Randomised, open, parallel-group
Follow-up	30 days
Patients	324 patients, aged 18–75 years. Time since onset of symptoms: < 6 h
Treatment regimen	Reteplase, 10 + 10 MU bolus doses separated by 30 min, or alteplase, 90-min infusion
Concomitant therapy	Aspirin and iv heparin in all cases
Results	The bolus regimen of reteplase was significantly better than the accelerated alteplase infusion in terms of infarct-related coronary artery patency and flow rates at 60 and 90 min after start. In addition, patients in the reteplase group required coronary angioplasty (PTCA) significantly less frequently than those in the alteplase group

RAPT
Ridogrel versus Aspirin Patency Trial

Authors	The RAPT investigators
Title	Randomized trial of ridogrel, a combined thromboxane A_2 synthase inhibitor and thromboxane A_2/prostaglandin endoperoxide receptor antagonist, versus aspirin as adjunct to thrombolysis in patients with acute myocardial infarction. The Ridogrel versus Aspirin Patency Trial (RAPT)
Reference	*Circulation* 1994;**89**:588–95
Disease	AMI
Purpose	To compare the effect of aspirin and ridogrel, a combined thromboxane A_2 synthase inhibitor and prostaglandin/ endoperoxide receptor antagonist, given as an adjunct to thrombolytic therapy, on coronary patency at predischarge angiography
Study design	Randomised, double-blind, parallel-group
Follow-up	7–14 days
Patients	907 patients, aged < 75 years. Time since onset of symptoms: < 6 h
Treatment regimen	On admission, ridogrel, 300 mg iv, or aspirin, 250 mg iv, then oral ridogrel, 300 mg bid, or oral aspirin, 160 mg once daily until discharge
Concomitant therapy	Streptokinase, 1.5×10^6 U/h
Results	A patent infarct-related vessel was found in 72.2% of patients treated with ridogrel and in 75.5% of patients treated with aspirin. The incidence of major clinical events was also similar for the two groups during hospital stay. In-hospital mortality rates were 6.4% in the ridogrel and 7.1% in the aspirin group. A 32% lower incidence of new ischaemic events was seen with ridogrel compared to aspirin (13% vs 19%; p < 0.025). More bleeding complications were noted in the ridogrel group

RED-LIP
Reduction in Lipid metabolism study

Authors	Sinzinger H, Pirich Ch, and the RED-LIP study team
Title	The RED-LIP study – Pravastatin in primary isolated hypercholesterolemia – an open, prospective, multicenter trial
Reference	*Wien Klin Wochenschr* 1994;**106**:721–7
Disease	Primary isolated hypercholesterolaemia (Fredrickson type IIa hyperlipoproteinaemia)
Purpose	To assess the therapeutic effect on total cholesterol, low-density lipoprotein (LDL), high-density lipoprotein (HDL), and triglycerides as well as safety of pravastatin in patients with primary hypercholesterolaemia
Study design	Open
Follow-up	3 months
Patients	715 patients (352 men, mean age 53.6 ± 10.3 years, and 363 women, mean age 58.6 ± 11.7 years) presenting with severe primary hypercholesterolaemia not responding to dietary counselling for 3 months. Additional patients included in the safety assessment (total = 1111 patients)
Treatment regimen	Pravastatin, 10 mg at bedtime. If the response was inadequate, the dose could be increased to 20 or 40 mg/day after 4 or 8 weeks of therapy
Results	Treatment with pravastatin led to significant decreases in total cholesterol (by 23.8%), LDL cholesterol (by 31.9%) and triglycerides (by 16.9%) together with a significant increase in the HDL cholesterol level (by 15%); the total cholesterol/HDL cholesterol ratio was reduced by almost 36%. By the end of treatment, 67.2% of 122 patients initially classed as being at high cardiovascular risk (including those with coronary heart disease) could be categorised in a lower risk group. Adverse reactions were infrequent and mainly involved gastrointestinal disturbances. Elevations of creatine kinase or transaminase levels were observed in only a few cases, and were reversible

REDUCE

Randomized, Double-blind, Unfractionated heparin and placebo-controlled, multicenter trial

Authors	Karsch KR, Preisack MB, Baildon R, Eschenfelder V, Foley D, Garcia EJ, Kaltenbach M, Meisner C, Selbmann HK, Serruys PW, Shiu MF, Sujatta M, Bonan R
Title	Low molecular weight heparin (reviparin) in percutaneous transluminal coronary angioplasty. Results of a randomized, double-blind, unfractionated heparin and placebo-controlled, multicenter trial (REDUCE trial)
Reference	*J Am Coll Cardiol* 1996;**28**:1437–43
Disease	Angina pectoris, stable or unstable
Purpose	To evaluate whether reviparin given intraarterially and iv during coronary angioplasty (PTCA) and then subcutaneously after PTCA can reduce the incidence of restenosis compared to treatment with unfractionated heparin or placebo
Study design	Randomised, double-blind, placebo-controlled
Follow-up	30 weeks
Patients	625 patients with single-lesion coronary artery obstructions suitable for PTCA
Treatment regimen	Reviparin, 10,000 U iv bolus before PTCA, followed by 10,500 U iv infusion over 24 h, then 3500 U bid sc for 28 days, or (control group) unfractionated heparin, as 10,000 U iv bolus before PTCA, followed by 24,000 U iv infusion over 24 h, then placebo sc for 28 days
Results	Treatment failure, defined as the occurrence of death, MI, bypass surgery or repeat PTCA in the observation period, was recorded in 33.3% of the reviparin group and 32% of the control group. There were no significant differences between these two groups with regard to the incidences of angiographic restenosis, angina requiring repeat PTCA, death, MI or the need for revascularisation surgery, or bleeding complications. Acute events immediately after PTCA (day 1) occurred in 3.9% of reviparin patients and 8.2% of control patients (p = 0.027), and emergency stent implantation in the acute stage was required in 6 reviparin patients and 21 control patients (p = 0.003)

REFLECT
Randomized Evaluation of Flosequinan on Exercise Tolerance study

Authors	Packer M, Narahara KA, Elkayam U *et al*
Title	Double-blind, placebo-controlled study of the efficacy of flosequinan in patients with chronic heart failure
Reference	*J Am Coll Cardiol* 1993;**22**:65–72
Disease	Heart failure
Purpose	To test the efficacy of flosequinan in patients with chronic heart failure
Study design	Randomised, double-blind, placebo-controlled
Follow-up	3 months
Patients	193 patients with chronic heart failure, NYHA class II or III and left ventricular ejection fraction < 40%
Treatment regimen	Flosequinan, 100 mg once daily, or placebo
Concomitant therapy	Digoxin and frusemide
Results	After 12 weeks, maximal treadmill exercise time increased by 96 s in the flosequinan group but by only 47 s in the placebo group (p = 0.022). Symptomatically, 55% of patients receiving flosequinan and 36% of patients receiving placebo benefitted from treatment (p = 0.018). Fewer patients treated with flosequinan had worsening heart failure requiring withdrawal from the study. However, by intention-to-treat analysis, 7 patients in the flosequinan and 2 patients in the placebo group died (p > 0.10). The mode of death was sudden in 7 patients (5 flosequinan, 2 placebo). Other adverse events were similar in the two groups
Comments	A similar study, the PROFILE (Prospective Randomised Flosequinan Longevity Evaluation) study, was terminated early because of excess deaths in the flosequinan group

REGICOR
Registre Gironí del COR

Authors	**(a)** Marrugat J, Antó JM, Sala J, Masiá R, and the REGICOR investigators **(b)** Sala J, Marrugat J, Masiá R, Porta M, and the REGICOR investigators
Titles	**(a)** Influence of gender in acute and long-term cardiac mortality after a first myocardial infarction **(b)** Improvement in survival after myocardial infarction between 1978–85 and 1986–88 in the REGICOR study
References	**(a)** *J Clin Epidemiol* 1994;**47**:111–8 **(b)** *Eur Heart J* 1995;**16**:779–84
Disease	MI
Purpose	To assess changes in 28-day and 3-year survival after a first MI between 1978–85 and 1986–88 in the REGICOR registry
Study design	Case review, epidemiological
Follow-up	3–12 years
Patients	All patients aged 25–74 years, resident in Girona (Spain) and admitted to a hospital with a coronary care unit between 1978 and 1988 with a definite diagnosis of first transmural MI. There were 1216 patients (1023 men and 193 women), with 834 in 1978–85 and 372 in 1986–88
Treatment regimen	Standard treatment
Results	New therapeutic modalities were adopted in the Girona coronary care unit in 1986, reflecting a general change in practice regarding the management of MI. Compared to the first period, patients admitted in the second period were more frequently hypertensive or diabetic, and more often had a history of angina. Patients in the second period had better 28-day survival than those in the first period; after adjusting for diabetes, hypertension, age and sex, the relative risk of 28-day mortality was 0.65 in the second period compared to the first, and this was largely due to lower severity of MI. However, the 3-year mortality of those surviving 28 days was the same in both periods (8.3%). Compared to men, women had a relative risk of 1.56 of dying in the acute phase of MI, mainly due to greater severity of infarction. Their relative risk of long-term mortality was 1.37, but in this case the cause was only partly related to severity of infarction

REGRESS
Regression Growth Evaluation Statin Study

Authors	**(a)** Jukema JW, Bruschke AVG, van Boven AJ, Reiber JHC, Bal ET, Zwinderman AH, Jansen H, Boerma GJM, van Rappard FM, Lie KI **(b)** de Groot E, Jukema JW, van Boven AJ, Reiber JHC, Zwinderman AH, Lie KI, Ackerstaff RA, Bruschke AVG **(c)** Jukema JW, Zwinderman AH, van Boven AJ, Reiber JHC, van der Laarse A, Lie KI, Bruschke AVG
Titles	**(a)** Effects of lipid-lowering by pravastatin on progression and regression of coronary artery disease in symptomatic men with normal to moderately elevated serum cholesterol levels. The Regression Growth Evaluation Statin Study (REGRESS) **(b)** Effect of pravastatin on progression and regression of coronary atherosclerosis and vessel wall changes in carotid and femoral arteries: a report from the Regression Growth Evaluation Statin Study **(c)** Evidence for a synergistic effect of calcium channel blockers with lipid-lowering therapy in retarding progression of coronary atherosclerosis in symptomatic patients with normal to moderately raised cholesterol levels
References	**(a)** *Circulation* 1995;**91**:2528–40 **(b)** *Am J Cardiol* 1995;**76**:40C–6C **(c)** *Arterioscler Thromb Vasc Biol* 1996;**16**:425–30
Disease	Myocardial ischaemia, coronary artery disease
Purpose	To assess the lipid-lowering effects of pravastatin in normocholesterolaemic men with myocardial ischaemia
Study design	Randomised, double-blind, placebo-controlled
Follow-up	2 years
Patients	884 men (434 placebo, 450 pravastatin), aged 40–70 years, with proven myocardial ischaemia and serum cholesterol levels of 155–310 mg/dl, about to undergo routine coronary arteriography
Treatment regimen	Pravastatin, 40 mg once daily, or placebo
Concomitant therapy	Dietary advice, other lipid-lowering agents not allowed and stopped minimum 6–12 weeks before start of trial
Results	Mean segment diameter decreased more in the placebo group than in the pravastatin group (0.10 mm vs 0.06 mm, p = 0.019). Median minimum obstruction diameter decreased more in the placebo group than in the pravastatin group (0.09 mm vs 0.03 mm, p = 0.001). At the end of follow-up, 89% of pravastatin-treated patients and 81% of the placebo-treated patients were without new cardiovascular events (p = 0.002). Lipid levels did not change in the placebo

group, but fell by 20% (total cholesterol), 29% (low-density lipoprotein cholesterol), and 7% (triglycerides) in the pravastatin group. High-density lipoprotein increased 10% in the pravastatin group. Co-treatment with pravastatin and a calcium antagonist slowed the progression of established atherosclerosis, and significantly decreased the formation of new lesions by 50% ($p = 0.0026$) compared to pravastatin without calcium antagonist. No such effects were found in the placebo group. No beneficial effect of calcium antagonists on clinical events was observed

REIN
Ramipril Efficacy In Nephropathy
Ongoing trial

Authors	**(a)** Gruppo Italiano Studi Epidemiologici in Nefrologia (G.I.S.E.N.) **(b)** The GISEN Group
Titles	**(a)** A long term, randomized clinical trial to evaluate the effects of ramipril on the evolution of renal function in chronic nephropathies **(b)** Randomised placebo-controlled trial of effect of ramipril on decline in glomerular filtration rate and risk of terminal renal failure in proteinuric, non-diabetic nephropathy
References	**(a)** *J Nephrol* 1991;**3**:193–202 **(b)** *Lancet* 1997;**349**:1857–63
Disease	Chronic non-diabetic nephropathy with proteinuria
Purpose	To compare the effects of treatment with ramipril and placebo on the rate of decline of glomerular filtration rate (GFR) in patients with chronic non-diabetic nephropathy and proteinuria. Secondary endpoints: 24-h proteinuria, end-stage renal events plus cardiovascular events and death, and lipid profile
Study design	Randomised, double-blind, placebo-controlled (2 years) plus open (3 more years)
Follow-up	Planned 2 years plus 3 years; part of patients ended < 2 years
Patients	352 patients, 186 with proteinuria 1.0–2.9 g/24 h (stratum 1) and 166 with proteinuria ≥ 3.0 g/24 h (stratum 2)
Treatment regimen	Double-blind phase: ramipril, 1.25–5 mg/day, or placebo Open phase: ramipril, 1.25 mg/day, if necessary increased to a maximum of 5 mg/day
Results	117 patients in stratum 2 had at least 3 GFR evaluations and were used for calculations. The mean rate of GFR decline per month was significantly lower in the ramipril-treated patients than in the placebo group, 0.53 vs 0.88 ml/min (p = 0.03). Urinary protein excretion decreased significantly (p < 0.01) by month 1 in the ramipril group and remained lower than baseline throughout the study period. There was no change in urinary protein excretion in the placebo group. The need for transplantation or dialysis and doubling of S-creatinine were significantly decreased in the ramipril group (p = 0.02). Blood pressure control and the overall number of cardiovascular events were simular in the two treatment groups. The study is continuing for stratum 1 patients

Comments   At the second planned interim analysis, the significant effect of ramipril on GFR decline in patients from stratum 2 led to a decision to break the code for these patients and make the final analysis

REPAIR
Reperfusion in Acute Infarction, Rotterdam study

Authors	Bouten MJM, Simoons ML, Hartman JAM, van Miltenburg AJM, van der Does E, Pool J
Title	Prehospital thrombolysis with alteplase (rt-PA) in acute myocardial infarction
Reference	*Eur Heart J* 1992;**13**:925–31
Disease	AMI
Purpose	To evaluate feasibility and safety of prehospital thrombolytic therapy administered by specially trained ambulance paramedics
Study design	Open
Follow-up	Acute study
Patients	226 patients, men aged < 75 and women 55–75 years, with chest pain and the requisite ECG criteria
Treatment regimen	Alteplase, 10 mg iv in 1 min, then 40 mg over 1 h and 50 mg over 2 h
Concomitant therapy	In hospital: heparin, 5000 U iv bolus, then 1000 U/h for at least 24 h. Aspirin, 600 mg orally, or 250 mg iv, then 100 mg orally on alternate days
Results	Prehospital thrombolytic therapy was initiated 100 ± 56 min after the onset of symptoms, and within 22 ± 9 min after ambulance arrival. Time gained by prehospital treatment was 47 min, in comparison to patients receiving thrombolytic therapy after hospital admission. 3 patients were defibrillated during transportation and 6 (3%) died after arrival in hospital. No bleeding complications occurred before hospital admission

RESOLVD
Randomized Evaluation of Strategies for Left Ventricular Dysfunction pilot trial

Authors	**(a)** McKelvie R, Yusuf S, Wiecek E, Tsuyuki R, Rouleau J, Held P, Lindgren E, Avezum A Jr, Maggioni A, Probstfield J **(b)** Yusuf S, Maggioni AP, Held P, Rouleau J-L
Titles	**(a)** A trial of combination neurohormonal blockade with an ACE inhibitor, a β-blocker, and an angiotension II blocker in patients with congestive heart failure (CHF) **(b)** Effects of candesartan, enalapril or their combination on exercise capacity, ventricular function, clinical deterioration and quality of life in heart failure: Randomized Evaluation of Strategies for Left Ventricular Dysfunction (Resolvd)
References	**(a)** In: Heart Failure '97 Second International Meeting organised under the auspices of the Working Group on Heart Failure. Cologne, Germany: European Society of Cardiology, 1997:**42** **(b)** *Circulation* 1997;**96**(suppl I):I-452
Disease	Congestive heart failure (CHF)
Purpose	To determine the efficacy and tolerability of monotherapy vs combination drug therapy in CHF patients
Study design	Randomised, 2-staged, factorial
Follow-up	4.5 months for stage I and 6 months for stage II
Patients	769 patients randomised in stage I and 426 patients in stage II
Treatment regimen	Stage I – Group A: candesartan cilexetil (subgroups – 4 mg, 8 mg, 16 mg, once daily), Group B: candesartan cilexetil (subgroups – 4 mg, 8 mg, once daily) plus enalapril (10 mg bid), Group C: enalapril alone (10 mg bid) Stage II – Metoprolol CR, uptitrated to 200 mg once daily, or placebo, given in addition to stage I therapy
Concomitant therapy	All other necessary medications, except: non-study ACE inhibitors or angiotensin II antagonists; non-study β-blockers in stage II
Results	Candesartan cilexetil and enalapril had similar effects on exercise capacity, ventricular function and neurohormones. The combination of candesartan cilexetil and enalapril improved ejection fraction and decreased ventricular volumes compared to the monotherapies. A similar result was obtained with metoprolol CR vs placebo

RISC
Research on Instability in Coronary artery disease

Authors	**(a)** The RISC group **(b)** Wallentin LC and the Research Group on Instability in Coronary Artery Disease in Southeast Sweden
Titles	**(a)** Risk of myocardial infarction and death during treatment with low dose aspirin and intravenous heparin in men with unstable coronary artery disease **(b)** Aspirin (75 mg/day) after an episode of unstable coronary artery disease: long-term effects on the risk for myocardial infarction, occurrence of severe angina and the need for revascularization
References	**(a)** *Lancet* 1990;**336**:827–30 **(b)** *J Am Coll Cardiol* 1991;**18**:1587–93
Disease	Unstable coronary artery disease
Purpose	To assess the effects of aspirin and/or heparin in patients presenting with unstable angina or non-Q-wave MI and to compare the long-term effects of aspirin and placebo in these patients
Study design	Randomised, double-blind, placebo-controlled
Follow-up	Aim 1 year, minimum 3 months
Patients	796 men (187 aspirin, 210 aspirin plus heparin, 198 heparin and 199 placebo), aged < 70 years. Time since onset of symptoms: 24–72 h
Treatment regimen	Aspirin, 75 mg/day for at least 3 months, and/or heparin, 30,000 U iv for 5 days, or placebo
Concomitant therapy	Metoprolol given to all patients unless contraindicated, and nitrates when needed. Calcium antagonists given if necessary
Results	Event rate (MI or death) in the group treated with oral placebo was 5.8% after 5 days, 13.4% after 1 month, and 17.1% after 3 months. Aspirin treatment reduced event rate at 5 days and thereafter by 57–69%. The risk ratio at 5 days for the aspirin group was 0.43, at 3 months 0.36 and at 1 year 0.52. Heparin had no significant influence on event rate, though the group treated with aspirin and heparin had the lowest number of events during the initial 5 days. Severe angina necessitating referral to coronary angiography was less common during aspirin therapy. Gastrointestinal symptoms with aspirin became more frequent after 3 months compared to placebo
Comments	The Safety Committee advised discontinuation of the trial after publication of ISIS-2 in August 1988, which demonstrated the beneficial effects of aspirin

ROBUST
Recanalization of chronically Occluded aortocoronary saphenous vein Bypass grafts with long-term, low dose direct infusion of Urokinase Trial

Authors	Hartmann JR, McKeever LS, O'Neill WW, White CJ, Whitlow PL, Gilmore PS, Doorey AJ, Galichia JP, Enger EL
Title	Recanalization of chronically occluded aortocoronary saphenous vein bypass grafts with long-term, low dose direct infusion of urokinase (ROBUST): a serial trial
Reference	*J Am Coll Cardiol* 1996;**27**:60–6
Disease	Coronary artery disease with chronically occluded bypass grafts and uncontrolled angina pectoris
Purpose	To evaluate the short-term efficacy and safety of prolonged, low-dose direct urokinase infusion in the recanalisation of chronically occluded saphenous vein bypass grafts
Study design	Open
Follow-up	6 months
Patients	107 patients (79% men), mean age 61 years, with coronary bypass graft occlusion. Most were seen within 1 month of occlusion, but others up to 6 months after occlusion
Treatment regimen	After initial angiography, an angiographic catheter was securely seated in the orifice of the occluded graft. An infusion wire was inserted at least 2 cm into the occlusion and urokinase was infused coaxially at 50,000 U/h proximally and distally (totally 100,000 U/h) for at least 24 h; the dose could be increased to 360,000 U/h if necessary. Repeat angiography was performed at 4–8 h, 22–26 h or at the completion of infusion. Balloon angioplasty was performed when the thrombus was resolved or no further improvement was seen
Concomitant therapy	Heparin during and after urokinase infusion in all cases
Results	Initial patency of the occluded graft was achieved in 74 patients (69%) with a mean infusion time of 25.4 h, and a mean urokinase dosage of 3.70 million units. Follow-up angiograms at 6 months were obtained in 40 patients, 16 of whom (40%) still had a patent graft. Angina was present at 6 months in 22% of patients with successful and 71% with unsuccessful recanalisation. Acute adverse events included 5 cases of MI, 18 of enzyme elevation, 4 of emergency coronary bypass surgery, and 3 of stroke. There were 7 deaths, all among patients with unsuccessful recanalisation. The clinical results may be improved further if the procedure is applied strictly according to protocol in patients with only one occluded vein graft

ROCKET
Regionally Organised Cardiac Key European Trial

Authors	Fox K, Pool J, Vos J, Lubsen J
Title	The effects of nisoldipine on the total ischaemic burden: the results of the ROCKET study
Reference	*Eur Heart J* 1991;**12**:1283–7
Disease	Coronary artery disease, silent ischaemia
Purpose	To define the prevalence of silent ischaemia in the general population and assess its therapeutic implications
Study design	Randomised, double-blind, crossover, placebo-controlled
Follow-up	2 weeks for each treatment
Patients	52 patients with ≥ 6 episodes of silent ischaemia in 48 h or a total duration of painless ST-segment depression of 30 min during 48 h
Treatment regimen	Nisoldipine, 5 mg bid or 10 mg once daily, or placebo
Concomitant therapy	19 patients were treated concurrently with β-blockers
Results	Neither dose of nisoldipine affected the workload that could be achieved nor did concurrent β-blockade. The rate pressure product at peak exercise and 1 mm ST-segment depression were not affected by nisoldipine, nor was the circadian distribution of ischaemic episodes

4S
Scandinavian Simvastatin Survival Study

Authors	**(a), (b)** and **(d)** The Scandinavian Simvastatin Survival Study group **(c)** Kjekshus J, Pedersen TR **(e)** Pedersen TR, Berg K, Cook TJ, Færgeman O, Haghfelt T, Kjekshus J, Miettinen T, Musliner TA, Olsson AG, Pyörälä K, Thorgeirsson G, Tobert JA, Wedel H, Wilhelmsen L **(f)** Reckless JPD **(g)** Jönsson B, Johannesson M, Kjekshus J, Olsson AG, Pedersen TR, Wedel H
Titles	**(a)** Design and baseline results of the Scandinavian Simvastatin Survival Study of patients with stable angina and/or previous myocardial infarction **(b)** Randomised trial of cholesterol lowering in 4444 patients with coronary heart disease: the Scandinavian Simvastatin Survival Study (4S) **(c)** Reducing the risk of coronary events: evidence from the Scandinavian Simvastatin Survival Study (4S) **(d)** Baseline serum cholesterol and treatment effect in the Scandinavian Simvastatin Survival Study (4S) **(e)** Safety and tolerability of cholesterol lowering with simvastatin during 5 years in the Scandinavian Simvastatin Survival Study **(f)** The 4S study and its pharmacoeconomic implications **(g)** Cost-effectiveness of cholesterol lowering. Results from the Scandinavian Simvastatin Survival Study (4S)
References	**(a)** *Am J Cardiol* 1993;**71**:393–400 **(b)** *Lancet* 1994;**344**:1383–9 **(c)** *Am J Cardiol* 1995;**76**:64C–8C **(d)** *Lancet* 1995;**345**:1274–5 **(e)** *Arch Intern Med* 1996;**156**:2085–92 **(f)** *PharmacoEconomics* 1996;**9**:101–5 **(g)** *Eur Heart J* 1996;**17**:1001–7
Disease	Coronary artery disease and mild or moderate hypercholesterolaemia
Purpose	To investigate whether long-term treatment with simvastatin in patients with serum total cholesterol levels between 5.5 and 8.0 mmol/l will reduce overall mortality. Secondarily, whether the incidence of major coronary artery disease events is reduced by simvastatin
Study design	Randomised, double-blind, placebo-controlled
Follow-up	Minimum 3 years, median 5.4 years
Patients	4444 men and women, aged 35–69 years, with coronary artery disease and serum total cholesterol between 5.5 and 8.0 mmol/l after 8 weeks of dietary treatment

Treatment regimen	Simvastatin, 20 mg once daily, or placebo. If serum cholesterol > 5.2 mmol/l at 6 or 18 weeks of therapy, simvastatin, 40 mg once daily, or placebo
Concomitant therapy	Dietary advice 8 weeks prior to randomisation
Results	Over a median of 5.4 years of follow-up, simvastatin produced mean changes in total cholesterol, low-density lipoprotein (LDL) cholesterol, and high-density lipoprotein (HDL) cholesterol of -25%, -35%, and +8%, respectively. In the placebo group 12% of patients died, in the simvastatin group 8%, a risk reduction of 30% (p = 0.0003) attributable to a 42% decrease in the risk of coronary death. 28% of patients in the placebo group and 19% in the simvastatin group had one or more major coronary events (risk reduction 34%, p < 0.00001). Active treatment lead to a 37% reduction in the risk of undergoing myocardial revascularisation procedures (p < 0.00001). A significant reduction in major coronary events was noted in 202 diabetic patients treated with simvastatin compared to placebo (p = 0.002), and in women and patients of both sexes ≥ 60 years. The relative risk reduction for major coronary events in the simvastatin group was 35% in the lowest quartile of baseline LDL cholesterol and 36% in the highest. Simvastatin significantly reduced the risk of major coronary events in all quartiles of baseline total, HDL and LDL cholesterol, by a similar amount in each quartile. The only clearly drug-related serious adverse event was a single reversible case of myopathy. Simvastatin use was associated with a 32% reduction in the total cost of hospitalisation compared to the use of placebo. The cost of simvastatin therapy per discounted life-year saved was £5502

SAFE
Safety After Fifty Evaluation

Authors	**(a)** Rich MW, LaPalio L, Shork A **(b)** LaPalio L, Schork A, Glasser S, Tifft C
Titles	**(a)** The Safety After Fifty Evaluation trial: evaluation of the safety and efficacy of antihypertensive therapy with metoprolol in patients 50 to 75 years of age: study design **(b)** Safety and efficacy of metoprolol in the treatment of hypertension in the elderly
References	**(a)** *Am Heart J* 1988;**116**:301–4 **(b)** *J Am Geriatr Soc* 1992;**40**:354–8
Disease	Mild to moderate hypertension
Purpose	To evaluate the short-term efficacy and safety of metoprolol alone or in combination with low-dose hydrochlorothiazide in patients with mild to moderate hypertension, aged 50–75 years
Study design	Open
Follow up	8 weeks
Patients	21,692 patients, aged 50–75 years (mean 60 ± 9 years). Diastolic blood pressure at entry: 90–104 mm Hg
Treatment regimen	Metoprolol, 100 mg/day, and, if necessary, after 4 weeks, hydrochlorothiazide, 25 mg/day
Results	Mean systolic and diastolic blood pressures decreased significantly after 4 weeks of therapy, from 162/95 to 148/87 mm Hg ($p < 0.001$). 58% of patients had satisfactory blood pressure control. At 8 weeks, a further decrease in blood pressure was seen (143/84 mm Hg). Blood pressure response was similar in all age groups. At the termination of the study, 50% of patients were continued on metoprolol monotherapy and 27% on combined therapy. Adverse events were reported in 4.5% of patients. Good or excellent tolerability was noted in 94% of patients

SALT
Swedish Aspirin Low-dose Trial

Authors	The SALT collaborative group
Title	Swedish aspirin low-dose trial (SALT) of 75 mg aspirin as secondary prophylaxis after cerebrovascular ischaemic events
Reference	*Lancet* 1991;**338**:1345–9
Disease	Cerebrovascular ischaemia
Purpose	To study the efficacy of aspirin, 75 mg/day, in preventing stroke and death after a transient ischaemic attack or minor stroke
Study design	Randomised, double-blind, placebo-controlled
Follow-up	12–63 months (median 32 months)
Patients	1360 patients who had suffered a transient ischaemic attack, minor ischaemic stroke, or retinal artery occlusion within the previous 3 months (676 aspirin and 684 placebo)
Treatment regimen	Aspirin, 75 mg/day, 30 min before breakfast, or placebo
Concomitant therapy	Products containing aspirin and non-steroidal anti-inflammatory drugs were not permitted. Paracetamol was prescribed for minor pains
Results	In the aspirin group, there was an 18% reduction in the risk of the primary outcome events, stroke or death (relative risk 0.82), compared to the placebo group. There was also a 16–20% reduction in the risk of the secondary outcome events (ie, stroke, two or more transient ischaemic attacks (TIA) within a week of each other necessitating a change of treatment, or MI) in the aspirin group compared to the placebo group

SAMI
Streptokinase Angioplasty Myocardial Infarction trial

Authors	O'Neill WW, Weintraub R, Grines CL *et al*
Title	A prospective, placebo-controlled, randomized trial of intravenous streptokinase and angioplasty versus lone angioplasty therapy of acute myocardial infarction
Reference	*Circulation* 1992;**86**:1710–7
Disease	AMI
Purpose	To assess the clinical usefulness of fibrinolysis as an adjunct to primary angioplasty in AMI, and to determine its impact on long-term patency and myocardial salvage
Study design	Randomised, open, parallel-group
Follow-up	6 months
Patients	122 patients (63 percutaneous transluminal coronary angioplasty, PTCA, and 59 PTCA plus streptokinase), aged ≤ 75 years. Time since onset of symptoms: ≤ 4 h
Treatment regimen	PTCA alone or combined with streptokinase, 1.5×10^6 U iv over 30 min, or placebo
Concomitant therapy	Heparin, 10,000 U iv bolus, oral aspirin, 325 mg/day. Oxygen, iv morphine or mepiridine, iv lidocaine. Diltiazem, 30–60 mg qid
Results	Overall, 86% of the treatment group underwent coronary angioplasty, it was successful in 95% of patients, there was no significant difference between the two groups. There were no differences in 24-h or 6-week ejection fractions between the two groups. At 6 months, arterial patency was 87% and coronary restenosis was present in 38% of patients, similar for both groups. Rates of reinfarction and mortality were also similar between the two groups. However, adjunctive iv streptokinase complicated the hospital course. Hospitalisation was longer and more costly. There were more bleeding complications and need for emergency coronary bypass surgery was greater for the streptokinase-treated patients

SAPAT
Swedish Angina Pectoris Aspirin Trial

Authors	Juul-Möller S, Edvardsson N, Jahnmatz B *et al*
Title	Double-blind trial of aspirin in primary prevention of myocardial infarction in patients with stable chronic angina pectoris
Reference	*Lancet* 1992;**340**:1421–5
Disease	Chronic angina pectoris
Purpose	Primary prevention of MI in patients with chronic stable angina pectoris
Study design	Randomised, double-blind, placebo-controlled
Follow-up	Mean 50 months (range 23–76 months)
Patients	2035 patients (1009 aspirin and 1026 placebo), aged 30–80 years, with exertional chest pain
Treatment regimen	Aspirin, 75 mg/day, or placebo
Concomitant therapy	Sotalol, 40-480 mg/day (mean 160 mg), for control of symptoms
Results	Compared to the placebo plus sotalol group, the aspirin plus sotalol group had a 34% reduction in MI and sudden death ($p = 0.003$). There was a significant reduction (22–32%) in vascular events, vascular death, stroke and total mortality in the aspirin plus sotalol group. Adverse events, including bleeding, were slightly more common in the aspirin group ($p = ns$)

SAVE
Survival And Ventricular Enlargement study

Authors	**(a)** Pfeffer MA, Braunwald E, Moyé LA *et al* **(b)** Rutherford JD, Pfeffer MA, Moyé LA, Davis BR, Flaker GC, Kowey PR, Lamas GA, Miller HS, Packer M, Rouleau JL, Braunwald E
Titles	**(a)** Effect of captopril on mortality and morbidity in patients with left ventricular dysfunction after myocardial infarction. Results of the Survival And Ventricular Enlargement trial **(b)** Effects of captopril on ischemic events after myocardial infarction. Results of the Survival and Ventricular Enlargement Trial
References	**(a)** *N Engl J Med* 1992;**327**:669–77 **(b)** *Circulation* 1994;**90**:1731–8
Disease	AMI
Purpose	To evaluate the efficacy of captopril, started 3–16 days after MI, in improving survival and preventing deterioration of left ventricular function
Study design	Randomised, double-blind, placebo-controlled
Follow-up	Mean 42 months (range 24–60 months)
Patients	2231 patients, aged 21–80 years, with left ventricular ejection fraction $\leq 40\%$, but no overt heart failure
Treatment regimen	Captopril, started 3–16 days after MI, titrated from 12.5 mg to 25 mg tid before hospital discharge. Where tolerated the dose was progressively increased to 50 mg tid
Concomitant therapy	Thrombolytic therapy when considered appropriate
Results	Mortality from all causes was significantly reduced in the captopril group compared to the placebo group. The reduction in risk was 19% ($p = 0.019$). The risk of recurrent MI was reduced by 25% ($p = 0.015$) and of death after recurrent MI by 32% ($p = 0.029$) captopril-treated patients compared to placebo-treated patients. Captopril-treated patients were less likely to require cardiac revascularisation procedures ($p = 0.01$), but hospitalisation for unstable angina was unaltered. When all 3 major coronary ischaemic events were considered together, captopril reduced the risk by 14% ($p = 0.047$). The following adverse events were more common for the captopril group: dizziness, taste alteration, cough and diarrhoea

SCRIP
Stanford Coronary Risk Intervention Project

Authors	Haskell WL, Alderman EL, Fair JM *et al*
Title	Effects of intensive multiple risk factor reduction on coronary atherosclerosis and clinical cardiac events in men and women with coronary artery disease. The Stanford Coronary Risk Intervention Project (SCRIP)
Reference	*Circulation* 1994;**89**:975–90
Disease	Coronary heart disease
Purpose	To compare the effects of a risk factor intervention programme and conventional therapy on prognosis in coronary heart disease
Study design	Randomised
Follow-up	4 years
Patients	300 patients with coronary artery disease (145 risk reduction and 155 usual care), aged ≤ 75 years
Treatment regimen	Drug therapy and behaviour modification programme to reduce risk factors for coronary heart disease, or usual care
Results	In the risk reduction group, there were significantly greater reductions in total cholesterol, low-density lipoprotein cholesterol levels, body mass index and calorie intake as fat, and significantly greater increases in high-density lipoprotein cholesterol levels and quality of life, than in the usual care group. The reduction in the internal diameter of diseased vessels was also significantly lower in the risk reduction group than in the usual care group

SECURE
Study to Evaluate Carotid Ultrasound changes in patients treated with Ramipril and vitamin E
Ongoing trial

Authors	Lonn EM, Yusuf S, Doris CI, Sabine MJ, Dzavik V, Hutchison K, Riley WA, Tucker J, Pogue J, Taylor W
Title	Study design and baseline characteristics of the Study to Evaluate Carotid Ultrasound Changes in Patients Treated with Ramipril and Vitamin E: SECURE
Reference	*Am J Cardiol* 1996;**78**:914–9
Disease	Cardiovascular disease
Purpose	To investigate the effects of ramipril and vitamin E on the rate of progression of atherosclerotic lesions in the carotid arteries
Study design	Randomised, double-blind, placebo-controlled, 3 × 2 factorial
Follow-up	4 years
Patients	732 patients ≥ 55 years at high risk of cardiovascular events, with documented history of significant cardiovascular disease, or with diabetes and additional risk factors
Treatment regimen	Ramipril, 2.5 mg/day, 10 mg/day, or placebo; plus vitamin E, 400 U/day, or placebo
Results	Not yet available, end of trial planned for late 1998
Comments	This is a substudy of HOPE, the Heart Outcomes Prevention Evaluation study

SESAIR
Studio Eparina Sottocutanea nell'Angina Instabile Refrattaria

Authors	Neri Serneri GG, Modesti PA, Gensini GF, Branzi A, Melandri G, Poggesi L, Rostagno C, Tamburini C, Carnovali M, Magnani B
Title	Randomised comparison of subcutaneous heparin, intravenous heparin, and aspirin in unstable angina
Reference	*Lancet* 1995;**345**:1201–4
Disease	Unstable angina
Purpose	To assess the effectiveness of sc heparin compared to heparin infusion and to aspirin in the management of myocardial ischaemia in patients with refractory unstable angina
Study design	Randomised
Follow-up	1 month
Patients	108 patients (69 men and 39 women), mean age 35–37 years, with unstable angina refractory to conventional antianginal treatment
Treatment regimen	(1) Heparin, 5000 U iv, followed by 1000 U/h. Dose was adjusted to maintain partial thromboplastin time (PTT) between 1.5 and 2 times the baseline. (2) Heparin, 5000 U iv, followed by 5000–10,000 U sc tid. The most appropriate dose was identified according to body weight and sex. Time of sc injection was adjusted according to PTT. (3) Oral aspirin, 325 mg/day
Concomitant therapy	Conventional antianginal therapy (aspirin, isosorbide dinitrate, nifedipine, metoprolol, nitroglycerin) in all patients, as required
Results	Aspirin treatment did not significantly alter the incidence of myocardial ischaemia as assessed by the frequency and duration of angina attacks. During the 3-day trial, heparin treatment led to significant improvement in ischaemia: in the infused heparin group the frequency of angina was reduced by 91%, the frequency of silent ischaemia by 56%, and the duration of ischaemia by 66%. The respective figures were 86%, 46% and 61% in the sc heparin group. The adverse effects included only 4 cases of minor bleeding complications (2 with aspirin and 2 with iv heparin)

SESAM
Study in Europe with Saruplase and Alteplase in Myocardial infarction

Authors	Bär FW, Meyer J, Vermeer F, Michels R, Charbonnier B, Haerten K, Spiecker M, Macaya C, Hanssen M, Heras M, Boland JP, Morice M-C, Dunn FG, Uebis R, Hamm C, Ayzenberg O, Strupp G, Withagen AJ, Klein W, Windeler J, Hopkins G, Barth H, von Fisenne JM
Title	Comparison of saruplase and alteplase in acute myocardial infarction
Reference	*Am J Cardiol* 1997;**79**:727–32
Disease	AMI
Purpose	To compare the effect of saruplase and alteplase on reocclusion rate within 24–40 h after start of thrombolytic therapy in patients with a new AMI. Secondary, to compare patency rates at 45 and 60 min after start of study therapy
Study design	Randomised, double-blind, double-dummy
Follow-up	24–40 h
Patients	473 patients, aged ≤ 70 years, with chest pain ≥ 30 min within the last 6 h
Treatment regimen	Saruplase, 80 mg iv or 20 mg iv bolus plus 60 mg infusion, or alteplase, 10 mg iv bolus plus 50 mg infusion/1 h plus 40 mg infusion/2 h
Concomitant therapy	Heparin, 5000 U bolus before the thrombolytic and 500 U bolus before catheterisation, plus infusion to activated partial thromboplastin time 1.5–2.5 × normal during 24–40 h, and aspirin, 80–120 mg/day
Results	Early patency rates (45 and 60 min after therapy start) were high for both saruplase and alteplase and not different. Reocclusion rates for both drugs were very low, and complication rates were similar

SHAPE

Study of Heparin and Actilyse Processed Electronically

Authors	Patterson DLH, Bailey RJ, Murray M *et al*
Title	Evaluation of patient benefit and resource use after early treatment of myocardial infarction with heparin and recombinant tissue type plasminogen activator (Actilyse): Study of Heparin and Actilyse Processed Electronically (SHAPE)
Reference	*Br Heart J* 1991;**66**:62
Disease	AMI
Purpose	To evaluate the effects of early treatment of MI with heparin and recombinant tissue type plasminogen activator (rt-PA) with respect to patient benefit and use of resources
Study design	Randomised, double-blind, placebo-controlled
Follow-up	12 months
Patients	594 patients (435 rt-PA and 159 placebo). Aim 3000
Treatment regimen	rt-PA, 100 mg, plus heparin, or placebo plus heparin
Results	There was no significant difference between the two groups with respect to patient benefit. Bleeding complications were seen in 12% of patients in the rt-PA group compared to 3% in the placebo group. The incidence of stroke was very low in both groups. There was little difference in the use of resources. In the rt-PA group, there was some increase in survival, but this was not significant
Comments	The trial was discontinued prematurely on ethical grounds

SHARP
Subcutaneous Heparin and Angioplasty Restenosis Prevention

Authors	Brack MJ, Ray S, Chauhan A, Fox J, Hubner PJB, Schofield P, Harley A, Gershlick AH
Title	The Subcutaneous Heparin and Angioplasty Restenosis Prevention (SHARP) trial. Results of a multicentre randomized trial investigating the effects of high dose unfractionated heparin on angiographic restenosis and clinical outcome
Reference	*J Am Coll Cardiol* 1995;**26**:947–54
Disease	Coronary artery disease
Purpose	To determine whether a high dose subcutaneous regimen of unfractionated heparin given for 4 months after coronary angioplasty (PTCA) can influence the subsequent rate of angiographic restenosis and the incidence of clinical events
Study design	Randomised, parallel-group clinical trial with blinded data analysis
Follow-up	4 months
Patients	339 patients (approx. 81% men), mean age approx. 56 years, who had undergone successful PTCA for angiographically demonstrated narrowing of one or more coronary arteries
Treatment regimen	After angioplasty under iv heparin cover, either unfractionated heparin, 12,500 U sc bid, or no heparin
Concomitant therapy	All patients received aspirin. Calcium antagonists, nitrates and β-blockers were given as required
Results	Repeat angiography was undertaken in 159 patients in the no-heparin group and 140 in the heparin group. Of these patients, 23 in the no-heparin group and 16 in the heparin group underwent angiography before 4 months because of the return of angina; the others were examined after 4 months. There were no significant differences between the treatment groups with regard to the decrease in minimal lumen diameter between the immediate post-angioplasty measurement and the follow-up measurement. Similarly, the two groups were comparable with regard to the incidence of clinical events and the presence of angina at 4 months

SHELL
Systolic Hypertension in the Elderly
Long-term Lacidipine trial
Ongoing trial

Authors	Malacca E, Gnemmi AE, Romagnoli A, Coppini A
Title	Systolic Hypertension in the Elderly: Long-term Lacidipine treatment. Objective, protocol, and organization
Reference	*J Cardiovasc Pharmacol* 1994;**23**(suppl 5):S62–6
Disease	Hypertension, cardiovascular events
Purpose	The efficacy of lacidipine-based treatment is to be compared to thiazide-like diuretic (chlorthalidone)-based treatment in elderly patients with isolated systolic hypertension
Study design	Randomised, blinded evaluation of endpoints, open
Follow-up	36–60 months
Patients	Aim 4800 patients, aged $\geq$ 60 years, with isolated systolic hypertension, defined as systolic blood pressure of $\geq$ 160 mm Hg with diastolic blood pressure of $\leq$ 95 mm Hg
Treatment regimen	Lacidipine, 4–6 mg/day initially, or chlorthalidone, 12.5–25 mg/day. If blood pressure was not controlled, fosinopril, 10 mg/day, was added in both groups
Results	Not yet available

SHEP
Systolic Hypertension in the Elderly Program

Authors	**(a)** SHEP Cooperative Research Group **(b)** Black HR, Curb JD, Pressel S, Probstfield JL, Stamler J, eds **(c)** Davis BR, Wittes J, Pressel S, Berge KG, Hawkins CM, Lakatos E, Moyé LA, Probstfield JL **(d)** Bearden D, Allman R, McDonald R, Miller S, Pressel S, Petrovitch H, and the SHEP Cooperative Research Group
Titles	**(a)** Prevention of stroke by antihypertensive drug treatment in older persons with isolated systolic hypertension. Final results of the Systolic Hypertension in the Elderly Program (SHEP) **(b)** Systolic Hypertension in the Elderly Program (SHEP) **(c)** Statistical considerations in monitoring the Systolic Hypertension in the Elderly Program (SHEP) **(d)** Age, race, and gender variation in the utilization of coronary artery bypass surgery and angioplasty in SHEP
References	**(a)** *JAMA* 1991;**265**:3255–64 **(b)** *Hypertension* 1991;**17**(suppl II):II-1–171 **(c)** *Control Clin Trials* 1993;**14**:350–61 **(d)** *J Am Geriatr Soc* 1994;**42**:1143–9
Disease	Isolated systolic hypertension
Purpose	To determine whether antihypertensive drug treatment reduces the risk of total stroke (both nonfatal and fatal) in men and women with isolated systolic hypertension, aged ≥ 60 years
Study design	Randomised, double-blind, placebo-controlled
Follow-up	Mean 4.5 years
Patients	4736 patients (57% women), aged ≥ 60 years (mean 72 years), with systolic blood pressure 160–219 mm Hg (mean 170 mm Hg) and diastolic blood pressure < 90 mm Hg (mean 77 mm Hg)
Treatment regimen	Chlorthalidone, 12.5 mg/day. If the systolic blood pressure goal was not achieved at follow-up, the dose of chlorthalidone was doubled and, if necessary, changed to atenolol, 25 mg/day (or reserpine, 0.05 mg/day, if atenolol contraindicated), also doubled if required
Concomitant therapy	Potassium supplements in all patients with serum potassium levels < 3.5 mmol/l at two consecutive visits
Results	At 5 years, the average systolic blood pressure was 155 mm Hg in the placebo group and 143 mm Hg in the active treatment group, and the average diastolic blood pressures were 72 mm Hg and 68 mm Hg, respectively. The 5-year incidence of total stroke was 5.2% in the active treatment group and 8.2% in the placebo group; the relative risk,

calculated by proportional hazards regression analysis, was 0.64 (p = 0.0003). The relative risk of clinical nonfatal MI plus coronary death, which was the secondary endpoint, was 0.73. Major cardiovascular events were also reduced (relative risk 0.68). The relative risk of death from all causes was 0.87. Patients > 75 years and women underwent fewer intensive cardiovascular interventions than did patients 60–75 years and men. Active treatment was significantly associated with decreased use of coronary artery bypass grafting and percutaneous transluminal coronary angioplasty in patients < 75 years with coronary heart disease

SIAM
Streptokinase In Acute Myocardial infarction trial

Authors	Özbek C, Dyckmans J, Sen S, Schieffer H
Title	Comparison of invasive and conservative strategies after treatment with streptokinase in acute myocardial infarction. Results of a randomised trial (SIAM)
Reference	*J Am Coll Cardiol* 1990;**15**(suppl A):63A
Disease	AMI
Purpose	To compare the effects of invasive and conservative strategies after treatment with streptokinase in patients with AMI
Study design	Randomised, open, parallel-group
Follow-up	21 days
Patients	324 patients with suspected AMI (166 in the conservative group and 158 in the invasive group). Time since onset of symptoms: ≤ 4 h
Treatment regimen	Streptokinase, 1.5×10^6 U iv over 1 h, together with either a conservative or invasive therapeutic strategy. Conservative strategy: no coronary arteriography or percutaneous transluminal coronary angioplasty (PTCA) during the first 21 days, and coronary arteriography only prior to discharge. Invasive strategy: transfer to tertiary hospital, early coronary arteriography 14–48 h after start of treatment and predischarge control coronary arteriography
Results	Global ejection fraction was $55 \pm 11\%$ in the conservative group and $55 \pm 10\%$ in the invasive group. Reinfarction occurred following PTCA in 1 patient in the conservative group and in 7 patients in the invasive group, and without PTCA in 27 patients in the conservative group and 11 patients in the invasive group. Total mortality was 10 in the conservative group and 14 in the invasive group

SLIP
Study on Lipids with Isoptin Press

Authors	Libretti A, Catalano M
Title	Lipid profile during antihypertensive treatment. The SLIP study
Reference	*Drugs* 1993;**46**(suppl 2):16–23
Disease	Mild to moderate hypertension
Purpose	To test the effects of verapamil and enalapril on plasma lipids in hypertensive patients
Study design	Randomised, parallel-group
Follow-up	6 months
Patients	931 patients (437 verapamil and 427 enalapril), aged < 70 years, with diastolic blood pressure 95–115 mm Hg
Treatment regimen	Verapamil sustained release, 240 mg once daily, or enalapril, 20 mg once daily
Concomitant therapy	For patients with diastolic blood pressure > 95 mm Hg after 1 month of monotherapy, enalapril, 20 mg once daily, was added to verapamil treatment, or hydrochlorothiazide, 12.5 mg once daily, was added to enalapril treatment. Additional therapy as required
Results	65.1% of evaluable patients (864) were successfully treated with monotherapy and 25.5% required combined therapy. Systolic and diastolic blood pressure and heart rate were significantly reduced by both verapamil and enalapril. Total cholesterol, triglycerides and low-density lipoprotein levels were significantly reduced by both treatments. High-density lipoprotein levels were significantly increased by verapamil but not by enalapril (p < 0.01). Adverse events occurred in 3.9% of patients receiving verapamil and 2.7% of patients receiving enalapril

SMILE
Survival of Myocardial Infarction Long-term Evaluation

Authors	**(a)**, **(b)**, and **(c)** Ambrosioni E, Borghi C, Magnani B
Titles	**(a)** The SMILE study: rationale, design, organization and definition of the outcomes **(b)** Survival of myocardial infarction long-term evaluation (SMILE) study: rationale, design, organization, and outcome definitions **(c)** The effect of the angiotensin-converting-enzyme inhibitor zofenopril on mortality and morbidity after anterior myocardial infarction
References	**(a)** *Ann Ital Med Int* 1993;**8**:230–4 **(b)** *Control Clin Trials* 1994;**15**:201–10 **(c)** *N Engl J Med* 1995;**332**:80–5
Disease	Anterior AMI
Purpose	To determine whether an angiotensin-converting enzyme inhibitor could reduce short-term mortality and occurrence of severe refractory congestive heart failure in patients with anterior MI not undergoing thrombolysis
Study design	Randomised, double-blind, placebo-controlled
Follow-up	6 weeks on treatment, 1 year of observation
Patients	1556 patients (784 placebo, 772 zofenopril) with no history of congestive heart failure and presenting < 24 h after onset of symptoms
Treatment regimen	Zofenopril, 7.5–30 mg bid, or placebo
Results	Incidence of death or severe congestive heart failure at 6 weeks was significantly reduced by zofenopril compared to placebo (7.1% vs 10.6%); the cumulative risk reduction was 34% (p = 0.018). The risk reduction with zofenopril was 46% (p = 0.018) for severe congestive heart failure and 25% (p = 0.19) for death. After 1 year, the mortality rate was significantly lower in the zofenopril group than in the placebo group (10.0% vs 14.1%); risk reduction was 29% (p = 0.011)
Comments	SMILE pilot study reported in: *Am J Cardiol* 1991;**68**:101D–10D

SMT
Stockholm Metoprolol Trial

Authors	**(a)** Olsson G, Rehnqvist N, Sjögren A, Erhardt L, Lundman T **(b)** and **(c)** Olsson G, Rehnqvist N **(d)** Olsson G, Odén A, Johansson L, Sjögren A, Rehnqvist N
Titles	**(a)** Long-term treatment with metoprolol after myocardial infarction: effect on 3 year mortality and morbidity **(b)** Evaluation of antiarrhythmic effect of metoprolol treatment after acute myocardial infarction: relationship between treatment responses and survival during a 3-year follow-up **(c)** Reduction in nonfatal reinfarctions in patients with a history of hypertension by chronic postinfarction treatment with metoprolol **(d)** Prognosis after withdrawal of chronic postinfarction metoprolol treatment: a 2–7-year follow-up
References	**(a)** J Am Coll Cardiol 1985;**5**:1428–37 **(b)** Eur Heart J 1986;**7**:312–9 **(c)** Acta Med Stand 1986;**220**:33–8 **(d)** Eur Heart J 1988;**9**:365–72
Disease	AMI
Purpose	To evaluate the effect of metoprolol on chronic ventricular arrhythmias, exercise performance and standard biochemical values, and to determine morbidity and mortality in different risk strata
Study design	Randomised, double-blind, placebo-controlled
Follow-up	3 years on therapy followed by 2–7 years after termination of therapy
Patients	301 patients (154 metoprolol and 147 placebo), aged < 70 years. Time since onset of AMI: 11–18 days
Treatment regimen	Metoprolol, 50 mg tid for first 3 days, then 100 mg bid
Results	There were non-significant reductions in the total number of deaths (23%) and the number of cardiac deaths (34%) in the metoprolol group. Metoprolol significantly reduced cardiac deaths in the subgroup of patients with a large infarct ($p < 0.05$) sudden death rates ($p < 0.05$) and the incidence of nonfatal reinfarction ($p < 0.05$). Atherosclerotic complications were significantly reduced ($p < 0.001$). In the group, there was an increase in complexity of arrhythmias ($p < 0.001$) and frequency of premature ventricular complexes ($p < 0.001$) with time. These increases were blunted in the metoprolol group. Of the patients with a history of hypertension, 41 were in the placebo group and 35 in the metoprolol group. The reduction in blood pressure was identical in both groups. Fatal and nonfatal events

occurred in 24 patients in the placebo group and 8 patients in the metoprolol group (p < 0.01). Exercise-induced ventricular arrhythmias were significantly more common in the placebo group during the initial 6 months. ST depression carried prognostic weight for reinfarction or death in the placebo group, but not in the metoprolol group. Following termination of metoprolol therapy, the mortality risk was doubled (Cox hazard model)

SOLVD
Studies Of Left Ventricular Dysfunction

Authors	**(a), (b)** and **(c)** The SOLVD investigators **(d)** Rogers WJ, Johnstone DE, Yusuf S, Weiner DH, Gallagher P, Bittner VA, Ahn S, Schron E, Shumaker SA, Sheffield LT **(e)** Pratt CM, Gardner M, Pepine C, Kohn R, Young JB, Greenberg B, Capone R, Kostis J, Henzlova M, Gosselin G, Weiss M, Francis M, Stewart D, Davis E, Yusuf S **(f)** Greenberg B, Quinones MA, Koilpillai C, Limacher M, Shindler D, Benedict C, Shelton B **(g)** Glick H, Cook J, Kinosian B, Pitt B, Bourassa MG, Pouleur H, Gerth W
Titles	**(a)** Studies of left ventricular dysfunction (SOLVD) – rationale, design and methods: two trials that evaluate the effect of enalapril in patients with reduced ejection fraction **(b)** Effect of enalapril on survival in patients with reduced left ventricular ejection fractions and congestive heart failure **(c)** Effect of enalapril on mortality and the development of heart failure in asymptomatic patients with reduced left ventricular ejection fractions **(d)** Quality of life among 5,025 patients with left ventricular dysfunction randomized between placebo and enalapril: the studies of left ventricular dysfunction **(e)** Lack of long-term ventricular arrhythmia reduction by enalapril in heart failure **(f)** Effects of long-term enalapril therapy on cardiac structure and function in patients with left ventricular dysfunction. Results of the SOLVD echocardiography substudy **(g)** Costs and effects of enalapril therapy in patients with symptomatic heart failure: an economic analysis of the studies of left ventricular dysfunction (SOLVD) treatment trial
References	**(a)** *Am J Cardiol* 1990;**66**:315–22 **(b)** *N Engl J Med* 1991;**325**:293–302 **(c)** *N Engl J Med* 1992;**327**:685–91 **(d)** *J Am Coll Cardiol* 1994;**23**:393–400 **(e)** *Am J Cardiol* 1995;**75**:1244–9 **(f)** *Circulation* 1995;**91**:2573–81 **(g)** *J Card Fail* 1995;**1**:371–80
Disease	Left ventricular (LV) dysfunction with and without congestive heart failure (CHF)
Purpose	To investigate whether enalapril improves long-term survival in patients with LV dysfunction with and without a history of overt CHF. Secondary objectives: to demonstrate its effects in different subgroups of patients, eg group according to plasma sodium, vasodilator treatment, ejection fraction, aetiology, and NYHA class. Also to study effects on LV function and volume, arrhythmias, quality of life, and pharmacoeconomy
Study design	Randomised, double-blind, placebo-controlled

Follow-up	> 3 years
Patients	Men and women aged 21–80 years, with LV ejection fraction ≤ 0.35. Prevention trial: 4228 patients (2111 enalapril and 2117 placebo) without overt CHF. Treatment trial: 2568 patients (1285 enalapril and 1284 placebo) with overt CHF
Treatment regimen	Enalapril, 2.5 or 5 mg bid initially, increased to 5 or 10 mg bid after 2 weeks (10 mg bid recommended)
Concomitant therapy	Other treatment not restricted, except for the use of non-angiotensin-converting enzyme (ACE) inhibitor vasodilators. Efforts were made to discontinue these drugs, unless clearly indicated, during the prerandomisation period; if coronary heart failure develops or worsens after randomisation, diuretics, digitalis, or non-ACE inhibitor vasodilators should be used first
Results	Prevention trial: There were 334 deaths in the placebo group and 313 in the enalapril group. This represents a risk reduction of 8% (p = 0.30). The reduction in mortality from cardiovascular causes was larger but still not statistically significant. However, the combined incidence of death and development of overt CHF showed a risk reduction of 29% (p < 0.001). Treatment trial: There were 510 deaths in the placebo group and 452 in the enalapril group. This represents a risk reduction of 16% (p = 0.0036). The greatest reduction was seen in the number of deaths attributed to progressive heart failure. The following analyses were performed in patients from both trials: – Quality of life was assessed in 2560 patients from the prevention trial and 2465 from the treatment trial. No apparent changes in quality of life for ≥ 1 year was observed in the patients treated with enalapril in the prevention trial and only modest benefits in quality of life occurred in the enalapril-treated patients in the treatment trial. – 734 of the patients underwent ambulatory ECG at baseline and at 4 and 12 months of therapy. There were no significant differences in ventricular arrhythmia development over 1 year between placebo- and enalapril-treated patients. – 301 patients underwent Doppler-echocardiographic evaluations before and at 4 and 12 months of therapy. LV end-diastolic and end-systolic volumes increased in placebo- but not in enalapril-treated patients (p < 0.05 for both). LV mass tended to increase in placebo patients and to decrease in enalapril-treated patients (p ≤ 0.001). – For the 48 months within the treatment trial, study participants who received enalapril lived an average of 0.16 undiscounted year longer than did patients who received placebo. The lifetime projection of this indicated that participants who received enalapril would be expected to live, on average, 0.40 year longer than those who received placebo. Within the trial, the patient receiving enalapril costed on the average about USD720 less than

the patient receiving placebo, due to higher costs for hospitalisations. In lifetime projections, the costs per year of life saved and per quality-adjusted year of life saved were estimated to be USD80 and USD115, respectively

Comments   In connection with the SOLVD studies a registry for patients with LV dysfunction and/or CHF has been composed. This registry is available for several kinds of evaluations, such as medications used and risk factor assessments

SPAF
Stroke Prevention in Atrial Fibrillation

Authors	**(a)** and **(b)** Stroke Prevention in Atrial Fibrillation study group investigators
Titles	**(a)** Preliminary report of the Stroke Prevention in Atrial Fibrillation Study **(b)** Stroke prevention in atrial fibrillation study. Final results
References	**(a)** *N Engl J Med* 1990;**322**:863–8 **(b)** *Circulation* 1991;**84**:527–39
Disease	Nonrheumatic atrial fibrillation
Purpose	To investigate the safety and efficacy of warfarin and aspirin (as separate treatments) for the primary prevention of ischaemic stroke and systemic thromboembolism in patients with atrial fibrillation unrelated to rheumatic valvular disease
Study design	Randomised, open (warfarin), double-blind (aspirin-placebo), placebo-controlled, parallel-group
Follow-up	Mean 1.3 years
Patients	1330 patients with atrial fibrillation. The group eligible to receive warfarin (group 1) comprised 627 patients (210 warfarin, 206 aspirin and 211 placebo) and the group not eligible to receive warfarin (group 2) comprised 703 patients (346 aspirin and 357 placebo)
Treatment regimen	Warfarin adjusted to prolong prothrombin time to achieve an international normalised ratio between 2.0 and 3.5, and/or aspirin, 325 mg/day
Results	In group 1, the rate of systemic stroke and systemic embolism was substantially reduced in those assigned to warfarin (2.3%/ year) compared to placebo (7.4%/year) (p = 0.01; risk reduction 67%). The risk of death or a primary event was reduced by 58% in those receiving warfarin (p = 0.01). There was also a 54% reduction in disabling ischaemic stroke or vascular death in those receiving warfarin compared to placebo. In all patients receiving aspirin (groups 1 and 2 combined), there were fewer primary events (3.6%/year; p = 0.02; risk reduction 42%) and an overall reduction in primary events or death of 32% (p = 0.02). The risk reduction for ischaemic strokes, transient ischaemic attacks and systemic emboli in this double-blinded portion of the study was 44% (p < 0.01). Disabling ischaemic stroke or vascular death was reduced by 22% (p = 0.33) in patients receiving aspirin compared to placebo
Comments	Due to the weight of evidence that both aspirin and warfarin were superior to placebo, the placebo arm of group 1 was terminated in November 1989

SPAF II
Stroke Prevention in Atrial Fibrillation II study

Authors	**(a)** Stroke Prevention in Atrial Fibrillation investigators **(b)** Ezekowitz MD, James KE
Titles	**(a)** Warfarin versus aspirin for prevention of thromboembolism in atrial fibrillation: Stroke Prevention in Atrial Fibrillation II study **(b)** Stroke Prevention in Atrial Fibrillation II study (letter)
References	**(a)** *Lancet* 1994;**343**:687–91 **(b)** *Lancet* 1994;**343**:1508–9
Disease	Atrial fibrillation
Purpose	To assess the differential effects of warfarin and aspirin in preventing ischaemic stroke in patients with atrial fibrillation in two age-groups
Study design	Randomised, open, parallel-group
Follow-up	Mean 2.3 years
Patients	1100 patients, 715 aged ≤ 75 years and 385 aged > 75 years
Treatment regimen	Warfarin, to give an international normalised ratio 2.0–4.5, or aspirin, 325 mg/day
Results	In the younger patients warfarin decreased the absolute rate of primary events by 0.7% per year compared to aspirin. The primary event rate per year was 1.3% with warfarin and 1.9% with aspirin (p = 0.24). Among older patients warfarin decreased the absolute rate of primary events by 1.2% per year compared to aspirin. The primary event rate per year was 3.6% with warfarin and 4.8% with aspirin (p = 0.39). In this older group the rate of all stroke with residual deficit (ischaemic or haemorrhagic) was 4.3% per year with aspirin and 4.6% per year with warfarin. In younger patients rates of major haemorrhage were 0.9% per year with aspirin and 1.7% per year with warfarin (p = 0.17). For older patients, the data were, respectively, 1.6% and 4.2% (p = 0.04). In older patients assigned to warfarin, the annual rate of intracranial haemorrhage was significantly higher than in younger patients (p = 0.05)
Comments	Randomisation was done separately for the two age-groups, ≤ 75 years and > 75 years. The randomisation procedure has been questioned, and the conclusion that for those < 75 years the event rate with aspirin is low enough to warrant its use in preference to warfarin

SPAF III
Stroke Prevention in Atrial Fibrillation III study

Authors	**(a)** Zabalgoitia M **(b)** Cowburn P, Cleland JGF
Titles	**(a)** Stroke prevention in atrial fibrillation III and trans-oesophageal echo study. Design and progress report **(b)** SPAF-III results
References	**(a)** *Eur Heart J* 1994;**15**(abstr suppl):28 **(b)** *Eur Heart J* 1996;**17**:1129
Disease	Atrial fibrillation
Purpose	To assess whether a combination of fixed, low-dose warfarin and aspirin is as effective as, but safer and better tolerated than, adjusted-dose warfarin in high-risk patients with atrial fibrillation (AF). Secondary objectives: to establish that an acceptably low rate of stroke ($< 3\%$ per year) can be achieved by aspirin alone in low-risk AF patients, and to evaluate transoesophageal echo (TEE) for selection of antithrombotic therapy
Study design	Not stated
Follow-up	3 years
Patients	1724 patients with atrial fibrillation, including 680 with no risk factors for the subsequent development of stroke (low-risk group) and 1044 with at least one risk factor (high-risk group). In the latter group, the mean age was 72 years and 45% of patients had heart failure
Treatment regimen	Low-risk patients: aspirin, 325 mg/day. High-risk patients: warfarin, at a dose sufficient to maintain the international normalised ratio (INR) between 2.0 and 3.0 (conventional anticoagulation therapy), or warfarin in a fixed dose of 0.5–3.0 mg/day, adjusted initially to give an INR of 1.2–1.5, plus 325 mg/day aspirin (low-dose warfarin + aspirin therapy)
Results	The low-risk trial is ongoing, and the high-risk trial was terminated prematurely due to an excess of strokes in the low-dose warfarin group. The annualised rate of primary events was 7.9% in the low-dose warfarin group and 1.9% in the conventional warfarin group. Conventional dose warfarin should be regarded as the optimal treatment for the majority of patients with atrial fibrillation

SPINAF
Stroke Prevention in Nonrheumatic Atrial Fibrillation

Authors	Ezekowitz MD, Bridgers SL, James KE *et al*
Title	Warfarin in the prevention of stroke associated with nonrheumatic atrial fibrillation
Reference	*N Engl J Med* 1992;**327**:1406–12
Disease	Nonrheumatic atrial fibrillation
Purpose	To investigate whether anticoagulation with warfarin would reduce the risk of stroke associated with nonrheumatic atrial fibrillation
Study design	Randomised, double-blind, placebo-controlled
Follow-up	3 years
Patients	571 men with chronic nonrheumatic atrial fibrillation, of whom 46 had had a previous cerebral infarction
Treatment regimen	Warfarin, given as 2 mg tablets to maintain an international normalised ratio of 1.4–2.8, or placebo
Results	For patients with no history of stroke receiving placebo, cerebral infarction occurred in 4.3% per year compared to 0.9% per year for the warfarin group. The risk reduction with warfarin was 0.79 (p = 0.001). The annual event rate for patients aged > 70 years was 4.8% in the placebo group and 0.9% in the warfarin group (risk reduction 0.79; p = 0.02). Cerebral infarction was more common among patients with a history of cerebral infarction, 9.3% per year in the placebo group and 6.1% per year in the warfarin group. Both major and minor haemorrhages were slightly more common in the warfarin group

SPIRIT
Stroke Prevention In Reversible Ischemia Trial

Author	Algra A
Title	SPIRIT: Bleeding complications in patients after cerebral ischemia treated with anticoagulant drugs
Reference	*Stroke* 1997;**28**:231
Disease	Transient ischaemia or ischaemic stroke
Purpose	To compare the efficacy and safety of daily aspirin and anticoagulant drugs in patients after a transient ischaemic attack or minor ischaemic stroke
Study design	Randomised, open, blind assessment
Follow-up	Planned 2.9 years; fulfilled 1200 person-years
Patients	Aim 3000 patients (1243 randomised)
Treatment regimen	Aspirin, 30 mg/day, or anticoagulant drugs to give an international normalised ratio of 3.0–4.4
Results	There was an excess of primary outcome events (death from all vascular causes, stroke, MI, or major bleeding complications) in the anticoagulant therapy group, 54/616 vs 26/627 in the aspirin group
Comments	The trial was stopped early, after about 1200 person-years, due to 36 major bleeding complications in the anticoagulant therapy group vs 5 in the aspirin group

SPRINT II
Secondary Prevention Reinfarction
Israeli Nifedipine Trial II

Authors	Goldbourt U, Behar S, Reicher-Reiss H *et al*
Title	Early administration of nifedipine in suspected acute myocardial infarction. The Secondary Prevention Reinfarction Israel Nifedipine Trial 2 study
Reference	*Arch Intern Med* 1993;**153**:345–53
Disease	AMI
Purpose	To evaluate the secondary prevention potential of nifedipine, titrated to 60 mg/day and administered as early as possible in the course of evolving AMI in patients at high risk
Study design	Randomised, double-blind, placebo-controlled
Follow-up	6 months
Patients	1006 patients (1358 randomised), aged 50–79 years. Time from admission: ≤ 48 h in 25% of patients and ≤ 3 h in 75% of patients
Treatment regimen	Nifedipine, 60 mg/day, reached within a 6-day titration period
Results	In the 1006 patients mortality was 18.7% for those randomised to nifedipine and 15.6% in those receiving placebo. This reflected an increased mortality of 7.8% compared to 5.5% during the first 6 days in the nifedipine and placebo groups, respectively. Among the 826 patients who continued the treatment for 6 months, mortality was similar in the nifedipine (9.3%) and placebo (9.5%) groups. Nonfatal MI occurred in 5.1% of patients in the nifedipine group and 4.2% of patients in the placebo group
Comments	After analysis of all 1358 randomised patients, an excess mortality was observed in the nifedipine group with 105 deaths (15.4%) compared to 90 deaths (13.3%) in the placebo group. This difference was entirely due to an excess in early (6-day) mortality with nifedipine. The study was discontinued as soon as this was known

SSSD
Spanish Study on Sudden Death

Authors	Navarro-López F, Cosin J, Marrugat J, Guindo J, Bayes de Luna A
Title	Comparison of the effects of amiodarone versus metoprolol on the frequency of ventricular arrhythmias and on mortality after acute myocardial infarction
Reference	*Am J Cardiol* 1993;**72**:1243–8
Disease	AMI
Purpose	To assess the efficacy of amiodarone vs metoprolol or no treatment to prevent death and sudden death in post-MI patients with left ventricular ejection fraction ≤ 45% and frequent ventricular arrhythmias
Study design	Randomised, open, controlled
Follow-up	Mean 2.8 years
Patients	368 patients, aged < 75 years, 10–60 days after AMI with left ventricular ejection fraction 20–45% and ≥ 3 ventricular premature complexes per hour
Treatment regimen	Amiodarone, 600 mg/day the first week, 400 mg/day the second week, then 200 mg/day, or metoprolol, 50–100 mg bid, or no treatment
Results	After a mean follow-up of 2.8 years, mortality in the amiodarone group (3.5%) did not differ significantly from that of untreated control subjects (7.9%) but was lower than that in the metoprolol group (15.4%, p < 0.006). The difference between the metoprolol group and the control group was not significant. Holter studies performed at 1, 6 and 12 months showed that both amiodarone and metoprolol reduced heart rate, but only amiodarone significantly reduced mortality due to ectopic beats

STAI
Studio della Ticlopidina nell'Angina Instabile

Authors	Balsano F, Rizzon P, Violi F *et al*
Title	Antiplatelet treatment with ticlopidine in unstable angina. A controlled multicenter clinical trial
Reference	*Circulation* 1990;**82**:17–26
Disease	Unstable angina pectoris
Purpose	To investigate whether ticlopidine influences the clinical course of unstable angina
Study design	Randomised, open, standard-care-controlled
Follow-up	6 months
Patients	652 patients (314 ticlopidine and 338 control) with 5 or more attacks of rest angina, with one of 15 min duration, in the week before admission to hospital
Treatment regimen	Ticlopidine, 250 mg bid, administered within 48 h of hospitalisation
Concomitant therapy	Conventional therapy with β-blockers, calcium antagonists and nitrates in all patients, including those on ticlopidine
Results	By intention-to-treat analysis, total mortality was 2.5% in the ticlopidine group and 4.7% in the control group, which represents a 46.8% reduction with ticlopidine (p = 0.139). Nonfatal MI occurred in 4.8% of patients in the ticlopidine group and 8.9% of patients in the control group, which represents a 46.1% reduction with ticlopidine (p = 0.039). Fatal and nonfatal MI was 5.1% in the ticlopidine group and 10.9% in the control group, a risk reduction of 53.2% (p = 0.006)

STARC
Studio Trapidil versus Aspirina nella Restenosi Coronarica

Authors	Maresta A, Balducelli M, Cantini L, Casari A, Chioin R, Fabbri M, Fontanelli A, Preti PAM, Repetto S, De Servi S, Varani E
Title	Trapidil (triazolopyrimidine), a platelet-derived growth factor antagonist, reduces restenosis after percutaneous transluminal coronary angioplasty. Results of the randomized, double-blind STARC study
Reference	*Circulation* 1994;**90**:2710–5
Disease	Coronary artery disease
Purpose	To assess the effects of trapidil in the prevention of angiographic restenosis after coronary angioplasty (PTCA)
Study design	Randomised, double-blind, controlled
Follow-up	6 months
Patients	384 patients (254 evaluated), aged 18–75 years, with functionally significant stenosis in one or more principal coronary arteries suitable for PTCA
Treatment regimen	Trapidil, 100 mg tid, or aspirin, 100 mg tid, both for 6 months
Concomitant therapy	Calcium antagonists, nitrates, β-blockers and paracetamol as required
Results	Restenosis occurred in 24.2% of trapidil patients and 39.7% of aspirin patients (p < 0.01). Clinical events were similar in the two groups, except that recurrence of angina was significantly more frequent in the aspirin group (43.7%) than in the trapidil group (25.8%). Six patients in each group dropped out due to adverse events

STILE
Surgery vs Thrombolysis for Ischemia of the Lower Extremity

Authors	The STILE investigators
Title	Results of a prospective randomized trial evaluating Surgery *Versus* Thrombolysis for Ischemia of the Lower Extremity. The STILE trial
Reference	*Ann Surg* 1994;**220**:251–68
Disease	Leg ischaemia
Purpose	To evaluate intra-arterial thrombolytic therapy as part of a treatment strategy for patients requiring revascularisation for leg ischaemia due to non-embolic occlusion of an artery or graft
Study design	Randomised, open
Follow-up	1 year
Patients	393 patients, aged 18–90 years, with signs or symptoms of worsening limb ischaemia within the past 6 months or with angiographically documented non-embolic arterial or bypass graft occlusion
Treatment regimen	Either the most appropriate surgical procedure or intra-arterial, catheter-directed thrombolysis with recombinant tissue plasminogen activator (rt-PA) or urokinase. rt-PA as a continuous infusion at 0.5 mg/kg/h for up to 12 h; urokinase as a bolus of 250,000 U followed by infusion at 4000 U/min for 4 h, then 2000 U/min for up to 36 h
Results	The catheter could not be correctly placed in 28% of patients who were randomised for thrombolysis, and these were considered to be treatment failures. Clinical outcomes, particularly amputation and persistent ischaemia, were better with thrombolysis than with surgery in patients whose ischaemia had lasted for ≤ 14 days before treatment, whereas the outcomes were better with surgery than with thrombolysis in patients whose ischaemia had lasted for >14 days before treatment. A significant reduction in planned surgery was obtained after thrombolysis. There was no difference in efficacy or safety between rt-PA and urokinase. A combination strategy of catheter-directed thrombolysis for acute limb ischaemia and surgical revascularisation for chronic limb ischaemia offers the best overall result

STIMS
Swedish Ticlopidine Multicentre Study

Authors	**(a)** Janzon L, Bergqvist D, Boberg J *et al* **(b)** Bergqvist D, Almgren B, Dickinson JP
Titles	**(a)** Prevention of myocardial infarction and stroke In patients with intermittent claudication; effects of ticlopidine. Results from STIMS, the Swedish Ticlopidine Multicentre Study **(b)** Reduction of requirement for leg vascular surgery during long-term treatment of claudicant patients with ticlopidine: results from the Swedish Ticlopidine Multicentre Study (STIMS)
References	**(a)** *J Intern Med* 1990;**227**:301–8 (erratum **228**:659) **(b)** *Eur J Vasc Endovasc Surg* 1995;**10**:69–76
Disease	Intermittent claudication
Purpose	To assess whether the incidence of MI, stroke and transient ischaemic attacks in patients with intermittent claudication can be reduced with ticlopidine
Study design	Randomised, double-blind, placebo-controlled
Follow-up	7 years
Patients	687 patients (346 ticlopidine and 341 placebo), aged < 70 years, with a history of intermittent claudication
Treatment regimen	Ticlopidine, 250 mg bid
Concomitant therapy	All patients were monitored for known cardiovascular risk factors, and received other treatment if necessary (eg, β-blockers, calcium antagonists and/or diuretics for hypertension; special diet and, if necessary, clofibrate for hyperlipidaemia; special diet and, when appropriate, oral hypoglycaemic agents for high blood glucose). Patients were advised not to take medication containing aspirin
Results	The number of endpoints (89 in the ticlopidine group and 99 in the placebo group) was 11.4% lower in the ticlopidine group (p = 0.24). The mortality rate was 29.1% lower in the ticlopidine group (64 deaths vs 89 deaths; p = 0.015), mainly due to a reduced mortality from ischaemic heart disease. On-treatment analysis showed significantly fewer endpoints in the ticlopidine group (47 vs 76; p = 0.017). Side-effects led to permanent withdrawal of treatment in more patients in the ticlopidine group (73 vs 26). The overall rate of first vascular reconstructive surgery was 2.4%/year. Ticlopidine reduced the need for vascular reconstructive surgery by about half (p < 0.01)

STONE
Shanghai Trial Of Nifedipine in the Elderly

Authors	Gong L, Zhang W, Zhu Y, Zhu J, 11 collaborative centres in the Shanghai area, Kong D, Pagé V, Ghadirian P, LeLorier J, Hamet P
Title	Shanghai Trial Of Nifedipine in the Elderly (STONE)
Reference	*J Hypertens* 1996;**14**:1237–45
Disease	Hypertension
Purpose	To assess the efficacy of nifedipine in elderly hypertensives
Study design	Single-blind, placebo-controlled
Follow-up	36 months, mean 30 months
Patients	1632 mainly Chinese patients (765 men and 867 women), aged 60–79 years, with systolic blood pressure ≥ 160 mm Hg or diastolic blood pressure ≥ 96 mm Hg.
Treatment regimen	After a 4-week placebo run-in period, nifedipine, 10 mg bid, increasing up to 60 mg as required for blood pressure control, or placebo. 74 patients with severe hypertension were switched from placebo to nifedipine
Concomitant therapy	Captopril and/or dihydrochlorothiazide, if required
Results	Blood pressure was reduced in both treatment groups, but the effect was significantly greater in the nifedipine group than in the placebo group, and the disparity increased with increasing duration of treatment. Compared to placebo, treatment with nifedipine led to a significant reduction in the relative risk for strokes and severe arrhythmia, and can be recommended for the management of elderly hypertensives

STOP-Hypertension
Swedish Trial in Old Patients with Hypertension

Authors	**(a)** Hansson L, Dahlöf B, Ekbom T, Lindholm L, Scherstén B, Wester P-O **(b)** Dahlöf B, Lindholm LH, Hansson L, Scherstén B, Ekbom T, Wester P-O **(c)** Dahlöf B, Hansson L, Lindholm LH, Scherstén B, Ekbom T, Wester P-O **(d)** Johannesson M, Dahlöf B, Lindholm LH, Ekbom T, Hansson L, Odéns A, Scherstén B, Wester P-O, Jönsson B
Titles	**(a)** Key learnings from the STOP-Hypertension study: an update on the progress of the ongoing Swedish study of antihypertensive treatment in the elderly **(b)** Morbidity and mortality in the Swedish Trial in Old Patients with Hypertension (STOP-Hypertension) **(c)** Swedish trial in old patients with hypertension (STOP-Hypertension): analyses performed up to 1992 **(d)** The cost-effectiveness of treating hypertension in elderly people – an analysis of the Swedish Trial in Old Patients with Hypertension (STOP-Hypertension)
References	**(a)** *Cardiovasc Drug Ther* 1990;**4**:1253–6 **(b)** *Lancet* 1991;**338**:1281–5 **(c)** *Clin Exp Hypertens* 1993;**15**:925–39 **(d)** *J Intern Med* 1993;**234**:317–23
Disease	Hypertension
Purpose	To determine whether pharmacological treatment of hypertension is beneficial in men and women aged 70–84 years, and to evaluate drug tolerance and effect on non-cardiac, cerebrovascular and total mortality
Study design	Randomised, double-blind, placebo-controlled
Follow-up	1–4 years, mean 25 months
Patients	1627 men and women (812 active treatment and 815 placebo), with systolic blood pressure 180–230 mm Hg and/or diastolic blood pressure 105–120 mm Hg, aged 70–84 years
Treatment regimen	Atenolol, 50 mg/day, or metoprolol CR/ZOC, 100 mg/day, or pindolol, 5 mg/day, or a combination of amiloride and hydrochlorothiazide, 2.5/25 mg/day
Concomitant therapy	If systolic blood pressure was ≥ 160 mm Hg and/or diastolic blood pressure was ≥ 95 mm Hg, the amiloride and hydrochlorothiazide combination was given in addition to atenolol, metoprolol CR/ZOC or pindolol, or vice versa
Results	Active treatment reduced blood pressure significantly more than placebo. At the last follow-up visit (ie, before primary endpoint/death or at study termination), supine blood pressure was 186/96 mm Hg in the placebo group and 167/87

mm Hg in the active treatment group. There were 40% fewer cardiovascular primary endpoints in the active treatment group (p = 0.0031), and 47% fewer fatal and non-fatal strokes (p = 0.0081), as well as a 43% reduction in total mortality (p = 0.0079). There was a total of 94 primary endpoints in the placebo group and 58 in the active treatment group. These effects became more pronounced as the study progressed. There were 132 secondary endpoints (ie, congestive heart failure, blood pressure > 230/120 mm Hg, transient ischaemic attacks or angina pectoris) in the placebo group compared to 40 in the active treatment group. The beneficial effects of active anti-hypertensive treatment were demonstrable up to the age of 84 years (ie, over the entire age range of patients in the study), and women benefitted from active treatment at least as much as men. A pharmaco-economic analysis indicated that treatment of elderly hypertensive men and women with β-blockers and/or diuretics is cost-effective

Comments The study was terminated prematurely after recommendation from the Safety Committee due to the positive outcome for patients on active treatments. All blinded medication was discontinued

STOP-Hypertension 2
Swedish Trial in Old Patients with Hypertension 2
Ongoing trial

Authors	**(a)** Dahlöf B, Hansson L, Lindholm LH *et al* **(b)** Lindholm LH, Hansson L, Dahlöf B, Ekbom T, Hedner T, de Faire U, Scherstén B, Wester P-O
Titles	**(a)** STOP-Hypertension 2: a prospective intervention trial of 'newer' versus 'older' treatment alternatives in old patients with hypertension **(b)** The Swedish Trial in Old Patients with hypertension-2 (STOP-hypertension-2): a progress report
References	**(a)** *Blood Press* 1993;**2**:136–41 **(b)** *Blood Press* 1996;**5**:300–4
Disease	Hypertension
Purpose	To evaluate classical antihypertensive agents, diuretics and β-blockers, vs the newer antihypertensive agents, lisinopril, enalapril, isradipine and felodipine, on cardiovascular mortality and clinical events, eg stroke, AMI and sudden death in elderly hypertensives. Secondary endpoints: new onset of heart failure, atrial fibrillation, diabetes mellitus, or hospitalisations
Study design	Prospective, randomised, open, blinded-endpoint (PROBE design)
Follow-up	4 years
Patients	6628 men (34%) and women (66%), aged 70–84 years, with blood pressure $\geq$ 180/105 mm Hg
Treatment regimen	(1) β-blocker/diuretic: metoprolol CR, 100 mg, atenolol, 50 mg, pindolol, 5 mg, or hydrochlorothiazide plus amiloride, 25 and 2.5 mg, in daily dosages. If uncontrolled, the diuretic combination is given to the β-blocker patients and vice versa (2) Calcium antagonist: felodipine or isradipine, both 2.5–5 mg daily. If uncontrolled, a β-blocker is added (3) ACE inhibitor: enalapril or lisinopril, both 10–20 mg daily. If uncontrolled, hydrochlorothiazide is added
Concomitant therapy	For patients not attaining the treatment goal of supine blood pressure $\leq$ 160/95 mm Hg, additional therapy with hydrochlorothiazide or one of the above β-blockers. For patients still not reaching the treatment goal, addition of an α-blocker
Results	Recruitment ended in end 1994. At 1 year, blood pressure in the whole cohort was lowered from 194/98 mm Hg to 167/85 mm Hg. At end 1995, 319 fatal events (all-cause) had been reported, corresponding to a mortality rate of 21.3/1000 person-years. The study is expected to be completed in 1999

SUTAMI
Saruplase and Urokinase in the Treatment of Acute Myocardial Infarction

Authors	Hoffmann JJML, Michels HR, Windeler J, Günzler WA
Title	Plasma markers of thrombin activity during coronary thrombolytic therapy with saruplase or urokinase: no prediction of reinfarction
Reference	*Fibrinolysis* 1993;7:330–4
Disease	AMI
Purpose	To document the course of thrombin-antithrombin III complex (TAT) and prothrombin fragments 1 and 2 (F_{1+2}) as markers of in vivo thrombin activity during thrombolysis with saruplase or urokinase
Study design	Randomised
Follow-up	72 h
Patients	543 patients, aged 20–75 years, with AMI < 6 h after onset of symptoms. 33 patients had signs of reinfarction
Treatment regimen	Saruplase, 20 mg iv bolus, then 60 mg over 1 h, or urokinase, 1.5×10^6 U iv in 5 min then 1.5×10^6 U over 1 h
Concomitant therapy	Heparin, 15 U/kg/h, started 30 min after the end of thrombolysis until coronary angiography, 24–72 h after treatment start
Results	Both drugs caused considerable systemic degradation of fibrinogen and the degree of systemic lysis was very similar. The median concentrations of both TAT and F_{1+2} significantly increased 3–6-fold after therapy. Following heparin administration, both parameters returned towards normal in most patients. At no time point studied was there any significant difference in these coagulation parameters between the patients with and without reinfarction

SWIFT
Should We Intervene Following Thrombolysis trial

Authors	SWIFT Trial Study Group
Title	SWIFT trial of delayed elective intervention v conservative treatment after thrombolysis with anistreplase in acute myocardial infarction
Reference	*BMJ* 1991;**302**:555–60
Disease	AMI
Purpose	To determine whether early elective angiography with a view to coronary angioplasty or bypass grafting of a stenosed infarct-related vessel improves the outcome in AMI treated by thrombolysis with anisoylated plasminogen streptokinase activator complex (APSAC, anistreplase)
Study design	Randomised, open, parallel-group
Follow-up	12 months
Patients	800 men and women (397 early angiography and 403 conservative care), aged < 70 years. Time since onset of symptoms: 3 h
Treatment regimen	Early coronary angiography with a view to angioplasty or coronary artery grafting, or angiography followed by intervention only if required for conventional clinical indications
Concomitant therapy	APSAC, 30 U iv over 5 min, immediately after entry; heparin, 1000 U/h, by continuous iv infusion started 4–6 h later and changed to oral warfarin when the prothrombin time was > 2.0; timolol, 1 mg/day, started before discharge
Results	At 12 months, the mortality rate in the intervention group was 5.8% and in the conservative care group 5.0% (p = 0.6). The reinfarction rates were 15.1% and 12.9%, respectively (p = 0.4). There were no significant differences in the incidence of angina or rest pain, or in left ventricular ejection fraction. Median hospital stay was 11 days in the intervention group compared to 10 days in the conservative care group (p < 0.0001)

SWISH
Swedish Isradipine Study in Hypertension

Authors	Jern S, Hansson L, Scherstén B *et al*
Title	Swedish Isradipine Study in Hypertension: evaluation of quality of life, safety, and efficacy
Reference	*J Cardiovasc Pharmacol* 1991;**18**(suppl 3):S7–8
Disease	Hypertension
Purpose	To compare the efficacy, tolerability and effects on quality of life of isradipine and atenolol in the treatment
Study design	Randomised, double-blind, parallel-group
Follow-up	24 weeks
Patients	549 patients, mean age 52 years, with diastolic blood pressure (DBP) > 90 mm Hg
Treatment regimen	Either isradipine, 1.25 mg bid, or atenolol, 50 mg once daily. Doses were doubled after 4 weeks if DBP > 90 mm Hg. If after 4 more weeks DBP > 90 mm Hg, isradipine, 1.25 mg bid, was added to atenolol and atenolol, 50 mg once daily, added to isradipine
Results	Both isradipine and atenolol as monotherapy produced significant decreases in blood pressure, though isradipine was slightly less effective. In both groups, 37% of patients reported adverse events, oedema being more common with isradipine, and fatigue, vertigo and cold extremities with atenolol. There were no significant differences between the compounds in quality of life profiles

SWISSI II
Swiss International Study on Silent Ischemia II
Ongoing trial

Authors	Erne P, Evequoz D, Zuber M, Yoon S, Bürckhardt D
Title	Swiss International Study on Silent Ischemia II (SWISSI II): study design and preliminary results
Reference	*Circulation* 1995;**692**(suppl I):I-80
Disease	Silent ischaemia post-AMI
Purpose	To compare the effects of coronary angioplasty (PTCA) and anti-ischaemic drug therapy on clinical events, ie angina pectoris, AMI, need for bypass grafting (CABG) or PTCA, and mortality, in patients with silent ischaemia after AMI
Study design	Randomised, open
Follow-up	At least 3 years
Patients	115 as per April 1995
Treatment regimen	Aloxyprinum, 600 mg/day, and bisoprolol, 10 mg/day, and combinations with amlodipine, 5–10 mg/day, and molsidomine, 8–24 mg/day, or PTCA
Results	In April 1995, 115 patients had been randomised, and had been followed-up for a mean of 1.5 years. No differences in the incidence of combined clinical endpoints were found

SWORD
Survival With Oral d-sotalol

Authors	**(a)** Waldo AL, Camm AJ, deRuyter H, Friedman PL, MacNeil DJ, Pitt B, Pratt CM, Rodda BE, Schwartz PJ **(b)** Waldo AL, Camm AJ, deRuyter H, Friedman PL, MacNeil DJ, Pauls JF, Pitt B, Pratt CM, Schwartz PJ, Veltri EP
Titles	**(a)** Survival with oral d-sotalol in patients with left ventricular dysfunction after myocardial infarction: rationale, design, and methods (the SWORD trial) **(b)** Effect of *d*-sotalol on mortality in patients with left ventricular dysfunction after recent and remote myocardial infarction
References	**(a)** *Am J Cardiol* 1995;**75**:1023–7 **(b)** *Lancet* 1996;**348**:7–12
Disease	AMI with impaired left ventricular function
Purpose	To test the hypothesis that the class III antiarrhythmic agent d-sotalol can reduce all-cause mortality in high-risk survivors of AMI. Secondary endpoints: cardiovascular mortality and arrhythmic events
Study design	Randomised, double-blind, placebo-controlled
Follow-up	Aim at least 18 months
Patients	3121 patients (aim 6400), aged $\geq$ 18 years, with left ventricular dysfunction (ejection fraction $\leq$ 40%) following AMI. Group I includes 915 patients with AMI 6–42 days before randomisation, with or without heart failure. Group II includes 2206 patients with AMI occurring > 42 days before randomisation and a history of overt heart failure
Treatment regimen	d-sotalol, 100–200 mg bid, or placebo
Results	At termination of the study there were 78 deaths among the d-sotalol patients (5.0%) and 48 deaths among the placebo patients (3.1%, p = 0.006). Significantly greater numbers of cardiac and arrhythmic deaths accounted for the increased mortality. In all subgroups of interest, patients on d-sotalol had a higher death rate than those on placebo
Comments	An interim analysis showed increased mortality among patients treated with d-sotalol, and termination of the trial was recommended by the data and safety monitoring board

Syst-China
Systolic hypertension in the elderly: Chinese trial
Ongoing trial

Authors	**(a)** Lisheng L **(b)** Wang JG, Liu G, Wang X, Zhang S, Sun M, Pan X, Jian M, Gong L, Thijs L, Staessen J, Fagard R, Liu L
Titles	**(a)** Effects of hypertension control on stroke incidence and fatality: report from Syst-China and post-stroke antihypertensive treatment **(b)** Long-term blood pressure control in older Chinese patients with isolated systolic hypertension: a progress report on the Syst-China trial
References	**(a)** *J Hum Hypertens* 1996;**10**(suppl 1):S9–11 **(b)** *J Hum Hypertens* 1996;**10**:735–42
Disease	Isolated systolic hypertension
Purpose	To assess whether nitrendipine, if necessary combined with captopril and hydrochlorothiazide, is suitable for maintaining long-term blood pressure control in older Chinese patients with isolated systolic hypertension. Furthermore, whether this therapy can reduce the incidence of stroke and other cardiovascular complications
Study design	Randomised, double-blind, placebo-controlled
Follow-up	At least 3 years
Patients	2379 patients, aged ≥ 60 years, with systolic blood pressure 160–219 mm Hg and diastolic blood pressure < 95 mm Hg
Treatment regimen	Nitrendipine, 10-40 mg/day, plus captopril, 12.5–50 mg/day, and hydrochlorothiazide, 12.5–50 mg/day if necessary, or placebo
Results	Blood pressure was reduced 8/3 mm Hg more in the active therapy group than in the placebo group

SYST-EUR
Systolic hypertension – Europe

Authors	**(a)** Amery A, Birkenhäger W, Bulpitt CJ *et al* **(b)** Celis H, Yodfat Y, Thijs L, Clement D, Cozic J, De Cort P, Forette F, Grégoire M, Heyrman J, Stibbe G, Van den Haute M, Staessen J, Fagard R
Titles	**(a)** SYST-EUR. A multicentre trial on the treatment of isolated systolic hypertension in the elderly: objectives, protocol, and organization **(b)** Antihypertensive therapy in older patients with isolated systolic hypertension: the Syst-Eur experience in general practice
References	**(a)** *Aging* 1991;**3**:287–302 **(b)** *Fam Pract* 1996;**13**:138–43
Disease	Isolated systolic hypertension
Purpose	To investigate whether antihypertensive treatment in elderly patients with isolated systolic hypertension results in a significant change in stroke morbidity and mortality. Secondary objective: to assess the effect of antihypertensive treatment in elderly patients with isolated systolic hypertension on quality of life and the incidence of multi-infarct dementia and whether 24-h blood pressure monitoring improves the prediction of cardiovascular complications
Study design	Randomised, double-blind, placebo-controlled
Follow-up	Planned 6 years, completed median 2 years
Patients	Aim 3000 patients, aged ≥ 60 years, with sitting diastolic blood pressure > 95 mm Hg and systolic blood pressure (SBP) 160–219 mm Hg. Only patients with primary hypertension were included
Treatment regimen	Nitrendipine, 10–40 mg/day, and if necessary enalapril, 5–20 mg/day, and hydrochlorothiazide, 12.5–25 mg/day, to reduce SBP < 150 mm Hg and by ≥ 20 mm Hg, or matching placebos
Concomitant therapy	Advice on non-pharmacological control of blood pressure (eg, weight reduction, salt and alcohol restriction)
Results	Results are available for 18 months' follow-up and 941 patients (485 active treatment, 456 placebo). A total of 40% of patients on active treatment achieved goal blood pressure compared to 15% on placebo (p < 0.001). More patients in the active treatment group remained on monotherapy than in the placebo group. At 1 year, in 421 patients (217 active treatment, 204 placebo) recruited and treated by family physicians, sitting systolic and diastolic blood pressures were significantly reduced by active treatment compared to placebo, fewer patients in the

placebo group remained on monotherapy and second and third line medications were started earlier in this group than in the active treatment group (p < 0.001 for all comparisons)

Comments

References describing the protocols of the side projects:

Quality of life
– Fletcher A, *Blood Pressure* 1993;**2**:45–50

Dementia
– Forette F, *Aging* 1991;**3**:373–82

24-h blood pressure
– Staessen J, *Aging Clin Exp Res* 1992;**4**:85–91

Mortality and morbidity
– Staessen JA *et al*, *Lancet* 1997;**350**:757–64

The trial was stopped in February 1997, as the second interim analysis showed a significant benefit for stroke

TACT
Ticlopidine Angioplastie Coronaire Transluminale

Authors	Bertrand ME, Allain H, Lablanche JM
Title	Results of a randomised trial of ticlopidine versus placebo for prevention of acute closure and restenosis after coronary angioplasty (PTCA). The TACT study
Reference	*Circulation* 1990;**82**(suppl 3):III-190
Disease	Coronary artery stenosis
Purpose	To investigate the effect of ticlopidine on acute closure and restenosis rate, 6 months after percutaneous transluminal coronary angioplasty (PTCA)
Study design	Randomised, double-blind, placebo-controlled
Follow-up	6 months
Patients	266 patients
Treatment regimen	Ticlopidine, 250 mg bid
Results	The acute closure rate was 16.2% in the placebo group and 5.1% in the ticlopidine group (p < 0.01). The restenosis rates were 40.7% and 49.6%, respectively (p = ns)

TAIM
Trial of Antihypertensive Interventions and Management

Authors	**(a)** Davis BR, Blaufox MD, Hawkins CM *et al* **(b)** Wassertheil-Smoller S, Blaufox MD, Oberman A *et al* **(c)** Langford HG, Davis BR, Blaufox MD *et al* **(d)** Wassertheil-Smoller S, Blaufox MD, Oberman AS, Langford HG, Davis BR, Wylie-Rosett J **(e)** Wassertheil-Smoller S, Oberman A, Blaufox MD, Davis B, Langford H **(f)** Davis BR, Oberman A, Blaufox MD, Wassertheil-Smoller S, Zimbaldi N, Kirchner K, Wylie-Rosett J, Langford HG
Titles	**(a)** Trial of antihypertensive interventions and management. Design, methods, and selected baseline results **(b)** Effect of antihypertensives on sexual function and quality of life: the TAIM study **(c)** Effect of drug and diet treatment of mild hypertension on diastolic blood pressure **(d)** The trial of antihypertensive interventions and management (TAIM) study. Adequate weight loss, alone and combined with drug therapy in the treatment of mild hypertension **(e)** The Trial of Antihypertensive Interventions and Management (TAIM) Study. Final results with regard to blood pressure, cardiovascular risk, and quality of life **(f)** Lack of effectiveness of a low-sodium/high-potassium diet in reducing antihypertensive medication requirements in overweight persons with mild hypertension
References	**(a)** *Control Clin Trials* 1989;**10**:11–30 **(b)** *Ann Intern Med* 1991;**114**:613–20 **(c)** *Hypertension* 1991;**17**:210–17 **(d)** *Arch Intern Med* 1992;**152**:131–6 **(e)** *Am J Hypertens* 1992;**5**:37–44 **(f)** *Am J Hypertens* 1994;**7**:926–32
Disease	Mild hypertension
Purpose	To assess the efficacy of various combinations of pharmacological and dietary intervention in the treatment of mild hypertension
Study design	Randomised, double-blind, placebo-controlled, factorial
Follow-up	Initially 6 months, then up to 3 years
Patients	878 patients (787 completed the 6-month study), aged 21–65 years, with diastolic blood pressure 90–100 mm Hg and body weight 110–160% of ideal; 587 (296 usual diet, 291 low-sodium/high-potassium diet) to 3 years
Treatment regimen	Nine treatment combinations comprising placebo, chlortha-lidone, 25 mg, or atenolol, 50 mg, and usual diet, weight loss, or sodium restriction/potassium supplementation. If adequate blood pressure control was not achieved,

additional therapy was given at 6 months, or sooner if emergency failure criteria were met; therapy was administered in a double-blind fashion with the same daily dose, one pill/day, as the initial regimen. Treatment failures were treated with additional, open-label medication

Results   The highest response rates (> 90%) were seen in the weight loss plus chlorthalidone and weight loss plus atenolol groups. β-blocker therapy alone achieved a greater reduction in diastolic blood pressure (DBP) than either the low-sodium diet or weight loss. Diuretic treatment achieved a reduction in DBP equivalent to that seen with either the low-sodium diet or weight loss. The combination of weight loss plus chlorthalidone produced a significantly greater reduction in blood pressure than weight loss alone; the effect of atenolol plus weight loss was similar, but not as great, and the result was not significantly different from atenolol alone. The combination of a low-sodium/high-potassium diet plus chlorthalidone had a minimal effect and a low-sodium/high-potassium diet plus atenolol had no effect in terms of lowering DBP. Thus, drug therapy, particularly with diuretics, was more effective than diet in reducing DBP, but weight loss was beneficial. Low-dose chlorthalidone or atenolol produced few side-effects, except in men. In those on their usual diets, problems related to impotence worsened in 28% of men receiving chlorthalidone compared to 11% of those receiving atenolol (p < 0.05) and 3% of those receiving placebo (p = 0.009). The low-sodium diet was associated with greater fatigue than either the usual or the weight-reducing diet. There was an increase in sleep problems associated with the low-sodium diet plus chlorthalidone compared to usual diet plus chlorthalidone. Weight loss was most beneficial in improving quality of life. At 3 years, the relative risk of failure (defined as a lack of blood pressure control requiring additional drugs) in patients on a low-sodium/high-potassium diet was 0.95 compared to the usual diet (p = 0.71)

TAMI-5
Thrombolysis and Angioplasty
in Myocardial Infarction – 5

Authors	(a) Califf RM, Topol EJ, Stack RS *et al* (b) Ward SR, Sutton JM, Pieper KS, Schwaiger M, Califf RM, Topol EJ
Titles	(a) Evaluation of combination thrombolytic therapy and timing of cardiac catheterization in acute myocardial infarction. Results of Thrombolysis and Angioplasty in Myocardial Infarction – phase 5 randomised trial (b) Effects of thrombolytic regimen, early catheterization, and predischarge angiographic variables on six-week left ventricular function
References	(a) *Circulation* 1991;**83**:1543–56 (b) *Am J Cardiol* 1997;**79**:539–44
Disease	AMI
Purpose	To compare combination thrombolytic therapy with monotherapy, and an aggressive with a deferred cardiac catheterisation strategy
Study design	Randomised, open, parallel-group, factorial
Follow-up	5–10 days, 6 weeks
Patients	575 men and women, aged < 76 years. Time since onset of AMI: 6 h
Treatment regimen	Urokinase, 1.5 x 10⁶ U iv bolus followed by 1.5 x 10⁶ U infusion over 90 min, recombinant tissue-type plasminogen activator (rt-PA), 100 mg over 3 h (given as a 6 mg bolus followed by 60 mg over 1 h then a 20 mg infusion in each of the subsequent 2 h), or combination therapy with urokinase, 1.5 x 10⁶ U over 1 h plus rt-PA, 1 mg/kg (10% given as a bolus and a maximum dose of 90 mg) over 1 h. Immediate catheterisation with angioplasty for failed thrombolysis, or deferred predischarge catheterisation between day 5 and day 10
Concomitant therapy	Aspirin, 325 mg/day orally. At the end of thrombolytic therapy, heparin infusion, 1000 U/h continued for at least 48 h; in the aggressive strategy, an additional 5000 U were given when vascular access was obtained or, if rescue angioplasty was attempted, the dose increased to at least 2000–5000 U/h. Prophylactic lignocaine, nitrates and angiotensin-converting enzyme inhibitors given as clinically indicated. β-blockers given only if indicated for hypertension, arrhythmia or ischaemia. Diltiazem, 30–60 mg tid throughout hospitalisation
Results	Global left ventricular ejection fraction was almost identical (54%) at predischarge catheterisation, irrespective of the catheterisation or thrombolytic therapy used (p = 0.98). Combination therapy with urokinase plus rt-PA was

associated with a lower rate of reocclusion (2%) compared to urokinase (7%) or rt-PA (12%) (p = 0.04), and a lower rate of recurrent ischaemia (25%) compared to urokinase (35%) or rt-PA (31%). Using a composite clinical endpoint (eg, death, stroke, reinfarction, reocclusion, heart failure, or recurrent ischaemia), combination therapy was associated with fewer adverse events (68%) than either urokinase (55%) or rt-PA (60%) alone (p = 0.04). There was no difference in bleeding complication rates with any thrombolytic regimen. The aggressive catheterisation strategy led to an overall early patency rate of 96% and a predischarge patency rate of 94%, compared to a 90% predischarge patency with the conservative strategy (p = 0.065). The aggressive strategy improved regional wall motion in the infarct region (-2.16 SDs/chord) compared to deferred catheterisation (-2.49 SDs/chord) (p = 0.004). The aggressive strategy led to fewer adverse outcomes than the conservative strategy (67% vs 55%; p = 0.004). No significant increase in use of blood products resulted from the aggressive strategy. 219 of the patients had interpretable paired predischarge and late left ventricular radionuclide ventriculographies available. Catheterisation strategy (acute or deferred) did not influence global or infarct zone function at 6 weeks. The early benefit on regional left ventricular function of acute catheterisation after thrombolysis did not persist at 6 weeks

TAMI-6
Thrombolysis and Angioplasty in Myocardial Infarction – 6

Authors	Califf RM, Vandormael M, Grines CL, George BS, Sanz ML, Wall T, O'Brien M, Schwaiger M, Aguirre FV, Young S, Popma JJ, Sigmon KN, Lee KL, Ellis SG, and the Thrombolysis and Angioplasty in Myocardial Infarction–6 Study Group
Title	A randomized trial of late reperfusion therapy for acute myocardial infarction
Reference	*Circulation* 1997;**85**:2090–9
Disease	AMI
Purpose	To determine outcome of reperfusion therapy 6–24 h after the onset of AMI
Study design	Randomised, double-blind, placebo-controlled
Follow-up	6 months
Patients	197 patients (71% men). Time since onset of AMI: 6–24 h
Treatment regimen	Recombinant tissue-type plasminogen activator (rt-PA), 100 mg iv over 2 h, or placebo. Patients with occluded infarct-related arteries at 24 h were randomised to angioplasty (PTCA) or no angioplasty
Concomitant therapy	Heparin and aspirin iv
Results	Infarct vessel patency was 65% in the rt-PA group compared to 27% in the placebo group (p < 0.0001), but the ejection fractions did not differ and the in-hospital mortalities were similar (9.4% vs 8.9%). There were no differences between the groups in ejection fraction or infarct zone regional wall motion at 1 or 6 months, and no difference in 6-month reinfarction rate or hospital readmission rate. The frequency of coronary artery bypass (CABG) within 6 months was higher in the rt-PA group. There were no differences between the groups with occluded coronary artery who had angioplasty or no angioplasty

TAMI-7
Thrombolysis and Angioplasty in Myocardial Infarction – 7

Authors	Wall TC, Califf RM, George BS *et al*
Title	Accelerated plasminogen activator dose regimens for coronary thrombolysis
Reference	*J Am Coll Cardiol* 1992;**19**:482–9
Disease	AMI
Purpose	To assess the efficacy of front-loaded dosing regimens of recombinant tissue-type plasminogen activator (rt-PA) to raise the 'plateau' of pharmacological coronary artery patency
Study design	Parallel-group
Follow-up	10 days
Patients	232 patients, aged 18–75 years. Time since onset of symptoms: ≤ 6 h
Treatment regimen	rt-PA: group A, 1 mg/kg over 30 min (10% bolus) plus 0.25 mg/kg over 30 min; group B, 1.25 mg/kg over 90 min (20 mg bolus); group C, 0.75 mg/kg over 30 min (10% bolus) plus 0.50 mg/kg over 60 min; group D, 20 mg bolus, 30 min wait plus 80 mg over 120 min; group E, 1 mg/kg over 30 min, plus urokinase, 1.5×10^6 U
Concomitant therapy	Aspirin, 325 mg/day. Heparin, 1000 U/h iv, after thrombolysis until repeat catheterisation. Metoprolol, 15 mg iv, in three divided doses unless contraindicated. Lignocaine, oxygen, morphine, nitrates
Results	The results of 219 patients were analysed. Patency and reocclusion rates at 90 min in group A were 63% and 11%, respectively; in group B, 61% and 3%; in group C, 83% and 4%; in group D, 72% and 3%; and in group E, 77% and 13.6%. Major clinical outcomes including death, reocclusion and reinfarction showed a tendency to be least with regimen C

TAMI-8
Thrombolysis and Angioplasty
in Myocardial Infarction – 8

Authors	Kleiman NS, Ohman EM, Califf RM *et al*
Title	Profound inhibition of platelet aggregation with monoclonal antibody 7E3 Fab after thrombolytic therapy. Results of the Thrombolysis and Angioplasty in Myocardial Infarction (TAMI) 8 pilot study
Reference	*J Am Coll Cardiol* 1993;**22**:381–9
Disease	AMI
Purpose	To establish evidence for physiologic activity and to study the safety of murine-derived monoclonal antibody (m7E3 Fab) in patients receiving recombinant tissue-type plasminogen activator (rt-PA)
Study design	Open
Follow-up	10 weeks
Patients	60 patients. Time since onset of symptoms: < 6 h. 10 patients treated with rt-PA were used as controls
Treatment regimen	Either 15 h after the start of rt-PA, m7E3 Fab iv as a bolus 0.10 mg/kg or 0.15 mg/kg or 0.20 mg/kg or 0.25 mg/kg; or 6 h or 3 h after the start of rt-PA, 0.15 mg/kg or 0.20 mg/kg or 0.25 mg/kg
Concomitant therapy	rt-PA, 60 mg iv over 1 h (10% bolus) and 20 mg over 2 h
Results	Receptor site blockade and inhibition of platelet aggregation to 20 µmol/l adenosine diphosphate were maximal at a dose of 0.25 mg/kg of m7E3 Fab. Major bleeding occurred in 15 (25%) m7E3 Fab treated patients and in 5 (50%) control patients. Recurrent ischaemia occurred in 8 m7E3 Fab treated patients and in 2 control subjects. Coronary angiography was performed in 43 patients (37 m7E3 Fab, 9 control). Infarct-related coronary artery patency was observed in 92% of m7E3 Fab treated patients and 56% of control patients

TAMI-9
Thrombolysis and Angioplasty in Myocardial Infarction – 9

Authors	Wall TC, Califf RM, Blankenship J, Talley JD, Tannenbaum M, Schwaiger M, Gacioch G, Cohen MD, Sanz M, Leimberger JD, Topol EJ, the TAMI 9 Research Group
Title	Intravenous Fluosol in the treatment of acute myocardial infarction. Results of the Thrombolysis and Angioplasty in Myocardial Infarction 9 trial
Reference	*Circulation* 1994;**90**:114–20
Disease	AMI
Purpose	To test the ability of Fluosol, a fluorinated hydrocarbon, to reduce reperfusion injury following MI, defined as ejection fraction, regional wall motion, infarct size, and clinical outcome
Study design	Randomised, open
Follow-up	14 days
Patients	430 patients (213 Fluosol)
Treatment regimen	Fluosol, 15 ml/kg, or no Fluosol
Concomitant therapy	Alteplase, 100 mg, iv heparin and aspirin, 324 mg po; iv atenolol unless contraindicated; iv morphine, glyceryl trinitrate and atropine at investigator's discretion
Results	There were no significant differences between the 2 groups in global ejection fraction, regional wall motion, or thallium infarct size. Fluosol-treated patients with anterior infarction had a non-significantly lower mean infarct size. Median infarct size, left ventricular ejection fraction and regional wall motion were similar. Mortality and stroke rates were similar in the 2 groups, but Fluosol-treated patients experienced less recurrent ischaemia. Fluosol-treated patients had more transient congestive heart failure and pulmonary oedema. There was no difference in haemorrhagic complications between the groups
Comments	An overview of the 10 TAMI trials (including TAMI UK) has been published, which reviews the history of the TAMI collaboration and discusses the individual trials and the larger analyses of results: Barsness GW, *J Interven Cardiol* 1996;**9**:89–115

TAPS
rt-PA–APSAC Patency Study

Authors	Neuhaus K-L, von Essen R, Tebbe U *et al*
Title	Improved thrombolysis in acute myocardial infarction with front-loaded administration of alteplase: results of the rt-PA–APSAC patency study
Reference	*J Am Coll Cardiol* 1992;**19**:885–91
Disease	AMI
Purpose	To compare a new front-loaded infusion regimen of 100 mg rt-PA with anisoylated plasminogen streptokinase activator complex (APSAC) on patency and reocclusion of infarct-related coronary arteries
Study design	Randomised
Follow-up	21 days
Patients	421 patients, aged 25–75 years, with AMI > 30 min and < 6 h in duration
Treatment regimen	Heparin 5000 U iv bolus, and rt-PA, 15 mg iv bolus, then 50 mg over 30 min and 35 mg over 60 min, or heparin, 5000 U iv bolus, followed by APSAC, 30 mg iv bolus over 5 min
Results	Coronary angiography 90 min after the start of treatment revealed a patent infarct-related artery in 84.4% of 199 patients given rt-PA vs 70.3% of 202 patients given APSAC (p = 0.0007). Early reocclusion, in 24–48 h, was documented in 10.3% of 174 patients given rt-PA vs 2.5% of 163 patients given APSAC. Reocclusion at 21 days was seen in 6.3% of 152 patients given rt-PA vs 6.3% of 159 patients given APSAC. In-hospital mortality was 2.4% in the rt-PA group and 8.1% in the APSAC group (p = 0.0095). There were more bleeding complications after APSAC

TAUSA
Thrombolysis and Angioplasty in Unstable Angina

Authors	**(a)** Ambrose JA, Almeida OD, Sharma SK, Torre SR, Marmur JD, Israel DH, Ratner DE, Weiss MB, Hjemdahl-Monsen CE, Myler RK, Moses J, Unterecker WJ, Grunwald AM, Garrett JS, Cowley MJ, Anwar A, Sobolski J **(b)** Mehran R, Ambrose JA, Bongu RM, Almeida OD, Israel DH, Torre S, Sharma SK, Ratner DE
Titles	**(a)** Adjunctive thrombolytic therapy during angioplasty for ischemic rest angina. Results of the TAUSA trial **(b)** Angioplasty of complex lesions in ischemic rest angina: results of the Thrombolysis and Angioplasty in Unstable Angina (TAUSA) trial
References	**(a)** *Circulation* 1994;**90**:69–77 **(b)** *J Am Coll Cardiol* 1995;**26**:961–6
Disease	Unstable angina pectoris
Purpose	To study the effect of urokinase before angioplasty on thrombus formation and ischaemia in patients with unstable angina
Study design	Randomised, double-blind, placebo-controlled
Follow-up	During hospital stay
Patients	469 patients (257 in phase I and 212 in phase II)
Treatment regimen	Phase I: urokinase, 250,000 U intracoronary during angioplasty, or placebo Phase II: urokinase intracoronary, 250,000 U pre- and 250,000 U post-angioplasty, or placebo
Concomitant therapy	Pretreatment with aspirin, then heparin to maintain activated clotting time > 300 s
Results	Angiographic endpoints of thrombus after angioplasty were non-significantly decreased by urokinase compared to placebo (13.8% vs 18.0%). Acute closure was significantly increased in the urokinase group (10.2% vs 4.3%, p < 0.02); this difference was more striking at the higher urokinase dose (p < 0.04) than at the lower dose of urokinase (p = ns). Adverse in-hospital clinical endpoints (ischaemia, infarction, or emergency coronary artery bypass surgery) were also increased with urokinase vs placebo (12.9% vs 6.3%, p < 0.02). Angiographic and clinical endpoints were worse with urokinase in unstable angina without recent infarction than with angioplasty after recent infarction. Complex lesions were associated with a higher abrupt closure rate than simple lesions (10.6% vs 3.3%, p < 0.003), and the abrupt closure rate of complex lesions was particularly high in the urokinase group (15.0% vs 5.9%, p < 0.03). Composite clinical endpoints were also significantly higher for complex lesions and urokinase

TEAHAT
Thrombolysis Early in Heart Attack Trial

Authors	**(a)** The Thrombolysis Early in Acute Heart Attack Trial study group **(b)** Risenfors M, Gustavsson G, Ekström L, Hartford M, Herlitz J, Karlson BW, Luepker R, Swedberg K, Wennerblom B, Holmberg S **(c)** Risenfors M, Hartford M, Dellborg M, Luepker R, Hjalmarsson Å, Swedberg K, Holmberg S, Herlitz J **(d)** Risenfors M, Zukauskiene I, Albertsson P, Hartford M, Lomsky M, Herlitz J **(e)** Risenfors M, Hartford M, Dellborg M, Edvardsson N, Emanuelsson H, Karlson BW, Sandstedt B, Herlitz J **(f)** Risenfors M, Herlitz J, Berg C-H, Dellborg M, Gustavsson G, Gottfridsson C, Lomsky M, Swedberg K, Hjalmarsson Å **(g)** Herlitz J, Dellborg M, Hartford M, Karlsson T, Risenfors M, Karlson BW, Luepker R, Holmberg S, Swedberg K, Hjalmarsson Å
Titles	**(a)** Very early thrombolytic therapy in suspected acute myocardial infarction **(b)** Prehospital thrombolysis in suspected acute myocardial infarction: results from the TEAHAT study **(c)** Effect of early intravenous rt-PA on infarct size estimated from serum enzyme activity: results from the TEAHAT study **(d)** Early thrombolytic therapy in suspected acute myocardial infarction – role of the electrocardiogram: results from the TEAHAT study **(e)** Effects on chest pain of early thrombolytic treatment in suspected acute myocardial infarction: results from the TEAHAT study **(f)** Early treatment with thrombolysis and beta-blockade in suspected acute myocardial infarction: results from the TEAHAT study **(g)** Mortality and morbidity 1 year after early thrombolysis in suspected AMI: results from the TEAHAT study
References	**(a)** *Am J Cardiol* 1990;**65**:401–7 **(b)** *J Intern Med* 1991;**229**(suppl 1):3–10 **(c)** *J Intern Med* 1991;**229**(suppl 1):11–18 **(d)** *J Intern Med* 1991;**229**(suppl 1):19–25 **(e)** *J Intern Med* 1991;**229**(suppl 1):27–34 **(f)** *J Intern Med* 1991;**229**(suppl 1):35–42 **(g)** *J Intern Med* 1991;**229**(suppl 1):43–51
Disease	AMI
Purpose	To determine whether early administration of recombinant tissue plasminogen activator (rt-PA) could favourably affect the outcome of suspected AMI
Study design	Randomised, double-blind, placebo-controlled
Follow-up	72 h, ECG at 1 month and 1 year, mortality at 1 year

Patients	352 patients with pain strongly indicative of AMI, aged < 75 years. AMI was diagnosed in 89% of the 352 randomised patients. Duration of symptoms: < 2.75 h
Treatment regimen	Heparin, 5000 U iv, followed by rt-PA, 10 mg iv bolus, then 40 mg over 48 min and 50 mg over 2.5 h
Concomitant therapy	Metoprolol, three doses of 5 mg iv at 2-min intervals followed by 200 mg/day, iv heparin and oral dicoumarol were given. Aspirin, 125 mg/day, was administered after the infusion
Results	rt-PA was associated with a significant decrease in infarct size and an increase in ejection fraction. No difference in exercise capacity could be detected. The effect of rt-PA on pain was studied in 312 patients. Compared to placebo, rt-PA resulted in a 43% reduction in mean total pain score (p < 0.0001), a 26% reduction in pain duration (p < 0.01) and a 33% reduction in morphine requirement (p = 0.01). In the prehospital setting, the median interval between onset and pain was 75 min, 45 min less than for subjects randomised in hospital. The prevalence of AMI was 42% in the prehospital group compared to 66% in the hospital group. Bleeding and cardiac complications were few and similar for both the hospital and prehospital groups. rt-PA reduced maximum lactate dehydrogenase isoenzyme 1 activity by 32% (p = 0.001 compared to placebo) only in patients with ST elevation in the initial ECG; this reduction was more pronounced in patients with previous ischaemic heart disease, above median age, and in those with a shorter delay in initiation of treatment. ST-segment changes and Q-wave development were similar in the rt-PA and placebo groups, but R-wave amplitude was higher after 1 month in patients given rt-PA. The infarction rate was not altered by rt-PA, but there was a shift towards a reduction in Q-wave infarction in these patients and infarct size was limited. Reduction in enzymically estimated infarct size by rt-PA was more pronounced in patients who also received metoprolol (p < 0.001) than in those with contraindications to β-blockade. Patients who also received metoprolol had a lower incidence of Q-wave infarction, congestive heart failure and ventricular fibrillation than those who did not receive metoprolol. Mortality at 1 year was not significantly different between the rt-PA and placebo groups (10.2% and 14.3%). In those with ST-segment elevation, however, 1-year mortality was 8% in the rt-PA group vs 18% in the placebo group (p < 0.05). Requirement for rehospitalisation, symptoms of angina and congestive heart failure, time of return to work and medication requirements were similar in the 2 groups

TEAM-2
Second Thrombolytic trial of Eminase (anistreplase) in Acute Myocardial infarction

Authors	**(a)** Anderson JL, Sorensen SG, Moreno FL *et al* **(b)** Karagounis L, Sorensen SG, Menlove RL, Moreno FL, Anderson JL
Titles	**(a)** Multicenter patency trial of intravenous anistreplase compared with streptokinase in acute myocardial infarction **(b)** Does thrombolysis in myocardial infarction (TIMI) perfusion grade 2 represent a mostly patent artery or a mostly occluded artery? Enzymatic and electrocardiographic evidence from the TEAM-2 study
References	**(a)** *Circulation* 1991;**83**:126–40 **(b)** *J Am Coll Cardiol* 1992;**19**:1–10
Disease	AMI
Purpose	To compare the therapeutic effects of anistreplase (APSAC) on patency soon after AMI with a standard thrombolytic regimen of iv streptokinase. This was to be achieved by determining absolute and relative reocclusion rates within 1–2 days after the two regimens and assessing anistreplase with respect to patient safety and tolerance
Study design	Randomised, double-blind, parallel-group
Follow-up	18–48 h (mean 28 h)
Patients	370 men and women (188 anistreplase and 182 streptokinase), aged < 76 years. Time since onset of AMI: < 4 h
Treatment regimen	Lyophilised anistreplase, 30 U over 2–5 min, plus streptokinase placebo, or streptokinase, 1.5×10^6 U over 60 min, plus anistreplase placebo
Concomitant therapy	Heparin, 5000–10,000 U as a loading dose, at the start of catheterisation and an iv infusion, usually initiated at 1000 U/h and continued for at least 24 h, after the angiogram. Administration of an antihistamine (diphenhydramine, 25–50 mg iv) was recommended before thrombolytic therapy. Additional concomitant medications given according to standard hospital practice
Results	Early total patency was high in both the anistreplase (72%) and streptokinase (73%) groups, and overall patency patterns were similar. 'Complete' (grade 3) perfusion of patent arteries was, however, seen more often in the anistreplase group (83%) than in the streptokinase group (72%) (p = 0.03). Early residual coronary stenosis in patent arteries was slightly less common in the anistreplase group than in the streptokinase group (mean stenosis diameter 74% vs 77.2%; p = 0.02). In patients with patent arteries without other early interventions, the risk of reocclusion

within 1–2 days was low (anistreplase 1 out of 96 patients, streptokinase 2 out of 94 patients). In-hospital mortality rates were comparable (anistreplase 5.9% and streptokinase 7.1%). Stroke occurred in 1 patient in the anistreplase group (0.5%) and 3 patients in the streptokinase group (1.6%). The incidence of other adverse events, which were uncommon, was similar in both groups. Patients with grade 2 flow had indices of MI similar to those in patients with an occluded artery. Only grade 3 flow, which was achieved in 56% of the combined patient groups, resulted in a significantly better outcome than that of other grades

TEAM-3
Third Thrombolytic trial of Eminase (anistreplase) in Acute Myocardial infarction

Authors	**(a)** Anderson JL, Becker LC, Sorensen SG *et al* **(b)** Anderson JL, Karagounis LA, Becker LC, Sorensen SG, Menlove RL
Titles	**(a)** Anistreplase versus alteplase in acute myocardial infarction: comparative effects on left ventricular function, morbidity and 1-day coronary artery patency **(b)** TIMI perfusion grade 3 but not grade 2 results in improved outcome after thrombolysis for myocardial infarction. Ventriculographic, enzymatic, and electrocardiographic evidence from the TEAM-3 study
References	**(a)** *J Am Coll Cardiol* 1992;**20**:753–66 **(b)** *Circulation* 1993;**87**:1829–39
Disease	AMI
Purpose	To compare the effects of treatment with anistreplase (APSAC) and alteplase (rt-PA) on convalescent left ventricular function, morbidity and coronary artery patency at 1 day in patients with AMI
Study design	Randomised, double-blind, controlled, double-dummy, parallel-group
Follow-up	1 month
Patients	325 patients (161 anistreplase and 164 alteplase), aged ≤ 75 years, with symptoms of AMI ≤ 4 h and ST-segment elevation
Treatment regimen	Anistreplase, 30 U/2–5 min iv, or alteplase, 10 mg iv bolus, 50 mg over 1 h, then 20 mg/h over 2 h. For patients weighing < 65 kg, 1.25 mg/kg total dose
Concomitant therapy	Heparin, 5000 U iv bolus 2 h after start of thrombolysis, then 1000 U/h, adjusted to activated partial thromboplastin times 1.5–2.5 times normal for 2 days. Oral aspirin 160–320 mg/day for 1 month
Results	Coronary artery patency at 1 day was high and similar in both groups (anistreplase 89%, alteplase 86%). At 1 month, ejection fraction averaged 50.2% in the anistreplase group and 54.8% in the alteplase group (p < 0.01). Ejection fraction showed a similar increase with exercise at 1 month and exercise times were comparable for both anistreplase and alteplase. Mortality was 6.2% for anistreplase and 7.9% for alteplase. Other events were also comparable for the two groups. Grade 3 perfusion was achieved in 74% of the total study population and predicted significantly better outcomes than lesser grades of flow

TEMS
Trimetazidine European Multicenter Study

Authors	Detry JM, Sellier P, Pennaforte S, Cokkinos D, Dargie H, Mathes P
Title	Trimetazidine: a new concept in the treatment of angina. Comparison with propranolol in patients with stable angina
Reference	*Br J Clin Pharmacol* 1994;**37**:279–88
Disease	Stable angina pectoris
Purpose	To compare the antianginal effect of trimetazidine with that of propranolol in patients with stable angina
Study design	Randomised, double-blind, controlled, parallel-group
Follow-up	3 months
Patients	149 men, mean age 57 years
Treatment regimen	Trimetazidine, 20 mg tid, or propranolol, 40 mg tid
Results	At 3 months, the antianginal effect obtained was similar in both groups, with no significant differences observed between the treatments with regard to effect on incidence of angina attacks, exercise endurance or time to 1 mm ST-segment depression during exercise. The heart rate x pressure product at rest and during peak exercise remained unchanged in the trimetazidine group but decreased significantly in the propranolol group. Treatment was withdrawn in 6 cases in the trimetazidine group and 12 in the propranolol group; 5 withdrawals in each group were due to deterioration of cardiovascular status. Although trimetazidine was as effective as propranolol, it seems to operate via a different mechanism of action not primarily dependent on a reduction in energy demand

TIBBS
Total Ischemic Burden Bisoprolol Study

Author	**(a)** and **(b)** von Arnim T
Titles	**(a)** Medical treatment to reduce total ischemic burden: Total Ischemic Burden Bisoprolol Study (TIBBS), a multicenter trial comparing bisoprolol and nifedipine **(b)** Prognostic significance of transient ischemic episodes: response to treatment shows improved prognosis. Results of the Total Ischemic Burden Bisoprolol Study (TIBBS) follow-up
References	**(a)** *J Am Coll Cardiol* 1995;**25**:231–8 **(b)** *J Am Coll Cardiol* 1996;**28**:20–4
Disease	Stable angina pectoris
Purpose	To compare the effects of bisoprolol to those of nifedipine, on transient myocardial ischaemia in patients with chronic angina pectoris
Study design	Randomised, double-blind, parallel-group
Follow-up	8 weeks on treatment, 1-year follow-up
Patients	330 patients (161 bisoprolol and 169 nifedipine) with stable angina pectoris, a positive exercise test and > 2 episodes of transient ischaemia during 48 h of Holter monitoring
Treatment regimen	Phase 1: bisoprolol, 10 mg once daily, or nifedipine SR, 20 mg bid, for 4 weeks Phase 2: bisoprolol, 20 mg once daily, or nifedipine SR, 40 mg bid, for 4 weeks
Results	In phase 1 of the trial, bisoprolol therapy reduced the mean number of transient ischaemic episodes from 8.1 ± 0.6 to 3.2 ± 0.4 per 48 h. Nifedipine reduced transient ischaemic episodes from 8.3 ± 0.5 to 5.9 ± 0.4 per 48 h. Total duration of ischaemia was reduced from 99.3 ± 10.1 to 31.9 ± 5.5 min per 48 h with bisoprolol and from 101 ± 9.1 to 72.6 ± 8.1 min per 48 h with nifedipine. Reductions were significant for both drugs; the difference between bisoprolol and nifedipine was also significant ($p < 0.0001$). Doubling of the dose in phase 2 of the trial had small additive effects. Only bisoprolol showed a marked circadian effect by reducing the morning peak of transient ischaemic episodes. Patients with a 100% response rate of transient ischaemic episodes during treatment had a 17.5% event rate (death, AMI, hospital admission for unstable angina pectoris) at 1 year compared to 32.3% for non-100% responders ($p = 0.008$). Patients receiving bisoprolol had a lower event rate at 1 year than those receiving nifedipine (22.1% vs 33.1%, $p = 0.033$)

TIBET
Total Ischaemic Burden European Trial

Authors	(a) The TIBET study group (b) Fox KM, Mulcahy D, Findlay I, Ford I, Dargie HJ (c) Dargie HJ, Ford I, Fox KM
Titles	(a) The Total Ischaemic Burden European Trial (TIBET): design, methodology, and management (b) Total Ischaemic Burden European Trial (TIBET). Effects of atenolol, nifedipine SR and their combination on the exercise test and the total ischaemic burden in 608 patients with stable angina (c) Total Ischaemic Burden European Trial (TIBET). Effects of ischaemia and treatment with atenolol, nifedipine SR and their combination on outcome in patients with chronic stable angina
References	(a) *Cardiovasc Drugs Ther* 1992;**6**:379–86 (b) *Eur Heart J* 1996;**17**:96–103 (c) *Eur Heart J* 1996;**17**:104–12
Disease	Mild, chronic, stable angina pectoris
Purpose	To investigate whether total ischaemic burden has important prognostic implications in patients with stable angina on standard antianginal treatments
Study design	Randomised, double-blind, parallel-group
Follow-up	1 year
Patients	682 men and women, aged 40–79 years, having had stable angina symptoms for at least 3 months and not evaluated for coronary artery bypass grafting
Treatment regimen	Atenolol, 50 mg bid, or nifedipine, 20 mg bid, or fixed combination atenolol-nifedipine, 50/20 mg bid. Patients on nifedipine with symptoms not adequately controlled were given further nifedipine, 20 mg bid
Results	All three treatments showed a comparable favourable influence on both the exercise test and Holter parameters when compared to placebo. Treatment effects were seen equally by exercise tests and ambulatory monitoring. There was a non-significant trend to a lower rate of hard endpoints (cardiac death, nonfatal MI, unstable angina) in the combination therapy group. There were no significant differences between groups for any of the measured ischaemic parameters, though combination therapy resulted in a greater fall in resting systolic and diastolic blood pressures than either treatment alone. The incidence of withdrawals was significantly greater in patients treated with nifedipine

TIMI II
Thrombolysis In Myocardial Infarction (Phase II)

Authors	**(a)** The TIMI study group **(b)** Mueller HS, Forman SA, Menegus MA, Cohen LS, Knatterud GL, Braunwald E **(c)** Aguirre FV, Younis LT, Chaitman BR, Ross AM, McMahon RP, Kern MJ, Berger PB, Sopko G, Rogers WJ, Shaw L, Knatterud G, Braunwald E
Titles	**(a)** Comparison of invasive and conservative strategies after treatment with intravenous tissue plasminogen activator in acute myocardial infarction. Results of the Thrombolysis in Myocardial Infarction (TIMI) Phase II trial **(b)** Prognostic significance of nonfatal reinfarction during 3-year follow-up: results of the Thrombolysis in Myocardial Infarction (TIMI) phase II clinical trial **(c)** Early and 1-year clinical outcome of patients' evolving non-Q-wave versus Q-wave myocardial infarction after thrombolysis. Results from the TIMI II study
References	**(a)** *N Engl J Med* 1989;**320**:618–27 **(b)** *J Am Coll Cardiol* 1995;**26**:900–7 **(c)** *Circulation* 1995;**91**:2541–8
Disease	AMI
Purpose	**TIMI II-A:** to compare the effects of immediate (2 h) and delayed (18–48 h) percutaneous transluminal coronary angioplasty (PTCA) or coronary artery bypass grafting (CABG) in patients with AMI treated with alteplase (rt-PA) **TIMI II-B:** to compare the effects of immediate iv vs delayed (from day 6) β-blockade in patients with AMI treated with alteplase
Study design	Randomised, open, parallel-group
Follow-up	1–3 years
Patients	3339 patients (1681 invasive treatment and 1658 conservative treatment), aged < 76 years. Time since onset of pain: < 4 h **TIMI II-A:** 195 patients immediate invasive treatment, 194 delayed invasive treatment and 197 conservative treatment **TIMI II-B:** 720 patients immediate metoprolol, iv initially then orally, and 714 delayed metoprolol started on day 6; 1514 patients were not eligible for β-blocker treatment and were randomised to delayed invasive treatment or conservative treatment as in TIMI II-A
Treatment regimen	Alteplase in all patients; total dose 150 mg in first 520 patients and 100 mg in subsequent patients. Invasive strategy comprised PTCA if appropriate, otherwise CABG. Conservative strategy comprised PTCA or CABG only in response to spontaneous or provoked myocardial ischaemia. Immediate metoprolol, three doses of 5 mg iv,

followed by 50 mg bid on day 1, then 100 mg bid, or 50 mg bid on day 6 followed by 100 mg bid

Concomitant therapy	Lignocaine, 1–1.5 mg/kg then 2–4 mg/min for > 24 h. Heparin, 5000 U bolus, followed by 1000 U/h iv, then on day 6 10,000 U sc 12-hourly. Aspirin, 80 mg/day from day 1 or 2 and 325 mg/day from day 6
Results	**TIMI II-A and TIMI II-B:** data from 1-year follow-up are available for 3316 patients. There was no difference in the incidence of death and nonfatal reinfarction when the invasive and conservative treatment groups were considered either together or individually. Anginal status at 1 year was also similar. Cardiac catheterisation and PTCA were performed more often in the invasive treatment group compared to the conservative treatment group. Fewer older patients (65–75 years) received early ($\leq$ 2 h) alteplase or were eligible for random assignment to immediate or deferred β-blocker therapy (p = 0.01). More older patients had multivessel disease (p = 0.001) and the highest 1-year mortality rate occurred in older patients. Early mortality and adverse clinical cardiac events were not significantly different after a conservative vs an invasive treatment strategy, regardless of whether the infarct type was Q wave or non-Q wave. Data from 2-year follow-up are available for 3187 patients and from 3-year follow-up for 2174 patients. The cumulative rates of death or reinfarction were similar for the invasive and conservative groups. Nonfatal reinfarction was a strong independent predictor of subsequent death
Comments	A selection of additional references are listed below: *JAMA* 1988;**260**:2849–58 *Circulation* 1990;**81**:1457–76 *Circulation* 1991;**83**:422–37 *Ann Intern Med* 1991;**115**:256–65 *Circulation* 1992;**85**:533–42 *J Am Coll Cardiol* 1993;**22**:1763–72 *Circulation* 1994;**90**:78–86 *Circulation* 1995; **92**:3575–6

TIMI III
Thrombolysis In Myocardial Ischemia (Phase III)

Authors	(a) and (b) The TIMI IIIA investigators (c) Anderson HV, Cannon CP, Stone PH, Williams DO, McCabe CH, Knatterud GL, Thompson B, Willerson JT, Braunwald E
Titles	(a) Early effects of tissue-type plasminogen activator added to conventional therapy on the culprit coronary lesion in patients presenting with ischemic cardiac pain at rest. Results of the Thrombolysis in Myocardial Ischemia (TIMI IIIA) trial (b) Effects of tissue plasminogen activator and a comparison of early invasive and conservative strategies in unstable angina and non-Q-wave myocardial infarction. Results of the TIMI IIIB trial (c) One-year results of the Thrombolysis in Myocardial Infarction (TIMI) IIIB clinical trial. A randomized comparison of tissue-type plasminogen activator versus placebo and early invasive versus early conservative strategies in unstable angina and non-Q wave myocardial infarction
References	(a) *Circulation* 1993;**87**:38–52 (b) *Circulation* 1994;**89**:1545–56 (c) *J Am Coll Cardiol* 1995;**26**:1643–50
Disease	Unstable angina or non-Q-wave MI
Purpose	To assess the effects of tissue-type plasminogen activator (rt-PA) added to conventional therapy on coronary angiographic findings (TIMI IIIA) and to determine the effects of thrombolytic therapy and of an early invasive strategy on clinical outcome (TIMI IIIB)
Study design	Randomised, double-blind, placebo-controlled
Follow-up	**TIMI IIIA**: 48 h **TIMI IIIB**: 6 weeks, follow-up contact at 1 year
Patients	1473 patients. Time since onset of symptoms: < 6 h. **TIMI IIIA:** 306 patients. **TIMI IIIB:** 1473 patients
Treatment regimen	Alteplase, 20 mg iv bolus then 0.8 mg/kg, total maximum dose 80 mg, or placebo
Concomitant therapy	Oxygen, oral metoprolol, 50 mg bid, oral diltiazem, 30 mg qid, and oral isosorbide dinitrate, 10 mg tid. Sublingual or iv glyceryl trinitrate, if required. Heparin, 5000 U iv bolus, then dose adjusted to maintain partial thromboplastin times at 1.5–2.0 control values. Aspirin, 325 mg once daily
Results	**TIMI IIIA:** for all patients, 25% of alteplase-treated and 19% of placebo-treated (p = 0.25) obtained improvements of ≥ 10% stenosis reduction or by two TIMI flow grades. ≥ 20% reduction of stenosis or improvement by two TIMI flow grades was seen for alteplase in 15% of all culprit lesions

vs 5% for placebo (p < 0.003). This latter improvement was more common with alteplase among lesions containing apparent thrombus (36% with alteplase vs 15% with placebo, p < 0.01), than it was among patients with a non-Q-wave MI (33% vs 8%, p < 0.005)

TIMI IIIB: the primary endpoint was death, MI, or failure of initial therapy at 6 weeks. This occurred in 54.2% of alteplase-treated and 55.5% of placebo-treated patients (p = ns). Fatal and nonfatal MI or reinfarction occurred in 7.4% of alteplase-treated and 4.9% of placebo-treated patients (p = 0.04). There were no intracranial haemorrhages in the placebo group vs 4 in the alteplase group. 18.1% of patients in the early conservative strategy group reached the endpoint vs 16.2% assigned to the early invasive strategy group (p = ns). However, the average length of hospitalisation was significantly lower in the latter group. Non-Q-wave AMI was predicted by the absence of prior angioplasty (odds ratio (OR) 3.3), duration of pain $\geq$ 60 min (OR 2.9), ST-segment deviation on qualifying ECG (OR 2.0), and recent-onset angina (OR 1.7). The percentage of patients with non-Q-wave AMI when 0, 1, 2, 3 or 4 risk factors were present were 7.0%, 19.6%, 24.4%, 49.9% and 70.6%, respectively (p < 0.001). Elevated fibrinogen level at the time of hospital admission was associated with coronary ischaemic events and a poor clinical outcome in the patients with unstable angina. Mortality and nonfatal reinfarction rates at 1 year were similar in the alteplase and placebo groups (12.4% and 10.6%, respectively), and in the early invasive and early conservative strategies (10.8% and 12.2%, respectively). Revascularisation at 1 year was more common with the early invasive than with the early conservative strategy (64% vs 58%, p < 0.001), related to the difference in angioplasty rates (39% vs 32%, p < 0.001). 30% of patients in each group had bypass grafting. Clinical status at 1 year was similar with both early treatment strategies. The cost of the early invasive strategy over the 6-week period has been estimated to be nearly 50% more than that of the early conservative strategy

| Comments | The TIMI III Registry was an observational study designed to investigate the natural history and response to treatment of patients with unstable angina or non-Q-wave MI. Important differences in the use of medical resources, as well as different outcomes, among different demographic groups, have been reported in *JAMA* 1996;**275**:1104–12 |

TIMI 4
Thrombolysis In Myocardial Infarction (Phase 4)

Authors	**(a)** Cannon CP, McCabe CH, Diver DJ *et al* **(b)** Gibson CM, Cannon CP, Piana RN, Breall JA, Sharaf B, Flatley M, Alexander B, Diver DJ, McCabe CH, Flaker GC, Baim DS, Braunwald E
Titles	**(a)** Comparison of front-loaded recombinant tissue-type plasminogen activator, anistreplase and combination thrombolytic therapy for acute myocardial infarction: results of the Thrombolysis in Myocardial Infarction (TIMI) 4 trial **(b)** Angiographic predictors of reocclusion after thrombolysis: results from the Thrombolysis in Myocardial Infarction (TIMI) 4 trial
References	**(a)** *J Am Coll Cardiol* 1994;**24**:1602–10 **(b)** *J Am Coll Cardiol* 1995;**25**:582–9
Disease	AMI
Purpose	To determine the best thrombolytic regimen from anistreplase (APSAC), front-loaded alteplase (rt-PA), or a combination of both agents
Study design	Randomised, double-blind
Follow-up	1 year
Patients	382 patients, aged < 80 years, with ischaemic pain for ≥ 30 min and ST-segment elevation. Time since onset of pain: < 6 h before treatment
Treatment regimen	Front-loaded alteplase, 15 mg bolus, then 0.75 mg/kg (up to 50 mg) infusion over 30 min, followed by a 0.50 mg/kg (up to 35 mg) infusion over 60 min; or anistreplase, 30 U bolus over 2–5 min; or alteplase, 15 mg bolus, then 0.75 mg/kg (up to 50 mg) infusion over 30 min, and anistreplase, 20 U bolus
Concomitant therapy	Heparin, 5000 U iv bolus then 1000 U/h infusion, aspirin, 325 mg once daily, metoprolol, iv then oral. Further treatment at the discretion of the physician
Results	Patency of the infarct-related artery at 60 min was significantly higher in alteplase-treated patients (77.8% vs 59.5% for anistreplase-treated patients and 59.3% for combination-treated patients). At 90 min, the incidence of infarct-related patency was significantly higher in alteplase-treated patients (alteplase vs anistreplase, p < 0.01; alteplase vs combination, p = 0.02). The rate of major haemorrhage was significantly lower for the alteplase-treated patients (10.9%) compared to the anistreplase-treated patients (21.8%) or the combination-treated patients (21.6%). The mortality rate at 6 weeks was 2.2% for the alteplase-treated patients, 8.8% for the anistreplase-treated patients (alteplase vs anistreplase, p = 0.02), and 7.2% for

the patients receiving combination therapy (alteplase vs combination, p = 0.06). By life-table analysis, mortality was 5.3% at 1 year for the alteplase group, 11% for the anistreplase group and 10.5% for the combination therapy group. The presence of TIMI grade 2 flow, ulceration, collateral vessels and greater percentage diameter stenosis at 90 min after thrombolysis were associated with significantly higher rates of infarct-related artery reocclusion by 18–36 h

TIMI 5
Thrombolysis In Myocardial Infarction (Phase 5)

Authors	Cannon CP, McCabe CH, Henry TD *et al*
Title	A pilot trial of recombinant desulfatohirudin compared with heparin in conjunction with tissue-type plasminogen activator and aspirin for acute myocardial infarction: results of the Thrombolysis in Myocardial Infarction (TIMI) 5 trial
Reference	*J Am Coll Cardiol* 1994;**23**:993–1003
Disease	AMI
Purpose	To assess the value of recombinant desulfatohirudin (hirudin) as adjunctive therapy to thrombolysis in AMI
Study design	Randomised, open
Follow-up	18–36 h
Patients	264 patients (157 hirudin and 79 heparin), aged 21–75 years. Time since onset of symptoms: < 6 h
Treatment regimen	Hirudin iv in one of four doses: 0.15 mg/kg bolus plus 0.05 mg/kg/h, or 0.1 mg/kg bolus plus 0.1 mg/kg/h, or 0.3 mg/kg bolus plus 0.1 mg/kg/h, or 0.6 mg/kg bolus plus 0.2 mg/kg/h; or heparin iv, 5000 U bolus plus 1000 U/h, adjusted to maintain an activated partial thromboplastin time of 60–90 s
Concomitant therapy	Front-loaded tissue-type plasminogen activator (rt-PA), 15 mg bolus, 0.75 mg/kg (up to 50 mg) iv over 30 min, then 0.50 mg/kg (up to 35 mg) iv over 60 min, and aspirin, 160 mg, then 160 mg/day. Metoprolol, nitrates and calcium antagonists at the discretion of the physician, and aspirin
Results	TIMI grade 3 flow in the infarct-related artery at 90 min and 18–36 h without death or reinfarction was achieved in 61.8% of hirudin-treated patients compared to 49.4% of heparin-treated patients (p = 0.07). All four doses of hirudin led to similar findings in the angiographic and clinical endpoints. At 18–36 h, 97.8% of hirudin-treated patients had a patent infarct-related artery compared to 89.2% of heparin-treated patients (p = 0.01). Reocclusion by 18–36 h occurred in 1.6% of hirudin-treated patients and 6.7% of heparin-treated patients (p = 0.07). Death or reinfarction occurred during the hospital period in 6.8% of hirudin-treated patients compared to 16.7% of heparin-treated patients (p = 0.02). Major spontaneous haemorrhage occurred in 1.2% of hirudin-treated patients vs 4.7% of heparin-treated patients (p = 0.09), and major haemorrhage at an instrumented site occurred in 16.3% and 18.4%, respectively (p = ns)

TIMI 6
Thrombolysis In Myocardial Infarction (Phase 6)

Author	Lee LV
Title	Initial experience with hirudin and streptokinase in acute myocardial infarction: results of the Thrombolysis In Myocardial Infarction (TIMI) 6 trial
Reference	*Am J Cardiol* 1995;**75**:7–13
Disease	AMI
Purpose	A pilot study to evaluate the safety of iv hirudin compared to iv heparin when given together with streptokinase and aspirin to patients with AMI
Study design	Randomised, open-label, parallel-group, comparative
Follow-up	6 weeks
Patients	193 patients, aged 21–75 years, seen within 6 h of the onset of symptoms
Treatment regimen	Heparin, 5000 U iv bolus followed by infusion at 1000 U/h, adjusted to a target activated partial thromboplastin time (aPTT) of 65–90 s, or iv hirudin; there were 3 hirudin dosage groups, ie a bolus of 0.15 mg/kg + infusion at 0.05 mg/kg/h, or 0.3 mg/kg + 0.1 mg/kg/h, or 0.6 mg/kg + 0.2 mg/kg/h. The infusion was continued for 5 days or until an earlier study endpoint was reached
Concomitant therapy	Streptokinase, 1.5×10^6 U iv infusion over 1 h, starting after the heparin or hirudin infusion, aspirin, 325 mg/day, and, if no contraindication to β-blockade, metoprolol
Results	The incidence of major haemorrhage was similar in all four treatment groups (5.5–6.5%). The composite incidence of unsatisfactory outcomes was also similar in all four treatment groups (32.2–37.3%), but the incidence of death, severe congestive heart failure, cardiogenic shock or nonfatal reinfarction was lower in the two higher hirudin dosage groups (9.7–11.3%) than in the lowest hirudin dosage group (21.6%) or in the heparin group (17.6). Hirudin provided consistent and effective anticoagulation and was as safe as heparin when administered together with streptokinase and aspirin

TIMI 7
Thrombin Inhibition in Myocardial Ischemia (Phase 7)

Authors	Fuchs J, Cannon CP, and the TIMI 7 investigators
Title	Hirulog in the treatment of unstable angina. Results of the Thrombin Inhibition in Myocardial Ischaemia (TIMI) 7 trial
Reference	*Circulation* 1995;**92**:727–33
Disease	Unstable angina pectoris
Purpose	To evaluate whether the effects of the direct thrombin inhibitor hirulog are dose-dependent in patients with unstable angina
Study design	Randomised, double-blind
Follow-up	6 weeks
Patients	410 patients (one-third women), mean age 60 years. 49% had a prior history of MI
Treatment regimen	Hirulog, iv infusion at 0.02, 0.25, 0.50 or 1.0 mg/kg/h for 72 h
Concomitant therapy	All patients received aspirin daily. Heparin was administered after the hirulog infusion at the discretion of the physician, and was used in 46% of cases
Results	The primary endpoint of unsatisfactory outcome (death, nonfatal MI, rapid clinical deterioration or recurrent ischaemic pain at rest) at 72 h showed a similar incidence in all four dosage groups (8.1%, 6.2%, 11.4% and 6.2%). However, the secondary endpoint of death or nonfatal MI at hospital discharge occurred significantly more frequently in the lowest dosage group than in the three higher dosage groups (10.0% vs 3.2%). Only 2 patients (0.5%) had a major haemorrhage attributed to hirulog
Comments	Based on the findings of the TIMI 7 trial, TIMI 8 was designed as a randomised, double-blind, multicentre trial to compare the efficacy and safety of hirulog to iv heparin in patients with unstable angina and non-Q-wave MI. It was planned to enroll 5300 patients with the acute ischaemic syndromes. Soon after enrollment began, the trial was discontinued for reasons unrelated to the drugs

TIMI 9A
Thrombolysis and thrombin Inhibition
in Myocardial Infarction (Phase 9A)

Author	Antman EM
Title	Hirudin in acute myocardial infarction. Safety report from the Thrombolysis and Thrombin Inhibition in Myocardial Infarction (TIMI) 9A trial
Reference	*Circulation* 1994;**90**:1624–30
Disease	AMI
Purpose	To compare the safety and efficacy of iv heparin versus the direct-acting thrombin inhibitor hirudin in patients with AMI undergoing thrombolysis
Study design	Randomised, double-blind, parallel-group
Follow-up	30 days
Patients	757 patients seen within 12 h from the onset of symptoms
Treatment regimen	Intravenous heparin or hirudin was administered following thrombolysis. Heparin, 5000 U bolus followed by infusion at 1000–1300 U/h, with titration to achieve a target activated partial thromboplastin time (aPTT) of 60–90 s. Hirudin, 0.6 mg/kg bolus followed by infusion at 0.2 mg/kg/h for 96 h
Concomitant therapy	Thrombolysis with streptokinase or tissue-type plasminogen activator over 60–90 min, oral aspirin daily
Results	Intracranial haemorrhage occurred in 1.7% of hirudin patients and 1.9% of heparin patients; non-intracranial spontaneous bleeding occurred in 7.0% of hirudin patients compared to 3.0% of heparin patients, but the incidence of bleeding at instrumented sites was 5.2% in both groups. Risk factors for major haemorrhage were older age and higher aPTT values, especially in the first 12 h after thrombolysis
Comments	The study was interrupted after the enrolment of 757 patients because the incidence of haemorrhage was greater than expected in both treatment groups. Instead TIMI 9B was started with lower drug doses

TIMI 9B
Thrombolysis and thrombin Inhibition in Myocardial Infarction 9B trial

Author	Antman EM
Title	Hirudin in acute myocardial infarction. Thrombolysis and Thrombin Inhibition in Myocardial Infarction (TIMI) 9B trial
Reference	*Circulation* 1996:**94**:911–21
Disease	AMI
Purpose	To compare the safety and efficacy of iv heparin versus the direct-acting thrombin inhibitor hirudin in patients with AMI undergoing thrombolysis
Study design	Randomised, double-blind, parallel-group
Follow-up	30 days
Patients	3002 patients (2247 men and 755 women), mean age approx. 60 ± 12 years, seen within 12 h from the onset of symptoms
Treatment regimen	Intravenous heparin or hirudin was administered before or immediately following thrombolysis. Heparin, 5000 U bolus followed by infusion at 1000 U/h for 96 h. Hirudin, 0.1 mg/kg bolus (not exceeding 15 mg) followed by infusion at 0.1 mg/kg/h (not exceeding 15 mg/h) for 96 h. The target activated partial thromboplastin time (aPTT) was 55–85 s, and the infusion rate of the study drugs could be adjusted in individual patients between 6 and 12 h after thrombolysis, if necessary
Concomitant therapy	Thrombolysis with streptokinase or tissue-type plasminogen activator over 60–90 min, oral aspirin daily
Results	The target aPTT was achieved significantly more consistently with hirudin than with heparin. The primary endpoint (death, nonfatal MI, severe heart failure, cardiogenic shock) at 30 days occurred in 11.9% of patients in the heparin group and 12.9% of those in the hirudin group. The rate of major haemorrhage was also similar in the two groups (5.3% vs 4.6%). Intracranial haemorrhage occurred in 0.9% of heparin patients and 0.4% of hirudin patients. Hirudin and heparin were thus equally effective and safe as adjunctive therapy to thrombolysis in AMI patients
Comments	A review of all TIMI trials has been published in *J Interven Cardiol* 1995;**8**:117–35

TOMHS
Treatment Of Mild Hypertension Study

Authors	**(a)** Mascioli SR, Grimm RH Jr, Neaton JD *et al* **(b)** Neaton JD, Grimm RH Jr, Prineas RJ *et al* **(c)** Liebson PR, Grandits GA, Dianzumba S, Prineas RJ, Grimm RH Jr, Neaton JD, Stamler J **(d)** Grimm RH Jr, Grandits GA, Cutler JA, Stewart AL, McDonald RH, Svendsen K, Prineas RJ, Liebson PR
Titles	**(a)** Characteristics of participants at baseline in the Treatment of Mild Hypertension Study (TOMHS) **(b)** Treatment of mild hypertension study. Final results **(c)** Comparison of five antihypertensive monotherapies and placebo for change in left ventricular mass in patients receiving nutritional-hygienic therapy in the Treatment of Mild Hypertension Study (TOMHS) **(d)** Relationships of quality-of-life measures to long-term lifestyle and drug treatment in the Treatment of Mild Hypertension Study
References	**(a)** *Am J Cardiol* 1990;**66**:32C–5C **(b)** *JAMA* 1993;**270**:713–24 **(c)** *Circulation* 1995;**91**:698–706 **(d)** *Arch Intern Med* 1997;**157**:638–48
Disease	Mild hypertension
Purpose	To evaluate and compare the effects of five active drug therapies, in addition to nutritional measures and exercise, in reducing blood pressure, side-effects, quality-of-life indices, and the incidence of ECG and echocardiographic abnormalities in patients with mild hypertension. Secondary objective: to compare the incidence of cardiovascular clinical events, including death, in patients receiving drugs as the first line of treatment with those receiving non-pharmacological treatment only
Study design	Randomised, double-blind, placebo-controlled, parallel-group
Follow-up	4.4 years
Patients	902 patients (62% men), aged 45–69 years (mean 55 years), with a diastolic blood pressure of 90–99 mm Hg or, if previously treated with antihypertensive drugs, 85–99 mm Hg
Treatment regimen	Acebutolol, 400 mg/day, or amlodipine, 5 mg/day, or chlorthalidone, 15 mg/day, or doxazosin, 1 mg/day for 1 month then 2 mg/day, or enalapril, 5 mg/day
Concomitant therapy	Measures to reduce weight, sodium intake and alcohol consumption, and to increase physical activity
Results	Blood pressure reductions occurred in all six groups, but were significantly greater for patients on active treatment

than on placebo. (Systolic blood pressure -15.9 vs -9.1 mm Hg, diastolic blood pressure -12.3 vs -8.6 mm Hg; $p < 0.0001$.) Death and major nonfatal cardiovascular events occurred slightly more often in the placebo group (7.3%) than in the treatment groups (5.1%; $p = 0.21$). Including all adverse events, 11.1% of the treatment and 16.2% of the placebo group were affected ($p = 0.03$). Differences among the five drug treatments did not consistently favour one treatment group in terms of regression of left ventricular mass (LVM), blood lipids and other outcome measures. The nutritional intervention plus placebo, with the emphasis on weight loss and reduction of dietary sodium, was as effective as dietary advice plus active treatment in reducing echocardiographically determined LVM, despite the smaller decrease in blood pressure in the placebo group. Chlorthalidone had a small additional effect in lowering LVM. Improvements in quality of life were observed in all groups but were largest in the acebutolol and chlorthalidone groups

TPT
Thrombosis Prevention Trial
Ongoing trial

Authors	**(a)** Meade TW **(b)** Meade TW, Roderick PJ, Brennan PJ, Wilkes HC, Kelleher CC **(c)** Meade TW, Miller GJ **(d)** Richards M, Meade TW, Peart S, Brennan PJ, Mann AH
Titles	**(a)** Low-dose warfarin and low-dose aspirin in the primary prevention of ischemic heart disease **(b)** Extra-cranial bleeding and other symptoms due to low dose aspirin and low intensity oral anticoagulation **(c)** Combined use of aspirin and warfarin in primary prevention of ischemic heart disease in men at high risk **(d)** Is there any evidence for a protective effect of antithrombotic medication on cognitive function in men at risk of cardiovascular disease? Some preliminary functions
References	**(a)** *Am J Cardiol* 1990;**65**(suppl C):7C–11C **(b)** *Thromb Haemost* 1992;**68**:1–6 **(c)** *Am J Cardiol* 1995;**75**:23B–6B **(d)** *J Neurol Neurosurg Psychiatry* 1997;**62**:269–72
Disease	Ischaemic heart disease
Purpose	To investigate the effect of low-dose warfarin and low-dose aspirin on the incidence of ischaemic heart disease in men at high risk
Study design	Randomised, double-blind, placebo-controlled, factorial
Follow-up	5 years (minimum)
Patients	5493 men, aged 45–69 years, in the top 20% of the ischaemic heart disease risk score distribution
Treatment regimen	Warfarin, 2.5 mg/day increasing by 0.5 mg/day or 1.0 mg/day at monthly intervals until the appropriate dose has been achieved for each individual (average dose 4.6 mg/day), and/or controlled-release aspirin, 75 mg/day, or placebo
Results	Results obtained so far pertain to bleeding complications. There was no difference between the three groups in the frequency of major bleeding episodes, which amounted to about 1 episode in 500 men per year. Intermediate and minor bleeding are more frequent with the combined warfarin-aspirin treatment than with the single treatments, and least with placebo. Intermediate bleeding episodes with combined therapy were mainly gastrointestinal, and may be related to the high doses of aspirin with conventional levels of anticoagulation. A subgroup of 405 men made tests of verbal memory, attention, abstract reasoning, verbal fluency, and mental flexibility. Verbal fluency and mental flexibility were significantly better in subjects taking antithrombotic medication than in those taking placebo

TRACE
Trandolapril Cardiac Evaluation

Authors	**(a)** Køber L, Torp-Pedersen C, Carlsen JR, Bagger H, Eliasen P, Lyngborg K, Videbæk J, Cole DS, Auclert L, Pauly NC, Aliot E, Persson S, Camm AJ **b)** Torp-Pedersen C, Køber L, Carlsen J **(c)** Køber L, Torp-Pedersen C, Ottesen M, Burchardt H, Korup E, Lyngborg K
Titles	**(a)** A clinical trial of the angiotensin-converting-enzyme inhibitor trandolapril in patients with left ventricular dysfunction after myocardial infarction **(b)** Angiotensin-converting enzyme inhibition after myocardial infarction: the Trandolapril Cardiac Evaluation study **(c)** Influence of age on the prognostic importance of left ventricular dysfunction and congestive heart failure on long-term survival after acute myocardial infarction
References	**(a)** *N Engl J Med* 1995; **333**:1670–6 **(b)** *Am Heart J* 1996;**132**:235–43 **(c)** *Am J Cardiol* 1996;**78**:158–62
Disease	AMI with left ventricular dysfunction
Purpose	To determine whether patients who have left ventricular dysfunction soon after AMI benefit from long-term ACE inhibition with trandolapril
Study design	Randomised, double-blind, placebo-controlled
Follow-up	24–50 months
Patients	1749 patients with left ventricular systolic dysfunction and an ejection fraction ≤ 35%. Time since AMI: 2–6 days
Treatment regimen	Trandolapril, 1 mg/day, or placebo
Results	There were 304 deaths (34.7%) in the trandolapril group and 369 (42.3%) in the placebo group (p = 0.001). Trandolapril also reduced the risk of death from cardiovascular causes, the risk of sudden death and the frequency of progression to severe heart failure (relative risk 0.75, 0.76 and 0.71, respectively), but not the risk of recurrent MI (relative risk 0.86). Assessment of the screening data showed that the 1-year and 3-year mortality rates increased sharply with increasing age. There was an excess 3-year mortality of 14% in patients aged ≤ 55 years, 24% in those aged 56–65 years, 25% in those aged 66–75 years and 28% in those aged ≥ 75 years. The relative importance of left ventricular systolic dysfunction and congestive heart failure as causes of death diminished with increasing age

TREND
Trial on Reversing Endothelial Dysfunction

Authors	Mancini GBJ, Henry GC, Macaya C, O'Neill BJ, Pucillo AL, Carere RG, Wargovich TJ, Mudra H, Lüscher TF, Klibaner MI, Haber HE, Uprichard ACG, Pepine CJ, Pitt B
Title	Angiotensin-converting enzyme inhibition with quinapril improves endothelial vasomotor dysfunction in patients with coronary artery disease. The TREND (Trial on Reversing ENdothelial Dysfunction) study
Reference	*Circulation* 1996;**94**:258–65
Disease	Coronary artery disease
Purpose	To determine whether treatment with quinapril can improve endothelial dysfunction in normotensive patients with coronary artery disease but no other confounding variables that affect endothelial dysfunction
Study design	Randomised, double-blind, placebo-controlled, parallel-group
Follow-up	6 months
Patients	129 patients (113 men and 16 women), mean age 58.6 ± 1.3 years, with documented coronary atherosclerosis requiring a nonsurgical revascularisation procedure, but not presenting hypertension, heart failure, cardiomyopathy or major lipid abnormalities
Treatment regimen	Quinapril, 40 mg once daily, or placebo
Concomitant therapy	Intracoronary acetylcholine during angiography and nitroglycerin bolus. Coronary angioplasty (PTCA), atherectomy, stent, or laser therapy before study treatment
Results	Endothelial function was assessed during angiography at baseline and after 6 months by measuring the constrictive response of target coronary segments to the intracoronary infusion of acetylcholine. At 6 months, the patients in the quinapril group but not those in the placebo group showed a significant net improvement by 10–20% in the coronary response to acetylcholine. In clinical terms, the patients treated with quinapril had a significant mean improvement in coronary artery diameter by 12.1%

TRIC
Thrombolysis during Instability in Coronary artery disease

Authors	Karlsson JE, Berglund U, Björkholm A *et al*
Title	Thrombolysis with recombinant human tissue-type plasminogen activator during instability in coronary artery disease: effect on myocardial ischemia and need for coronary revascularization
Reference	*Am Heart J* 1992;**124**:1419–26
Disease	Unstable coronary artery disease
Purpose	To investigate the effect of iv recombinant tissue-type plasminogen activator (rt-PA) on myocardial ischaemia, coronary lesions and the cumulative rate of coronary revascularisation, MI and death in patients with unstable coronary artery disease
Study design	Randomised, double-blind, placebo-controlled
Follow-up	1 month
Patients	205 men, aged 40–70 years, with unstable coronary artery disease on admission to the coronary care unit
Treatment regimen	rt-PA, 1 mg/kg (maximum dose 100 mg) iv infusion. Half the dose over 1 h, remaining over 3 h
Concomitant therapy	Oral aspirin, 225 mg first dose, then 75 mg/day. Heparin, 5000 U iv bolus before rt-PA, 1000 U/h after treatment for 36–48 h, then heparin, 10,000 U subcutaneously bid for 4 days. Oral metoprolol and, if necessary, nitrates and calcium antagonists
Results	There were no significant differences in the number of deaths, MIS or emergency revascularisations between the rt-PA and placebo groups. Myocardial ischaemia was reduced by treatment with rt-PA compared to placebo both at discharge, 53% compared to 70% ($p = 0.02$) and at 1 month, 61% compared to 80% ($p = 0.005$). Signs of myocardial ischaemia during exercise tests were reduced at discharge in the rt-PA group, 51% compared to 68% in the placebo group ($p = 0.03$) and after 1 month 48% compared to 62% ($p = 0.09$)

UK-TIA
United Kingdom Transient Ischaemic Attack study

Authors	**(a)** UK-TIA study group **(b)** Slattery J, Warlow CP, Shorrock CJ, Langman MJS
Titles	**(a)** United Kingdom transient ischaemic attack (UK-TIA) aspirin trial: final results **(b)** Risks of gastrointestinal bleeding during secondary prevention of vascular events with aspirin – analysis of gastrointestinal bleeding during the UK-TIA trial
References	**(a)** *J Neurol Neurosurg Psychiatry* 1991;**54**:1044–54 **(b)** *Gut* 1995;**37**:509–11
Disease	Transient ischaemic attack or minor ischaemic stroke
Purpose	To evaluate the clinical efficacy of long-term aspirin in a conventional antithrombotic dose and to determine whether a lower dose is as effective
Study design	Randomised, blind, placebo-controlled
Follow-up	1–7 years (mean 4 years)
Patients	2435 patients of whom 73% were men (815 high-dose aspirin, 806 low-dose aspirin and 814 placebo), mean age 59.8 years, thought to have had a transient ischaemic attack or minor ischaemic stroke
Treatment regimen	Aspirin, 600 mg bid or 300 mg once daily, or placebo
Results	Compliance with therapy was about 85%. The risk of non-fatal MI, nonfatal major stroke, vascular death or non-vascular death was 18% lower in the two aspirin groups than in the placebo group (2p = 0.01). There was no definite difference in response to therapy between aspirin, 1200 mg/day, and aspirin, 300 mg/day, except that the lower dose was significantly less gastrotoxic. For upper gastrointestinal bleeding the odds ratio was 3.3 for the lower dose vs 6.4 for the higher dose. The risk of hospitalisation because of bleeding was increased in the high-dose group. Bleeding was more likely from duodenal than from gastric ulcers and was more likely early in treatment. The risk of lower gastrointestinal bleeding was also increased by both doses of aspirin (odds ratio 1.8 for low dose vs 1.5 for high dose)

UNASEM
Unstable Angina Study using Eminase

Authors	Bär FW, Verheugt 380 FW, Col J *et al*
Title	Thrombolysis in patients with unstable angina improves the angiographic but not the clinical outcome. Results of UNASEM, a multicenter, randomized, placebo-controlled, clinical trial with anistreplase
Reference	*Circulation* 1992;**86**:131–7
Disease	Unstable angina pectoris
Purpose	To study the value of thrombolysis in unstable angina
Study design	Randomised, double-blind, placebo-controlled
Follow-up	During hospital stay
Patients	159 patients, aged 30–70 years, with unstable angina but no previous infarction
Treatment regimen	Anistreplase, 30 U iv over 5 min, or placebo
Concomitant therapy	Nitroglycerin iv, heparin, 5000 U iv bolus, then 1000 U/h during cardiac catheterisation. β-blocking agents or calcium antagonists according to local protocol. Aspirin, 300 mg/day
Results	Angiography was performed before study medication was given and 24–48 h afterwards. A significant decrease in stenosis diameter occurred between the first and second angiogram in the anistreplase group compared to the placebo group (11% vs 3%, p = 0.008). However, no beneficial clinical effects of thrombolytic treatment were found. Bleeding complications were significantly higher in patients who received thrombolytic therapy

USIM
Urochinasi per via Sistemica nell'Infarto Miocardico

Authors	Rossi P, Bolognese L
Title	Comparison of intravenous urokinase plus heparin versus heparin alone in acute myocardial infarction
Reference	*Am J Cardiol* 1991;**68**:585–92
Disease	AMI
Purpose	To compare the effects of iv urokinase plus heparin with heparin alone in AMI
Study design	Randomised, open, parallel-group
Follow-up	16 days
Patients	2201 patients (1128 urokinase plus heparin and 1073 heparin alone). Time since onset of symptoms: < 4 h
Treatment regimen	Urokinase, 1 x 10^6 U iv bolus repeated after 60 min, and/or heparin, 10,000 U iv bolus, followed by 1000 U/h for 48 h
Concomitant therapy	Oral anticoagulant drugs, aspirin or subcutaneous calcium-heparin were permitted after the second day of therapy
Results	At 16 days, overall hospital mortality was 8.0% in the urokinase plus heparin group, and 8.3% in the heparin group (p = ns). Mortality in patients with anterior AMI was 10.5% and 13.9%, respectively (p = ns; relative risk 0.73). The incidence of major bleeding and the overall incidence of stroke were similar in the two groups. The rates of major in-hospital cardiac complications (eg, reinfarction, postinfarction angina) were also similar in both groups

VHAS
Verapamil in Hypertension Atherosclerosis Study
Ongoing trial

Authors	**(a)** Zanchetti A, Magnani B, Dal Palù C **(b)** Zanchetti A
Titles	**(a)** Atherosclerosis and calcium antagonists: the VHAS **(b)** Vascular complications in hypertension: the VHAS study
References	**(a)** *J Hum Hypertens* 1992;**6**(suppl 2):S45–8 **(b)** *Cardiovasc Drugs Ther* 1995;**9**:529–31
Disease	Hypertension and atherosclerosis
Purpose	To compare the antihypertensive efficacy of verapamil and chlorthalidone and to evaluate the effect of the two drugs on carotid wall thickness and carotid plaques
Study design	Randomised, double-blind for 6 months, then open, parallel-group
Follow-up	2 years, 4 years for the subgroup
Patients	1464 patients, aged 40–65 years, with hypertension. A random subgroup of 500 patients will be evaluated for atherosclerotic lesions by ultrasonography
Treatment regimen	Verapamil SR, 240 mg once daily, or chlorthalidone, 25 mg once daily
Results	Not yet available
Comments	Baseline data for 440 patients in the subgroup undergoing investigation by ultrasonography show a high prevalence (67.5%) of asymptomatic carotid alterations

V-HeFT I
Vasodilator-Heart Failure Trial I

Authors	Cohn JN, Archibald DG, Ziesche S *et al*
Title	Effect of vasodilator therapy on mortality in chronic congestive heart failure. Results of a Veterans Administration cooperative study
Reference	*N Engl J Med* 1986;**314**:1547-52
Disease	Chronic congestive heart failure
Purpose	To determine whether two widely employed vasodilator regimens altered life expectancy
Study design	Randomised, double-blind, placebo-controlled
Follow-up	0.5–5.7 years (average 2.3 years)
Patients	642 men (183 prazosin, 186 hydralazine plus isosorbide dinitrate, and 273 placebo), aged 18–75 years (mean 58 years)
Treatment regimen	Either prazosin, 5 mg qid (2.5 mg qid for first 2 weeks), or hydralazine, 75 mg qid (37.5 mg qid for first 2 weeks), plus isosorbide dinitrate, 40 mg qid (20 mg qid for first 2 weeks), or placebo
Concomitant therapy	Digoxin and diuretic therapy permitted. Long-acting nitrates, calcium antagonists, β-blockers or antihypertensive drugs other than diuretics not permitted
Results	During follow-up, there were 91 deaths (49.7%) in the prazosin group, 72 deaths (38.7%) in the hydralazine plus nitrate group and 120 deaths (44.0%) in the placebo group. At 1 year, the cumulative mortality rate was 12.1% in the hydralazine plus nitrate group and 19.5% in the placebo group, which represented a 38% reduction with hydralazine plus nitrate. The cumulative mortality rates at 2 years were 25.6% in the hydralazine plus nitrate group and 34.3% in the placebo group, and at 3 years the rates were 36.2% and 46.9%, respectively. Left ventricular ejection fraction rose significantly at 8 weeks and at 1 year in the hydralazine plus nitrate group, but not in the other groups
Comments	Combined data from V-HeFT I and V-HeFT II reported in: *Circulation* 1993;**87**(suppl 6):1–117 *J Am Coll Cardiol* 1996;**27**:642–9

V-HeFT II
Vasodilator-Heart Failure Trial II

Authors	Cohn JN, Johnson G, Ziesche S *et al*
Title	A comparison of enalapril with hydralazine-isosorbide dinitrate in the treatment of chronic congestive heart failure
Reference	*N Engl J Med* 1991;**325**:303–10
Disease	Heart failure
Purpose	To compare the efficacy of enalapril with hydralazine plus isosorbide dinitrate in heart failure
Study design	Randomised, double-blind
Follow-up	0.5–5.7 years (average 2.5 years)
Patients	804 patients (403 enalapril and 401 hydralazine plus isosorbide dinitrate)
Treatment regimen	Enalapril, 20 mg/day, or hydralazine, 75 mg qid, plus isosorbide dinitrate, 20 mg qid
Concomitant therapy	Digoxin and diuretics
Results	Mortality in the enalapril group was significantly lower than in the hydralazine plus isosorbide dinitrate group (p = 0.016), which was due to a lower incidence of sudden death in the enalapril group. The reduction in blood pressure was significantly greater in the enalapril group during the first 13 weeks. Ejection fraction was significantly increased in both groups, but after 13 weeks was greater in the hydralazine plus isosorbide dinitrate group. Oxygen consumption at peak exercise was increased significantly in the hydralazine plus isosorbide dinitrate group after 13 weeks and after 6 months, but not in the enalapril group. After 1 year, oxygen consumption began to decline in both groups. An increased incidence of headache was noted in the hydralazine plus isosorbide dinitrate group, and of symptomatic hypotension and cough in the enalapril group
Comments	Combined data from V-HeFT I and V-HeFT II reported in: *Circulation* 1993;**87**(suppl 6):1–117 *J Am Coll Cardiol* 1996;**27**:642–9

V-HeFT III
Vasodilator-Heart Failure Trial III

Authors	(a) Cohn JN (b) Boden WE, Ziesche S, Carson PE, Conrad CH, Syat D, Cohn JN
Titles	(a) Vasodilators in heart failure. Conclusions from V-HeFT II and rationale for V-HeFT III (b) Rationale and design of the Third Vasodilator-Heart Failure Trial (V-HeFT III): felodipine as adjunctive therapy to enalapril and loop diuretics with or without digoxin in chronic congestive heart failure
References	(a) *Drugs* 1994;**47**(suppl 4):47–58 (b) *Am J Cardiol* 1996;**77**:1078–82
Disease	Heart failure
Purpose	To evaluate the addition of the vasodilator calcium antagonist, felodipine, to the angiotensin-converting enzyme inhibitor, enalapril, on cardiac function
Study design	Randomised, double-blind, placebo-controlled
Follow-up	Up to 42 months, mean 18 months
Patients	450 patients with NYHA class II-III congestive heart failure
Treatment regimen	Felodipine, 5 mg bid, or placebo; digoxin or placebo
Concomitant therapy	Enalapril plus loop diuretics
Results	Results presented in: Cohn JN, *Circulation* 1997;**96**:856–63
Comments	The digoxin phase was ended earlier than planned, due to results from RADIANCE and PROVED, showing the efficacy of digoxin

WARIS
Warfarin Reinfarction Study

Authors	Smith P, Arnesen H, Holme I
Title	The effect of warfarin on mortality and reinfarction after myocardial infarction
Reference	*N Engl J Med* 1990;**323**:147–52
Disease	MI
Purpose	To determine the effects of warfarin on mortality, reinfarction and cerebrovascular events after MI
Study design	Randomised, double-blind, placebo-controlled
Follow-up	Average 37 months
Patients	1214 patients (607 warfarin and 607 placebo), who had recovered from MI, aged < 75 years. Mean time since MI: 27 days
Treatment regimen	Warfarin adjusted to prolong prothrombin time to achieve an international normalised ratio between 2.8 and 4.8
Concomitant therapy	All patients received standard medical therapy (including β-blockers) in hospital according to local guidelines. To reduce the risk of bleeding, all patients were advised not to take aspirin or other antiplatelet drugs
Results	The total number of deaths was 94 patients in the warfarin group and 123 patients in the placebo group, representing a 24% reduction with warfarin (p = 0.02). Reinfarction occurred in 82 patients in the warfarin group and 124 patients in the placebo group, representing a 34% reduction with warfarin (p = 0.0001). Cerebrovascular events occurred in 20 patients in the warfarin group and 44 patients in the placebo group, representing a 55% reduction with warfarin (p = 0.0015)

WOSCOPS
West Of Scotland Coronary Prevention Study

Authors	**(a)** The West of Scotland Coronary Prevention Study group **(b)** The WOSCOPS Study group **(c)** Shepherd J, Cobbe SM, Ford I, Isles CG, Lorimer AR, Macfarlane PW, McKillop JH, Packard CJ **(d)** The WOSCOPS Study Group
Titles	**(a)** A coronary primary prevention study of Scottish men aged 45–64 years: trial design **(b)** Screening experience and baseline characteristics in the West of Scotland Coronary Prevention Study **(c)** Prevention of coronary heart disease with pravastatin in men with hypercholesterolemia **(d)** West of Scotland coronary prevention study: implications for clinical practice
References	**(a)** *J Clin Epidemiol* 1992;**45**:849–60 **(b)** *Am J Cardiol* 1995;**76**:485–91 **(c)** *N Engl J Med* 1995;**333**:1301–7 **(d)** *Eur Heart J* 1996;**17**:163–4
Disease	Hypercholesterolaemia
Purpose	To test whether 5 years of pravastatin treatment leads to a reduction in MI
Study design	Randomised, double-blind, placebo-controlled
Follow-up	5 years (mean 4.9 years)
Patients	6595 men, aged 45–64 years, with low-density lipoprotein (LDL) cholesterol ≥ 4.0 and ≤ 6.0 mmol/l and no history of MI
Treatment regimen	Pravastatin, 40 mg each evening, or placebo
Concomitant therapy	Smoking and dietary advice during the whole study
Results	Pravastatin lowered plasma cholesterol levels by 20% and LDL cholesterol by 26% whereas there was no change with placebo. There were 248 definite coronary events (nonfatal MI or death from coronary heart disease) in the placebo group and 174 in the pravastatin group (relative risk reduction with pravastatin 31%, $p < 0.001$). There were similar risk reductions with pravastatin for nonfatal MI (31% reduction, $p < 0.001$), death from coronary heart disease (33% reduction, $p = 0.042$) and death from all cardiovascular causes (32% reduction, $p = 0.033$). There was no excess of deaths in the pravastatin group, and the risk of death from any cause was reduced by 22% in the pravastatin group ($p = 0.051$)

WWICT
Western Washington Intracoronary Streptokinase Trial

Authors	**(a)** Kennedy JW, Ritchie JL, Davis KB, Stadius ML, Maynard C, Fritz JK **(b)** Cerqueira MD, Maynard C, Ritchie JL, Davis KB, Kennedy JW
Titles	**(a)** The Western Washington randomised trial of intracoronary streptokinase in acute myocardial infarction. A 12-month follow-up report **(b)** Long-term survival in 618 patients from the Western Washington streptokinase in myocardial infarction trials
References	**(a)** *N Engl J Med* 1985;**312**:1073–8 **(b)** *J Am Coll Cardiol* 1992;**20**:1452–9
Disease	AMI
Purpose	To compare the efficacy of intracoronary streptokinase with that of conventional therapy in patients with recent AMI
Study design	Randomised, open, standard-care-controlled
Follow-up	**(a)** 1 year **(b)** 3–8 years (mean 5.8 years)
Patients	250 patients (134 streptokinase and 116 placebo), aged < 75 years. Time since onset of symptoms: ≤ 12 h
Treatment regimen	Streptokinase, intracoronary infusion of 4000 U/min (average 286,000 ± 77,000 U over 72 ± 44 min)
Concomitant therapy	Heparin and then warfarin throughout the hospital stay
Results	**(a)** During the first 30 days, 37% of patients in the streptokinase group and 11.2% of patients in the control group died (p = 0.02). During the first year, there were 11 deaths (8.2%) in the streptokinase group and 17 deaths (14.7%) in the control group (p = 0.10). When a minor imbalance between the two groups in the ejection fraction and infarct location was adjusted by logistic regression, the difference in 1-year mortality became significant (p = 0.03). **(b)** Survival at 3 years was 84% in the streptokinase group and 82% in the control group, and for the total period there was no significant survival benefit (p = 0.16). Generally there was a higher survival rate for patients with an inferior infarction than for patients with an anterior infarction but no overall survival benefit from streptokinase treatment
Comments	Included in the long-term follow-up were 368 patients from the Western Washington Intravenous Streptokinase in Myocardial Infarction Trial (WWIST). For further details see following reference: Kennedy JW, Martin GV, Davis KB *et al*, *Circulation* 1988;**77**:345–52 (erratum 1037)

Appendix

Trials without a main entry in this edition

In this fourth edition of *What's What*, the main section is devoted to major trials in cardiovascular medicine, listed by their acronyms. Some studies which do not have an entry in the main pages of *What's What* are listed in briefer form in this Appendix. These are smaller trials or older trials and some which predominantly deal with epidemiology, diet or surgery.

ABC Alpha Beta Canada
Hypertension 1994;**24**:241–8

AMIS Aspirin Myocardial Infarction Study
JAMA 1980;**243**:661–9

ANBP Australian National Blood Pressure study
Lancet 1980;**i**:1261–7

APSIM APSAC dans l'Infarctus du Myocarde
J Am Coll Cardiol 1989;**13**:988–97

ARIS Anturan Reinfarction Italian Study
Lancet 1982;**i**:237–42

ART Anturane Reinfarction Trial
N Engl J Med 1980;**302**:250–6

ASIS Angina and Silent Ischemia Study
J Am Coll Cardiol 1993;**21**:1605–11

ATEST Atenolol and Streptokinase Trial
Eur Heart J 1989;**10**(suppl):117

BARI Bypass Angioplasty Revascularization Investigation
N Engl J Med 1996;**335**:217–25

BBPP Beta-Blocker Pooling Project
Eur Heart J 1988;**9**:8–16

BECAIT Bezafibrate Coronary Atherosclerosis Intervention Trial
Lancet 1996;**347**:849–53

BENESTENT Belgian Netherlands Stent
J Am Coll Cardiol 1996;**27**:255–61

BENESTENT II Belgian Netherlands Stent II
Circulation 1996;**93**:412–22

BEPS Belgian Eminase Prehospital Study
Eur Heart J 1991;12:965–7

BEST β-blocker Stroke Trial
BMJ 1988;**296**:737–41

Bogalusa Heart Study
Ann NY Acad Sci 1997;**817**:189–98

CAPS Cardiac Arrhythmia Pilot Study
Am J Cardiol 1988;**61**:501–9

CAPTIN Captopril before reperfusion in acute myocardial infarction
J Am Coll Cardiol 1993;**21**:371A

CARDIA Coronary Artery Risk Development in Young Adults study
Circulation 1996;**93**:60–6

CASIS Canadian Amlodipine/Atenolol in Silent Ischemia Study
J Am Coll Cardiol 1995;**25**:619–25

CAST Chinese Acute Stroke Trial
Lancet 1997;**349**:1641–9

CATS Canadian American Ticlopidine Study
Lancet 1989;**i**:1215–20

CDP Coronary Drug Project
JAMA 1975;**231**:360–81

CNR-OD1 Italian CNR multicentre prospective study OD1
Eur Heart J 1989;**10**:292–303

CONVINCE Controlled Onset Verapamil Investigation of Clinical Endpoints
Ann NY Acad Sci 1996;**783**:278–94

Copenhagen AFASAK Copenhagen Atrie Flimmer Aspirin Antikoagulation study
Lancet 1989;**i**:175–9

Copenhagen City Heart Study
Am J Hypertens 1997;**10**:634–9

CRAFT Catheterization/Rescue Angioplasty Following Thrombolysis study
J Am Coll Cardiol 1991;**17**(suppl A):276A

CRAFT-I Controlled Randomized Atrial Fibrillation Trial
J Am Coll Cardiol 1993;**21**:478A

DANAMI Danish trial in Acute Myocardial Infarction
Circulation 1997;**96**:748–55

DART Diet And Reinfarction Trial
Eur Heart J 1992;**13**:166–70

DAVIT I Danish Verapamil Infarction Trial I
Cardiology 1994;**85**:259–66

DHCCP Department of Health and Social Security Hypertension Care Computing Project
J Hum Hypertens 1997;**11**:205–11

DRS Diltiazem Reinfarction Study
J Am Coll Cardiol 1990;**15**:940–7

DURAC Duration of Anticoagulation trial
J Int Med 1994;**236**:143–52

EARS European Atherosclerosis Research Study
Int J Epidemiol 1994;**23**:465–71

EAST Emory Angioplasty versus Surgery Trial
Am J Cardiol 1997;**79**:1453–9

ECASS European Cooperative Acute Stroke Study
JAMA 1995;**274**:1017–25

ECCE Effects of Captopril on Cardiopulmonary Exercise parameters post myocardial infarction
Herz 1993;**18**:424–9

ECSG-1 European Cooperative Study Group for recombinant tissue-type plasminogen activator
Lancet 1985;**i**:842–7

ECSG-2 European Cooperative Study Group for recombinant tissue-type plasminogen activator
Lancet 1985;**ii**:965–9

ECSG-3 European Cooperative Study Group for recombinant tissue-type plasminogen activator
Am J Cardiol 1987;**60**:231–7

ECSG-4 European Cooperative Study Group for recombinant tissue-type plasminogen activator
Lancet 1988;**i**:197–203

ECSG-5 European Cooperative Study Group for recombinant tissue-type plasminogen activator
BMJ 1988;**297**:1374–9

ECST European Carotid Surgery Trial
Lancet 1991;**337**:1235–43

ECTIM Enquête Cas-Témoins de l'Infarctus du Myocarde
Eur Heart J 1995;**16**:348–53

EIS European Infarction Study
Eur Heart J 1984;**5**:189–202

EPSIM Enquête de Prévention Secondaire de l'Infarctus du Myocarde
N Engl J Med 1982;**307**:701–8

FEMINA Felodipine and Metoprolol In stable effort-induced Angina
J Am Coll Cardiol 1996;**27**(suppl A):72A

GABI German Angioplasty Bypass-surgery Intervention trial
Topol EJ, ed. Textbook of interventional cardiology. Chapter 12.
Saunders, 1990:240–53

GAUS German Activator Urokinase Study
J Am Coll Cardiol 1988;**12**:581–7

GCP German Cardiovascular Prevention study
Prev Med 1996;**25**:135–45

GEMT German Eminase Multicentre Trial
Am J Cardiol 1988;**62**:347–51

GPP Göteborg Primary Prevention trial
Eur Heart J 1986;**7**:279–88

GRECO German study with recombinant t-PA in coronary occlusion
J Am Coll Cardiol 1994;**24**:55–60

HARP Harvard Atherosclerosis Reversibility Project
Lancet 1994;**344**:1182–6

Honolulu (Hawaii) Heart Program
Arterioscler Thromb Vasc Biol 1997;**17**:760–8

HPT Hypertension Prevention Trial
Arch Intern Med 1990;**150**:153–62

HYNON Hypertension Non-drug treatment cooperative study
Eur Heart J 1989;**10**(suppl):307

IASSH Italian Acute Stroke Study – Haemodilution
Lancet 1988;**i**:318–21

IMPACT International Mexiletine and Placebo Antiarrhythmic Coronary Trial
J Am Coll Cardiol 1984;**4**:1148–63

INTERSALT International cooperative investigation of electrolytes and blood pressure
Hypertension 1991;**17**(suppl I):I-9–15

IPPPSH International Prospective Primary Prevention Study in Hypertension
J Hypertens 1985;**3**:379–92

LAARS LDL-Apheresis Atherosclerosis Regression Study
Circulation 1996;**93**:1826–35

LIT Lopressor Intervention Trial
Eur Heart J 1987;**8**:1056–64

LRC-CPPT Lipid Research Clinics Coronary Primary Prevention Trial
JAMA 1994;**272**:1455–6

LRT Lovastatin Restenosis Trial
Am J Cardiol 1996;**78**:221–4

MADAM Moexipril as Antihypertensive Drug After Menopause
Hypertension 1997;**29**:843–4

MILIS Multicenter Investigation for Limitation of Infarct Size
Am J Cardiol 1986;**57**:1236–43

Minnesota Heart Health Program
Am J Epidemiol 1996;**144**:351–61

Minnesota Heart Survey
Ann Epidemiol 1993;**3**;483–7; *Arch Intern Med* 1997;**157**:873–81

NAMIS Nifedipine Angina Myocardial Infarction Study
Circulation 1984;**69**:728–47

PACT Philadelphia Association of Clinical Trials
Am J Cardiol 1989;**63**:37B–41B

PAIMS Plasminogen Activator Italian Multicenter Study
J Am Coll Cardiol 1989;**13**:19–26

PAIMS-2 Plasminogen Activator Italian Multicenter Study–2
J Am Coll Cardiol 1992;**20**:520–6

PAMELA Pressioni Ambulatoriali e Loro Associazioni
J Cardiovasc Pharmacol 1994;**23**(suppl 5):S12–5

PARAGON Platelet IIb/IIIa Antagonist for the Reduction of Acute coronary
syndrome events in a Global Organization Network
J Am Coll Cardiol 1997;**29**:410A

PARIS I Persantine-Aspirin Reinfarction Study (Part I)
Circulation 1980;**62**:449–61

PARIS II Persantine-Aspirin Reinfarction Study (Part II)
J Am Coll Cardiol 1986;**7**:251–69

PARK Prevention of Angioplasty Reocclusion with Ketanserin
Circulation 1993;**89**:1588–601

PAS Polish Amiodarone Study
J Am Coll Cardiol 1992;**20**:1056–62

PATS Prehospital Administration of t-PA Study
R I Med J 1991;**74**:405–8

PATS Post-stroke Antihypertensive Treatment Study
Chin Med J 1995;**108**:710–7

PHICOG Philadelphia Cooperative Group trial
Clin Ther 1989;**11**:94–119

Physicians' Health Study
Am Heart J 1991;**122**:1588–92

POSCH Program on the Surgical Control of the Hyperlipidemias
Ann Surg 1996;**224**:486–500

PROFILE Prospective Randomized Flosequinan Longevity Evaluation study (study stopped prematurely because of excess mortality; see p 122, 266)

PROVED Prospective Randomized Study of Ventricular Failure and the Efficacy of Digoxin
J Am Coll Cardiol 1993;**22**:955–62

RESTORE Randomized Efficacy Study of Tirofiban for Outcomes and Restenosis
J Am Coll Cardiol 1996;**27**:536–42

RITA Randomized Intervention Treatment of Angina trial
Circulation 1996;**94**:135–41

SCATI Studio sulla Calciparina nell'Angina e nella Trombosi ventricolare nell'Infarto
Lancet 1989;**ii**:182–6

SESAM Study in Europe of Saruplase and Alteplase in Myocardial Infarction
Am J Cardiol 1997;**79**:727–32

Sixty-Plus Reinfarction Study
Lancet 1980;**ii**:989–94

SMART Study of Medicine vs Angioplasty Reperfusion Trial
J Am Coll Cardiol 1994;(suppl):225A

SPAA Studio sulla Pressione Arteriosa nell'Anziano
Eur Heart J 1992;**13**:178–82

SPIC Studio Policentrico Italiano Cardiomiopatie
Il Cuore 1994;**11**:187–93

SPRINT Secondary Prevention Reinfarction Israeli Nifedipine Trial
Eur Heart J 1988;**9**:354–64

STAMP Systemic Thrombolysis in Acute Myocardial infarction with Pro-urokinase and urokinase
J Am Coll Cardiol 1990;**15**(suppl A):3A

Stanford Five-City Project
Am J Epidemiol 1990;**132**:629–46

STARS St. Thomas' Atherosclerosis Regression Study
J Cardiovasc Pharmacol 1995;**25**(suppl 4):S11–9

START Saruplase Taprostene Acute Reocclusion Trial
Eur Heart J 1993;**14**:1118–26

TAMI-1 Thrombolysis and Angioplasty in Myocardial Infarction – 1
Coron Artery Dis 1994;**5**:611–5

TAMI-2 Thrombolysis and Angioplasty in Myocardial Infarction – 2
Circulation 1988;**77**:1100–7

TAMI-3 Thrombolysis and Angioplasty in Myocardial Infarction – 3
Circulation 1989;**79**:281–6

TAMI-4 Thrombolysis and Angioplasty in Myocardial Infarction – 4
J Am Coll Cardiol 1989;**14**:877–84

TASS Ticlopidine Aspirin Stroke Study
N Engl J Med 1989;**321**:501–7

TEAM-I Trial of Eminase in AMI
J Am Coll Cardiol 1988;**11**:1153–63

Tecumseh Blood Pressure Study
JAMA 1990;**264**:354–8

THAMES Tenormin in Hypertension And Myocardial ischemia
Epidemiological Survey
Eur Heart J 1993;**14**:1622–8

TIARA Timolol en Infarto Agudo, Republica Argentina
Circulation 1987;**76**:610–7

TICO Thrombolysis In Coronary Occlusion
Eur Heart J 1992;**13**:770–5

TIMI 1 Thrombolysis In Myocardial Infarction (Phase I)
Circulation 1987;**76**:142–54

TIMI 10A Thrombolysis In Myocardial Infarction (10A-Phase I)
Circulation 1996;**93**:843–6

TIMS Tertatolol International Multicenter Study
Am J Hypertens 1989;**2**:296S–302S

TOHP-I Trials Of Hypertension Prevention–I
Ann Epidemiol 1995;**5**:85–107

TOHP-II Trials Of Hypertension Prevention–II
Ann Epidemiol 1995;**5**:130–55

TOPS Treatment Of Post-thrombolytic Stenoses study
Circulation 1992;**86**:1400–6

TPAT Tissue Plasminogen Activator Toronto trial
J Am Coll Cardiol 1989;**13**:1469–76

TRENT Trial of Early Nifedipine Treatment
BMJ 1986;**293**:1204–8

TRIMM Triggers and Mechanisms of Myocardial infarction study
Circulation 1991;**84**(suppl):VI-62–7

TTOPP Thrombolytic Therapy in an Older Patient Population
Circulation 1990;**82**(suppl III):III-666

VERDI Verapamil versus Diuretic
BMJ 1989;**299**:881–6

Worcester Heart Attack Study
Am Heart J 1990;**119**:996–1001

Author index

General index

α-blockers **14**, **364**
α-tocopherol **71**, **117**
Abciximab **51**, **105**, **107**
ACE inhibitors **3**, **14**, **16**, **60**, **68**, **74**, **86**, **96**, **97**, **110**, **127**, **142**, **163**, **166**, **273**, **315**
Acebutolol **19**, **355**
Acute myocardial infarction *see* AMI
Adipose tissue **117**
Albuminuria **86**
Aldactone **259**
Aloxyprinum **319**
Alteplase **30**, **95**, **103**, **140**, **146**, **160**, **179**, **184**, **186**, **218**, **233**, **236**, **255**, **261**, **262**, **272**, **287**, **288**, **328**, **329**, **330**, **331**, **333**, **336**, **339**, **344**, **346**, **348**, **349**, **359**
AMI **10**, **12**, **13**, **28**, **29**, **42**, **47**, **52**, **63**, **66**, **69**, **82**, **84**, **89**, **91**, **92**, **95**, **112**, **140**, **141**, **144**, **150**, **160**, **169**, **172**, **173**, **176**, **177**, **178**, **180**, **181**, **186**, **189**, **191**, **204**, **208**, **213**, **218**, **233**, **236**, **244**, **260**, **261**, **262**, **263**, **281**, **283**, **287**, **293**, **295**, **297**, **316**, **319**, **320**, **328**, **332**, **333**, **336**, **338**, **344**, **348**, **352**, **353**, **357**, **362**, **369** *see also* MI
Amiloride **170**, **224**, **314**
Amiodarone **9**, **34**, **38**, **47**, **56**, **72**, **75**, **99**, **104**, **137**, **307**
Amlodipine **5**, **14**, **21**, **48**, **245**, **319**, **355**
Angina pectoris **8**, **20**, **46**, **48**, **54**, **59**, **82**, **167**, **216**, **229**, **265**, **282**, **340**, **341**, **342**
Angina pectoris (unstable) **32**, **113**, **155**, **158**, **191**, **252**, **308**, **334**, **346**, **359**, **361**
Angiotensin II antagonists **96**, **273**
Angiotensin-converting enzyme inhibitors *see* ACE inhibitors
Anistreplase **10**, **11**, **23**, **100**, **103**, **144**, **174**, **179**, **260**, **317**, **338**, **339**, **348**, **361**
Antiarrhythmics **38**, **56**, **104**, **115**, **116**, **123**, **137**, **194**, **226**
Anticoagulants **10**, **93**, **176**, **247**, **305**
Antioxidants **71**, **117**
APSAC **11**, **23**, **91**, **92**, **100**, **103**, **174**, **179**, **317**, **333**, **361**
Arrhythmia **35**, **37**, **45**, **55**, **61**, **63**, **72**, **75**, **93**, **115**, **123**, **194**, **226**, **235**, **301**, **302**, **303**, **304**, **307** *see also* atrial and ventricular
Aspirin **2**, **10**, **24**, **25**, **32**, **36**, **45**, **50**, **51**, **54**, **81**, **92**, **93**, **107**, **112**, **136**, **140**, **150**, **154**, **163**, **172**, **178**, **179**, **180**, **182**, **183**, **199**, **210**, **231**, **235**, **263**, **280**, **282**, **302**, **305**, **309**, **356**, **360**
Atenolol **7**, **64**, **97**, **149**, **153**, **177**, **188**, **216**, **224**, **257**, **290**, **292**, **314**, **318**, **326**, **342**
Atherectomy **106**, **254**
Atherosclerosis **1**, **22**, **25**, **43**, **67**, **71**, **76**, **77**, **97**, **118**, **124**, **128**, **185**, **187**, **215**, **232**, **238**, **243**, **254**, **269**, **290**, **363**
Atrial fibrillation **36**, **45**, **93**, **123**, **134**, **235**, **301**, **302**, **303**, **304**

Quinapril **3**, **254**, **358**
Quinidine **37**

Ramipril **12**, **13**, **53**, **86**, **161**, **165**, **214**, **241**, **257**, **271**, **285**
Recombinant tissue plasminogen activator *see* rt-PA
Reinfarction **82**, **112**, **316**
Renal failure **110**
Reperfusion injury **332**
Reserpine **225**, **292**
Restenosis **54**, **108**, **112**, **131**, **206**, **287**, **289**, **309**
Reteplase **169**, **261**, **262**
Reviparin **265**
Ridogrel **263**
Risk factors **22**, **29**, **70**, **118**, **148**, **201**, **237**
rt-PA **30**, **92**, **93**, **94**, **95**, **103**, **112**, **146**, **150**, **160**, **172**, **179**, **184**, **186**, **233**, **236**, **255**, **272**, **288**, **310**, **328**, **329**, **330**, **331**, **333**, **349**, **359**

Saruplase **190**, **234**, **247**, **287**, **316**
Simvastatin **124**, **193**, **278**
Smoking **134**, **225**
Sotalol **34**, **115**, **116**, **320**
Spirapril **15**, **60**
Stenting **102**
Streptokinase **27**, **98**, **138**, **140**, **146**, **169**, **174**, **176**, **178**, **179**, **184**, **198**, **199**, **247**, **281**, **293**, **333**, **338**, **369**
Stroke **2**, **27**, **50**, **93**, **94**, **182**, **198**, **199**, **221**, **228**, **235**, **280**, **304**, **305**, **321**, **360**
ST-segment elevation **92**
Sudden death **134**
Sulodexide **173**
Sulotroban **210**

Thiazides **195**
Thrombolysis **92**, **93**, **94**, **100**, **112**, **144**, **260**, **261**, **262**, **272**, **287**, **328**, **336**
Thromboxane **210**
Thromboxane A$_2$-receptor blocker **54**
Ticlopidine **102**, **308**, **311**, **324**
Trandolapril **357**
Transient ischaemic attack **183**, **360**